Twentieth-Century
CIVILIZATION

*the text of this book is printed
on 100% recycled paper*

About the Author

Kerry Davidson was born in Water Valley, Mississippi. He received his A.B. degree from Morehouse College, his M.A. from the University of Iowa, and his Ph.D. from Tulane University. He has taught at Prairie View A. & M. College and chaired the history departments of Southern University in New Orleans and Fisk University. He is currently Assistant Commissioner for Academic Affairs, Louisiana Board of Regents.

Twentieth-Century
CIVILIZATION

KERRY DAVIDSON

BARNES & NOBLE BOOKS

A DIVISION OF HARPER & ROW, PUBLISHERS

New York, Hagerstown, San Francisco, London

For BETTY and THERESA

FIRST BARNES & NOBLE BOOKS edition published 1976

LIBRARY OF CONGRESS CATALOG CARD NUMBER: 74–21814

STANDARD BOOK NUMBER: 06–460146–3 (paperback)

STANDARD BOOK NUMBER: 06–480188–8 (hardcover)

76 77 10 9 8 7 6 5 4 3 2 1

Contents

Maps

Preface

This book examines the developments and interactions of the world's major civilizations. Although the twentieth century is the focus of study, efforts are made to place more recent occurrences in a broader historical perspective.

World history during the twentieth century has been more truly global than any history that has preceded it. By the end of the nineteenth century, Western civilization, with the nation-states of Western Europe as its mainsprings, had achieved political, scientific, economic, and in many cases, cultural dominance of the globe. Because of this preponderance, the two major European wars that were fought in this century expanded until they became worldwide. At the end of World War II, international power relations had altered dramatically since the period before World War I. In 1914, the issues of war and peace were decided by two hostile military alliances that, with the exception of Russia, were centered in Western and Central Europe. By mid-century, these critical questions were resolved by two superpowers, the United States and the Soviet Union, both of which lay outside of Western Europe. The evolution and consequences of these events are among the central themes treated.

Review questions and supplementary readings for each chapter are included at the end of the book for individual and classroom use.

1

The Supremacy of Europe

Through the shadow of the globe we sweep into
the younger day;
Better fifty years of Europe than a cycle of Cathay.
—Tennyson

At the beginning of the twentieth century, these words reflected the assumption of most Europeans and many non-Europeans that European civilization was incomparably superior to any other. The foundation for this view was the unsurpassed economic and political power of the European nations, an ascendancy that had manifested itself during the early period of imperialism (1500–1763) through the extension of European power and civilization into North and South America. Portugal, Spain, France, and Great Britain were the leading exploring and colonizing states. Although European political control over most of the Americas had been weakened or lost during the eighteenth and nineteenth centuries, the economic, intellectual, and cultural influences of Europe remained. By the late nineteenth century, the drama of the new imperialism was being played on the stages of Asia, the Middle East, Africa, and the Pacific. Great Britain and France led the way in the scramble for territory, while enfeebled Spain and Portugal were replaced by the recently united, powerful, and aggressive German Empire. The political and economic supremacy of European states was the result of a convergence of historic trends, the most significant of which were the evolution of strong nation-states and the continuing revolutions in science, technology, and industry.

SCIENCE AND TECHNOLOGY

Nineteenth-century science was a guiding force of European civilization. The unique attribute of its adherents was a claim to precise and provable knowledge of reality. The measurable achievements of science seemed to support this assumption. Scientific discoveries continually sparked inventions that, when applied to industry, agriculture, and medicine, led to a rapidly increasing population and a rising standard of living. Europeans believed that the continuing ability of science to harness the forces of nature for the purposes of man would ensure individual and social progress. This rationalist thinking permeated not only established sciences, such as mathematics, biology, and physics, but all areas of intellectual life. However, by the end of the nineteenth century, important discoveries and new theories in the natural and social sciences raised serious doubts about some scientific premises. These doubts, like the rationalist premises they challenged, were reflected in philosophy, literature, and the arts.

Theory of Evolution. The scientific theory that had the most widespread impact upon intellectual thought during the half century before World War I was Charles Darwin's theory of evolution, developed in *On the Origin of Species* (1859) and *Descent of Man* (1871). The first book advanced the thesis that existing species of life on earth have evolved from simple forms through a process of *natural selection*. In order to survive, organisms compete within and outside of their species for food and shelter. Some organisms are born with qualities that better equip them in this struggle. These live longer and reproduce more, passing their advantageous features on to their young. Over a number of generations, these successful variations become common characteristics, resulting in the evolution of new species. In *Descent of Man*, Darwin not only interpreted human history as subject to the same laws of natural selection, but he also concluded that the human struggle was interrelated with the struggle of other organisms and that man's ancestors were probably monkey-like animals.

Medicine. Scientific discoveries were the basis for medical progress. The most notable achievement was Louis Pasteur's germ theory, which laid the foundations for the field of bacteriology. A French chemist, Pasteur (1822–1895) advanced the idea that infection from bacteria caused many diseases. Aided by Robert Koch (1843–1910), a German bacteriologist who discovered the tuberculosis bacillus, Pasteur developed antibodies effective in the control of a silkworm disease, tuberculosis in cows, and rabies in humans. Following acceptance by scientists of the germ theory, improvements were made in antiseptic techniques, primarily by a British surgeon, Joseph Lister (1827–1912). For most of the nineteenth century, surgical patients in even the best hospitals were fortunate if possibly fatal diseases did not infect them. Lister discovered that most of the infectious microorganisms could be destroyed by exposing everything coming into contact with a wound to moderate amounts of carbolic acid. Other notable medical advances included the discovery of the X-ray by Wilhelm Röntgen (1845–1923), a German professor; the application of anesthesia (first used in 1842 by Dr. Crawford Long, an American physician); and the discovery of the nutritional value of vitamins.

Physics. Physical theories pertaining to the nature of matter and energy probe secrets of nature so profound that they have always had implications for diverse areas of intellectual thought. Until the late nineteenth century, most scientists believed that ideas based upon the theories of Sir Isaac Newton (1642–1727) gave the final answers to questions related to movement in space. Newton's laws of gravitation rested on the theory that the actions of bodies in the universe conformed to laws that could be mathematically understood and expressed. This was the basis for philosophies that assumed the orderliness of the universe and the rationality of man. During the late nineteenth century, however, discoveries relating to the composition of matter and the transmission of energy began to undermine Newton's premises. In 1887, Albert Michelson and Edward Morley, two American scientists, demonstrated that the ether through which light was assumed to pass did not exist. The publication in 1902 of the discovery of Ernest Rutherford (1871–1937) and Frederick Soddy (1877–1956) that radium, thorium, and uranium are constantly disintegrating refuted the theory that elements are unchangeable. Through additional experiments conducted in atomic science, the German physicist Max Planck (1858–1947) concluded in 1900 that energy is transmitted in particles instead of in waves, as had been traditionally thought.

Building upon the findings of these scientists, Albert Einstein (1879–1955) presented two revolutionary theories, a special theory of relativity (1905) and a general theory of relativity (1915). The central point of Einstein's speculation was the assumption that absolute motionlessness is nonexistent in the universe. Since there are no fixed objects, no basis exists for formulating constant principles of space and time; they are relative to the position and speed of the observer. Einstein's theories refuted the hypothesis underlying Newton's laws of gravitation, which held that heavenly bodies always move in an orderly and predictable fashion. They also raised questions about rationalist philosophies. Men could no longer be so certain that their discerning capacities could master a universe found to be infinitely more complex than they had assumed.

Anthropology. Like psychology, anthropology was established as a separate discipline during the late nineteenth century when scholars undertook the task of understanding human races and cultures. Their research was furthered by travels to Africa, the Pacific Islands, and the Americas. Their conclusions undermined notions of racial and cultural superiority that the theories of Darwin were being used to support. Instead, anthropologists taught that no absolute yardsticks are available to measure the cultures that arise from man's adaptation to varying environments. In *The Golden Bough* (1890), for example, Sir James Frazer illustrated the similarities between Christianity and primitive religions, concluding that neither was superior.

ECONOMICS

The Industrial Revolution was the governing force in Europe's and the world's economic life. During the early stages of industrialization, from around 1750 to 1850, Great Britain led the way in establishing a factory system and in large-scale production and trade. The revolution significantly altered its character between 1870 and World War I. Large-scale industrialization spread from Great Britain to the United States, France, and Germany, in addition to other areas of Europe. As a consequence, Great Britain's position as the world's foremost importing power was seriously challenged. Movements toward intensive manufacture gave birth to huge and increasingly complex business and labor organizations. In addition, new sources of power accelerated the production and marketing of manufactured goods. As a result of a decline in the death rate and a rise in standards of living, increased population was one immediate effect of expansive industrialization. Philosophical justification was given to these transformations by laissez-faire economic liberalism. This creed held that capitalism, the profit motive, and free trade were responsible for harnessing the natural and human resources that made economic progress possible.

Science and Industry. The combination of science, technology, and production has been the key feature of modern industry. Under one roof, industries have experts who can isolate and define problems, scientists who can formulate theories for resolving them, and engineers who can develop the technology to put these theories into practice. For example, the problem of producing high-grade steel from iron ore was solved through successive improvements in techniques of metallurgy. Since steel is harder and longer-lasting than iron, it soon became the most widely used construction material, and hence the period after 1870 has been termed the *age of steel*. Electricity was the most notable new source of energy. Experimentation by two British scientists, Michael Faraday (1791–1867) and James Maxwell (1831–1879), resulted in the discovery that steam- and water-driven dynamos could be used to convert mechanical into electrical energy. Chemical discoveries also generated entirely new industries, including the manufacture of explosives, perfumes, dyes, and laxatives.

Monopoly Capitalism. By the 1880s, business operations in highly industrialized countries were increasingly characterized by the spread of huge corporations. Large and small investors, attracted by prospective profits and laws that limited their liability, purchased stock in varied enterprises. Diverse types of mergers appeared. Some industries attained *vertical integration,* meaning that all functions from the accumulation of raw materials to the refinement of finished products were gathered under unified management. *Horizontal integration* was accomplished through a combination of businesses engaged in the same industry. Corporations frequently created joint directorates to pool their administrative resources. In the United States, this form of merger was called a *trust;* in Europe it was called a *cartel.* Through these consolidations, business leaders eliminated lesser competitors and amassed unparalleled fortunes and power. Production costs were lowered as new techniques lessened duplication and inefficiency. While making cheaper products available for most segments of the population, mass production brought about increasing depersonalization in labor-management relations.

Labor Organizations. European workers organized politically and economically on a national and international scale during the second half of the nineteenth century. Male workers won the franchise in all the principal industrial countries. To pool their strength, they organized a Labour party in England and socialist parties in continental countries. These parties, particularly those on the Continent, were heavily influenced by the doctrines and theories of Karl Marx (see p. 9). The Second International, an association of socialist groups from various nations, was founded in 1889. Workers used their recently established political leverage to challenge the crippling restrictions that hindered the development of labor unions in most countries. In Great Britain, unions in 1874–1875 were granted the rights to strike, to picket peaceably, and to collect funds for their operations. French workers had won similar rights by 1884. Although unions in Germany achieved the right to bargain collectively in 1896, governmental regulations still restricted their ability to picket and strike. However, German workers possessed another vehicle to make their influence felt, since most were members of the Social Democratic party, which by 1914 had become Europe's largest socialist party. The most tangible effects of labor's growing political and economic strength were programs of social legislation, which by the beginning of World War I had ameliorated working conditions in most industrialized countries.

Urbanization.   The migration of people from rural areas to cities, a direct result of industrialization, has been the most significant population movement in modern history. By 1914, urbanized areas included more than 50 percent of the population in Britain, Belgium, and Germany and about 50 percent in France. This trend was accompanied by the emergence of new social groups and values. Factory workers, the most numerous element of the urban population, were often dissatisfied with inadequate housing and monotonous working conditions. It was in their name that labor unions and parties registered social protest. Since the impersonality of the factory was transferred to other urban institutions, the sense of community that characterized smaller towns was lacking. The dominant social group was the middle class, or bourgeoisie, usually subdivided into upper, middle, and lower components. From this class were derived the cities' politicians and industrialists, as well as members of the professions of law, medicine, journalism, and education. These groups had replaced the landed aristocracy in size, wealth, and influence. As an outgrowth of its political and economic sway, the middle class set manners, tastes, and cultural styles.

MILITARY FORCES

At the beginning of the twentieth century, European armies and navies were the unquestioned world masters. Great Britain ruled the seas, and the German Empire possessed the most awesome power on land. It was no accident that these nations were also leaders in science and industry, for military strength in large part had emerged from these transforming forces. The rise in population that accompanied industrialization made more men available for military service, while technological advances lessened manpower needs in industry and agriculture. Mass-production techniques made it possible to arm, transport, supply, and shelter soldiers while maintaining the living standard of the civilian population. More directly, the same energy, skills, and organization that ran the factories were placed at the service of war ministries. Areas that had not felt the full impact of industrialization could not hope to resist the extension of European influence and power. European nations had not only the ability but also the will to create strong military machines. The prevailing view that a nation's security and possibly its survival depended on military preparedness was inculcated in classrooms, in exhortations by government leaders, and in popular novels and the press.

Widespread enthusiasm for military superiority resulted—a phenomenon reflected in the changing character of armies. Prussia's army served as the model for the rest of Europe, since most observers believed that its superior numbers, organization, and planning had brought about Prussia's easy victories over Denmark in 1864, Austria-Hungary in 1866, and France in 1870. With the exception of Great Britain, whose island position allowed it to rely on a small professional army and a superior navy, other European states after 1870 followed the example of Prussia by adopting universal military conscription. The Prussian general staff, consisting of highly trained military specialists who formulated mobilization plans to prepare for future wars, was also widely imitated. In an age of strong nationalistic sentiments, military leaders were exalted as a special caste endowed with the responsibility of protecting the nation's honor. This glorification, especially in the German Empire, permitted military leaders to exercise a wide-ranging influence over diverse governmental policies.

POLITICS

Europe's political life was dominated by nation-states whose principal objective was to accumulate and protect national power. They claimed complete autonomy over their territory and the recognition of this sovereignty in their dealings with other nations. The strongest nations were Great Britain, Germany, and France. In these countries, the scientific and industrial revolutions had contributed to national power not only the most advanced energy and products but also rational attitudes and organizational skills. In wealth and power, these countries had eclipsed Portugal, Spain, and Italy, where some of the principal characteristics of nation-states had first developed. In the

1800s, the political trend in industrialized states was the transfer of governmental control from the landed aristocracy to representatives of the middle classes. By the early 1900s, movements for political and economic democracy were threatening to further transfer the locus of power to those who spoke in the name of the laboring masses. From right to left, the European political spectrum was divided into conservative, liberal, and socialist parties.

Conservatism. European conservatism was historically identified with rule by an elite whose status was determined by tradition and whose wealth was centered in land. Most conservatives viewed society as a slowly evolving organism that was creative and progressive as long as no sudden or artificial interruptions interfered with its natural growth. Accordingly, conservatives subordinated individual rights to general community needs, asserting the primacy of society over the individual. The principal spokesmen for these views were representatives of the nobility, military, and the higher echelons of the bureaucracy and clergy. Distrustful of the middle and lower classes, they considered rule by a hereditary monarch the best form of government. In the Western European states of Great Britain, France, and Belgium, conservative rule had been supplanted by the decisive victory of the middle class; however, in Central and Eastern Europe, including the large German, Austro-Hungarian, Ottoman, and Russian empires, conservatives were still holding uncertain grips on the reins of power.

Liberalism. In contrast with conservatives, liberals were positive that large numbers of free men, particularly those of education and property, were capable of controlling their destinies while simultaneously promoting social progress. Recognizing that unlimited individual freedom could threaten others, liberals attempted to organize parliamentary institutions that would concurrently guarantee and limit individual rights. They generally supported free trade, representative government, and the freedoms of press, speech, and religion. To secure these goals, they opposed high tariffs, emphasized the need for popularly elected legislatures, supported the supremacy of law over the caprices of men, favored written constitutions that clearly defined the functions of government, and advocated the separation of governmental powers in order to make it difficult for the interests of a few to predominate. Their ideas and institutions achieved widespread popularity in the mid-nineteenth century. By the opening of the twentieth century, liberals were being attacked from two sides. With renewed vigor, conservatives condemned liberal parties and the middle classes who supported them for an overemphasis on secular yardsticks of progress and for producing industrialization that worsened relations among the social classes. The chief threat to liberal rule, however, came from the emerging strength of socialist parties on the Left.

Socialism. Liberals helped create the conditions that produced socialist parties. On one hand, they controlled the capitalist economic system, which generated widespread disaffection among laboring classes. On the other hand, they supported programs of increased political and economic democracy, which encouraged the emergence of mass movements. Socialism slowly evolved from a utopian reformist period during the early and middle portions of the nineteenth century to a national and international movement that by the end of the century many adherents considered scientific. The ideas of Karl Marx (1818–1883), a German philosopher, became socialism's strongest intellectual current. Marxists believed that the middle classes exercised dictatorial control through the parliamentary institutions they erected and manipulated. As working conditions deteriorated and wealth became progressively concentrated in fewer capitalist hands, a life-and-death struggle between the laboring (proletariat) and middle (bourgeoisie) classes would ensue. Marxists were certain that a victorious revolution of the workers would inevitably result, replacing the dictatorship of the bourgeoisie with that of the proletariat, which itself would eventually be replaced by a classless society.

The socialist movement was soon faced with fraternal strife between orthodox and revisionist Marxists. Revisionists agreed in general with Marx's ideas without fully accepting his conclusions. They observed that in many places, the economic conditions of the laboring classes were improving rather than decaying. Political suffrage had already been won by workers in some Western countries, and revisionists concluded that this movement could be accelerated if socialist parties would concentrate on reforming nations from within, thereby through evolutionary means achieving a socialist society. This controversy raged in the socialist parties of Germany and France, which by 1914 were Europe's largest. In national congresses and at meetings of the Second International, orthodox revolutionary Marxists usually won the right to incorporate their ideas in party programs. In spite of their Marxist dogma, however, on the eve of World War I, national parties were generally following revisionist practices, contending for pragmatic bread-and-butter reforms.

DOMINANT EUROPEAN NATIONS

Richly endowed with natural resources and advantages, Great Britain, France, and Germany were the dominant European nations. These states were leaders in science, industry, and world politics. The primacy of Great Britain and France had been established during the seventeenth and eighteenth centuries; Germany's arrival as a world power followed the achievement of political unity in 1871.

Great Britain. At the beginning of the twentieth century, Great Britain was still enjoying the fruits of its economic and political gains won during the two preceding centuries. Many of the industrial techniques that undergirded the Industrial Revolution had first been tested in its factories. Although it was seriously challenged, and in some categories surpassed, by the economic advances of Germany and the United States, about a third of the world's trade still passed through British ports. Geography had served England well; ample coal supplies provided energy for factories, and numerous rivers and streams facilitated internal communication and transportation. As an island nation possessing the world's strongest navy, Great Britain was also protected from the invasions of foreign armies that dotted the history of every other European country.

End of Isolation. By 1900, the preeminent European powers, with the exception of Great Britain, were divided into two rival alliance systems. Since 1882, Germany, Austria-Hungary, and Italy had been bound by the Triple Alliance; and since 1894, France and Russia had been attached in a Dual Alliance. British statesmen feared most an attack by the Dual Alliance powers, resulting from intense rivalries between Russia and Great Britain in the Mediterranean, the Persian Gulf, and the Indian Ocean. Having halfheartedly and unsuccessfully attempted to formulate an alliance with Germany, Great Britain then turned for assistance against Russia to Japan, a nation itself at odds with Russia over Korea and Port Arthur. According to provisions of an Anglo-Japanese treaty signed in 1902, Great Britain recognized Japan's preeminence in Korea and agreed to assist Japan in a Russo-Japanese war if a third power came to the assistance of Russia. In return, Japan agreed to protect British interests in China and the Pacific.

The French became alarmed, calculating that their alliance with Russia might force them into an unwanted war against Great Britain. Franco-British negotiations were stimulated by desires in both countries to resolve long-standing colonial differences. The result was the

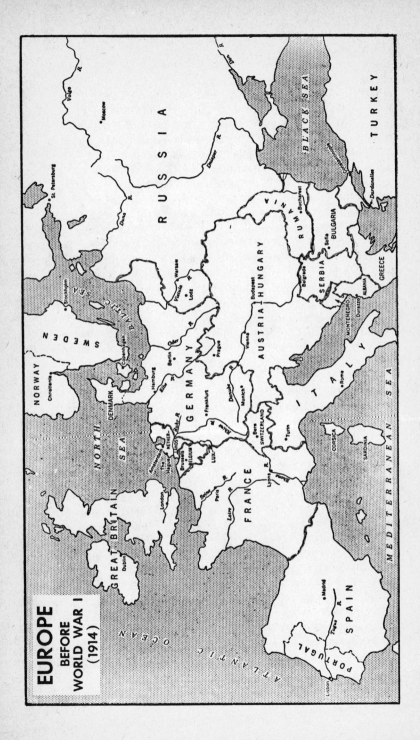

EUROPE
BEFORE
WORLD WAR I
(1914)

Entente of 1904, which reconciled outstanding differences without effecting a formal alliance. The principal agreement was over territories in North Africa. France conceded Egypt and the Sudan as British spheres of influence, and Britain acknowledged French primacy in Morocco. By 1906, Germany had replaced Russia as Britain's major antagonist. First, Russia revealed its ineptness as a potential foe through its humiliating defeat in the war with Japan (see pp. 45–46, 49), and second, Britain moved further from Germany, when it supported France during the Franco-German dispute over Morocco in 1905–1906.

Conservative Decline. The Conservative party ruled in Great Britain from 1895 to 1905 under the premierships of Lord Salisbury (1895–1902) and Arthur Balfour (1902–1905). During Balfour's years in office, three controversial issues dominated domestic politics. First, the Taff-Vale judgment by the House of Lords in 1901 ruled that businesses could sue unions for the damages resulting from illegal strikes. This decision led to unprecedented political organization and resistance by labor leaders. Second, the Education Act of 1902 provided that voluntary schools would be supported by tax funds as were state schools. Although Anglicans heartily supported the act, predictable opposition was proclaimed by Nonconformists, who did not maintain church schools of their own. Their opposition was organized into an active and adamant Passive Registers' League. Finally, Colonial Secretary Joseph Chamberlain made a series of speeches in which he challenged Britain's long-standing tradition of free trade. He maintained that the existing depression in agriculture could be remedied by imposing duties on foreign foodstuffs while allowing goods from the Dominions and the colonies to enter British ports either duty-free or at lower rates. Forced to resign from the cabinet in 1903 because his views on tariff reform differed from Balfour's, Chamberlain then proceeded to seriously divide the Conservative party by organizing a Tariff Reform League, which sponsored his continued campaign for a protective tariff.

Establishment of Liberal Rule. Free trade, an economic creed shared by Conservatives and Liberals, had been British policy since 1860, when Liberals had helped dismantle protective trade barriers. Chamberlain's campaign thus allowed Liberals to fight on their favorite historical battlegrounds, restoring unity to a party that had been badly divided over the issues of Irish home rule and imperial quests. Liberals exploited the potential unpopularity of protective tariffs by arguing that they would result in higher prices, greater inequalities of income, and business inefficiencies. Balfour resigned from the leadership of his badly divided and besieged party in December 1905. The next prime minister, Liberal leader Sir Henry Campbell-Bannerman, organized one of the ablest cabinets in British history. Included were Herbert Asquith, chancellor of the exchequer; Sir Edward Grey, foreign secretary; David Lloyd George, president of the Board of Trade; and Winston Churchill as undersecretary for the colonies. In elections to the House of Commons in 1906, voters supported this government by returning 401 Liberal to 132 Conservative members. Liberals maintained a parliamentary majority until the beginning of World War I.

Domestic Reforms. While Liberals were upholding laissez-faire in international trade, they were abandoning the idea as it applied to the relationship between governmental power and economic conditions at home. Instead of viewing the state as a passive overseer of business activities, Liberals developed the theory of the state as an active regulator of forces affecting the living conditions of the masses. They were persuaded by parliamentary studies showing that vast segments of the population, living on subsistence wages, were overwhelmed by the vagaries of unemployment and ill health. Liberals received support for their reform program from Labour representatives and also from the Irish Nationalists (in return for a promise of Liberal support for Irish home rule).

Although reform bills passed the House of Commons, the House of Lords either radically revised them or rejected them outright. Differences between the two houses produced a major constitutional struggle in 1909 when the House of Lords refused to pass a budget, presented by the chancellor of the exchequer David Lloyd George, which would have required greatly increased taxation of the wealthy. After an election in 1910 affirmed popular support for their program, Liberals forced passage of the Parliament Act of 1911. It expressly forbade the House of Lords to veto revenue or appropriations bills, while other measures voted by the Commons could be delayed no longer than two years. Between 1905 and 1914, Liberals succeeded in enacting legislation for health and unemployment insurance, progressive income and inheritance taxes, and a minimum wage.

Germany. Before 1871, German lands were divided into numerous political units, comprising principalities and townships of varied size and power. The two predominant states, Prussia and Austria, had emerged as rivals for leadership of a united Germany. The movement to achieve political unification was an outgrowth of the nationalism generated by German resistance to Napoleon's invasions. During the revolutions of 1848, democratic and liberal elements attempted unsuccessfully to create a constitutional monarchy headed by the king of Prussia. German unity was finally accomplished under Prussian leadership and through Prussian arms during the period from 1864 to 1871. Prussian policies were formulated by Otto von Bismarck, minister-president since 1862, who deliberately provoked three wars in order to achieve his goal. The first war, which ended in an easy Austro-Prussian victory over Denmark in 1864, brought the duchies of Schleswig and Holstein under Austrian and Prussian administration. The second war, in 1866, produced a quick Prussian defeat of Austria. This eliminated Austria as a rival and allowed Prussia to create the North German Confederation. Prussia's third victory, over France in 1870–1871, completed the process of German unification. The south German states thereupon joined the North German Confederation to create the German Empire with the Prussian king as kaiser and Bismarck as chancellor.

Sham Constitutionalism.   Before World War I, the German Empire was governed by a constitution (adopted in 1871) that provided for a federal state comprising the kingdoms of Prussia, Bavaria, Saxony, Württenburg, eighteen lesser states, three free cities, and the territory of Alsace-Lorraine. There was a two-chamber legislature: All adult males could vote for members of the lower chamber (Reichstag); delegates to the upper chamber (Bundesrat) were appointed by the various federal states. Because of the dominance of Prussia inside the empire, the promises of federalism and democracy were never implemented. In contrast with the English parliamentary system, the chancellor and other imperial officials were responsible to the emperor rather than to the legislature, and these officials commanded the initiative in both foreign and domestic affairs. The Reichstag usually considered only those matters submitted to it by the ministers. In any case, the assent of the Bundesrat was required before Reichstag bills became law; and in this chamber, 17 of the 58 votes belonged to Prussia, a kingdom dominated by conservative landowning and military groups. Finally, the supreme responsibility for maintaining internal order and national defense rested with Prussian soldiers.

Political Parties.   The German political spectrum included six parties. The Conservative party occupied the extreme right. Primarily Protestant and strongest among the Prussian landed aristocracy, its members exalted service to the monarch and state and usually opposed liberal reforms. The Free Conservative party included both large industrialists and landowners. Although the two parties shared many common views, the Free Conservatives advocated more nationalistic policies than the Prussian-oriented Conservatives did. The Catholic Center party, occupying the middle of the road, played a major role in German politics until Hitler's rise to power. Generally favoring constitutional monarchy and limited social reform, this party united Catholics of varied political views.

To the left of these groups were two liberal parties, the National Liberals and the Progressives, both heirs of the Prussian Progressive party. They had parted company during the 1860s, when the National Liberals supported Bismarck's forcible methods to achieve unification, which the Progressives opposed. Dominated by anticlerical and free-trade middle-class groups, the National Liberals were the leading party from 1871 to 1877. The faction-ridden Progressives comprised representatives from the lower middle class and the bureaucracy, who combined vigorous opposition to militarism, socialism, and centralized authority with demands for genuine parliamentary rule. The Social Democratic party, which by 1914 had become the strongest party in the Reichstag, occupied the extreme left. During the 1870s and 1880s, Bismarck had attempted unsuccessfully to cripple the budding Socialist movement with repressive laws while he enticed workers with welfare reforms to maintain support of the imperial government. The Social Democrats evolved in a manner that combined a commitment to Marxist principles of revolution with a willingness to work within the Reichstag for gradual reforms.

Weltpolitik. Bismarck, who guided the empire's foreign affairs from 1870 to 1890, viewed Germany as a territorially satiated power that should concentrate on consolidating its gains. Since France was Germany's principal enemy, his diplomacy focused on developing a system of alliances designed to isolate France from the other major continental powers, thus deterring it from waging a revengeful war against Germany. After 1890, German foreign policy changed dramatically. The new emperor, William II (r. 1888–1918), made himself the controlling voice in foreign affairs by dismissing Bismarck in 1890 and reducing the authority of chancellors who succeeded him. Arrogant and temperamental, William II assumed that, having attained an eminent world position, Germany was entitled to all the trappings appropriate to its "place in the sun." This meant that, like Britain and France, Germany should become a colonial power. The continuing search for raw materials and areas of capital investments, which was a result of German industrial growth, further encouraged the quest for colonies.

Germany's ambitious designs required that a more robust navy be added to its army, which was already the most powerful on the continent. On the emperor's orders, American naval officer Alfred Thayer Mahan's imposing work, *The Influence of Sea Power upon History, 1660–1783* (published in 1890), was translated into German; it had a direct impact upon Germany's naval policies. Mahan argued that great nations throughout history had used sea power to acquire and defend colonies and trade routes while simultaneously protecting the nation from invasion. Admiral Von Tirpitz, William's state secretary for naval affairs, set out to build the kind of sea power that Mahan advocated. Under his leadership, the Navy League was organized to encourage popular support for measures that would ensure Germany's naval greatness, and several naval expansion bills were enacted. When Great Britain in 1906 constructed the *Dreadnought,* a ship designed to be the most powerful on the seas, Germany built more powerful ships of the *Dreadnought* type.

The policy of *Weltpolitik* achieved its principal objectives. By 1914, Germany had acquired a colonial empire that included areas of North Africa, the Middle East, and Asia. Other nations feared and respected the unpredictable and frequently confusing German voice in world affairs.

Economy. The political unification of Germany was a powerful stimulant to economic development. During the half century before World War I, the nation was transformed by the forces of industrialization. As a latecomer to the Industrial Revolution, Germany was able to utilize the most advanced techniques from Great Britain, the United States, and France and was soon challenging them in the volume of its trade, banking, and foreign investments. Accelerated exploitation of Germany's rich coal and iron deposits provided the basis for an iron and steel industry that by 1914 was the most productive in Europe. Owing to its scientific achievements, Germany was a world leader in the newer electrical and chemical industries. Electrical power was used for a greater variety of industrial purposes in Germany than in any other country, while new synthetic products and synthetic substitutes for old products were impressive fruits of the unsurpassed union of German science, technology, and industry. Industrialization and increasing urbanization were paralleled by a growing population and rising standards of living.

France. From 1870 to 1914, the dominant political trend in France was a gradual move toward the Left. During the formative years of the Third Republic (1870–1875), Republican deputies replaced Monarchists as the leading group in the French Assembly. From 1879 to 1899, the strings of political power were in the hands of Moderate Republicans, whose notable achievements included an expansion of France's colonial empire and secularization of the French educational system.

The Boulanger and Dreyfus Crises. Two crises during this period threatened to topple the Republic. From 1887 to 1889, General Georges Boulanger campaigned for authoritarian rule by attempting to unite diverse sources of discontent under his leadership. He won a succession of by-elections in efforts to build support for the general elections of 1889. But when informed by the minister of the interior that some of his actions constituted treasonable offenses against the Republic, Boulanger fled to Belgium, and his crusade quickly crumbled.

The Dreyfus affair, which followed, shook the foundations of the Republic to a much greater degree. Alfred Dreyfus, a Jewish army captain, was accused in 1894 under dubious circumstances and convicted of treason. Frenchmen then coalesced into large Dreyfusard and anti-Dreyfusard groups. The anti-Dreyfusards were dominated by conservative army and church leaders who hoped to weaken or overthrow the Republic; most republicans and socialists sided with the Dreyfusards, led by the novelist Émile Zola. Fearful that militant reactionary groups threatened the Republic, the Dreyfusards combined in 1899 to form a coalition government, and Dreyfus was pardoned, although his conviction was not reversed until 1906. The new cabinet was headed by Moderate René Waldeck-Rousseau, but Radicals held most cabinet positions and continued to be the dominant group in parliament from 1899 to 1914.

Domestic Politics. The Left coalition, which held power from 1899 to 1905, provided France with an unusually stable period of government. Only two cabinets ruled during the period; the first (1899–1902) was headed by Waldeck-Rousseau and the second (1902–1905) by Émile Combès. (The average life of cabinets during the Third Republic [1870 to 1940] was only nine months.) The coalition focused its attention on legal revisions designed to weaken the conservative opposition. Military changes calculated to democratize army affairs and to encourage a greater degree of loyalty to the Republic among military men were instituted. Because of the role of church groups in attacking Dreyfus, as well as the strong anticlerical views of many republicans and socialists, the government then instituted fundamental reforms in church-state relations. According to the Associations Law of 1901, church orders were prohibited from operating without governmental authorization. Efforts to remodel religious institutions were crowned by the Separations Law of 1905, which severed all relations between church and state.

Socialists soon became disenchanted with the failures of the bourgeois-dominated coalition to enact progressive social legislation, and in 1905, the Socialist party withdrew from the coalition. Following their departure, Radicals depended upon the assistance of Moderate Republicans and Independent Socialists to retain their control of the government.

The years from 1906 to 1910 were marked by labor unrest, including a succession of strikes, frequently accompanied by violence. The campaign was climaxed by an abortive effort of leaders of the General Confederation of Labor (C.G.T.), a national federation of labor unions, to transform a 1910 railroad strike into a general strike. Radical cabinets countered labor agitation by slowing the pace of welfare reforms and by repressing combative acts with the military, judicial, and administrative powers at the government's disposal. The principal figures in the government were Georges Clemenceau, who served as premier from 1906 to 1909; Joseph Caillaux, a financial expert who headed a cabinet in 1911 and 1912; and Aristide Briand, an adaptable Independent Socialist who led three cabinets during the period from 1909 to 1914. A call for the unity of workers in all countries and the denunciation of bourgeois wars were the principal themes of the labor movement. These sentiments antagonized patriotic Frenchmen, thereby stimulating a revival of nationalistic sentiments and movements during these years of recurring European tensions.

Foreign Affairs. As a result of Bismarck's shrewd manipulations, France was isolated in Europe during the 1870s and 1880s. But after Bismarck's dismissal in 1890, the understanding that he had maintained between Germany and Russia was allowed to lapse. Four years later, the diplomatic isolation of France was ended by the signing of the Dual Alliance, which bound France with Russia. Differences between Britain and France were later compromised in the Entente Cordiale of 1904. After Anglo-Russian differences were resolved in 1907, the key alliance system of the Triple Entente was completed between Britain, France, and Russia. The generation before World War I witnessed widespread French colonial expansion as spacious new empires in Asia and Africa were added to older colonies in the West Indies, the Indian Ocean, and Algeria. By 1914, the population of the French Empire exceeded that of France, and the territory that France ruled overseas was considerably larger than the French homeland. Only the British could boast of more dispersed and extended colonial possessions.

Economy. There were two dominant economic trends between 1870 and 1914, both for France and for the rest of Europe. The 1870s and 1880s witnessed a decline in prices, particularly in agriculture, together with a steady growth in industrial output. From the 1890s to World War I, high tariffs on imported foodstuffs, rising prices, and accelerated industrial expansion were dominant factors. Rapid industrialization hastened the processes of production, foreign investment, and urbanization in France, as well as in Germany and Great Britain. In France, however, a much higher percentage of the population remained agricultural workers. Hence the nation was more self-sufficient in foodstuffs than its competitors were. By the turn of the century, France had become the world's leading exporter of iron ore, with a thriving trade in wine and a variety of other luxury items, and France's foreign investments were exceeded only by those of Britain. French citizens enjoyed a higher standard of living than the people of any other continental country.

THE IMPACT OF EUROPEAN DOMINANCE

There were several discernible patterns of European supremacy overseas. In North and South America and Australia, large numbers of European émigrés established dependencies and successfully challenged the natives for territorial control. In time, these Europeans became the dominant group politically and in most cases numerically. India and Africa represented a second pattern. There, smaller numbers of Europeans emigrated and established control over large populations in which native stock remained predominant. A third trend was more indirect. Europeans penetrated other areas economically and militarily, but natives maintained the semblance of political autonomy, along with their languages, religions, and customs. These semicolonial areas included the Chinese and Ottoman empires and small nations like Afghanistan and Iran. In these ways, European civilization and culture were spread over the entire globe.

The Americas. European colonies in North and South America were won during the sixteenth and seventeenth centuries and lost during the eighteenth and nineteenth. In time, Old World immigrants and their descendants became the dominant element in all areas. At first, most Europeans immigrated, when possible, to the colonies controlled by their own country. Thus, the white population became overwhelmingly Spanish and Portuguese in South America and French and British in North America. Before the 1890s, emigration to North America flowed principally from countries in northwestern Europe; after that period, emigration came primarily from southern and eastern Europe. When they arrived in the New World, Europeans encountered Indian populations that were concentrated in areas of South America and more sparsely located in North America. In order to fill the need for labor, large numbers of African slaves were shipped to both North and South America. In the United States, descendants of slaves constituted the largest group of non-Europeans (about 10 percent). In South America, Indians were the largest non-European group, and descendants of slaves ranked third in the total population.

Colonial Revolts. Most colonies in the Americas achieved their independence through a series of rebellions. The successful revolt of the English colonies (1776 to 1781) served as the political and intellectual model for other colonies. Colonial uprisings were further encouraged by the tumult in Europe during the French Revolution and the Napoleonic Wars (1789 to 1815), which weakened the reins of imperial control by forcing colonial powers to concentrate their energies on national survival.

Inspired by the leadership of General Simón Bolívar and aided by Great Britain, between 1815 and 1825 the following sovereign states were carved out of areas that had been colonies of Spain: Colombia, Venezuela, Panama, Ecuador, Bolivia, Chile, Peru, and Mexico. In contrast with the other revolutions, which were violent, Brazil won its independence from Portugal peaceably in 1822.

At the beginning of the twentieth century, Canada remained the largest and most powerful dependent territory in the Americas. However, following uprisings of Canadian provinces during 1837, Great Britain had granted the Canadians Dominion status, which included a considerable degree of self-government. After independence, the dominant trends in the United States were toward political unity, national stability, and representative government. In Latin America, by contrast, separatist tendencies produced greater divisions and resulted in the widespread and unstable rule of dictators in the various countries.

Enduring European Influence. Although the ties of empire had been broken or weakened, the economic, intellectual, and cultural influences of Europe remained preeminent in the Americas. European nations continued to provide industrial products and serve as markets for much of the foodstuffs and raw materials produced in the new countries. Surplus capital enabled investors from England, Germany, and France to dominate the economies of weaker Latin American countries. The flow of European capital helped the United States become one of the world's leading industrial powers by the end of the nineteenth century. Indian and Negro influences remained considerable, but European-based culture dominated formerly colonial areas. With the exception of Portuguese Brazil, the Spanish language and religious heritage reigned supreme in Latin America. Throughout most of the nineteenth century, Americans continued to imitate European tastes and fashions. But by the beginning of the twentieth century, the attitudes and skills required to conquer a continent had combined with European influences to produce a new American, who was more individualistic, democratic, and optimistic than his European counterpart.

Asia. India, China, and Japan, the foremost Asian nations, reacted differently to Western influences and penetrations. In India, the absence of a strong central government permitted the British East India Company to establish and expand its influence by exploiting divisions among local rulers. By the mid-nineteenth century, aggressive leaders of the trading company had made British mastery of India complete. In China and Japan, the impact of European civilization occurred later and was less overwhelming. China was forcibly opened to Western influence as the result of two trade wars with Britain (1839–1842 and 1856–1858). In these conflicts and in a later war with Japan (1894–1895), the inability of China to resist onslaughts by a major power was clearly demonstrated. As a result, by the end of the nineteenth century, powerful nations in Europe and Asia had forced China to yield portions of its territory and national rights, and its ports were opened to foreign commerce. But because a number of powers were competing, no single state was able to conquer China as Britain had succeeded in mastering India. Western influences were also penetrating Japan. But unlike India and China, Japan was able to resist political domination by other nations.

India. The initial British impact in India was economic. First, trade in spices and textiles was established; then, various other crops, including indigo, saltpeter, and hemp, were imported from India in large quantities. As the British East India Company gained control over the rich provinces of Bengal, Bihar, and Orissa and subsequently expanded its territorial hegemony outward from them, the forms of exploitation became both political and economic. Company officials collected taxes and made laws, and Indian rulers imitated many of their administrative and military techniques. Recognizing the changing role of the British East India Company, the British Parliament established direction over its policies during 1773 and 1774, revoked the company's special trading privileges in 1833, and placed India completely under the control of the British government after a mutiny of Indian (Sepoy) troops in 1857.

Cultural influences accompanied this expanding political and economic penetration. British officials eliminated the custom of suttee, in which Indian women burned themselves on the funeral pyres of their husbands. Between 1823 and 1919, a comprehensive educational system was established. Patterned after the English model and using the English language, it included both secondary schools and universities. Among an educated Indian minority, the traditional barriers of language and custom were thus weakened or eliminated. The imposition of a greater degree of political and linguistic unity, combined with the infiltration of Western political ideas, furthered Indian agitation for self-government. Consequently, the British government in 1909 permitted a minority of the propertied and educated natives, comprising separate Hindu and Muslim electorates, to elect a majority of the members of the legislative councils in each province and a minority of the viceroy's Legislative Council.

China. Convinced that their own civilization was superior, the Chinese were reluctant to adopt Western ideas. Even after their military defeats at the hands of Great Britain between 1842 and 1858, the government did little to institute the military and economic techniques that would have better equipped China to compete with foreign powers. The small minority of intellectuals willing to modernize were overwhelmed by the conservatives in high places who dogmatically rejected imitations of the West. China's receptivity to new ideas broadened after its military defeat by Japan (1895–1896) and encouraged European powers to make additional grabs for Chinese territory. Following these acquisitions, foreign powers controlled China's coastal cities and many of its inland waterways. Sympathetic to demands of the younger Chinese intellectuals for reforms, in 1898 the young Emperor Kuang-hsu introduced decrees intended to encourage industrial expansion, to introduce a school system on the Western model, and to institute civil service examinations. This Hundred Days Reform failed after a conservative reaction forced the retirement of the emperor and the execution of six reformers.

The supporters of the ruling Manchu dynasty blamed China's problems on the imperial powers who were depriving China of seaports and resources. Accordingly, conservative organizations encouraged the development of antiforeign movements. In 1900, a secret society known as the *Boxers* embarked on a violent campaign to rid China of foreign influences. After besieging the foreign legations in Peking, the Boxers were easily suppressed by an international army that included troops from the European powers, the United States, and Japan.

Following the failure of reform from above, the sentiment grew that only a more fundamental social and political revolution could initiate the changes needed to save China from dismemberment. Although the revolution came in 1911, the question of what kind of government would succeed the Manchu dynasty was unsettled on the eve of World War I. Principal antagonists were Dr. Sun Yat-sen, leader and founder of the republican Kuomintang party, and Yan Shin-k'ai, China's strongest military leader.

Japan. Like China, Japan had remained largely isolated from Western influences until the middle of the nineteenth century. In 1854, the year after a display of naval power in Japan's Edo Bay by an American fleet under the command of Commodore Matthew Perry, the Japanese were persuaded to open two ports to American ships. Japan's contacts with the West convinced it of the need to adopt Western methods and techniques in order to avoid foreign domination. Beginning in 1867, a spectacular series of constitutional, industrial, educational, and military reforms enabled Japan by the end of the nineteenth century not only to resist aggression but also to develop and pursue imperial ambitions of its own (see pp. 47–49).

Africa. During the late nineteenth century, Africa was partitioned by a daring scramble for territory among the European powers. Except for coastal trading stations, the only sizable colonial holdings in 1880 were French Algeria and British South Africa. Most of Africa remained alien to whites and to European culture. But by 1914, the only sizable areas that had escaped European control were Ethiopia and American-dominated Liberia. The rush for imperial conquest was preceded by a period of exploration, climaxed between 1849 and 1873 by the exploits of an Englishman, David Livingstone. The colonial pace was set by King Leopold of Belgium, who called an international conference at Brussels in 1876, ostensibly for the altruistic purpose of spreading civilization to Africa. Under Leopold's direction, the Brussels Conference set up the International Association for the Exploration and Civilization of Central Africa. Henry M. Stanley, a journalist and explorer, entered the service of the Belgian king, who soon made his real intentions in Africa known. Between 1879 and 1884, Stanley persuaded a multitude of African chieftains in the Congo basin to sign papers transferring ownership of their tribal lands to the International Association of the Congo, an agency Leopold had created.

As other nations entered the race, the tempo of expansionist activity accelerated. Having invaded Tunis in 1881, the French established control over lands north of the Congo River during the early 1880s. In 1884, Germany acquired domination over Southwest Africa, Togoland, and Cameroun. In addition to making advances in Egypt, the British concluded an agreement with Portugal to thwart Belgian and French penetrations of the Congo. The two governments signed a treaty in 1884 providing joint control over navigation on the Congo River and recognizing Portuguese claims to sovereignty over the river's mouth. Meanwhile, colonial antagonisms were intensifying rivalries among European countries. To encourage the amicable settlement of disagreements, Bismarck convened an international conference held at Berlin (1884–1885). The leading European states agreed that nations should publicize their intent before annexing land, that territorial occupation would be the prerequisite to a recognized claim, and that arbitration would be sought to resolve disputes. Nonetheless, numerous international disputes followed the Berlin Conference, and some produced incidents that periodically threatened to erupt into large-scale warfare.

In addition to dispersed British possessions and French supremacy in the north and west, varied German, Portuguese, Belgian, and Italian holdings made Africa a patchwork quilt of imperial possessions. The most widely applied forms of government to evolve in Africa were the British system of *indirect rule* and the French method of *assimilation*. Indirect rule permitted the natives to maintain their traditional institutions under the direction of British officials. Executive and legislative functions were delegated to chiefs and their councils, and native courts were allowed to hear civil and criminal cases. Consequently, an African elite in most British colonies acquired practical knowledge of governmental problems and administration. However, this policy perpetuated a cultural barrier between Europeans and natives. In contrast, the French theory of assimilation held that colonial areas were an integral part of metropolitan France and that Africans should be taught to accept French political and cultural institutions and attitudes. In actual practice, Africans retained some of their historical political institutions under French rule (just as they did under British rule) because there were too few Frenchmen available to administer France's enormous possessions.

Nevertheless, in most respects, European intrusions had a subversive effect on Africans. The impact was more profound in Africa than in Asia, where highly developed religious and philosophical systems provided greater resistance to Western pressures. Culturally, the African's attitudes and predispositions were radically transformed. Schools established by missionaries inculcated Western history and ideas while teaching Africans to despise their own history and social structure. The introduction of Christianity along with the complex of Western conventions and taboos undermined African attitudes toward ancestor-worship, tribal relations, and the group basis of marriage, family life, and sex. Economically, African self-sufficiency was destroyed. Africans were forced by methods often incredibly barbaric and cruel to work on plantations controlled by Europeans. The colonial boundaries devised by imperial powers bore little resemblance to historic tribal locations and organizations. In some cases, the lands of a single tribe were apportioned among three European powers. The loss of the chiefly religious and political authority increased the weakening of tribal bonds. Above all, the European prevalence deeply and negatively affected the African's self-image. Forced to adjust to diverse facets of another civilization, he often developed an abiding sense of the inferiority of his own.

CULTURE

The standards of European culture that had the most direct impact in other lands were primarily urban and middle class. Capitalists and their sons dominated the economic life in all the leading European nations, and in Britain, France, and Belgium, they achieved mastery of the political machinery as well. Middle-class industrialists set the tone for tastes, manners, and morals. The qualities that this dynamic class advanced in their religion, work, philosophies, and private lives were reflected in the pictures they painted and admired, the music they composed and enjoyed, and the novels and dramas they wrote and read. Characteristics of patience, abstinence, and thrift were frequently combined with attitudes of rationalism. During the late nine-

teenth century, these outlooks in literature and the arts encouraged
naturalist and realist trends. During the decades preceding World
War I, as the evils of industrialization became more real, and as the
revolutions in science, psychology, and anthropology challenged
older premises, all dimensions of the intellectual world were shaken.
Rationalism and naturalism were challenged by the forces of impressionism and expressionism. In most countries, these old and new
trends, often combined in the works of single artists, existed side
by side.

Religion. The secularizing forces of science and industry during
the late nineteenth century placed churches on the defensive. Among
Protestants, Catholics, and Jews, church membership became divided
between liberals, who were willing to make doctrinal and practical
adjustments to scientific and industrial influences, and conservatives,
who defended the immutability of religious teachings and practices. In
the Protestant faith, this battle was shaped by a struggle between
modernists, who de-emphasized the importance of biblical miracles, and
fundamentalists, who insisted on a literal interpretation of the Bible.
Because of its unified and dominant hierarchy, the Catholic church
suffered less serious divisions. Campaigns against modern heresies were
waged by Popes Pius IX (1846–1878), Leo XIII (1878–1903), and
Pius X (1903–1914). Pope Leo XIII, however, formulated an 1891
encyclical *Rerum Novarum* ("Concerning New Things"), which laid
the foundation for a greater degree of social and political involvement
by Catholics. It called upon the faithful to ameliorate those features
of both socialism and capitalism that were materialistic or that
deprived workers of fair treatment. Secularizing forces also divided
Judaism. Reform Jews were increasingly willing to seek greater assimilation into the wider community. This trend was countered not only
by Orthodox Judaism but also by the rise of nationalism (Zionism)
among Jews and by defensiveness against widespread anti-Semitism.

Evolution and Religion. Darwin's theories (see p. 2) became a
testing ground between the forces of science, technology, and industry
on the one hand and the dogmas of traditional religious faiths on the
other. These ideas helped dethrone man from the unique position in
the universe that religion and philosophy had for centuries accorded
him. Before Darwin, geologists had developed theories that calculated
the earth to be much older than biblical accounts suggested. Scholarly
critics, furthermore, had already pointed out the inconsistencies in
different scriptural versions of great events such as the Creation and
the Flood, had raised questions regarding the authenticity of certain

biblical sources, and had showed that Christianity had drawn upon pagan and other religious traditions. Evolutionary theories cast additional doubts upon assumptions that a divine will operated freely in natural and societal affairs, thereby encouraging a tendency to treat biblical stories as mere legends rather than divinely inspired truths.

Social Darwinism. Despite the religious uproar caused by Darwin's theory of evolution, his views accorded well with the temper of a competitive and aggressive age. Particularly attracted to his ideas were individuals, social groups, and nations that occupied superior positions in society. They adamantly justified their exalted positions on the grounds that the forces of natural selection had proved them the fittest to survive. This reasoning was encouraged by thinkers like British philosopher Herbert Spencer, who contended that governments would discourage excellence and progress if they interfered with the natural principles of selection. Applying these precepts, many middle- and upper-class spokesmen argued against reform laws designed to improve the condition of the masses. Racists, moreover, contended that the process of natural selection established the superiority of Aryans over Slavs and of whites over blacks. Darwin's broad ideas were also used to defend diverse and often contradictory political and economic philosophies. Capitalists and imperialists upheld the principles of monopoly in business and rule by powerful nations over weaker ones. At the same time, Marxists, who opposed capitalist economics and imperialist quests, claimed the concept of unceasing strife as support for their belief in a continuing class struggle.

Arts. Romanticism, the energizing intellectual force of the early nineteenth century, gradually yielded to realism and naturalism after the 1850s. Romanticism had directed its appeal to emotions and sentiments. Assuming that human nature was essentially good, romanticists ignored the often depressing economic and social conditions to seek the beauty and excitement they found in the past or in their own fertile imaginations. By contrast, realists and naturalists were determined to depict life honestly and objectively, to portray human character in its ignoble as well as its noble manifestations. Realism and naturalism were stimulated by the squalid industrial conditions and the rising popularity of scientific attitudes. But like the romanticism they replaced, these trends had limitations. New theories of the natural and social sciences led to an awareness that reality could not easily be depicted in systematic and objective terms. Consequently, some artists during the period from 1870 to 1914 were seeking alternative modes and standards of expression. Their quest produced a rich variety of experimental techniques, including impressionism, postimpressionism, and expressionism.

Painting. With Paris as the creative center, successive innovations in painting developed from 1860 to 1914. Traditional principles of painting, rigidly enforced by art academies and supported by conventional tastes, had followed standard rules for subject matter and technique. Heroism, mythology, and religion were among the common themes depicted on canvas. Painters believed that they could best achieve their goal of portraying reality by painting indoors, shading and toning rather than applying pure colors. Beginning in the 1860s, these rules were progressively violated by impressionist, postimpressionist, and expressionist schools. Led by Claude Monet (1840–1926) and Auguste Renoir (1841–1919), impressionist painters attempted to capture the subjective impressions that images made upon their eyes rather than to follow external rules for what scenes should look like. To them, reality was what "the eye actually saw." Impressionists demonstrated a greater willingness than traditional artists to depict ordinary life in varied ways, to use pure colors to show contrasts of light and dark, and to convey motion in their works. Postimpressionists, led by Paul Cézanne (1839–1906), Paul Gauguin (1848–1903), and Vincent van Gogh (1853–1890), continued these experiments and introduced a higher degree of abstraction. They revolted against efforts of both realists and impressionists to attempt to portray reality at all.

During the decades preceding World War I, these developments produced two related trends. One of these, called *expressionism*, carried further the abstractionist tendencies of postimpressionism. Perspective and accuracy in reproduction were unimportant to expressionist painters. They used color and form to convey emotions and psychological experiences even more than the postimpressionists did. Some of their studies revealed sympathy for oppressed people. The principal expressionist groups were two German schools, *Die Brücke* ("The Bridge") and *Der Blau Reiter* ("The Blue Rider"), and a French school, *les fauves* ("the wild beasts"). Another major modernist movement was cubism, as reflected in the works of Pablo Picasso (1881–1973). Cubists were influenced by the efforts of Paul Cézanne to give symmetry to paintings by emphasizing geometric form. They believed that objects in nature could be reduced to the shapes of the cones, cylinders, and spheres that underlie them. Expressionism and cubism represented irreparable breaks with an artistic tradition that had emphasized perspective and objectivity. Paintings were becoming more turbulent and confused, reflecting the anxieties and uncertainties of the modern age.

Literature and Drama. The principal dramas and novels of the late nineteenth century departed from the nostalgic longing, the idealism, and the sentimentality that had characterized romantic literature. Literary trends shared the quest of a scientific and industrial age for objective truth. Realist writers attempted impartial portrayals of the world around them. Abandoning conventional themes, they were frequently critical of the conditions and taboos that produced social and personal problems. Some notable realist works included Gustave Flaubert's treatment of a discontented wife in *Madame Bovary* (1857) in France, Leo Tolstoy's deglorification of Napoleon's campaigns in *War and Peace* (1866) in Russia, and Thomas Hardy's descriptions of individuals waging a losing struggle against social forces in *Jude the Obscure* (1895) in England. In drama, the powerful works of Henrik Ibsen, a Norwegian, attacked the harmful effects of middle-class conventions on individuals. By the turn of the century, realist trends had culminated in a movement called *naturalism* that attempted to use systematic study and observation as a way of scientifically arriving at truths. Although Ibsen's works were influenced by this school, its foremost exponent was Émile Zola, a French writer, who carefully detailed the lives of a middle-class family in his twenty-volume work, *Les Rougon-Macquart* (1871–1893). In poetry, the symbolist movement, which developed in France and had repercussions in Russia (see p. 46), encouraged the abandonment of inflexible patterns.

By World War I, the drama and the novel were being influenced by the same expressionist forces that had revolutionized painting. Many playwrights and novelists sought to revitalize a society they considered materialistic and decadent. Efforts were made to probe psychological depths, to achieve particular emotional impacts, and to explore the writer's anxieties and doubts about his world. Techniques inevitably became more unconventional. The Russian dramatist Anton Chekhov effectively used the introspection of his characters and their seemingly random remarks to convey the disintegration of Russia's aristocracy in *The Cherry Orchard* (1904). Thomas Mann, a German novelist, revealed in *Büddenbrooks* (1901) the uncertainty behind the façade of bourgeois confidence by chronicling progressive decay in several generations of a middle-class German family. In France, Marcel Proust's *Remembrance of Things Past* (1913–1927), a multi-volume psychological novel, portrayed the failings of the French upper class. Among the works most characteristic of expressionist trends were *The Trial* (1925) and *The Castle* (1926) by Prague novelist Franz Kafka. Both novels express a stark nightmare of bewilderment as the protagonists search for understanding in a callous and apathetic world.

Music.   Music was less responsive than the other arts to the forces sweeping urban society. The works of older masters, including Mozart, Beethoven, and Schubert, continued to dominate concerts, and romantic music remained the prevailing choice of audiences. In Germany, Richard Wagner's strongly nationalistic operas appealed to a wide following at the music festivals he organized at Bayreuth, while the more traditional romantic style of Johannes Brahms attracted rival support. Nationalism was also evident in the romantic symphonies of the Russian composer Pëtr Ilich Tchaikovsky. Despite the prevalence of tradition, however, there were notable impressionistic innovations during the decade before World War I. The negative reactions of some musicians to the heavy orchestration of romantic music encouraged the development of new styles. In France, Claude Debussy's (1862–1918) subtle and poetic dissonances contrasted with Wagner's massive music dramas. Clearly influenced by Debussy's departures, the dissonances of Igor Stravinsky (1882–1971), a Russian composer who emigrated to the United States, were even sharper and more primitive in sound. Arnold Schönberg (1874–1951), a Viennese composer, was more revolutionary in approach than either Debussy or Stravinsky. Writing for small chamber groups, he rejected the harmonies and repetitious themes characteristic of romanticism and adopted a consciously atonal system.

2
Challenges to European Supremacy

The supremacy of Europe was based upon the acceptance and application of concepts in science, industry, and politics that could also elevate other nations to greatness. It was only natural that qualities which had made Europe irresistible would be imitated elsewhere. Although their stages of development varied widely, by the twentieth century, the United States, Japan, and Russia were successfully harnessing the forces of science and industry and had become towering powers. The United States posed the principal challenge to Europe. Indeed, the stream of European immigration begun in the colonial period and continuing throughout the nineteenth century had made the United States an extension of European civilization. As a result of rapid industrial expansion after the Civil War, the United States had become the world's foremost industrial producer by the eve of World War I. Having conquered a continent, many Americans were now ready and eager to participate in the game of world politics as practiced by the European powers. Japan and Russia, on the other hand, were Asian nations in their traditional cultures and modes of thought. Their decisions to accept Western ideas were the result of deliberate efforts to match the West's superiority. Although Western influences upon the course of Russian history dated back to the seventeenth century, the scientific and industrial revolutions in Russia were still in their formative stages on the eve of World War I. Japan's acceptance of Western science and technology was more dramatic and more thorough. Still a tradition-bound society during the early 1800s, Japan evolved after the 1860s into the most modernized nation in Asia.

UNITED STATES

American foreign policy was generally isolationist throughout most of the nineteenth century. With attention centered on the conquest of continental territories and the related controversies over slavery and states' rights that culminated in a bloody civil war, American statesmen had little reason to become actively involved in European affairs. However, the nation's industrial emergence by the end of the century had effects that made continued isolation unlikely. The increasing export of capital and the gradual acquisition of overseas territories inevitably became important considerations in U.S. foreign policy. In addition, the rise of Germany and Japan altered the world balance of power in ways that created greater threats to American interests and security. Furthermore, influential segments of public opinion were impressed by the race of European states for markets and empires. Popular newspapers, the lectures and writings of Admiral Mahan (see p. 16), and such politicians as Theodore Roosevelt and Senator Henry Cabot Lodge urged Americans to become rivals for the power and glory being accumulated by Europe. Between 1890 and 1914, these influences brought about the end of America's isolation. The United States acquired territory beyond its continental boundaries, and its voice became more audible in international affairs.

Beginnings of Imperialism.   America's expanding role in world politics was manifested by developments in the Pacific, the Far East, and South America. The Treaty of Wanghia (1844) with China and a commercial treaty with Japan (1854) increased U.S. trade in those areas. American investors and naval experts were attracted to the Samoa and Hawaiian islands, which were strategically important as way stations to the Far East. U.S. control in Samoa included a coaling station at Pago Pago Harbor, acquired in 1878. Several crises involving American, British, and German rivalries in the islands were resolved when Germany and the United States divided them in 1899. Although American involvement in Hawaii led to white domination by 1890, Hawaiian nationalists succeeded in acquiring control of the government in 1891. Because this development threatened U.S. interests, local Americans organized the overthrow of the native government in 1893. Aware that the new regime sponsored by the Americans lacked popular support, President Grover Cleveland refused to recognize it. After prolonged controversy, Hawaii was annexed to the United States by a joint resolution of Congress in 1898.

Arguments for extending U.S. influence applied more forcefully in

South America than in the Pacific; in South America, strategic considerations were clearer, and economic investments were greater. U.S.
special interests in Latin America had been continually reiterated since
the Monroe Doctrine (1823) proclaimed that the United States would
regard as an unfriendly act the annexation or colonization of additional territory in the Americas by European powers and, conversely,
that the United States would not interfere in European affairs. More
teeth were added to the Monroe Doctrine during a series of confrontations between the United States and European nations in the
1880s and 1890s. One such dispute involved border territories between
independent Venezuela and British Guiana (1895). President Cleveland
sided with Venezuela, and his threats of war persuaded Great Britain
to accept arbitration.

Spanish-American War.   America's war with Spain was a landmark
in the emergence of the United States as an imperial and world power.
Events leading to the war began with the Cuban Revolution of 1895.
Violent resistance to Spanish rule erupted in response to Spain's
tyrannical and corrupt administration of the island. Moreover, the
imposition of American import duties on Cuban sugar in 1894 created
widespread misery by reducing the island's chief source of wealth.
Public opinion in the United States, already sympathetic toward a
colony fighting against the aristocratic rule of an Old World power,
was further inflamed as a result of press accounts. Although atrocities
and cruelties were plentiful on both sides, the New York *World*, published by Joseph Pulitzer, and the New York *Journal,* published by
William Randolph Hearst, competed for circulation by distorting and
fabricating stories of Spanish brutalities. Any chance for the United
States to avoid active involvement was lessened by two events early
in 1898. On February 9, Hearst's *Journal* published a letter written by
Dupuy de Lôme, the Spanish minister in Washington, that cast
aspersions on President William McKinley. This indignity was followed
by American condemnation of Spain for the mysterious sinking of the
American battleship *Maine* in the Havana harbor on February 15.
These events and public pressures persuaded a still-reluctant President
McKinley to ask Congress for a declaration of war against Spain.
Congress responded affirmatively on April 20.

The stated American objective at the outset was to free Cuba
from Spanish control without annexing it. However, as the war progressed, different aims evolved. On May 1, 1898, an American fleet
under the command of Commodore George Dewey destroyed the
Spanish fleet in the Philippines. By August 13, an American expedi-

tionary force completed the conquest of Manila, the principal city in
the Philippines. But the decisive battles were fought in Santiago de
Cuba, a port city. On July 3, an American naval force completely
destroyed a Spanish fleet in the Santiago de Cuba harbor; and two
weeks later, the Spanish land forces in Santiago surrendered. Meanwhile, American soldiers were completing the occupation of Puerto
Rico.

On August 12, a thoroughly vanquished Spain agreed to relinquish
its dominance in Cuba, to cede Puerto Rico and Guam to the United
States, and to settle the problems of the Philippines at a conference
to be convened in Paris in October. American delegates to the conference, carrying out what McKinley later described as a mandate from
God, surprised the Spanish representatives by demanding complete
control of the Philippines. Recognizing that they could no longer
continue the war, the Spanish negotiators yielded to these demands
in the Treaty of Paris. After a bitter public and congressional debate,
the Senate ratified this treaty on February 6, 1899. The United States
had now extended its sway beyond its continental perimeters. Puerto
Rico, Guam, and the Philippines had been annexed; and although
Cuba remained technically independent, the United States exercised
considerable control over the island's domestic and foreign policies.

Far Eastern Policies. The annexation of the Philippines, added to
America's commercial interests in China and Japan, increased American involvement in the Orient. This role broadened markedly during
the two decades preceding World War I. China's defeat in the Sino-
Japanese War (1894–1895) accelerated the race among world powers
for acquisition of its territory. This was a threat to the U.S. policy of
protecting its interests in China by upholding equal trading rights and
China's territorial integrity. Accordingly, in 1899, Secretary of State
John Hay addressed a series of notes to the major powers, requesting
that they respect the trade prerogatives of other nations within their
spheres of influence and that they uphold the rights of Chinese officials
to collect tariffs in these same areas. Although he received noncom-
mital replies, Hay announced this Open Door policy as an accomplished fact. Hay's defense of China's sovereignty during the nationalist
uprising (Boxer Rebellion) in 1900 (see p. 23) helped discourage
the imperial powers from further expropriations of territory on the
Asian mainland.

America's expanding world role was conspicuously demonstrated after
Japan's decisive defeat of Russia in 1905 (see pp. 45–46, 49). Responding to a suggestion from the Japanese, President Theodore Roosevelt

offered to serve as a mediator in the peace negotiations; and during August and September 1905, he helped iron out the peace agreements at Portsmouth, New Hampshire. The Japanese were unhappy with the compromise arrangements and left Portsmouth embittered at Roosevelt, whose efforts nevertheless won him the Nobel Peace Prize. The Japanese were further antagonized by the San Francisco Board of Education's policy of segregating Oriental students. Roosevelt's so-called gentlemen's agreement with Japan in 1907 helped to smooth over these differences. Its terms included Japan's consent to limit immigration to the United States and a pledge by the city of San Francisco to end segregation. This concord laid the groundwork for the Root-Takahira Agreement (1908), under which both nations agreed to respect each other's interests and the status quo in China.

Caribbean Policies. During the administrations of Theodore Roosevelt (1901–1909), Wiliam Howard Taft (1909–1913), and Woodrow Wilson (1913–1921), U.S. involvement in Caribbean affairs broadened considerably. The difficulties encountered in the Caribbean seemed to justify the apprehensions of many Americans that the problems of empire would prove unduly burdensome. In Puerto Rico, the only Caribbean area that the United States actually possessed, military occupation ended in 1900, and civilian government was established under the terms of the Foraker Act. The United States reserved the right to appoint the governor and upper house of the legislature, but local citizens were authorized to elect members of the lower house. Because of the island's meager resources and a rapidly increasing population, most Puerto Ricans continued to live in abject poverty.

American troops did not complete their withdrawal from Cuba until 1902, after a Cuban constitutional convention had formulated a representative governing system. The American government in later years repeatedly used threats of intervention to coerce the Cuban government; and at the request of Cuban authorities, who were threatened by an insurrection, American occupation troops returned to the island from 1906 to 1909. Because the production of sugar was Cuba's chief industry, the favorable conditions of importation granted by the United States discouraged the diversification of agriculture and the emphasis on industrialization that would have improved the island's economic health.

U.S. policies in the Caribbean also centered on the building of an isthmian canal, the exclusion of European military intervention in Caribbean affairs, and the promotion of American economic interests. Having decided that the canal's route should be across the Colombian province of Panama, President Theodore Roosevelt became infuriated when, in 1903, the Colombian Senate rejected U.S. demands. He subsequently supported a revolution that established the independence of the Republic of Panama, with which he negotiated a treaty granting the United States perpetual sovereignty over an area ten miles wide. The canal was opened to traffic in 1914 and completed in 1920. To prevent Europeans from intervening militarily when the weak Caribbean republics defaulted on their debts, Roosevelt devised a policy that became known as the *Roosevelt Corollary* to the Monroe Doctrine: When arbitration failed, the United States assumed the responsibility of protecting European nationals and their financial interests. In 1909, Roosevelt was succeeded by William Howard Taft, whose principal objective both in the Caribbean and in the Far East was to relate foreign policy to overseas investments. Taft's policies (labeled *dollar diplomacy*) were, like those of Roosevelt, accompanied by frequent military interventions, resulting in the growing alienation of the countries to the south. President Woodrow Wilson's efforts to encourage constitutional government and stability in South America produced a series of new interventions between 1912 and 1917.

Progressivism.   The period in American history from the end of the Spanish-American War to the beginning of World War I is conventionally labeled the *Progressive era*. Progressives were generally urban middle-class reformers who campaigned to ensure that America's industrial growth and enlarging role in foreign affairs would not destroy its political and economic democracy. Progressivism was never a unified movement; rather, it was a shifting aggregation of individuals and groups seeking diverse goals. Throughout the 1880s and 1890s, a variety of reformers, including a dissident Republican group called the *Mugwumps,* had favored broadening the requirement of competitive examinations for federal service as a means of countering the power of corrupt political machines. Progressives also inherited the struggle to regulate large corporations that had characterized the Granger and Populist agitation of the 1860s and 1890s. The crusade generated steam around the turn of the century after a variety of *muckraking* articles in popular magazines had exposed diverse political, economic, and social ills.

The impact of the Progressives was felt at the city, state, and national levels. City reformers focused their attention on demands that states grant municipalities home rule so that local governments would be better equipped to resolve community problems through expanded powers of regulation and taxation. Unable in most cases to persuade state legislatures to relinquish these closely guarded powers, reformers subsequently struggled to win control at the state level. At the same time, they supported measures to make state and local governments more responsive. The secret ballot and primary elections would increase voter independence and participation in the selection of candidates; the initiative, referendum, and recall would provide more direct control over legislation and elected officials. Robert La Follette (1855–1925) of Wisconsin was the most famous of the state Progressives. A succession of reforms, known collectively as the *Wisconsin Idea,* were enacted during his terms as governor (1900–1906). He then served three terms in the Senate, where he campaigned for Progressive legislation at the national level.

Progressives became increasingly aware that some economic and social ills could be remedied only through national action. As the movement broadened during the period from 1900 to 1916, reform-minded candidates were chosen by both major political parties. Progressive ideas helped shape policies during the administrations of Republicans Theodore Roosevelt and William Howard Taft and during the first administration of Democrat Woodrow Wilson. The reformist program pursued by Theodore Roosevelt included suits to dissolve some trusts, legislation to minimize railroad abuses, and regulation of the production and sale of meats, foods, and drugs. Roosevelt was also a staunch champion of conservation. He sponsored measures for land reclamation and placed many mineral and forest lands in the public domain. Although Taft, who was Roosevelt's handpicked successor, continued some of his predecessor's policies, he and Roosevelt parted company in 1909 over a conservation issue. This dispute split the Republican party during the 1912 election, enabling Woodrow Wilson, governor of New Jersey, to be elected president.

Wilson began his administration with a program of domestic reform labeled the *New Freedom.* The first item on this agenda was a reduction in tariff rates. Passed after a bitter congressional battle, the Underwood Act of 1913 carried through the most drastic reductions of import duties since the Civil War. Fundamental banking and currency changes were also achieved in 1913. The Federal Reserve Act created a national system to regulate both private and national banks. In 1914, two laws to regulate trusts were enacted. A Federal Trade Commission was established and empowered to investigate corporate practices and to issue cease and desist orders against manipulations unfairly interfering with trade, and the Clayton Act outlawed a variety of transactions, including price discrimination and interlocking directorates. A series of laws greatly expanded federal aid to agriculture. The Smith-Lever Act (1914) established grants-in-aid to improve farming methods; the Federal Highway Act (1916) provided aid to states for construction of rural roads; and the Smith-Hughes Act (1917) set up grants-in-aid for vocational education in rural areas.

Economy and Society.   In America, as in Europe, industrialization had a more far-reaching impact upon society than any other force. From the mid-nineteenth century to World War I, the United States, like Germany, was transformed from a predominantly agricultural to a primarily urban nation. A continuous stream of immigrants provided manpower for factories controlled by some of the nation's most able and energetic men. Attracted by the wealth and power available to those who organized and managed the discovery and exploitation of natural resources, these captains of industry accumulated unprecedented profits as the nation's markets broadened with the territorial expansion westward to the Pacific. By justifying aggressiveness and material yardsticks, businessmen set the intellectual and moral tone of the period. Mark Twain's satirical novel *The Gilded Age* (1873) provided an enduring label for the late nineteenth century; it focused on the greed, corruption, and naked acquisitiveness that characterized the era.

Mass Production.   In order to maximize trade and profits, industrial leaders concentrated on production for a mass market. Henry Ford was a leader and prophet of this trend. The key to Ford's success was the development of assembly-line methods, which were soon copied by businessmen in other industries. The manufacturing process was divided into related series of small tasks, each performed repeatedly by an individual worker, who thus quickly became an expert at an easy-to-learn skill. Ford helped create a mass market by raising the daily wages of his workers and then took advantage of that market by selling cars at low prices. Automotive transportation demonstrated how technological innovations can revolutionize habits and tastes; urban and rural areas were brought closer together, and work and leisure habits were radically transformed.

Education.   Larger enrollments and widespread curriculum changes were the dominant trends in education. In secondary schools, increased enrollment resulted not only from an expanding population but also from the freeing of children from the burdens of early employment. The expansion of higher education was encouraged by federal land grants to states for the support of agricultural and mechanical training and by the vast sums donated to private schools by business tycoons.

During Charles William Eliot's presidency (1869–1909), Harvard led the way in curriculum innovations at the college level. Course offerings, which had consisted of the classics, mathematics, and philosophy, were broadened to include a greater emphasis on the natural and social sciences, modern languages, and the fine arts; and the elective system was extended to include such courses. Eliot also placed law, medicine, and engineering schools on a graduate basis by raising entrance requirements and lengthening residence periods. Most other colleges and universities imitated these developments.

Literature. Schools of literature were commonly categorized by writers' reactions to the economic and social transformations of their day. Many novelists of the late nineteenth century were romantics who dealt only superficially with social conditions. Mark Twain and William Dean Howells, the giants of American literature during this period, provided more realistic portrayals.

Twain (born Samuel Langhorne Clemens) combined western humor with social criticism. *The Gilded Age* (see p. 38) was followed by *The Innocents Abroad* (1869), a tale of American tourists in Europe. Twain's literary masterpieces, *The Adventures of Tom Sawyer* (1876) and *Adventures of Huckleberry Finn* (1885), both focused on small-town and boyhood life. The works of William Dean Howells, especially his best-known novel, *The Rise of Silas Lapham* (1885), explored the impact of industrialization upon social classes, the emergence of social problems, and the rise of business leaders to political power.

These realist trends dominated the Progressive era (1900 to 1914) because reformers considered public exposure the precondition for rectifying social ills. Thus, Frank Norris described unscrupulous business practices among California railroad employers in *The Octopus* (1901) and among Chicago grain speculators in *The Pit* (1903). Few muckraking novels achieved more direct results than Upton Sinclair's *The Jungle* (1906). Sinclair's picture of unsanitary conditions in Chicago's meat-packing industry prompted passage of federal meat-inspection legislation in the same year.

Art and Architecture. Historically, American painting, sculpture, and architecture had imitated European styles and trends. Many American artists had received their training in French and German schools, and some became expatriates, living in Paris, Munich, or Rome. Although these trends were still evident, distinctive American contributions were made during the generation preceding World War I, when two American painters, Thomas Eakins (1844–1916) and

Winslow Homer (1836–1910), divorced themselves from European themes. Eakins, a talented portrait painter, was noted for the realism in his works; Homer, dealing exclusively with American scenes, painted bold and majestic canvases of the sea and maritime life. Augustus Saint-Gaudens (1848–1907), the greatest American sculptor of the era, also freed his art form from European bonds. His statues of American generals and statesmen were notable for their native authenticity. In architecture, Gothic was the dominant American style after the Civil War. But America's most gifted architect, Louis Sullivan (1856–1924), departed radically from this tradition, adopting the principle that "form follows function."

Mass Culture. Technological and industrial advances made it increasingly possible for varied forms of reading and amusements to reach an ever-expanding audience. Football, baseball, and boxing became popular spectator sports. Various parts of the country were entertained by traveling circuses, led by the Barnum and Bailey Circus, which was established in 1881. Theatrical fare ranged from the traditionally popular plays of Shakespeare to the light operas of Gilbert and Sullivan and vaudeville shows. Horatio Alger emerged as an enduring part of the American legend by writing 119 books, most describing how hardworking boys from humble upbringings achieved wealth and happiness. Cheap and spectacular paperback *dime novels* were popular among American youth. The newspaper and magazine audience was transformed from a few highly educated readers to the masses. Not surprisingly, low prices and sensationalism were commonly used to build and maintain circulation. Among newspapers, this was notably true of New York's *Journal* and *World,* both of which demonstrated a flair for stories built on rumor and scandal. Some mass-circulation magazines, including *McClure's Magazine, Cosmopolitan, Collier's,* and *Everybody's Magazine,* also featured articles exposing corruption in business and politics.

RUSSIA

Geographically and culturally, the Russian Empire developed on the boundary between Europe and the Orient. During the period between 1238 and 1480, Russia was controlled by Asiatic Mongols, or Tartars, who established a tradition of authoritarian rule, maintaining virtually no contact with the West. By 1480, the emerging principality of Moscow had cast off Tartar rule and began the so-called gathering of lands that made it the center of the new Russian state.

By the seventeenth century, Western ideas had penetrated at least Russia's educated and ruling inner circles. This impact became more pronounced during the eighteenth and nineteenth centuries. A succession of Russian rulers, notably Peter the Great, Catherine the Great, and Alexander II, introduced Western ideas and institutions in their efforts to consolidate and extend Russia's power. East-West alternatives generated continuing debates over the direction in which Russia should evolve; these discussions formed the central theme in Russian society during the two decades preceding World War I. In its religion, governing structure, and customs, this large empire remained Oriental; yet, the forces of industry and democracy that had transformed Europe had already begun to change Russia's character.

Government. From 1613 to 1917, Russia's emperors (*czars*) belonged to the Romanov dynasty. The czar was the sovereign figure in Russian society; all institutions and men were subordinated to his will and power. Supreme jurisdiction over both secular and religious affairs was the source of his pervasive authority. The czar's secular dominance was derived from the Tartar tradition of dictatorial rule and also from the use of absolute power by the princes of Moscow to extend their territory and authority. His religious authority was derived from claims of guardianship over Orthodox Christianity asserted by the princes of Moscow and later the rulers of Russia following the fall of Constantinople to the Turks in 1453. The czar's decisions were considered divinely inspired, and no area of Russian life was excluded from his intervention. As a consequence, rights constitutionally protected in most Western countries, including those of representative government and the freedoms of assembly, religion, press, and speech, had few roots in Russia.

There were three czars between 1855 and 1917: Alexander II (r. 1855–1881), Alexander III (r. 1881–1894), and Nicholas II (r. 1894–1917). The reign of Alexander II, who was known as the *czar-liberator,* was characterized by major reforms. The most significant was the emancipation of serfs in 1861, a step that directly affected the status of over 50 million peasants. In the following years, the population was granted a limited degree of self-government through the creation of local assemblies and boards (*zemstvos*). Other changes produced a reorganization of the empire's administrative and military structure. After escaping several assassination attempts, Alexander II was killed by a bomb in 1881. His successors, Alexander III and Nicholas II, blamed his assassination on the agitation and militancy that they were convinced his reforms had inspired. Therefore, during the last two decades of the nineteenth century, they implemented policies of generalized repression and counterreform. They were heavily influenced by a reactionary government official, Konstantin Pobedonostsev, who aimed to reverse any policies that threatened Russia's religious, social, and political traditions. During these years, social discontent became widespread. The reforms instituted by Alexander II had done little to improve the quality of life for most peasants, and some groups had become convinced that fundamental improvements were unlikely to occur unless the czarist system itself was altered.

Revolution of 1905. The Revolution of 1905 evolved from domestic discontent that was intensified by Russia's badly fought war with Japan (see pp. 45–46, 49). Revolutionary events were sparked by an incident on January 22, 1905 (Bloody Sunday). A group of 200,000 workingmen, led by a priest, Father Georgi Gapon, gathered peaceably to petition Czar Nicholas II for civil liberties, representative government, and economic reforms. When they refused to disperse, police fired into the unarmed crowd, killing 130. Popular outrage produced a rising wave of industrial strikes and riots and peasant disorders. In a number of cities, workers' councils (*soviets*) were established to coordinate strike and military activities. By mid-October, Socialist and liberal groups had united to produce a general strike that immobilized the country. The government was now persuaded to make important concessions. A manifesto issued by the czar on October 30, 1905, promised civil liberties and an elected legislature (*Duma*).

Political Parties. Russian political parties were organized into liberal and Socialist groups. These divisions were encouraged by the impact of late nineteenth-century industrialization on bourgeois and proletarian class consciousness. The October Manifesto served to clarify the policies of liberal and Socialist factions.

Those liberals who supported the government's concessions were known as *Octobrists*. Led by Vasilii Maklakov, they feared that revolutionary methods would destroy all chances for democratic and peaceful reforms. Liberals who agreed to participate in elections and serve in the legislature but continued to demand a constituent assembly were known as *Constitutional Democrats* (*Kadets*). Their leader, Pavel Milyukov, argued that because the manifesto included no fundamental reforms, liberals should maintain their opposition to the government.

Socialists were organized into *Social Democratic* and *Socialist Revolutionary* parties. The Social Democrats were Marxists who, in 1903, divided into two factions. The *Bolshevik* faction, led by Lenin, favored a small disciplined party of professional revolutionaries; the *Menshevik* faction supported a larger, more democratic association. Mensheviks joined with the liberal groups to participate in the Duma, but Bolsheviks pursued their goal of revolution. The Socialist Revolutionaries, although also influenced by Marxist ideas, were heirs of Russia's populist tradition and derived most of their strength from rural areas. The party was formed in 1901 under the leadership of Viktor Chernov. Like Social Democrats, the Socialist Revolutionaries divided over the October Manifesto. After a party congress (1905–1906) voted to boycott the Duma, disenchanted conservatives who supported cooperation and extremists who favored terrorist tactics left the party and formed their separate organizations.

Political Trends. Although the legal duration of a Duma was five years, four Dumas were chosen between 1906 and 1917. The first two (1906–1907) were dominated by representatives of the Kadet and leftist parties, and it proved impossible for the government's conservative ministers and the legislature to cooperate. To resolve the impasse, the czar authorized the dissolution of both Dumas. The first Duma had convened only two months before Nicholas II decreed its fate in July 1906. Following its dissolution, 200 deputies, most of them Kadets, gathered in the Finnish city of Viborg and issued a manifesto appealing to the population to oppose the government's decree by resisting the draft and refusing to pay taxes. An apathetic Russian citizenry declined to heed this call. Imperial officials jailed all signatories of the Viborg Manifesto and forbade them to serve in subsequent Dumas.

Elections to the second Duma were held during February 1907. Kadet membership decreased from 184 to 99, but the total strength of parties on the Left rose from 124 to 216, partly because of a decision by the Socialist Revolutionaries to participate fully in the elections. The second Duma was convened in March 1907 but was dissolved three months later. Like the first Duma, it had demonstrated an uncomfortable militancy toward the czar and his ministers. Invoking his supreme authority, Czar Nicholas II, advised by his talented and aggressive minister Pëtr Stolypin, arbitrarily changed the electoral procedures. The objective was to create a more pliable Duma by severely reducing representation of workers and peasants while increasing the strength of the gentry to about half the legislative seats.

These changes swiftly produced the desired results. The third Duma (1907–1912) was agreeable enough to be maintained for its full term, and the fourth Duma endured from 1912 until the Revolution of 1917. Although the relative strength of the Octobrists had been reduced, the government depended upon their support to maintain a legislative majority; thus, they exercised a constant and decisive influence. The failure to produce a genuinely representative lawmaking body increased the alienation of the intelligentsia from the government. At the same time, reform-minded leaders had to contend with astute government policies that combined ameliorative measures with repressive acts.

Economy. Russian industrialization slowly gathered steam in the 1870s and 1880s and then rapidly accelerated from 1890 to 1910. The emancipation of the serfs encouraged many landless peasants and those with small holdings to break their rural bonds. As a result, the industrial labor force expanded from less than 1 million in 1865 to more than 3 million by 1900. As a latecomer to large-scale industrialization, Russia had the advantage of being able to adopt the most advanced technology from Britain, the United States, and Germany. Western capital investment, aggressively sought by Sergei Witte, minister of finance from 1892 to 1903, also played an essential role in Russia's economic development. Witte further pursued policies that enabled Russia to export more than it imported and thus accumulate a gold reserve. Impressive results were also achieved in the heavy industries. Numerous railroads were constructed, and rapid increases were noted in the production of iron, steel, coal, and petroleum.

In spite of the nation's industrial advances, peasants constituted about three-fourths of the population in 1900. Emancipation of the serfs had produced complex and uneven results. Although most peasants received land with their freedom, roughly half the tillable soil, generally including the better lands, remained in the hands of the nobility. Because the government had compensated landowners for those acres lost through land allotments to former serfs, the freed peasants were in turn expected to reimburse the government through long-term redemption payments. Actual control over the land was placed in the hands of village authorities rather than individual farmers. The village elders and administrative officials were assigned the responsibility for collecting taxes and providing army recruits. Communal bonds were so strong that the liberated serfs neither traveled beyond nor withdrew from the village unless permitted to do so by the elders. This system perpetuated primitive methods of agricultural production and prevented the development of a healthy peasant economy.

After 1900, the most significant agricultural reforms occurred during Stolypin's premiership (1906–1911). Stolypin's goal was to combine repression of widespread terrorist activities with the development of a stronger and more conservative agricultural class. He believed that this could be done by breaking up the peasant communes and encouraging independent peasant proprietorship. Legislation implementing his ideas was enacted in 1906, 1910, and 1911. By 1907, financial relief was extended to peasants through the elimination of land-redemption payments. A series of measures made it possible for individual peasants to receive allotments of consolidated units of property from the commune while gentry landholdings were preserved. In addition, it was made easier for peasants to migrate from one section of the country to another, to buy land, and to receive common justice.

Foreign Policy. Several considerations had decisive influences on Russian foreign policy. Russia's historical territorial ambitions aimed to ensure control over access routes to the Baltic and Black seas and to establish frontiers that provided security against invasion. During the reign of Nicholas II, the country's attention was focused southward as a result of a combination of circumstances. Access to the Black Sea was less secure than access to the Baltic, and a virulent Pan-Slav movement, combined with Russia's role as protector of the Orthodox church, placed the nation culturally closer to the Balkan areas. The pursuit of foreign policy objectives evolved in the context of the conflicting ambitions of European powers. By supporting the policies of Bismarck during the 1860s and 1870s, Russia sought to secure German support for its Balkan ambitions against the competing aims of Austria-Hungary and Great Britain. After these efforts failed, Russia turned to an 1894 defensive alliance with France and to a 1907 understanding with Great Britain that resolved outstanding differences by demarcating spheres of influence in mutually disputed areas. However, by the eve of World War I, the opposition of European powers had prevented Russia from realizing its goal of dominating the Straits and the eastern Balkans.

Russia's territorial designs also included areas of Central Asia and the Far East. In Central Asia, Russian expansion brought it face to face with the rival ambitions of Great Britain. On several occasions before the Triple Entente of 1907 (see pp. 54–55), Russo-British competition in Iran and British fears that Russian expansion threatened India almost precipitated war between the two powers. In the Far East, Japan's imperial dreams were Russia's foremost obstacle, with Manchuria and Korea the key areas of conflict. Russia had established its influence in northern Manchuria after 1896 by constructing the Chinese Eastern Railway and in southern Manchuria in 1898 by obtaining a twenty-five-year lease for the part of the Liaotung Peninsula that included Port Arthur. The Japanese government offered a compromise whereby Russia's interests would be recognized in northern Manchuria if Russia would concede Japan's primacy in southern Manchuria and Korea. When the Russians refused their offer, Japan began hostilities (February 1904) in a war that resulted in the annihilation of Russia's fleet in the Far East and the triumph of Japanese armies in Manchuria. Although the defeats were disastrous and humiliating for Russia, compromise arrangements were established by the Treaty of Portsmouth, which ended the war in September 1905.

Culture.   Russian culture experienced a golden age during the period from 1860 to 1890 and a silver age from the 1890s to World War I. The golden age was characterized by educational changes that produced an expansion in the number of schools and in enrollment on all levels. Notable contributions were made in the sciences, including chemistry, mathematics, physics, biology, and physiology. The pinnacle of Russian cultural achievement, however, was in literature. The undisputed masters were Ivan Turgenev (1818–1883), Fëdor Dostoevski (1821–1881), and Leo Tolstoi (1828–1910). Between 1858 and 1881, Turgenev wrote six novels portraying Russian society, particularly developments among the intelligentsia. *Fathers and Sons* (1862) is considered his masterpiece. Dostoevski's greatest novels were *Crime and Punishment* (1866), *The Idiot* (1868–1869), *The Possessed* (1871), and *The Brothers Karamazov* (1880). His special talent was his ability to perceive those qualities that constituted the Russian character and in doing so to reveal much about the psychological makeup of all men. Leo Tolstoi's major novels were *War and Peace* (1866), a panoramic story centering on the Napoleonic War of 1812, and *Anna Karenina* (1875–1877), the tragedy of a woman who defies society's conventions.

The silver age exhibited excellence in a variety of art forms. The short stories of Anton Chekhov (1860–1904) and Maksim Gorki's novel *The Lower Depths* (1903) maintained the high standards of Russian prose. Superb poetry was created by a series of poetic schools. The most famous were the *symbolists,* so named because they emphasized the sound and symbolic significance of words. Among the leaders of this school were Aleksandr Blok and Andrei Bely. Other artistic schools included acmeists, who emphasized precision in the use of words, and futurists, who attempted to discover the potentials of the Russian language by transcending conventions. Modern trends in music and the ballet paralleled those in art. The works of Igor Stravinsky

(1882–1971), Sergei Rachmaninoff (1873–1943), Pëtr Tchaikovsky (1840–1893), and Nikolai Rimski-Korsakov (1844–1908) were the best known.

JAPAN

Japan's development was a dramatic example of what a determined Asiatic nation could do when confronted by threats of Western imperialism. During the Meiji period (1868–1912), Japan was transformed from a feudal state into one of the world's leading industrial and military powers. Having achieved a high degree of modernization by the 1890s, Japanese leaders then embarked upon an expansionist program on the Asiatic mainland and fought successful wars against China and Russia. Between these wars, Japan's recognition as a major power was confirmed by a defensive alliance with Great Britain. Before World War I, Japan's growing power and prestige had persuaded the Western states to relinquish earlier treaty concessions that infringed upon its sovereignty.

Economy. Japanese leaders recognized that economic advancement was the prerequisite for national strength. Programs were therefore instituted to achieve agricultural and industrial development, with primary emphasis on industrialization. The government spent vast sums to acquire Western models, ideas, and experts for the purpose of reorganizing Japan's industrial life and the educational system needed to sustain it. Between 1870 and 1900, government subsidies further resulted in the replacement of a virtually obsolete merchant marine with over 1,200 modern steamers. State revenue was necessarily expanded through foreign loans, higher taxes, and the creation of government monopolies. The most rapid economic growth was in the textile industries, with silk and cotton exports accounting for over half the nation's total. Significant progress was also made in the heavy industries and in the production of machine tools. The banking system was renovated, and other financial institutions were created to accommodate the expanding trade. Population increases and the growth of urban centers inevitably followed Japan's rapid industrial progress.

Chinese-Japanese War. By the 1890s, Japan's strides toward modernization had generated imperial ambitions among its leaders. Their first goal was to secure the independence of Korea, which the Chinese considered a dependent state. The Chinese-Japanese War erupted after Japanese forces sunk a British ship that was transporting Chinese troops to Korea (July 1894). Most observers considered Japan's chances for

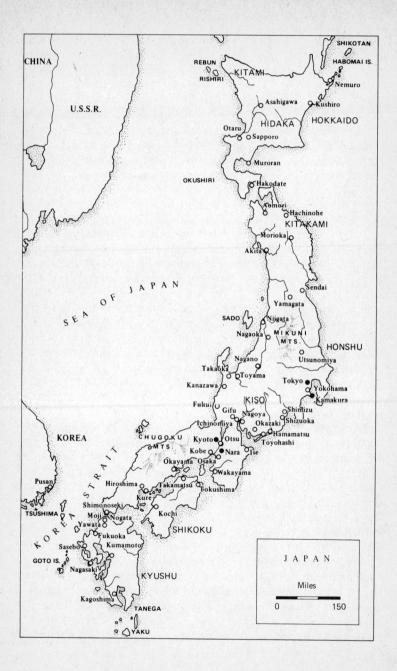

CHINA

U.S.S.R.

SHIKOTAN

HABOMAI IS.

REBUN

RISHIRI

KITAMI

Nemuro

Asahigawa

Kushiro

HIDAKA

HOKKAIDO

Otaru

Sapporo

Muroran

OKUSHIRI

Hakodate

Aomori

Hachinohe

KITAKAMI

Morioka

Akita

SEA OF JAPAN

Sendai

Yamagata

SADO

Niigata

MIKUNI

Nagaoka

MTS.

HONSHU

Nagano

Utsunomiya

Takaoka

Toyama

Kanazawa

Tokyo

Yokohama

KISO

Kamakura

Fukui

Gifu

Nagoya

Shimizu

Ichinomiya

Okazaki

Shizuoka

KOREA

CHUGOKU

Kyoto

Otsu

Hamamatsu

MTS.

Kobe

Nara

Toyohashi

Okayama

Osaka

Ise

Wakayama

Pusan

Hiroshima

Takamatsu

Tokushima

TSUSHIMA

Kure

Kochi

Shimonoseki

SHIKOKU

Moji

Nogata

Yawata

Fukuoka

Kumamoto

Sasebo

GOTO IS.

Nagasaki

KYUSHU

Kagoshima

TANEGA

YAKU

J A P A N

Miles

0   150

victory slim because the Chinese armies were far superior numerically. But the better-trained, -organized, and -equipped Japanese soldiers quickly forced the Chinese armies to retreat northward out of Korea; meanwhile, a Chinese fleet was decisively defeated near the mouth of the Yalu River (Sept. 1894). The Japanese occupation of Southern Manchuria (Nov. 1894) aroused Chinese fears that Japanese forces would reach the capital of Peking. Under the Treaty of Shimonoseki (April 1895), China recognized Korean independence and ceded to Japan the Liaotung Peninsula, Formosa, and the Pescadores. As a result of this victory, Japan became generally recognized as the dominant nation in Asia.

Russo-Japanese War. Events soon deprived Japan of gains won during the Chinese-Japanese War. Five months after the Treaty of Shimonoseki was signed, the intervention of Russia, France, and Germany compelled Japan to restore to China the Liaotung Peninsula, including the important harbor of Port Arthur. In 1898, the Russians acquired a twenty-five-year lease over the strategically located Liaotung Peninsula. After 1895, Russian influences were also replacing those of Japan in Korea. In 1903, Japanese leaders offered to compromise their differences with Russia. Interpreting fruitless negotiation as Russia's rejection of their terms, the Japanese abruptly attacked Russian forces at Port Arthur (February 8, 1904). In the ensuing war, Russia suffered successive humiliating defeats on land and sea. According to terms of the Treaty of Portsmouth (September 1905), Russia accepted Japan's paramount interest in Korea, transferred to Japan its lease over the Liaotung Peninsula, and ceded to Japan the southern half of the island of Sakhalin. This victory was even more impressive than Japan's defeat of China because Russia was considered a stronger adversary. It had become clear that any nations with interests in the Far East would have to respect the Japanese presence there.

Political Reforms. Influenced by Western models, Japan instituted a series of reforms during the 1880s. In 1885, a cabinet was established, headed by a minister-president with broad powers resembling those of the German chancellor. The Privy Council, an advisory body patterned after the English example, was created in 1888. The crowning Japanese political reform was the emperor's promulgation of a new constitution in February 1889. This document granted citizens property rights and the freedoms of religion, speech, and association. A two-house legislature (*Diet*) was created. Delegates to the House of Peers were chosen either from members of the nobility, by imperial appointment, or by selection by their peers. Members of the House of

Representatives were popularly elected by voters who possessed high property qualifications. Legislative elections were held in July 1890, and the first Diet convened in November of that year.

Nevertheless, the Japanese government remained oligarchic and authoritarian. The emperor, whose powers were still regarded as divine, appointed ministers responsible to him rather than to the legislature. The emperor and his ministers were entirely responsible for decisions concerning foreign affairs, including diplomacy, war, and treaty making. Furthermore, the emperor had sole authority to convoke and dissolve the Diet, whose powers were narrowly circumscribed. The Constitution required legislative approval of all budgets; nevertheless, if the Diet refused to adopt a new budget, the previous one remained in effect. The Diet also possessed lawmaking powers, but these were carefully defined and limited by the Constitution. And although no bill could become law without the emperor's sanction, emergency imperial decrees had the effect of law.

Religion. Shinto, founded on ancestor and nature worship, and Buddhism, an import from India by way of China, were the traditional Japanese religions. Followers of Shinto believed that the sun-goddess was the ancestress of all Japanese emperors, who were therefore deified. An individual's ancestors were also considered caring gods to be accorded honor and worship. Imposing no rigid rituals or moral code, the Shinto cult assumed a high degree of virtue in its adherents. The Mahayana branch of Buddhism, rich in moral philosophy and colorful ceremonies, was a major influence in transmitting Chinese culture into Japan. Highly metaphysical, Buddhism seeks to help each believer complete a process to free him from earthly desires, thereby enabling him to attain Nirvana, a mystical absorption into a spiritual state envisaged by most Japanese believers as a paradise comparable to the Christian Heaven. The Japanese warrior sects favored Zen Buddhism, which required mental and physical discipline and stressed intuitive oneness with nature. Although there were numerous individual conversions to Christianity, Shintoism and Buddhism remained Japan's dominant religious faiths.

Cultural Change. Japanese historians usually consider the period from 1870 to 1914 one of civilization and enlightenment. Various aspects of Japanese culture were affected by efforts to modernize the nation. Changes in everyday habits were brought about by the development of a modern postal system and the use of Western products. Baseball and tennis became fashionable sports. Japan's traditionally hierarchical society was seriously weakened by the flow of Western ideas and attitudes. For example, the preeminent place of the former warrior caste (samurai) was undermined by new government officials. Movements to achieve political rights and freedoms accompanied the broadening influence of Christianity. Learned societies such as the Meiroku-sha, patterned on Western models, facilitated communication among Japanese scholars. Following the impact of intellectual and cultural change, a fertile period in literature and the arts developed during the 1880s and 1890s.

Theater and Arts. Traditional Japanese theater and arts received much of their shape and substance from the influences that accompanied the importation of Buddhism from China and Korea. Ancient plays, called *No,* combined spiritual and human themes in stories that inevitably ended tragically. Japanese drama glorified suicide as a way out of trouble and frowned on the display of love through even the most modest physical contact. Although devotees of these plays usually opposed the introduction of works reflecting contemporary themes, such works became popular during the late nineteenth century.

Similarly, a struggle between the old and the new affected artistic traditions. Historically considered handmaidens of religion, the best painters and sculptors had concentrated on pictures and carvings of Buddha and other gods. Both these traditional and contemporary emphases were reflected in the curriculum of the Tokyo Fine Arts School, founded in 1889. The school was housed in two buildings, one teaching sculpture and painting (divided after 1896 into Japanese and European) and the other specializing in the minor arts, including engraving, casting, lacquering, and drawing. Students followed a course of study lasting five years.

Literature. The introduction of Western literature sparked widespread imitations among Japanese writers during the Meiji period. Adaptations of naturalism and realism encouraged analytic treatments of social and national problems. Recurring themes included the impact of modernization, the conflict between Eastern and Western ideas, and Japan's role as an emerging world power. Natsume Sōseki (1867–1916) and Mori Ōgai (1862–1922) were leading naturalist writers. Sōseki's novel *Kokoro* [Mind] depicted the fruitless life of an intellectual obsessed with daily duties and routines. Mori Ōgai was an army surgeon who used his scientific training as a basis for exploring various psychological problems. His spiritual turmoil, resulting from the interaction of old concepts with modern ideas, was evidenced in a 1912 work titled *Ka No Yō Ni* [As if].

INTERNAL EUROPEAN THREATS

Although external rivals existed, no single nation or combination of states could threaten Europe's supremacy in the early twentieth century. Immediately more serious were the internal problems that caused disharmony within and among European countries. Industrialization and nationalism proved simultaneously the most constructive and destructive social forces. Quests for wealth and for national security and glory led to rivalries between nations over markets, colonies, and the sizes of armies and navies. These conflicts encouraged the formation of opposing alliance systems, making it likely that a major conflict would involve most of the principal powers. Industrialization and nationalism had also created severe discontent within nations. Some economic and ethnic groups on the Continent, dissatisfied with a status quo that denied their goals, were threatening to dissolve national bonds and create new political and social systems that would enable them to realize their aspirations.

Nationalism.   Europe comprised over twenty nations, each claiming absolute sovereignty over its peoples, territories, and affairs. Each government attempted to promote its national ambitions by maximizing its strengths while taking advantage of other nations' weaknesses. When peaceful methods failed, national leaders considered aggressive actions, including war, justifiable ways of promoting and defending their countries' interests. During most of the nineteenth century, the major powers had been able to avoid general clashes among themselves through a policy of periodic consultation called the *concert of Europe*. Several considerations complicated this practice during the second half of the century. Traditional relations among European states were dramatically altered by the formation of the German Empire and the growing power of Russia. In addition, as nationalistic and economic rivalries intensified, international conflicts became increasingly abrasive.

The nation-state had demanded and won the highest allegiance and respect of most of its citizens. The English, Germans, French, and Russians, influenced by patriotic teachings, exhortations of ultranationalistic leaders, and theories of social Darwinism and racism, were separately persuaded that they were God's specially chosen people. They felt singularly honored when their nation was praised and pointedly offended when it was rebuffed or insulted. These assumptions were reflected in strong nationalist sentiments that were moderately restrained in England but overtly expressed on the Continent through a patriotic revival in France and through the Pan-German and Pan-Slav movements, which crossed national boundaries. There was widespread popular support for policies that justified increases in military forces as necessary to defend the nation and promote its expansion. National groups who had not achieved unity and statehood or whose independence was undermined by the presence of foreign powers were least willing to accept the status quo. These discontented peoples, who were concentrated in the Balkans and the multinational empires of Austria-Hungary and Turkey, posed more serious threats to European peace than the established powers did because they had even fewer inhibitions about the use of force to attain their goals.

Austria-Hungary. The Austro-Hungarian Empire comprised heterogeneous peoples and lands collected by the Hapsburg dynasty since the sixteenth century. Two minority groups dominated the empire: the Germans in Austria and the Magyars in Hungary. Although Slavs constituted a numerically larger group, they were deeply divided by language, culture, and history. Czechs, Slovaks, Poles, Serbs, Ruthenians, and Croats frequently hated each other as much as they despised the Germans or the Magyars. Italians and Romanians also constituted sizable ethnic groups within the empire. Since 1867, Austria-Hungary had been ruled as a dual monarchy in which the kingdoms of Austria and Hungary administered their internal affairs through separate legislatures: the Austrian Reichsrat and the Hungarian Diet. Matters that commonly affected both kingdoms, including foreign affairs, defense, and imperial finance, were regulated by joint ministries. Both kingdoms were ruled by the same monarch; the Hapsburg emperor of Austria also reigned as king of Hungary.

National divisions were the dominant feature of the empire. Germans and Magyars found it difficult to communicate with each other and impossible to assimilate their subject nationalities. In Austria, the Czech problem was by far the most critical. The Czechs, located in Bohemia, were an economically advanced people with a proud history and culture. Their most vocal demand was for a triple monarchy in which Bohemia would be equal to Austria and Hungary. Although Austria made meaningful concessions to the Czechs and other nationalities, these failed to fulfill rising nationalist aspirations. The Magyars of Hungary were even less tolerant toward the nationalities they subjugated. Only the Croats were permitted to have their own legislature, courts, and schools. Romanians, Slovaks, and Serbs were subjected to a harsh and continuing policy of cultural Magyarization. As the national groups became more demanding, the Austro-Hungarian Empire was repeatedly shaken with internal strife.

Ottoman Empire. The Ottoman, or Turkish, Empire, comprising lands in Europe and Asia, was also a mixture of antagonistic nationalities. Commonly called the *Sick Man of Europe,* the empire had been forced during the nineteenth century to relinquish territories to some of its subject nationalities. This dismemberment began with Serbia and Greece (1829), followed by Romania and Montenegro (1878). Since the Congress of Berlin (1878), the Turkish provinces of Bosnia and Herzegovina had been administered by Austria-Hungary. Additional reductions in Turkish territory occurred in July 1908, when the sultan's corrupt and despotic government was overthrown by the Young Turks, who established a Western-style parliamentary system. Fearing that a revitalized central government would be able to restore its authority, Bulgaria declared its independence from Turkey on October 5, and Austria-Hungary formally annexed Bosnia and Herzegovina a day later. Europe's Sick Man continued to live despite these nationalist and imperialist amputations, partly because the major powers could not decide how to divide the spoils and partly because the nationalities within the empire had never effectively united.

Alliance Systems. By the eve of World War I, Europe was divided into two rival alliance systems: the Triple Alliance and the Triple Entente. Impetus for the formation of permanent European alliances had been provided by Otto von Bismarck, the German chancellor from 1871 to 1890. Fearful that France would form a coalition against Germany in order to regain the provinces of Alsace and Lorraine, which were lost during the Franco-Prussian War (1870–1871), Bismarck attempted to isolate France by allying Germany with powers that might join France in alliances. Because Britain and France were already at odds over colonial questions, Bismarck directed his diplomatic efforts toward winning the friendship of Austria and Russia. The three powers were first joined in the Three Emperors' League (1873–1878). However, it proved difficult for Germany to ally with Austria and Russia simultaneously because these two nations were repeatedly engaged in bitter Balkan conflicts. Bismarck chose between the two in 1879 by signing the Dual Alliance with Austria-Hungary against Russia. Each signatory pledged to come to the assistance of the other if either was attacked by Russia and to remain neutral if either was attacked by a power other than Russia. Germany's position against France was strengthened in 1882 when the Italians, angered by the French seizure of Tunisia, joined with Germany and Austria to transform the Dual Alliance into the Triple Alliance. Germany and Austria agreed to aid Italy if it was attacked by France, and Italy was to assist Germany in case of a French attack. Prompted by fears of Russia, Romania joined the Triple Alliance in 1883 through a secret treaty with Austria-Hungary.

In the meantime, Russia and Germany parted company during the 1890s. Bismarck had managed to maintain both the Dual Alliance and Russian friendship by reviving the Three Emperors' League from 1881 to 1887 and, after it dissolved, by signing a separate Reinsurance Treaty with Russia (1887). After forcing Bismarck out of office in 1890, Emperor William II refused to renew the Reinsurance Treaty. Because they were both now isolated, France and Russia gravitated toward each other despite their political and cultural differences. A vague friendship established in 1891 was followed by a mutual-defense alliance in 1894. According to its terms Russia promised to aid France if it was attacked by Germany or by Italy supported by Germany, and France promised to aid Russia if it was attacked by Germany or by Austria-Hungary supported by Germany. Anglo-French and Anglo-Russian concords in 1904 and 1907 transformed this alliance into the Triple Entente.

International Crises. Between 1905 and 1913, Europe was plagued by a series of crises that threatened to engage the major powers in open warfare. The first developed in 1905. According to the Anglo-French Entente Cordiale of 1904, the British had recognized Morocco as a French sphere of influence. Because Germany had not been consulted about this matter, William II decided to undermine the Entente Cordiale and demonstrate simultaneously that the German voice had to be heard on colonial questions. Therefore, in March 1905, he landed at the Moroccan port of Tangier, demanded that the Anglo-French agreement be set aside, and called for an international conference to decide the fate of Morocco. Although the French government yielded and agreed to a conference at Algeciras in 1906 to settle the Moroccan question, German actions ultimately strengthened rather than weakened the Entente Cordiale. Sir Edward Grey, the British foreign secretary, strongly implied in his communications to the German ambassador that Britain would support France in case of a Franco-German war. Because of British support, France emerged from the Algeciras Conference with a tightened grip on Morocco.

A second crisis was incited in 1908 when Austria-Hungary formally annexed Bosnia and Herzegovina. This move followed an agreement between Count von Aehrenthal, the Austro-Hungarian foreign minister, and Aleksandr Izvolski, the Russian foreign minister, that Russia would defend the annexation if Austria would support increased Russian access to the Bosporus and Dardanelles straits. The Slavic nation of Serbia had long wanted to include the kindred peoples of Bosnia and Herzegovina under its control. At the same time, Britain resented any efforts to undermine the new Turkish government, which had begun to initiate liberal reforms in 1908. When Izvolski learned that sentiment in Russia was also strongly opposed to Austrian annexation, he denied his agreement with Aehrenthal and called for an international conference to resolve the matter. Britain now came to the assistance of Russia, and Germany gave strong support to Austria-Hungary. The dilemma was finally resolved in 1909 when Russia and Serbia, yielding to German and Austrian threats, agreed to recognize Austrian annexation of the two provinces. Neither Serbia nor Russia ever forgot these humiliations, and both nations feverishly accelerated propaganda and preparations for a war that they considered either likely or inevitable.

Less than three years later, problems in Morocco again threatened to trigger a European war. In 1911, as a result of civil disorders, French troops were sent to the Moroccan capital of Fès, ostensibly to protect the lives of foreigners. Fearing that France would establish a protectorate over the area, the German government dispatched the warship *Panther* to the Moroccan port of Agadir. This action gave rise to British fears that a compromise accepting German control over parts of Morocco would endanger British access routes to South Africa and India. The British government informed Germany that the matter could not be peaceably resolved unless Britain's interests were respected. Because neither side wanted war, a compromise was reached, conceding Germany control over a large part of the French Congo and, in exchange, giving France a free hand in Morocco. Patriotic feelings in France were so intense during this controversy that the conciliatory ministry of Joseph Caillaux was replaced by a strongly nationalistic government headed by Raymond Poincaré. As an outgrowth of the Moroccan dispute, the naval race between Germany and Great Britain accelerated. Alliance lines were hardening, and European states were becoming progressively more suspicious of their rivals' intentions.

The final crises before World War I occurred in the Balkans. Determined to free their national groups still under Turkish dominance, a coalition of states, comprising Bulgaria, Greece, Montenegro, and Serbia, organized the Balkan League in 1912. As the league made military preparations, the Turkish government and the major powers joined in promises of reform. Members of the Balkan League rejected these overtures and opened war against Turkey in October 1912. In a short time, they overran Macedonia and penetrated to within twenty-five miles of Constantinople, forcing Turkey to sign the Treaty of London in May 1913. However, this settlement proved transient because the victors soon began fighting over the spoils. In the Second Balkan War (June-July 1913), Bulgaria was opposed by the forces of Serbia, Greece, Montenegro, Romania, and Turkey. Facing these formidable odds, Bulgaria agreed to a redistribution of territory in the treaties of Bucharest and Constantinople. Although Turkey regained Adrianople, most of its remaining European possessions were divided among the nations that had precipitated the two Balkan wars.

3

World War I

World War I marked a turning point in European and world history. Since the end of the Napoleonic battles in 1815, Europe had been free from general warfare. The Crimean, Franco-Prussian, and Balkan conflicts had all ended without irreparable damage to the European state system. During this century of relative peace, Europe attained impressive achievements in science, industry, world power, and culture. But events in July and August 1914 redirected the talents and energies of the European people. For four dramatic years, they dedicated their highest skills to the requirements of self-preservation and destruction of the enemy. Although the war was fought primarily on European soil, it was truly a global affair; over a score of nations throughout the world were involved. It was also a *total war*, requiring the mobilization of all segments of a nation's population. At first, there was optimism in all quarters that a few major battles would end the struggle in a matter of weeks. This mood soon changed to one of pessimism and horror as the war lengthened into stalemates of attrition.

ALLIANCE SYSTEMS AND THE OUTBREAK OF WAR

The nationalities problem in the Balkans generated the incident that ignited World War I. The most explosive controversy involved bitter rivalries between Serbian nationalists and the rulers of Austria-Hungary. Among the Slavic peoples of the Ottoman Empire, Serbians had been the most successful in achieving national independence. Their goal was a Greater Serbia that would include other southern Slavs. Because many of these Slavs remained under the dominance of Austria-Hungary, relations between Serbia and the Hapsburg state progressively deteriorated. Serbian envy intensified in 1878 when Austria-Hungary expanded its control over Slavic peoples by gaining the right to administer Bosnia and Herzegovina, and when Austria formally annexed these two provinces in 1908, the Serbs were outraged. The conflict between Serbia and Austria had wider, more ominous implications. Throughout the nineteenth century, Russia had justified repeated interventions in the affairs of southeastern Europe on the grounds that it was the protector of the Slavic cause and the Orthodox faith in the Balkans. The Austrian Empire, of course, was closely allied with Germany. Thus, a serious crisis between Serbia and Austria would bring other powers into play, thereby testing the prior commitments of Europe's alliance systems.

Assassination at Sarajevo. The event that provided the catalyst for global warfare occurred in Sarajevo, the capital of Bosnia. On June 28, 1914, Archduke Francis Ferdinand, heir to the Austrian throne, was conducting a state visit to Bosnia in an effort to strengthen its relations to the Hapsburg dynasty. Several hours after an earlier bomb attempt failed, the archduke and his wife were shot to death by a member of a Serbian nationalist organization called the Black Hand. Although the actual role of the Serbian government was unclear, the leaders of Austria decided to use this incident to justify punitive measures against Serbia. Austria's goal was to secure its empire by crushing Serbia's anti-Austrian terrorist and propaganda campaign. Having obtained a promise of unqualified German support (the so-called blank check), the Austrian government, on July 23, 1914, presented Serbia with a harsh ultimatum. Serbia was to end all anti-Austrian propaganda and other activities, dismiss from service the military and administrative personnel engaged in such matters, and take legal action against frontier authorities assumed to be a part of the assassination conspiracy. Austro-Hungarian officials were to participate in the investigations related to these actions, even though they would take place on Serbian soil. Serbia was given forty-eight hours to indicate unconditional acceptance of these terms, which would in effect have made Serbia a dependent state of Austria.

Serbia responded on July 25, a few hours before the deadline. In a conciliatory and evasive message that made a favorable impression in most European countries, including Germany, the Serbian government conditionally accepted most of the Austrian demands. Nevertheless, a war party led by Austrian Foreign Minister Count Leopold von Berchtold was determined to stop at nothing less than the military chastisement of Serbia. Convinced by Berchtold, Emperor Francis Joseph I ordered a declaration of war against Serbia on July 28. The Austrians planned for a short war that would be confined to Austria and Serbia.

Russia's reaction, however, made such a localized conflict unlikely. Encouraged by promises of French support and determined to maintain its prestige and influence in the Balkans, the Russian government on July 30 ordered a general mobilization of its forces against Germany and Austria.

The cast of characters grew speedily. The German kaiser, after attempting unsuccessfully to persuade the Russian czar to stop massing his forces, declared war on Russia (August 1). Because German military plans in case of a war against Russia or Russia aided by France were predicated on the speedy and surprise deployment of troops, the German government demanded that France make its intentions known immediately. Receiving no satisfactory response, Germany declared war on France (August 3). On the same day, Germany began an invasion of Belgium, whose neutrality Britain had historically supported. Although Britain had no binding commitment to either side, British sentiments and understandings were with France and Russia. Consequently, Britain declared war on Germany (August 4).

Central Powers.   By coming to Austria's aid, Germany demonstrated the value of the Dual Alliance (1879). Although Italy's membership had transformed the Dual Alliance into the Triple Alliance, the Italian government formally declared its neutrality. Italy's technical excuse was that Austria's aggressive acts voided any Italian obligations to help Austria fight a defensive war. In reality, Italy hesitated because promises of Austrian territory that Italy wanted were not forthcoming and because it feared British attacks along the Italian coastline. Romania, an ally of Austria, also declared its neutrality. Both Italy and Romania maintained negotiations with both sides. Turkey was the only nation to join Germany and Austria in 1914. This attraction to the Central Powers was natural because Russia was Turkey's traditional foe; furthermore, German influence had grown steadily at Constantinople during the late nineteenth century. As a result of the close relationship between Germany and Austria, the Central Powers enjoyed a unity of military direction that eluded their foes until 1918. Throughout the war, Germany was the dominant partner. In addition to industrial and military weaknesses, Austria was plagued by the continuing problem of dissident nationalities.

Allies.   As the war began, the Allies included members of the Triple Entente (Britain, France, and Russia) and the lesser powers of Serbia, Montenegro, and Belgium. Japan also sided with the Allies. Britain's 1902 alliance with Japan, renewed in 1905 and 1911, obligated each nation to protect the other's interests in the Far East. Inspired by dreams of building an empire in Asia while the European powers struggled among themselves, Japan delivered an ultimatum to Germany (August 15, 1914), demanding that Germany withdraw its warships from Asian waters and relinquish control of the Chinese territory of Kiaochow. When Germany refused to bow to these demands, Japan declared war (August 23). The pooled strength of Allied nations appeared superior to the combined forces of Germany, Austria, and Turkey. France possessed the Entente's most powerful army; Britain was master of the seas; Japan was the dominant nation in Asia; Russia was the most populous country in Europe. But Russia's numerical strength was also its weakness because the inefficient Russian economy made it impossible to feed and supply both the troops and the civilian population adequately. Furthermore, the Allied states lacked the contiguous borders and the unified command that facilitated transportation and communication between Germany and Austria.

LAND WARFARE, 1914 TO 1917

When hostilities began, German armies assumed the offensive. In accordance with the carefully formulated Schlieffen Plan, Germany initially aimed at a holding action against the slower-moving Russian armies. This plan dictated that the critical assault in the West be made, not along the heavily fortified Franco-German border, but through Belgium into northern France. In a vast encircling movement, the German army's powerful right wing would attack the French army on its left and force it to retreat toward the Swiss frontier. The execution of this strategy was obstructed by a rapid Russian attack that led the German commander, General Helmuth von Moltke, to send two army corps from his right wing to defend East Prussia. In neither the East nor the West did the 1914 offensives succeed. Nevertheless, the early campaigns proved the most fluid of the war until 1918. From 1915 to 1917, the conflict that all sides had planned as one of movement settled into deadlocked trench warfare.

Western Front. Despite temporary halts, the German advance through Belgium proceeded; and after twenty days of fighting, German armies were ready to begin their invasion of France. The French commander, General Joseph Joffre, had shifted his strongest armies toward the Belgian frontier, where they were joined on August 22 by a British expeditionary force. Unable to stop the German onslaught, whose immediate goal was the capture of Paris, the Allied armies retreated for over 100 miles; by the first week in September, northeast-

ern France was under German control. Joffre decided to assume the
offensive at the Marne River, and the First Battle of the Marne was
fought from September 5 to 12, 1914. Taking advantage of Germany's
overextended supply lines, heroic efforts by the French soldiers hurled
the German armies backwards. Joffre's strategy had thus saved Paris
and produced the first conclusive encounter of World War I. German
forces retreated to deeply entrenched positions along the Aisne River,
which left them in control of Belgium and northern France, both rich
in mineral resources and highly developed industrially.

Battle positions were stabilized during the winter of 1914–1915. The
infantry on both sides dug trenches and fortified their positions with
impaling networks of barbed wire along a front that extended for over
300 miles. Although each side attempted forward thrusts, troops on
the defensive had all the advantages. Offensive units would begin with
artillery bombardments, followed by waves of infantrymen who would
go over the top of their trenches with fixed bayonets and hand gre-
nades. To achieve their goal, they had to penetrate wire barricades and
destroy well-entrenched machine-gun emplacements. Even when successful, the attackers suffered heavy casualties while forcing opposing
troops to retreat only a few miles. Supplemented by reserves, the defenders dug new trenches and were prepared to fight again. The French
learned this lesson hardest and last. In offensives during the summer
and fall of 1915, they lost about 600,000 men and gained little terrain; the battle lines remained virtually intact.

Eastern Front.   The war along the Eastern front was always less
intense and more fluid than the war in the West. Military operations
spanned vaster territories, making it more difficult for troops to become well entrenched. Decisive battles in the East during 1914 followed a Russian offensive into East Prussia, Germany's most exposed
position. Two Russian armies were involved: the First Army, under
the direction of General Pavel Rennenkampf, and the Second Army,
commanded by General Aleksandr Samsonov. Enmity between the
two generals resulted in inadequate coordination of troops, allowing a
wide gap to develop between their forces. Rennenkampf's First Army
advanced while Samsonov's Second Army procrastinated in the rear.
This weakness was exploited by German armies under two of the
war's ablest commanders, Field Marshal Paul von Hindenburg and his
chief of staff, General Erich Ludendorff. By the end of August, the
German forces had surrounded the Second Army, capturing over
120,000 men, and Samsonov committed suicide. Rennenkampf's forces
were then defeated and pursued into Lithuania. Meanwhile, Austria

was engaging the armies of both Russia and Serbia. As the Russians advanced into Galicia, Austria was meeting surprisingly determined opposition from the Serbians. By the end of 1914, the Russian invasion had been blunted by the arrival of German forces; but the Serbians stubbornly continued their resistance.

During 1915, the tide of battle on the Eastern front turned in favor of the Central Powers. First, the Allies attempted to gain control over Constantinople and the Balkans by seizing the Dardanelles. Their objectives were to force Turkey out of the war and to encourage Romania, Bulgaria, and Greece to join the Allied cause. Supervised by German officers, the Turks repelled each Allied effort to gain mastery of their forts. After suffering 150,000 casualties, the Allies terminated the campaign. Meanwhile, the Central Powers were conducting successful offensives. German and Austrian military leaders decided to relieve the pressure on Austria-Hungary by dealing Russia a decisive blow. Their drive, which opened in April, succeeded in forcing the Russians almost completely out of Austria-Hungary by the end of July. Suffering food and munitions shortages in addition to enormous casualties, the Russians were compelled to relinquish all Poland and part of Lithuania during the fall. In November, a German and Austro-Hungarian force also conquered Serbia, which had twice previously routed invading Austrian armies.

Attrition. In 1916, both sides developed schemes designed to break the impasse in the West and bring the war to a triumphant end. Plans for the Central Powers were formulated by General Erich von Falkenhayn, who had replaced Moltke as chief of staff. Falkenhayn was positive that the exhausted and vulnerable French forces could be defeated by a concentrated attack on one key and symbolic point. He chose for his purpose the famous fortress and city of Verdun, which formed a salient in the French front. The battle began in February with a blistering German artillery bombardment, and it raged for six months. Inspired by the war cry "They shall not pass," the French forces repeatedly repelled German onslaughts.

The French were assisted in June by two Allied offensives that forced the Germans to divert men and materials from Verdun. Seven German divisions were rushed to the East in response to a new Russian drive into Galicia while the British began an Allied offensive on the Somme River in an attempt to break through German lines. None of these offensives succeeded. At Verdun and on the Somme, the superiority of defensive over offensive units was again demonstrated. At the end of the Verdun struggle, each side had lost over 300,000 men, but the Germans had won only a few square miles of territory. The Somme offensive, lasting from July to November, cost the Germans 500,000 casualties and the Allies over 600,000 yet resulted in only minor shifts in positions along the battle line. After a brilliant counterattack in Austria-Hungary, the Russian advance in the East was repelled by the Germans. Despite optimistic predictions from both sides, 1916 did not prove to be a turning point in the war.

NAVAL WARFARE, 1914 TO 1917

Naval warfare was more conclusive than the struggles on land. Despite fierce prewar competition from Germany, British superiority gave the Allies continual mastery over the seas. The Allies established an effective blockade around the German and Austrian coastlines early in the war, thwarting the movement of German warships and virtually halting the Central Powers' seaborne commerce. British naval superiority also enabled the Allies to seize German colonies in Asia and the Pacific. However, the Germans enjoyed greater success in the oceans' depths. By 1917, their production and use of the submarine had accelerated, making it a potentially decisive weapon in the war. The critical naval struggle, therefore, was between the British blockade and the German efforts to destroy it and introduce a counterblockade through the use of submarines. Both measures were executed in ways that violated international law and infringed the rights of neutrals.

British Blockade.   The purpose of the British blockade was to strangle the Central Powers economically. Because Germany was a highly industrialized nation, its population and factories were dependent on continual imports of raw materials and foodstuffs. According to the specifications of international law, sanctioned by the Congress of Paris in 1856, a blockading power was authorized to stop only shipments of contraband goods, which were defined as including items that could clearly be labeled munitions and certain raw materials used to produce military equipment. Noncontraband goods, including foodstuffs, were supposed to pass freely through a blockade so that it would be impossible for a nation to deny essential goods to its enemy's citizens or to interfere with civilian production. However, because these were precisely the results the British hoped to achieve, they gradually eliminated the distinction between contraband and noncontraband items. They claimed the right not only to stop all neutral ships headed for German ports but also to regulate all imports into the neutral countries of Scandinavia and the Netherlands on the grounds that these goods were frequently destined for resale to Germany. The most serious violations of neutrality affected America's trade with Europe, and President Woodrow Wilson registered strenuous and bitter protests against them. However, sympathies in the United States were on the side of the Allies, and relations between the two powers were never broken.

Battle of Jutland.   The naval encounter known as the Battle of Jutland occurred off the coast of Norway on May 31, 1916, when a German scouting fleet ventured into the North Sea hoping to decoy a British squadron into a fight with the German High Seas Fleet. Informed by their intelligence services of this plan, the British schemed instead to lure the main German force into an encounter with the British Grand Fleet. The Grand Fleet, under the command of Admiral John Jellicoe, was made up of over 150 ships and constituted Great Britain's most formidable military force. By late afternoon, the British had succeeded in separating the German High Seas Fleet from their Helgoland base, but the Germans managed to penetrate the British formation and return to their home waters. During the encounter, the British suffered twice as many casualties as the Germans did and lost fourteen ships; the Germans lost eleven. But the Germans' miscalculations had risked destruction of the High Seas Fleet. They never made such a venture again, leaving British command of the seas intact.

Submarine Warfare.   The procedures of international law required that suspicious merchant ships be searched, seized, and escorted to a port. But this was difficult to apply to the smaller submarine, a novel instrument of warfare. What the submarine could do effectively was sink the ship it attacked, as demonstrated by German successes against British warships in 1914. The German admiralty therefore calculated that the use of submarines against both warships and merchant ships, Allied and neutral, would produce a weakening of the British blockade. In February 1915, the German government designated the waters around the British Isles a war zone in which submarine warfare would be unrestricted. After a stern warning from President Wilson that Germany would be held accountable for the loss of American vessels or lives, on May 7, 1915, German submarines torpedoed the British passenger ship *Lusitania.* Although the vessel was also transporting munitions from the United States to Britain, the American public was outraged because 139 Americans were among the 1,138 persons who drowned. This sinking and subsequent submarine attacks aroused bitter reactions from the American government. German leaders were unwilling at this stage to provoke the United States into formally joining the Allies, particularly because the use of submarines was not succeeding in destroying the British blockade. On September 1, 1915, the German government announced that it would cease surprise submarine attacks on unarmed vessels.

CHANGES IN THE CHARACTER OF THE WAR

Between the outbreak of war and 1917, no alliance changes were in themselves significant enough to alter power relations dramatically. Developments during 1917, however, brought hopes to each side that the deadlock could be broken in its favor. The collapse of the czarist regime in March 1917 created false optimism in Britain and France that the Russians would fight in a more inspired manner under a parliamentary system. But following the second Russian Revolution in November 1917, the Bolshevik rulers fulfilled their promise to take Russia out of the war altogether, allowing the Central Powers to concentrate their military operations in the West. Meanwhile, however, an American declaration of war against Germany provided the Allies with an even mightier and more energetic ally. The crucial question was whether American assistance would reach Europe quickly enough and in sufficient quantities to offset Germany's strengthened position in the West. These events also clarified ideological alignments. After Russia's withdrawal, the principal Allied nations were Western democracies fighting against the more aristocratic regimes of Germany and Austria. In addition, two avenues for achieving peace were competing for the loyalties of the European peoples: President Wilson's campaign to "make the world safe for democracy" and Lenin's alternative of peace without annexations, to be achieved through Socialist revolution.

Entry of the United States.   The predominant American attitude at the beginning of the war was to avoid entanglement. President Wilson expressed this view on August 4, 1914, by issuing a proclamation of neutrality, and he later advised Americans to be impartial in thought as well as action. Regardless of this stated policy, however, sentiments in the United States were never neutral. Austria's harsh ultimatum to Serbia, Germany's invasion of neutral Belgium, and Germany's campaign of submarine warfare all drew American sympathies to the Allied cause. Furthermore, in its cultural and political heritages, the United States was closer to Britain and France than to other European countries. Nevertheless, the isolationist mood was so deeply ingrained that the United States was unlikely to enter the conflict except in response to gross infringements of its neutral rights. Americans reacted vehemently to both British and German violations of their free access to the seas, but they objected most bitterly to Germany's submarine warfare, which involved the loss of American lives. Thus, on several occasions in 1915 and 1916, President Wilson responded to the submarine attacks by threatening to sever relations with Germany; and in 1916, he persuaded the Germans to halt unrestricted submarine warfare.

The reversal of this decision in 1917 precipitated the chain of events leading to American involvement. Hindenburg and Ludendorff had become convinced that land forces could not achieve an early victory and that submarine warfare was the only way of compelling the Allies to accept peace terms. The German leaders recognized that this decision would force the United States to join the Allies. But they believed that submarine attacks could bring Britain to her knees within six months and that a year or more would elapse before the United States could train, equip, and transport large numbers of troops and supplies to Europe. On January 31, 1917, the German government announced that unrestricted submarine warfare in the waters surrounding the British Isles would be renewed. All ships, Allied and neutral, were subject to attack without notice.

President Wilson promptly severed relations with Germany (February 3) but postponed further steps until Germany actually implemented its announced policy. In the midst of these developments, public opinion in the United States was further infuriated by the disclosure on March 1, 1917, of a note sent by German Foreign Minister Arthur Zimmermann to the German delegate in Mexico. In case of a German-American war, he was instructed to offer Mexico the return of lost territories in the American Southwest in exchange for a Mexican alliance against the United States. Next came a series of reported submarine attacks, culminating, on March 16, in the news that three American ships had been sunk by German torpedoes. Responding to widespread demands for retaliation, President Wilson, in a speech delivered to a joint session of Congress on April 2, proclaimed:

> *The right is more precious than peace, and we shall fight for the things which we have always carried nearest to our hearts—for democracy, for the right of those who submit to authority to have a voice in their own Governments, for the rights and liberties of small nations, for a universal domination of right by such a concert of free peoples as shall bring peace and safety to all nations and make the world itself at last free.*

Congress reacted by voting a declaration of war on April 6.

Withdrawal of Russia. The Russian Revolutions of 1917 (see chapter 4) were induced by the government bankruptcy that the war had revealed and magnified. No government met the test of war more ineffectively than the czarist regime did. Corruption, secrecy, and inefficiency permeated the imperial family and all levels of the bureaucracy. Army morale was lowered as soldiers were sent to battle with equipment that was inadequate or in short supply. Russian armies fared well against the forces of Austria-Hungary, but inevitable disaster followed when they faced the better-disciplined and better-equipped German soldiers. By the end of 1916, Russia had lost over 2 million men and suffered over 4 million additional casualties. Military discouragements and defeats fed civilian discontent, which was further intensified by food shortages. Despite the growing schism between the autocracy and the masses, no reforms were instituted in the government or the society in order to establish a consensus in support of the war. Above all, there was an absence of inspired leadership to defend and justify these cruel sacrifices. Widespread opposition led, in March 1917, to the overthrow of the czarist system, which was replaced by the bourgeois Provisional Government appointed by the Duma. During the spring of 1917, another military campaign ended in failure; and in November 1917, the Bolsheviks, who promised peace and reform, seized power from the Provisional Government. Although forced to accept harsh terms, the Bolsheviks fulfilled their peace promises by first agreeing to an armistice (December 15, 1917) and by later signing the Treaty of Brest Litovsk (March 3, 1918) with Germany.

Evolving War Aims. At the start of the war, the common objective of all belligerents was to protect and preserve their national security. But the shifting fortunes of battle and the ever-increasing sacrifices that citizens were called upon to endure soon generated a broadening of most countries' war aims. Throughout the struggle, Austria-Hungary's dominant goal remained the achievement of a Balkan settlement that would resolve the empire's internal difficulties. Of all protagonists, Germany developed the most ambitious plans for territorial expansion. Military leaders, supported by broad segments of the population, envisioned the extension of Germany's frontiers to include Belgium and northern France in the west and Poland and other satellite states in the east. In addition to protecting the interests of Serbia and extending its influence in the Balkans, Russia expressed interest in establishing a protectorate over Poland. Similarly, the

French added the establishment of a buffer state west of the Rhine to their predictable hopes of recovering Alsace-Lorraine. British goals were to ensure Belgium's independence, to weaken Germany by destroying its fleet and redistributing its colonies, and to reestablish the rule of law in international affairs. The United States, having no design on territorial conquests in Europe, hoped to guarantee freedom of the seas, to devise a peace of reconciliation, and to create a world organization that would resolve international conflicts peaceably or with a minimum of bloodshed.

Through secret negotiations, leagued nations bargained to obtain firm commitments that their war aims would be honored in postwar settlements. With the exception of the United States, this practice was particularly popular among the Allied nations, whose governments were able to formulate independent war policies. Secret treaties were less prevalent among the Central Powers because Germany's supremacy during the war would have meant German dominance of any peace settlements if the Central Powers were victorious. Neutral nations willing to join the fray were particularly well situated to define their war aims in advance, making acceptance of them the precondition for entering the war. Thus, Italy joined the Allies after being promised the Austrian provinces of southern Tirol, Trieste, Istria, and Dalmatia in the secret Treaty of London (1915). Romania was enticed to fight against the Central Powers by Allied assurances under the Treaty of Bucharest (1916) that it would receive Transylvania, Bucovina, Banat, and a sizable section of the Hungarian plain. Italy became a partner in the series of clandestine agreements with Britain, France, and Russia that partitioned Turkey (1915 and 1916). In a February 1917 concord, France supported Russian claims against the Central Powers; in return, Russia supported the French annexation of Alsace-Lorraine, Saarland, and the Rhineland from Germany. To obtain Japanese naval assistance in the Far East, Great Britain agreed to Japan's acquisition of Germany's Pacific islands and rights in Shantung. These secret agreements hampered efforts to reach a peace settlement once the war had ended.

After the Bolsheviks seized power in November 1917, they invited all belligerents to conclude peace by applying the principles of no annexations or indemnities. When the other Allies rejected these conditions, the Bolsheviks began independent negotiations with Germany in January 1918 that terminated the war in the East two months later. Under these circumstances, Allied leaders felt compelled to restate and redefine their wartime objectives. The most influential statement was President Wilson's peace program, announced in January 1918, comprising the following Fourteen Points:

1. Open covenants of peace, openly arrived at
2. Absolute freedom of navigation upon the seas in peace and in war
3. The removal, so far as possible, of all international economic barriers
4. Guarantees that national armaments would be reduced to the lowest point consistent with domestic safety
5. An impartial adjustment of colonial claims, giving equal weight to the interests of the populations and governments concerned
6. The evacuation of all conquered Russian territory
7. The evacuation and restoration of Belgium
8. The evacuation and restoration of formerly French territory, including Alsace-Lorraine, to France
9. The readjustment of Italian frontiers along clearly recognizable lines of nationality
10. The granting of autonomy to the subject nationalities of Austria-Hungary
11. Evacuation and restoration of Romania, Serbia, and Montenegro, with Serbia accorded free access to the sea
12. The Turkish portions of the Ottoman Empire to be assured a secure sovereignty, the other nationalities under Turkish rule to have independence, and the Dardanelles to be open to the commerce of all nations under international guarantees
13. An independent Polish state to be erected, with free and secure access to the sea
14. A general association of nations to be formed for the purpose of affording mutual guarantees of political independence and territorial integrity to great and small states alike

HOME FRONTS

As the illusion of a speedy war was dispelled, it became evident that the war would have a pervasive and lasting effect upon European society. In response to the demands of national security, the state became the supreme arbiter of how the resources of belligerent nations would be allocated. Government control of politics, the econ-

omy, and society was progressively expanded into spheres normally
considered the domains of individual choice. Varying systems of boards
and commissions were used to coordinate diverse aspects of the war
effort. Draft boards enforced military conscription, and as the need for
manpower became insatiable, women revolutionized their role by
assuming civilian and military jobs traditionally reserved for men. Business competition and labor agitation were subordinated to the requirements of a singleminded and sustained national industrial effort. In all
countries, propaganda was designed to sustain home morale, to convert
neutrals, and to weaken the enemy's will to fight. By 1917, war
weariness immensely complicated the task of arousing and maintaining
popular support. Socialists and pacifists were campaigning for an end
to the slaughter through an immediate peace without victory, annexations, or indemnities.

France.   The French greeted the outbreak of war with widespread
enthusiasm. The moderate cabinet of René Viviani was transformed
into the *union sacrée,* a coalition government headed by a succession
of premiers and including representatives of every political group, from
conservative to Socialist. At first, this coalition deferred to the judgment of General Joffre, the army's commander in chief. After Joffre
was replaced by General Robert Nivelle in late 1916, the pendulum of
power swung back toward the politicians, who began exercising a
greater influence over both military and domestic affairs. As casualty
lists grew while the conflict remained deadlocked, morale weakened,
and disunity became widespread. In the spring of 1917, entire army
units refused to obey orders to go over the top. At home, Socialists
and leftist Radicals became progressively disenchanted with the coalition politics that made them supporters of the war. The disgruntled were
led by Joseph Caillaux, a prewar Radical premier, who campaigned
vigorously for a negotiated peace. These divisions, which revived
traditional enmities between Left and Right, tore the coalition asunder.
As a consequence, President Poincaré, in November 1917, assigned the
premiership to the able, obstinate, and patriotic Clemenceau, who ruled
in a dictatorial fashion until the end of the war. Under his inspiring
and intolerant leadership, French morale was raised, resistance was
stiffened, and vocal opponents of the war were either intimidated or
sent to jail.

Germany.   In Germany, as in France, the outbreak of warfare
produced a truce among political parties. Despite the disapproval of a
few left-wing socialists, all political parties in the Reichstag voted war
credits on August 4, 1914. After this vote, the already weak Reichstag

left the conduct of the war entirely up to military leaders and imperial officials. Power soon gravitated to the supreme command, which was dominated by Hindenburg and Ludendorff. After the dismissal of Chancellor Theobald von Bethmann-Hollweg in 1917, the supreme command exercised dictatorial power. The new chancellor, Georg Michaelis, was a pliable tool of army leaders. Under military and conservative domination, Germany was clearly fighting for territorial acquisitions. As in France, socialists and many liberals became increasingly disheartened with the war effort. In July 1917, Social Democrats, Progressives, and Centrists united to force passage of a peace resolution in the Reichstag. The resolution urged the government to seek a peace of reconciliation without territorial conquests and also to undertake democratic reforms at home. Although it deepened the political cleavage within Germany, the peace resolution failed to alter the policies of Germany's military dictators.

Great Britain. In contrast with Germany, civilian dominance over the military prevailed in Britain throughout the conflict. Britain began the war with a Liberal government headed by Herbert H. Asquith and supported by both the Irish Home Rule party and the Labour party. Conservatives, led by Andrew Bonar Law, called a political truce and agreed to postpone the elections due in 1915. In 1916, Asquith broadened his ministry to include eight Conservatives in the cabinet of twenty-two. Asquith, with his gentle and compromising temperament, was ill suited for the ruthless decision making that characterized the great war leaders. An accumulation of frustrations and military setbacks by the end of 1916 led to a reorganization of the government. The new premier was the energetic and decisive David Lloyd George, who had earlier served as chancellor of the exchequer, minister of munitions, and secretary of state for war. Most Liberals followed Asquith into retirement, creating a split that accelerated the Liberal party's postwar decline. Although he remained nominally a Liberal, Lloyd George's coalition cabinet was dominated by Conservatives. A small inner cabinet, including Lloyd George and four other men, formulated war policies.

Austria-Hungary. Austria's traditional society and economy, like Russia's, were less well prepared than those of more highly industrialized countries for a long and weakening war. Austria's position was precarious throughout the war. Internally, stability was possible only if the Magyars and the subject nationalities sustained the war effort; externally, the defense of Austria was continually dependent upon the superiority of German arms. Pervasive war weariness took its toll during 1917 and 1918. The Austrian prime minister, Count Karl von Stürgkh, was assassinated in October 1916. A month later, Emperor Francis Joseph I died, ending an unprecedented reign of sixty-eight years. Social dislocations made it increasingly difficult for the new emperor, Charles I, to maintain Hapsburg rule. Hungary, which normally exported food to Austria, withheld supplies, demanding compensation in manufactured goods; concurrently, the two kingdoms argued over the deployment of troops. The subject nationalities were also stirring. By May 1917 the Czechs and Yugoslavs were demanding that the Dual Monarchy be made a federal state; at the same time, the Slovaks, Romanians, and Croats were urging political concessions from Hungary. As the campaigns of 1918 were being prepared, Austria-Hungary had already begun to disintegrate.

United States. The United States entered World War I when the tide of battle was flowing in favor of the Central Powers. Effective participation required the mobilization of the nation's resources to sustain the transfer of men and supplies to fight a war over 3,000 miles away. An unprecedented degree of government regimentation inevitably followed. The Selective Service Act (May 1917) required young men to register for military duty. Soon after the declaration of war, Congress created a propaganda agency called the Committee on Public Information to keep morale high by constantly rekindling the fires of patriotism. The Espionage Act (June 1917) and the Sedition Act (May 1918) imposed fines and prison sentences for behavior considered disloyal. The War Industries Board, administered by Bernard Baruch, was accorded authority to establish priorities for industrial production and distribution. Other boards were created to formulate policies for shipping, food, fuel, railroads, and labor. Unwilling to finance the war entirely through higher taxes, the government borrowed over $21 million through four bond drives. President Wilson encouraged Americans to justify sacrifices "to make the world safe for democracy."

END OF THE WAR

Although the events of 1917 failed to end the war, they did set the stage for the final drama. Despite heavy losses inflicted by German submarines, the British were able to preserve control of the seas by using a variety of antisubmarine devices, including radar, depth charges, and the convoy system. Nevertheless, Allied plans to break the deadlock also failed. On the Western front, a French offensive was launched in

April 1917 by General Robert Nivelle. Losses were so heavy against the well-entrenched German armies that some French units mutinied, persuading the French government to replace Nivelle with the more cautious Henri Philippe Pétain. During the final campaigns of 1917, the principal battlefield advantages were won by the Central Powers. Combined German-Austrian armies forced the Italians into a disastrous retreat at Caporetto (October 1917). A British offensive into Flanders (November-December 1917) gained but then lost a few miles of territory; nevertheless, the British demonstrated how devastating their newly invented tanks were when used in mass formation. The significance of 1917 was that the Central Powers, although predominant in the East, failed to conclude the war in the West on their terms. Superior reserves, national resources, and industrial superiority made time the ally of the Allies. As 1918 began, German leaders fully recognized that their only hope of victory was to end the war quickly.

Last German Offensives. After the conclusion of the peace of Brest Litovsk (March 1918), which took Russia out of the war, Germany completed an ominous and fateful transference of troops from the Eastern to the Western front. Ludendorff convinced Hindenburg and the kaiser that a spring offensive would defeat Britain and France before American support could have a conclusive impact. Because this drive would dissipate Germany's remaining military resources, Ludendorff realized that it would bring either speedy victory or inevitable defeat. Three German armies were involved in the attack, which lasted from March to May. Successive German assaults achieved breakthroughs at Amiens, Ypres, and the Chemin des Dames. In desperation, Allied leaders subordinated the suspicions that had thwarted coordinated efforts throughout the war and made French General Ferdinand Foch the supreme Allied commander. By the end of May, Ludendorff's strategy had for the second time brought German troops to the Marne, less than forty miles from Paris. It had also used up German reserves of supplies and men. The battles of June and July, therefore, would decide the outcome of the war.

Collapse of the Central Powers. General Foch, a leading exponent of the theory that military victory depended upon the maintenance of unrelenting offensives, was finally able to execute this theory with brilliant success. Although few American troops had arrived in Europe during 1917, the rate progressed; and by the spring of 1918, approximately 275,000 were arriving each month. When combined with the rapid production of British ammunition, planes, and tanks, American aid shifted the balance in manpower and supply strength to the Allies, a development that Germany hastened by ambitious and weakening thrusts. American units saw action in June at Château-Thierry and were used to bolster French forces for the expected German onslaught on the Marne. The Second Battle of the Marne (July 1918) was as decisive as its predecessor had been. Having gained the initiative, Foch commanded incessant counterattacks all along the Western front, until by mid-September, the Germans had relinquished the territory they had gained in the spring.

Seeking a final victory, Foch ordered a general Allied advance that produced significant penetrations of Germany's defensive perimeter. In the South and the Near East, the Allies were also successful. An Allied advance begun in mid-September soon forced Bulgaria and Turkey to armistices, liberated Serbia, and threatened the territory of Hungary. The Italian defeat of Austria at Vittorio Veneto in late October hastened the disintegration of the Austro-Hungarian Empire. Rejecting a last-minute effort by Emperor Charles to create a federal state, the Hungarians and subject nationalities had divided the empire into its component parts. With capitulation their only realistic choice, the Hapsburgs signed an armistice on November 3. By late September, Ludendorff's will to fight had also been broken. In response to his request, a government headed by the liberal Prince Max of Baden was instructed to sue for peace and assumed office early in October. Internal discontent grew, and this government was replaced on November 9 by a ministry led by Friedrich Ebert and dominated by Social Democrats. This ministry ended the war on November 11, 1918, by signing the peace terms that Marshal Foch had earlier dictated.

EFFECTS OF WORLD WAR I

World War I produced consequences of tremendous magnitude. Two empires, the Russian and the Austro-Hungarian, had crumbled. Because of dislocations in these nations and in those that maintained their traditional governments, the tasks of reorganization and reconstruction were enormous. Governments had spent billions of dollars to wage the struggle, producing inflated prices that undermined some of the social classes that had stabilized European society in the past. Over 31 million casualties were suffered, including 9 million killed. Some of Europe's most energetic, idealistic, and able men had been killed. Many of those who survived had been changed, some into disenchanted, unemployed, and alienated veterans who continued to exalt military virtues. The combinations of wartime regimentation, economic hardships, and general disenchantment caused a decline of liberal values in politics and economics. As an outgrowth of wartime transformations, totalitarian societies and movements became a prominent feature of European society.

4

The Russian Revolutions of 1917

There were two Russian revolutions in 1917. The first in March* resulted in the overthrow of the czarist regime and its replacement by the Provisional Government, dominated by representatives of middle-class parties. The following November, this interim government was itself displaced by revolutionaries whose representatives spoke in behalf of the masses. Because groups on the Left were deeply divided, it was uncertain where government power would finally be centered. Events soon resolved this question in favor of the Bolsheviks, engineers of the November coup and most extreme of the revolutionary parties. They were favored with extraordinary leaders, notably Nikolai Lenin, who addressed himself directly to the nation's pressing problems and dealt effectively with opposition groups on all levels.

PREREVOLUTIONARY RUSSIA

Early in the twentieth century, there were signs that Russia was developing in a manner that paralleled the evolution of nations in Western Europe. Conspicuous industrial and agricultural progress was being made; a parliamentary system was instituted; and impressive advances were evident in education and the arts. Nevertheless, diverse segments of Russian society had accumulated a long list of grievances against the czarist autocracy. Peasants, industrial workers, and the

* The Julian (Old Style) calendar used in Russia through 1917 was thirteen days behind the Gregorian (New Style) calendar prevalent in Western countries. New Style dates are used throughout this chapter.

intelligentsia were all disenchanted with the hesitant efforts to reform Russia's traditional government and society. During the Russo-Japanese War (see pp. 45–46, 49), military failures had intensified civilian discontent and generated revolutionary plotting. However, by granting parliamentary concessions, the imperial government had maintained its essential authority intact. Beginning in 1914, another war, this one immensely more devastating and weakening, again caused mounting dissatisfaction. By 1917, the czarist system had thoroughly discredited itself. Corruption, inefficiency, and intrigue aggravated the effects of the war, which were worse in Russia than in any other country.

Dumas. The Revolution of 1905 (see p. 42) was intended to reform rather than overthrow the czarist system. Essentially middle class in character, its primary demands were constitutional government and individual liberty. The czar's most important concession was that a representative legislative body, the Duma, be created in Russia for the first time. When liberal majorities were elected to the first two Dumas, Nicholas II, aware that the worst dangers had passed, decided in 1907 to create a conservative Duma artificially. As a consequence of this arbitrary act, the Duma was prevented from developing into a genuine constitutional body.

Relations between the Duma and imperial officials worsened as the war progressed. At first, the political groups in the Duma, like those in the parliamentary bodies of other countries, greeted the war effort with general enthusiasm and support. But military reverses and economic strains weakened confidence in the government, causing dissident Duma members to form a Progressive bloc in 1915. Led by Pavel Milyukov, the Progressive coalition included representatives of all parties except the extremes of Right and Left and delegates from the State Council. This moderate coalition unsuccessfully pressured imperial officials to enact reforms embracing a greater degree of political, religious, and economic liberty. By the end of 1916, further alienation had occurred over the czar's refusal to appoint a ministry acceptable to the Duma or to grant other concessions. At the same time, uneasiness about the war effort spread. The intransigent and unusually inept prime ministers chosen by Nicholas II caused further deterioration of his relations with the Duma.

Imperial Family. As the result of the czar's uninspiring and impotent decision making, any remaining popular loyalty to the Romanov dynasty was dissipated by the end of 1916. Against the advice of army and civilian leaders, Nicholas had succeeded his uncle, Grand Duke Nicholas, as supreme military commander in 1915. Thereafter, he spent almost all his time at the war front. Although key domestic decisions still required his assent, the czar relied heavily upon the advice of his wife, Empress Alexandra, an ultraconservative and a religious zealot. She in turn was heavily influenced by Grigori Rasputin, a puzzling and persuasive holy man of peasant birth, who she believed could guide the destiny of Russia while saving her son from hemophilia. Rasputin's advice exercised a pivotal influence upon government policies, including the appointment, control, and dismissal of top officials. Confidence in the Russian government, at home and abroad, on the Right as well as on the Left, reached its nadir. In a desperate effort to save the dynasty, a group of nobles assassinated Rasputin in December 1916.

War and Social Discontent. The crisis in leadership was directly related to Russia's military failures and economic collapse, which became overwhelming during the third year of the war. Although arms production had increased by 1916, many Russian soldiers during 1915 had been forced to face German artillery with only their bayonets. Some were sent into battle with orders to obtain their arms by retrieving those of the slain. Bandages, medicine, and rations were frequently in short supply or nonexistent. Desertion reached astronomical figures, and the large number of Russians taken as prisoners of war was partly attributable to demoralization. News of military disasters fed the flames of civilian discontent, which further intensified as housing conditions worsened and wages lagged behind inflated prices. By 1916, these grievances were combined with extensive food shortages. Labor unrest inevitably followed. Striking workers numbered over half a million in 1915 and grew to nearly a million in 1916. In addition, ethnic groups in the areas temporarily won from Austria, as well as those within Russia, were antagonized by the government's refusal to make concessions to their demands. The disintegrative effects of the long war were thus breaking the bonds of dynasty, religion, and tradition that had held the large empire together.

MARCH REVOLUTION

During February 1917, rising disorders induced the government to take extraordinary measures in order to protect itself in the capital. Security was in the hands of the Petrograd garrison, over 150,000 strong but composed mostly of inexperienced troops. Under these circumstances, the imperial regime's final crisis was sparked by the events of March 8 (February 23, Old Style) during demonstrations celebrating the Socialist Women's Day. Protesting food shortages, demonstrators and about 70,000 striking workers joined in the streets. As the crowds swelled, the czar, who was at the war front, sent orders to the Petrograd commandant to end the disruptions immediately. On March 10, troops in the capital mutinied and joined the mob. To eliminate a forum for the disaffection, the czar on March 11 ordered the Duma dissolved. But on March 12, the Duma defied the czar's orders and set up a committee to speak for its members and to attempt to form a new government. That same evening, the Petrograd Soviet was founded to articulate views of the masses. Having gained complete control of Petrograd during March 13 and 14, the insurgents agreed that the Duma should establish a new government.

Provisional Government.   Nicholas II abdicated on March 15, ending the Romanov dynasty, which had ruled Russia for over 300 years. While the establishment of a new permanent government awaited the election of a constituent assembly, the monarchy was immediately replaced by the Provisional Government, organized and dominated by liberal parties in the Duma. Prince Georgi E. Lvov, the zemstvo leader, assumed the positions of prime minister and minister of interior. The influential Milyukov, spokesman for the Kadets, became minister of foreign affairs. Other distinguished figures included Octobrist Aleksandr I. Guchkov, the minister of war, and Aleksandr Kerenski, the minister of justice and the only Socialist in the cabinet. The Provisional Government was quickly accepted in Russia and speedily recognized by the Western democracies. The new regime soon instituted creditable liberal reforms. Constitutional freedoms were broadened; local governments were democratized; liberties were extended to ethnic minorities; and legislation was enacted to improve the conditions of labor. Yet, the Provisional Government failed to resolve the two dilemmas that had helped destroy the Romanov dynasty: Russia's disastrous participation in the war and the intense land hunger of the peasantry.

Petrograd Soviet.   Inspired by the memory of similar organizations that formed spontaneously during the 1905 Revolution, workers councils (*soviets*) were organized throughout Russia during March and April 1917. Representing urban workers, peasants, and soldiers, they followed the lead of the Petrograd Soviet, which quickly asserted its authority. Moderate Socialists, Mensheviks, and Socialist Revolutionaries dominated the soviets. Considering the March Revolution bourgeois, these groups concluded that industrial conditions would have to advance gradually before a Socialist revolution could be launched. The first All-Russian Congress of Soviets met in Petrograd in June 1917.

Representing over 350 local organizations, delegates included 285 Socialist Revolutionaries, 245 Mensheviks, and 105 Bolsheviks. The Congress chose an executive committee, which assumed control of the Petrograd militia and the direction of food distribution.

Emergence of Lenin. The Bolshevik leader Vladimir Ilich Ulyanov, better known as Nikolai Lenin, was to be a pivotal figure in Russian and world history. Following the Revolution of 1905, Lenin left Russia to live abroad as a professional revolutionary. The events of 1917 found him in Switzerland. He finally arrived at Finland Station in Petrograd on April 16, after securing permission from the kaiser's government to cross German territory. German officials calculated that the fiery Bolshevik would spread discontent on the home front, thereby helping to disrupt Russia's war effort, and they were right. Lenin publicly identified the Provisional Government with the monarchy it purported to replace, and he condemned it for the continuing war and its associated problems. The Bolsheviks offered a program that included an immediate general peace, land reform, nationalization of production and distribution, and the transference of power from parliamentary institutions to the soviets. Unlike Menshevik and Socialist Revolutionary leaders, Lenin thought that conditions in Russia were ripe for a Socialist revolution, beginning with the seizure of power by peasants and industrial workers.

Dilemmas of the Provisional Government. The Provisional Government dealt inadequately with Russia's monumental problems. Wrongly assessing the popular mood, the government was confident that democratic reforms would persuade the people to combine their energies in a patriotic war effort. The liberal regime also erred in its delay in calling a constituent assembly, especially because major reforms such as a land settlement for the peasants were contingent upon the approval of that body. Government stability was further undermined by the rival prestige of the Petrograd Soviet and administrative disruptions following the disaffection of many czarist officials. During May 1917, continuing difficulties led to a government reorganization that represented a shift to the political Left. Milyukov and Guchkov, ministers of foreign affairs and war, respectively, were forced to resign because they were identified with policies of loyalty to the Allies. Two Socialist Revolutionaries and two Mensheviks were brought into the cabinet, and Socialist Revolutionary Aleksandr Kerenski became minister of war.

July Crisis. The July crisis was the aftermath of a disastrous campaign on the southwestern front. Although the reorganized cabinet had committed itself to a strictly defensive war and a peace without victory,

Kerenski trusted that a major military offensive would both reflect and enhance loyalty to the revolution. Launched on June 29, the advance scored initial successes in Galicia. By the first week of July, however, German and Austrian counterattacks had broken through the Russian lines and turned Kerenski's thrust into a disorderly retreat. Discipline evaporated as entire units refused to fight; some regiments killed the officers who ordered them to fight. When added to the nation's other aggravating problems, the military collapse encouraged popular agitation during the July Days. Large crowds, including soldiers from the Petrograd garrison, demanded acceptance of the Bolshevik program and the immediate transfer of power to the Petrograd Soviet's Central Executive Committee. The Provisional Government retaliated by accusing the Bolsheviks of treason, and Lenin was forced to flee to Finland. The rebellion failed because the Bolsheviks had not yet gained enough support within the army or the nation as a whole. The Provisional Government was again reshuffled, with Kerenski replacing Prince Lvov as prime minister.

Kornilov Coup. Uprisings on the Left incited a vigorous reaction from the Right. Early in September, General Lavr Kornilov ordered a contingent of troops to advance upon Petrograd, apparently in order to seize power. At first, for motives still unclear, Kerenski encouraged Kornilov, but misunderstandings developed between the two. Kerenski charged Kornilov with mutiny and appealed for popular support to halt the counterrevolution. The advancing troops disbanded before reaching their destination, but both the army and the government had been weakened in the process. The Provisional Government was reorganized for the last time on October 8. With Kerenski remaining as premier, Socialists now headed ten of the sixteen ministries. The Bolsheviks profited most from the Kornilov episode; their leaders were freed, and many Bolsheviks were armed to help defend the capital. Popular support broadened for the Socialist extremes, as peasants, urban workers, and soldiers dreaded a counterrevolution that would restore the oppressive features of the czarist regime.

NOVEMBER REVOLUTION

Although they remained a minority in the nation as a whole, Bolsheviks had won majorities in the key soviets of Petrograd and Moscow. In these same nerve centers, they had generated considerable support among labor unions and the military, allowing them to form a disciplined strike force. During October 1917, Lenin decided that conditions favored the overthrow of the Provisional Government. On October 23, the Bolshevik Central Committee voted in favor of an armed insurrection to coincide with the convening of the All-Russian Congress of Soviets. They anticipated that a favorable vote from this Congress would dramatize popular ratification of the revolution. Final planning was directed by Leon Trotsky, chairman of the Petrograd Soviet, who had risen rapidly in the revolutionary ranks.

The Provisional Government crumbled with as little resistance as the czarist system it had replaced. Both regimes had been thoroughly discredited by their inability to end the war or to wage it successfully and by their unwillingness to institute broad social reforms. During the night of November 6, the military revolutionary committee directed armed units to occupy the public buildings, bridges, and railway terminals in Petrograd. The next day, Kerenski left the capital in search of loyal troops to suppress the insurrection; he was never to return. On November 7 (October 25, Old Style), central elements in the drama were enacted at the Winter Palace, where the Provisional Government was convening. By late afternoon, the weakly defended palace had been surrounded by Petrograd soldiers, sailors from the Kronshtadt naval base, the workers' Red Guards, and guns from the cruiser *Aurora*. During the night of November 7–8, the Bolsheviks arrested and imprisoned all members of the Provisional Government who had not escaped.

Second All-Russian Congress of Soviets. The Bolsheviks used the second All-Russian Congress of Soviets to cloak their seizure of power with the air of legality. It met for two days, beginning on November 7. At the opening session, moderate Socialists still held an absolute majority. However, the Socialist Revolutionaries and Mensheviks withdrew from the Congress, declaring that it should not convene in the atmosphere created by the siege of the Winter Palace. This gave the Bolsheviks an absolute majority in the Congress, although it had clearly become nonrepresentative of the entire nation.

Two decrees on peace and the agrarian problem, drafted by Lenin, were unanimously adopted. The Decree of Peace called for a democratic end to the war, requesting an immediate truce and a settlement without annexations or indemnities. The Land Decree promised fulfillment for the historical yearnings of the Russian peasantry by confiscating all land on behalf of the peasantry without compensation, thereby destroying the foundation of the aristocracy. Councils of peasants at the village level were delegated the authority to execute the decree. Lenin was well aware that by sponsoring the Land Decree, he had adopted the heart of the Socialist Revolutionary party's program. In making this shrewd move, he gained indispensable support for the revolution from the largest segment of the population. The Bolsheviks had thus outmaneuvered both the Provisional Government and their revolutionary competitors. Under the guise of transferring power to the soviets, Bolshevik leaders were in fact gathering the reins of power for themselves. On the same day, the Congress organized the first Soviet government, the Council of People's Commissars. With Lenin as chairman, other notable figures included Aleksei Rykov, commissar of the interior; Leon Trotsky, commissar of foreign affairs; Joseph Stalin, commissar for nationality affairs; and Anatoli Lunacharski, commissar of education.

Constituent Assembly. Following the overthrow of a government, revolutionaries in liberal Western countries commonly convened constituent assemblies. It was widely held that a nation's constitution should be written by a popularly elected assemblage especially chosen for that purpose. The Provisional Government had committed itself throughout to the same procedure; yet, elections were repeatedly postponed. They did not take place until over two weeks after the Bolsheviks assumed power. Viewed by diverse groups as the really legitimate sovereign body, the Constituent Assembly convened in Petrograd in January 1918. Included among the 707 delegates were 370 Socialist Revolutionaries, 170 Bolsheviks, 40 Left Socialist Revolutionaries, and 34 Mensheviks. Socialist Revolutionaries possessed an absolute majority and elected their leader, Viktor Chernov, chairman of the assembly. In anticipation of this development, Lenin had devised a subterfuge to bypass the popular verdict. Since the left-wing Socialist Revolutionaries had merged with the Bolsheviks, he proclaimed, the Socialist Revolutionaries no longer existed as a party. Accordingly, Bolshevik leaders deployed troops who quickly dispersed the Assembly and thereby defeated the first serious challenge to Bolshevik authority. The function of making a constitution was transferred to the All-Russian Congress of Soviets, a body that the Bolsheviks now dominated.

TREATY OF BREST LITOVSK

The Bolshevik call for an immediate peace was coupled with the expectation that wartime dislocations would make the Russian Revolution the prelude to Socialist revolutions in other European countries. While Russian leaders anxiously and fruitlessly awaited word that the

German government had been replaced by a revolutionary Socialist regime, protracted armistice and peace negotiations went on. Two weeks after the revolution, Trotsky sent the foreign ambassadors in Petrograd a note proposing an immediate armistice on all fronts. The Allies rejected Trotsky's overtures, but the Central Powers, who would benefit immensely if Russia withdrew from the war, responded with urgent speed. Armistice negotiations were begun at Brest Litovsk on December 3, and an armistice between Russia and the Central Powers went into effect two days later. Negotiations of peace terms resumed on December 22, 1917. Russian delegates realized that their foes possessed undisputed military superiority. If they rejected harsh German terms, further invasions of Russian territory could threaten Bolshevik control at home. Conversely, if punitive terms were accepted, a rebellion by indignant Russian patriots could also threaten the revolutionary regime. Bolshevik leaders therefore ordered their delegates to procrastinate in the hope that the predicted Socialist insurrection in Germany would be forthcoming.

The territorial aims of the Central Powers broadened as the negotiations proceeded. In addition to claiming the Russian territory their troops already occupied, including the areas of Poland, Kurland, and Lithuania, the kaiser demanded control over Livonia and Estonia. Impatient with Russia's delays, the Central Powers on February 9, 1918, renewed their stringent terms in the form of an ultimatum, which Trotsky, who headed the Russian delegation, refused to accept. The following day, Trotsky returned to Petrograd, declared the war ended, and announced a deliberately ambiguous formula described as "no war, no peace." Thus provoked, Germany resumed the offensive on February 18. The next day, the Bolshevik's badly divided Central Committee capitulated and agreed by a 7-to-6 vote to accept the conditions of February 9. The Germans responded with new and even harsher demands in the form of an ultimatum to be answered within forty-eight hours. At Lenin's insistence, the humiliating terms were accepted, and the Treaty of Brest Litovsk was signed on March 3. According to its provisions, Russia yielded control over the Ukraine, Poland, Finland, Lithuania, Estonia, and Latvia. In each of these border areas, a German-controlled puppet state was erected. Additionally, Russia ceded the districts of Ardahan, Kars, and Batum to Turkey. In sum, Russia lost over one-fourth of its population and was forced to relinquish territory acquired over a period of two centuries. But Germany's defeat in the war made these articles of peace transitory.

CONSEQUENCES OF THE REVOLUTIONS

During 1917, government power passed from the hands of the czarist regime to the bourgeois-dominated Provisional Government to the Socialists. The Bolsheviks, the most extreme Socialist group, engineered the November Revolution and rapidly accumulated dictatorial powers. Collaboration with the right-wing Socialist Revolutionaries ended during the fiasco of the Constituent Assembly, and the troubled alliance with the left-wing Socialist Revolutionaries terminated during squabbles over the Brest Litovsk treaty. In order to deal with their opponents on both the Left and the Right, the Bolsheviks established a secret police force (*Cheka*) that became an instrument of oppression and terror. Nongovernment centers of power such as trade unions and the press were soon brought under party dominance. Although they were much influenced by ideological fervor, the qualities that characterized the Bolsheviks in their rise to power were a capacity for audacious decision making combined with an unusual ability to improvise. Three years of civil war remained before the Bolsheviks, under Lenin's leadership, finally consolidated their authority and stabilized their regime. Nevertheless, the two revolutions that brought them to power in 1917 proved decisive for Russia and were the most significant for the world since the French Revolution of 1789.

5

Europe's Quest for Security, 1919 to 1929

The 1920s were dominated in Europe by the effects of World War I. All states were faced with uncommon social dislocations. In the economic realm, the ravages of war had resulted in severe agricultural and industrial underproduction, and the adjustments to a peacetime economy generated widespread unemployment and inflation. From within and without, there were persistent challenges to those nations that possessed traditional or newly fashioned liberal institutions. The necessities of wartime regimentation had created precedents that diminished respect for individual rights and the free-enterprise system. With the rise of fascism in Italy and communism in Russia, democracy's most implacable foes obtained influential power bases. In most nations that remained liberal, with the notable exception of Great Britain, the authoritarian sentiments of fascism and communism were echoed by influential and discontented minority groups. The postwar settlements further divided European states into conservative powers, which had profited from the conditions of peace, and revisionist states, which favored a remodeling of the peace terms. The conservative states included France, Great Britain, Poland, and the successor states of Czechoslovakia and Yugoslavia; the revisionist nations were Germany, Russia, Austria, Hungary, and Italy.

During the period from 1919 to 1923, unstable conditions persisted as governments grappled with unresolved postwar problems. Efforts to ensure collective security through the peace settlements failed because the victorious powers adhered to different definitions of national security. To Great Britain, it meant a revived and orderly Europe with which to trade; to France, guarantees against future German aggression; and to the United States, despite the internationalist goals of Woodrow Wilson, it increasingly meant a withdrawal to American shores. During the period from 1924 to 1929, the twin goals of peace and prosperity seemed closer to fulfillment. Some of the abrasive features of the reparations problems were eased, and Germany again became a member in good standing of the Western community. In many places, business revivals produced a rise in living standards. Pacts were signed containing pledges of mutual security and the renunciation of war. However, events were soon to demonstrate that the euphoria encouraged by these developments rested on assumptions and foundations less sound than they seemed.

By 1920, the victorious Allies had formulated separate treaties for each of the defeated Central Powers. Although collectively known as the *Peace of Paris,* most of these treaties bore the names of the small towns near Paris where they were signed. The Treaty of Versailles with Germany was the first, the most far-reaching, and the most influential of the settlements. Other pacts included the Treaty of Saint-Germain with Austria, the Treaty of Trianon with Hungary, and the Treaty of Neuilly with Bulgaria. The final concord reached at Paris was the Treaty of Sèvres with Turkey. It was never implemented, however, because nationalist Turks staged an uprising against its exacting terms. After a period of fighting, the Allies drafted a new and more lenient peace arrangement, the Treaty of Lausanne. Although peace terms varied widely, each of the Paris treaties imposed the same burdens upon the vanquished foe: losses of territory, limitations of military power, and payment of reparations.

PARIS PEACE CONFERENCE

As a tribute to the extraordinary sacrifices borne by France during the war, Paris was chosen as the site for the peace conference. Delegates from twenty-seven nations, representing the victorious Allied and Associated powers, assembled for the first session on January 18, 1919. In theory, all conference decisions required general approval; nevertheless, plenary sessions did not make major decisions. Instead, the superior organ was the Council of Ten, consisting of two representatives from each of the five major Allied nations (the United States, Britain, France, Italy, and Japan). Within the council, key influence was exercised by the representatives of the Big Four, including Woodrow Wilson from the United States, David Lloyd George from Great Britain, Georges Clemenceau from France, and Vittorio Orlando from Italy. During the first two months, conference activities focused on the council's secret negotiations with delegates of affected states who came to advance their national claims. To assist its investigations, the council appointed special committees to conduct preliminary studies of the perplexing problems being confronted. These influential bodies, which eventually totaled fifty-eight, then made their recommendations to the Big Four. Thus, the major considerations at Paris were the domestic political strengths, the conceptions of national interest, the temperaments, and the visions of the principal Allied leaders.

It was Woodrow Wilson who emerged as the spokesman for a peace based upon principles of reconciliation. On the basis of his Fourteen Points (see p. 70), Germany had accepted the armistice terms that ended the war. The Democratic president traveled to Paris with uncertain support from the American electorate; in the 1918 elections, Republicans had won control of both houses of Congress. The most formidable opposition to a Wilsonian settlement came from David Lloyd George and Georges Clemenceau, both of whom possessed more definite mandates from their citizens. In Great Britain's so-called khaki election of December 1918, Lloyd George had won reelection by promising punitive anti-German terms. In the same month, the French Chamber of Deputies had voted confidence in Clemenceau's ministry by the impressive margin of 386 to 88. An uncompromising realist, Clemenceau viewed his mission at the conference as that of obtaining the security against Germany that his countrymen passionately desired. Deliberations among these three men produced the critical decisions at the conference. Prime Minister Orlando of Italy assumed a subordinate role in the negotiations.

TREATY OF VERSAILLES

The Treaty of Versailles, which ended the war with Germany, radically altered the political map of Europe. Few peace settlements have stirred as much controversy. It was a subject of bitter dispute at the conference and among contemporaries and has remained a bone of contention among historians. The most controversial provisions were Article 231, which assigned guilt for the war to Germany, and the requirement for German reparations payments based upon this assumption. Germans labeled the treaty a *diktat* because they were not allowed to participate in its formulation and because their only alternatives were complete acceptance or total rejection. When news of the harsh terms arrived from Paris, German nationalists attempted to persuade their government to reject ratification. But depleted German resources would not permit a resumption of the war, and German delegates chose their only realistic option by signing the treaty on June 28, 1919. The location chosen for the occasion was the Hall of Mirrors in the Palace of Versailles. For Germans, this setting made the peace even more humiliating because forty-eight years earlier, the founding of the German Empire had been proclaimed in the same place.

League of Nations. The human and material losses of the First World War led to general demands for the creation of an international assembly dedicated to the peaceful resolution of crises among nations. Establishment of the League of Nations was the priority item on Woodrow Wilson's program, and it was at his urging that the Covenant of the League of Nations was attached as a preamble to the Treaty of Versailles. Because the settlement with Germany was viewed as the conference's weightiest task, Wilson calculated that the League's chances would be enhanced if nations were required to accept it in order to implement the peace terms with Germany. Not surprisingly, Wilson was named chairman of the special commission that wrote the League Covenant. When the commission presented its draft, considerable resistance was evidenced in the United States on the grounds that American participation would jeopardize the special prerogatives claimed by the United States under the Monroe Doctrine. After Wilson sponsored revisions to eliminate this objection, the League Covenant was approved by a plenary session on April 28, and it became the first twenty-six articles of the Treaty of Versailles.

The key organs of the League were the Assembly and the Council. The Assembly was a deliberative body in which each member state had one vote and a maximum of three representatives. The Council's membership was designed to represent the principal states. Provisions were made for five permanent and four nonpermanent members. But the United States eventually declined participation in the League, and there were only four permanent members (Japan, France, Great Britain, and Italy). They increased to five when Germany was admitted to the League in 1926. The Assembly and the Council were both assigned the responsibility for dealing with "any matter within the sphere of the authority of the League or affecting the peace of the world." At the same time, some functions were delegated to the Assembly alone, and others were vested exclusively in the Council. Among the Assembly's special prerogatives were the selection of nonpermanent members of the Council, the admission of League members, and the ratification of amendments to the Covenant. Reserved for the Council were the functions of formulating disarmament plans and charting courses of action relating to serious international disputes. The League Covenant also created a permanent Secretariat, the World Court, and the International Labor Organization. The League was a pioneering attempt to reduce the anarchy of international politics, but it was seriously weakened by the unwillingness of nations to diminish meaningfully their national sovereignty.

Germany's Boundaries.   Germany was first of all eliminated as a colonial power. The Versailles treaty required the German government to renounce control of its overseas territories. The issue was whether the German colonies, as well as those of Turkey, would be annexed outright by other powers or administered under League supervision. Japan was the strongest advocate of outright annexation; Wilson, of League supervision. The Big Four accepted Wilson's position in principle and created a *mandate* system that divided confiscated colonies into three classes (A, B, and C) based upon assessments of their progress toward independence. The League exercised virtually no supervision over the administration of class C areas. These included both the German colonies in the Pacific that were annexed by Japan, Australia, and New Zealand and Southwest Africa, which was placed under the control of the Union of South Africa. A much greater degree of League regulation was exerted over class B mandates, including most of the former German colonies in Africa. These six mandates were divided among France, Britain, and Belgium. The class A designation, accompanied by only nominal League supervision, was reserved for the Arab lands formerly governed by Turkey, which were placed under the mandate of Britain and France but intended to be autonomous at an early date.

The problem of Germany's home boundaries was immensely more troublesome. The simplest decision was that Alsace and Lorraine, which Germany had wrested from France in 1871, should be restored to France. The principal antagonists on other questions were Clemenceau on one side and Wilson and Lloyd George usually on the other. Although at times their differences seemed irreconcilable, they reached compromises on outstanding questions. With French security as his guiding star, Clemenceau focused his strongest claims on Germany's western borders, demanding the creation of an autonomous buffer state from German territory on the left bank of the Rhine. Wilson and Lloyd

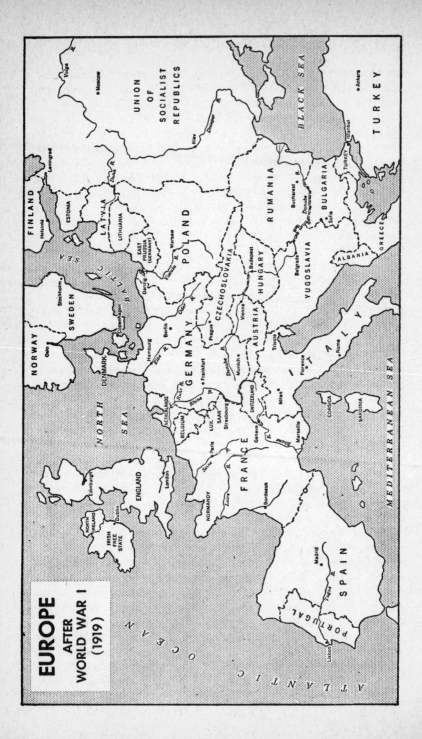

EUROPE
AFTER
WORLD WAR I
(1919)

George rejected this plan, arguing that resulting German discontent would plant the seeds of a future war. Clemenceau was persuaded to yield after Wilson and Lloyd George agreed to Allied occupation of the Rhineland for fifteen years and promised British and American aid to France in case of an unprovoked German attack. Clemenceau also sought French annexation of the Saar basin, an area northeast of Lorraine that had some of the richest coal beds on the Continent. Wilson and Lloyd George were willing to accept French dominance in the area, but they opposed outright political annexation. France was accorded control over the coal mines for fifteen years, during which the League would supervise the Saar territory. In 1935, the natives of the area would decide their political future through a plebiscite.

Germany suffered far more severely in the reshaping of its eastern boundaries. During the war, the Allies had promised to reconstitute the state of Poland, which Prussia, Russia, and Austria had partitioned between 1772 and 1795. They had also pledged that this revived nation would have a "free and secure access to the sea." By the end of the war, this scheme was being promoted as a way to erect strong buffer states against Russian bolshevism. The problem was that of deciding what the boundaries of Poland would be. To provide access to the Baltic Sea, Polish leaders, energetically supported by Clemenceau, favored a corridor through the province of West Prussia that would include both banks of the lower Vistula and the city of Danzig. Lloyd George opposed this plan because it would separate East Prussia from the rest of Germany and place Danzig, a predominantly German city, under Polish control. The final compromise required Germany to renounce most of its provinces of Posen and West Prussia. A Polish sea corridor through West Prussia was provided, with Danzig established as a free city under League of Nations supervision. Plebiscites were held in the most highly contested districts, including Allenstein, Marienwerder, and Upper Silesia. According to the disputed results, Germany was awarded most of the contended territory and population, but the areas received by Poland contained the richest economic resources.

German Disarmament. Stringent restrictions were designed to render Germany incapable of again becoming an aggressive military power. The German army was limited to 100,000 men; the general staff was eliminated; and compulsory military training was forbidden. To limit the number who received military training, officers and privates were required to enlist for twenty-five and twelve years, respectively. In addition, the Allies occupied the left bank of the Rhine, and the right bank was demilitarized for thirty miles. Naval activity was similarly curtailed. Personnel quotas were set, and Germany was permitted only six battleships, six cruisers, twelve destroyers, and twelve torpedo boats. The principal part of the German fleet was to be surrendered to the Allies. The manufacture of offensive weapons, including arms, munitions, and submarines, was forbidden. Germany was also required to pay the cost of Allied control commissions created to enforce these terms.

German Reparations. The reparations question was intimately bound with the most passionate emotions unleashed by the war. The German government and people had been depicted by Allied propaganda machines as the incarnation of international crime. In Great Britain and France, where wartime devastation was immense, popular expressions were "hang the Kaiser" and "squeeze the German lemon." Lloyd George and Clemenceau were thus supported by national moods that sought not only to ensure security against German aggression but also to punish and humiliate Germany. All Allied leaders pronounced Germany guilty for causing the war and accordingly held it accountable for the losses and damages their nations had suffered. Nevertheless, crucial differences developed over whether Germany should be required to pay restricted or total reparations. Lloyd George and Clemenceau insisted upon total reparations, including both costs for the destruction perpetrated by Germany's military forces and the expenses incurred by the Allies in waging the war. Wilson countered this scheme by supporting reparations limited to directly inflicted damages.

The final reparations arrangements demonstrated the extent of the British and French victories on this question. As an initial payment, Germany was instructed to furnish the Allies with specified commodities. These included the transfer of most of its merchant fleet; the delivery of large quantities of coal to France, Belgium, and Italy; the transfer of sizable quantities of farm animals, machines, and construction materials to France and Belgium; and the surrender of all property that German citizens owned abroad. Despite strenuous American objections, future payments were made intentionally ambiguous and indefinite. Although Germany was required to pay $5 billion by May 1921, neither a total payment nor a specified period of payment was fixed under the Versailles treaty. Instead, the Reparations Commission was established to fix a final sum by the May 1921 deadline. If Germany defaulted on its payments, the Allied governments assumed the right to use economic or other reprisals to ensure compliance. Given Germany's prostrate economic condition and the importance of a

healthy German economy to Europe's postwar recovery, these astronomical demands were unrealistic. When added to the war-guilt proviso, they heightened the feeling among Germans that their national
honor had been insulted. Most Germans considered escape from these
terms essential to regaining national self-respect.

UNITED STATES AND THE TREATY OF VERSAILLES

American opposition to the Versailles treaty came from varied
sources. Friends of Germany and many liberals considered the treaty
too harsh; others condemned what they interpreted as its leniency.
The bitterest attacks centered on the Covenant of the League of Nations, and among its most hated sections was Article 10, which bound
members of the League to guarantee each other's territorial integrity
and political independence. Wilson soon discovered that the League
Covenant, the instrument that he trusted would rectify any defects in
the Paris settlements, would become the focus of Senate attacks on the
Versailles treaty.

Senate Divisions. The Senate was divided into four groups during
the struggle over ratification. The *bitter-enders,* led by William E.
Borah of Idaho and Hiram Johnson of California, were irreconcilably
opposed to U.S. involvement in any world organization. At the opposite extreme were the Wilson Democrats, who favored ratification
with few, if any, modifications. In between were the mild and the
strict reservationists. Those who had mild reservations, including both
Republicans and Democrats, favored the League in principle but supported limitations on American involvement. Those with strict reservations, a group of Republicans led by Henry Cabot Lodge, who was
chairman of the Senate Foreign Relations Committee, supported ratification only if a series of amendments were added to the League Covenant. These reservations were designed to provide a limited and reluctant American involvement on the one hand and Republican credit
for the League on the other.

Rejection of the Treaty. The Treaty of Versailles was voted on
three times by the Senate, and each time, its supporters failed to obtain
the two-thirds majority required for ratification. Although sentiments
in the Senate and the nation were predominantly in favor of it, the
League was rejected because the Wilson Democrats and the strict
reservationists refused to compromise. Viewing Lodge's reservations
as an impairment to the League and a challenge to his political and
moral leadership, an ailing President Wilson instructed the Democratic

minority to repudiate the treaty rather than approve it with qualifications. Their negative votes, when combined with those of the bitter-
enders, doomed the treaty. Confident that the majority of Americans
supported his position, Wilson encouraged voters to make the 1920
elections a referendum on acceptance or rejection of the League and
the Versailles treaty. Republicans were thus disposed to interpret Warren Harding's overwhelming victory as a popular mandate against the
treaty. Support for the League subsequently waned, and on July 2,
1921, the United States ended the state of war with Germany through
a joint resolution of Congress. Defeat of the Versailles treaty signaled
a fateful American return to isolationism.

LESSER TREATIES

The Austro-Hungarian, Russian, and Ottoman empires were among
the major casualties of World War I; independent states were carved
out of areas over which they had maintained hegemony. Finland, Estonia, Latvia, and Lithuania won autonomy during the turbulent first
years of Bolshevik rule in Russia. The Paris conference further helped
to draw a new map for Eastern Europe by deciding the borders of
those lands that had previously been controlled by the defeated powers.
To a considerable degree, Allied representatives followed the lead of
nationalist groups that established squatters' rights over territory at
the end of the war. This was the case particularly in Austria-Hungary,
where the Czechs and Yugoslavs had already formed their own states.
At the same time, the Paris conference immeasurably assisted the evolution of national independence in those areas that remained under Turkish rule by making them class A mandates of the League of Nations.
Decisions affecting the former lands of Austria-Hungary and Turkey
were contained in the separate treaties concluded with Austria, Hungary, Bulgaria, and Turkey.

Saint-Germain.   Under the terms of the Treaty of Saint-Germain,
Austria accepted the loss not only of the former empire's dependent
peoples but also of some of its German-speaking citizens. Reduced to
its Alpine and Danubian provinces, Austria retained fewer than 7 million of its former 30 million inhabitants. In an effort to cultivate a
favorable audience at Paris, the Austrian delegates argued that their
country, like Czechoslovakia and Yugoslavia, was a successor state to
the Austro-Hungarian Empire. They attempted to call the nation
German Austria in the hope that it would eventually achieve unity
(*Anschluss*) with the new German Republic. However, the Allies re-

fused to accept these maneuvers, and Austria was compelled to share responsibility for the war with Germany and was forbidden to take any action that would compromise its independence without the express consent of the League's Council. Some of the settlement's other key provisions were modeled after the Treaty of Versailles. Except for three patrol boats, Austria was forced to surrender its navy; its army was reduced to 30,000 men. In addition, Austria, like Germany, was required to pay reparations as determined by the Reparations Commission.

The most difficult problem of assigning Hapsburg territory involved the Treaty of London (1915), which persuaded Italy to fight on the side of the Allies. According to its secret terms, to which the United States had never acceded, Italy was promised Austrian territory near the head of the Adriatic, including the Trentino region and the city of Trieste. By the end of the war, Italy had added the strategically located port of Fiume to its demands. The principal opposition to Italy's claims came from the newly created state of Yugoslavia and from the American delegation. Wilson was willing to concede Italian claims over the Trentino and Trieste, but he categorically rejected the demand for Fiume, which was populated overwhelmingly by Croats and Slovenes and, in addition, was the best available seaport for the Yugoslav state. Wilson even made a rare appeal to the Italian people in an effort to obtain their support against the leaders of their own government, but he was unsuccessful. Unable to persuade Wilson to yield, and incensed by his efforts to undermine their support at home, Italy's Premier Orlando and Foreign Minister Sidney Sonnino withdrew their delegation for two weeks. The peace conference was unable to resolve the problem of Fiume, and the matter was left to direct negotiations between Italy and Yugoslavia.

Trianon. The Hungarian kingdom, like the Austrian, was divided by its constitutent national groups as Allied victory appeared imminent. The Magyars had themselves broken with the Dual Monarchy by proclaiming their independence in October 1918. Because of continuing domestic turmoil, highlighted by a Communist government's acquisition of power in March 1919, it was not until November 1919 that the Hungarians had created a government which the Allies were willing to recognize. The terms of the Trianon treaty awarded Hungarian territory to every state that surrounded it. Hungary was reduced from a kingdom of 125,000 square miles and 20 million people to an area of 35,000 square miles and 8 million people. Yugoslavia, Czechoslovakia, Romania, and even Austria profited by Hungary's losses. Yugoslavia received Croatia and part of the Banat of Temesvár; Romania was granted the remainder of the Banat region, Transylvania, and other portions of Hungary to the west; Czechoslovakia acquired Slovakia and Ruthenia; and Austria was awarded the German area of West Hungary. The Hungarians were also subjected to reparations and military limitations. Their navy was reduced to three patrol boats and their army to 35,000 men.

Neuilly. Compared with the other Paris settlements, the treaty concluded with Bulgaria at Neuilly-sur-Seine was unusually generous. Its most critical strategic loss was Western Thrace, which the Allies transferred to Greece, thereby denying the Bulgarians their only direct access to the Aegean Sea. Some border districts were also ceded to Yugoslavia in order to increase that state's security by affording it control over strategically located mountain passes. The standard military and reparations provisions were added. Bulgaria was required to surrender its navy and reduce its army to 20,000 men, and reparations payments were finally fixed at $445 million.

Sèvres and Lausanne. The Treaty of Sèvres with Turkey was the final peace settlement concluded at Paris. Several states, including Russia, Great Britain, France, and Italy, had staked claims to Ottoman territory through secret treaties during the war. For a variety of reasons, these clandestine agreements were difficult to implement. They were revealed and condemned by the Russian Bolsheviks following their seizure of power in 1917. Their execution was opposed by the United States, which had never been a party to them. At the same time, Great Britain, France, and Italy disagreed over how the territories should be allocated. According to the concords eventually reached, Turkey was required not only to relinquish sovereignty over the Arab lands but also to surrender parts of its Asia Minor homeland. The most important Arab lands were made mandates of Britain and France, with Palestine, Mesopotamia, and Transjordan assigned to Great Britain and Syria awarded to France. Other articles awarded the Arab state of Hejaz its independence; internationalized the Straits; transferred the areas of Smyrna, Thrace, Adrianople, and Gallipoli to Greece; and compelled Turkey to surrender the Dodecanese Islands and Rhodes to Italy.

The sultan's helpless government at Constantinople, which was well within the range of Allied guns, reluctantly accepted these stringent terms. However, a nationalist movement based at Ankara defied the sultan and the Allies, proclaiming that those areas inhabited by an

Ottoman Muslim majority (Turks and Kurds) should remain under Turkish sovereignty. Mustafa Kemal, popular hero of the Gallipoli campaign (see p. 63), led the patriotic crusade to revise the Sèvres treaty. Because the Allies had already withdrawn most of their forces from the Near East, they accepted a Greek offer to lead in suppressing the Kemalist armies. After failing to capture Kemal's government at Ankara, the Greek armies were defeated at Smyrna in September 1922. At this point, the Allies agreed to void the Sèvres treaty and negotiate another settlement. The terms of the Treaty of Lausanne (July 1923) restored to Turkey most of the lost areas. Although the independence of the Arab states was maintained, the government at Constantinople regained control of Anatolia, Smyrna, and most of Eastern Thrace. As an added concession to the nationalists, reparations were abolished. At the same time, freedom of navigation was to apply in the Straits, where military fortifications were forbidden. The Lausanne treaty was the only one that the Allies negotiated with a defeated foe and the only instance in which a nationalist reaction forced an immediate revision of peace terms.

EXECUTION OF THE SETTLEMENTS

The Treaty of Versailles, the most important of the Paris settlements and the model for the others, has been criticized for falling between two extremes. First, the conditions applicable to Germany contained vengeful features that violated the Wilsonian principles upon which Germany's agreement to an armistice was based. The reparations requirements were considered by some the most unrealistic of these provisions. Soon after the Versailles treaty was signed, the British economist John Maynard Keynes referred to the economic settlement as a "Carthaginian" peace and argued that it would be impossible to implement. Too punitive to conciliate, the treaty was also too lenient to disable Germany permanently. From the very beginning, all segments of German public opinion were dedicated to revising the diktat's hated terms. The maintenance of a high degree of unity among the principal Allies was the most effective way to counter efforts of Germany and other aggrieved nations to revise the Paris settlements. Yet, the United States had rejected the League and during the 1920s withdrew from an activist role in European affairs. With the British also hesitant, the French were frequently left alone to enforce the Paris settlements.

LEAGUE OF NATIONS AND COLLECTIVE SECURITY

There were weighty presences as well as notable absences when delegates to the First Assembly of the League of Nations convened in Geneva during November 1920. Thirty-one Allied and Associated states became original members by affixing their signatures to the peace treaties. The membership of thirteen neutral nations was also welcomed. Included were all the Allied states of Europe, the British dominions, the newly created successor states of Eastern Europe, the Latin American nations, Liberia, Persia, and Hejaz. The most conspicuous absence, that of the United States, seriously weakened the League's prestige and authority and left Britain and France as the world organization's major powers. Although none of the enemy states was initially included, Austria and Bulgaria were accepted as members in 1920; Hungary, in 1922; Germany, in 1926; and Turkey, in 1932. An outcast among nations, the Soviet Union was not admitted to the League until the 1930s. Bolshevik leaders denounced the League as a Western agency designed to promote capitalist aggression. The problem of collective security was obviously complicated at the outset by the refusal or the inability of some of the world's major powers to attend and participate. Eventually, treaties embodying the principle of mutual security were applied in limited spheres through direct negotiations among the powers involved.

Treaty of Mutual Assistance and the Geneva Protocol. During the first few years of the League's operation, French leaders sponsored proposals designed to strengthen the organization's Covenant, principally in its provisions for common action against aggressors. Article 10 pledged League members to help preserve each other's territorial integrity and political independence against external aggression. Article 11 made any matter relating to war the common concern of the entire League and committed the body to taking actions deemed essential for the preservation of peace. Article 16 further noted economic and military sanctions that League states could employ against nations that threatened or violated the peace. France, which had been subjected to German invasions twice within a half century, was concerned that the League Covenant did not bind all members to take the actions prescribed and that sanctions were not inevitably brought into play when aggression occurred. Most League members also recognized that the League's goal of general disarmament was impractical unless more effective machinery for mutual security was created.

In an attempt to overcome these weaknesses, the League adopted the Draft Treaty of Mutual Assistance in 1923. This treaty obligated all signatory powers to assist a member nation under attack once the League Council declared that such a situation existed. Some nations, including France, Japan, and Italy, indicated their acceptance of the draft treaty's provisions. A majority in the League Assembly, however, registered their disapproval, objecting particularly to the treaty's failure to define aggression and its delegation of complete responsibility for designating an aggressor to the League Council. The Geneva Protocol, presented to the Fifth Assembly of the League of Nations in 1924, was designed to overcome these criticisms. It stipulated that all international legal disputes must be submitted to the World Court and that nonlegal discords must be referred to the League Council for arbitration. Any affected nation that refused to submit to this machinery would automatically be labeled an aggressor, thereby subjecting itself to economic and military sanctions from League states. Both treaties failed to be adopted, primarily because of opposition from Great Britain and the dominions. The British were traditionally adverse to any binding arrangements automatically entangling them in continental problems that might or might not affect their vital interests.

Achievements of the League. Although its failures were more dramatic and memorable, the League of Nations proved eminently successful in promoting matters of general humanitarian concern. Without international machinery for enforcement, the League's success in these spheres depended upon its ability to cultivate and appeal to the enlightened citizenry of the leading countries. Among the programs that gained broad support were the extension of aid to prisoners of war and refugees and the periodic granting of financial aid to selected nations (such as Austria) that were faced with recurring economic crises. On the basis of numerous studies, League agencies cultivated international cooperation in the areas of health, labor, and trade. Intellectual cooperation was also stimulated through the scholarly and artistic exchanges that the League advanced. Arbitration machinery established by the international body was successful in mediating several ruptures involving secondary or defeated states. The 1921 plebiscite held in Upper Silesia to decide the border between Germany and Poland was conducted under League auspices. From 1921 to 1922, League arbitrators helped ease a controversy between Sweden and Finland over the Åland Islands by granting the area's independence under Finnish administration. In 1925, League arbitrators resolved a border clash between Greece and Bulgaria.

Locarno Treaties. The circumstance that led to the Locarno conference was the advent to power during the mid-1920s of two conciliatory leaders, Gustav Stresemann in Germany and Aristide Briand in France. Stresemann sought détente between the two nations in the hope of moderating some of the Versailles restrictions upon Germany. As a concession from his government, he indicated its willingness to sign with France an agreement of mutual guarantee and nonaggression. Germany would recognize its current boundaries with France and Belgium as permanent, subject to international guarantees. To formulate such an arrangement, delegates from Great Britain, Italy, Belgium, Poland, and Czechoslovakia joined representatives of France and Germany at Locarno, Switzerland, in October 1925. Seven treaties emerged from this conference. First, under the Treaty of Mutual Guarantee (the Locarno Pact), Germany, France, and Belgium agreed to respect their existing frontiers. They further renounced the use of war against each other except in self-defense or in compliance with the League Covenant. Britain and Italy consented to serve as guarantors of the arrangement. Four other treaties separately bound Germany on the one hand and France, Belgium, Czechoslovakia, and Poland on the other to resolve mutual differences through arbitration. Finally, two treaties that France signed with Poland and Czechoslovakia pledged the signatories to aid each other in case Germany violated the agreements affecting their respective interests. Significantly, the Locarno treaties ensured only the integrity of Germany's western boundaries. Even in their most conciliatory moment, the German people refused to concede the loss of their eastern territory that had been sanctioned by the Versailles treaty. Nevertheless, to a Europe in which recurring tensions and recriminations had followed four years of warfare, the so-called spirit of Locarno engendered a wave of optimism and enthusiasm.

Pact of Paris. The Pact of Paris was known as the Kellogg-Briand Pact for its sponsors, American Secretary of State Frank B. Kellogg and French Prime Minister Aristide Briand, who in 1927 proposed a general antiwar treaty. The resulting document was signed in Paris in August 1928 by delegates from fifteen countries, who renounced war as an instrument of national policy and promised to resolve differences peaceably. Within a few years, representatives of sixty-two nations had affixed their signatures to this document. But because no machinery was set up to compel enforcement, the Pact of Paris did little more than create, for a brief span, the attractive illusion that war had been outlawed. The pact's actual effect was to motivate nations that decided to wage military struggles to do so on an unannounced and undeclared basis.

Disarmament. Plans to achieve mutual security were inevitably bound up with the question of disarmament. Pledges of arbitration and guarantees of territorial integrity would have little meaning in the face of fears and tensions resulting from an arms race. Recognizing this, Allied leaders at the Paris peace conference decided first to impose severe arms limitations on the defeated powers. The League of Nations was then given a mandate to formulate general disarmament plans. But once the war had ended, the victorious powers were unwilling to institute comprehensive limitations on their own armaments. Hopes were raised when the Washington Conference of 1921–1922 restricted the numbers and tonnage of capital ships and aircraft carriers of the signatory powers (Great Britain, the United States, Japan, France, and Italy). However, other efforts within and outside of the League during the 1920s proved nonproductive or achieved only modest results. Meanwhile, in 1925, the League had appointed a preparatory commission to lay the groundwork for the World Disarmament Conference, which convened in Geneva during 1932 and 1933 (see pp. 219–220).

REPARATIONS AND WAR DEBTS

Relations between France and Germany posed the most severe threat to European and world peace. The most disturbing problem between the two historical antagonists was the question of reparations. In addition to the exorbitant reparations required of Germany, World War I produced other debts of staggering proportions. The United States was the principal creditor nation, having loaned over $10 billion to Allied countries. Great Britain, especially during the early years of the war, had advanced huge sums to the Allies, but this total was less than Britain had borrowed from the United States. Accordingly, in the interest of reviving trade while liquidating its war debt, Britain proposed to cancel all wartime bills owed Britain if the United States would do likewise. Successive American governments rejected this proposal, which would have placed the major responsibility for financing the war on American taxpayers. At the same time, those nations in debt to the United States and Great Britain (with the exception of Russia, where the Bolsheviks renounced obligations incurred by the czars) contended that they could honor their obligations only to the extent that reparations payments were forthcoming from Germany. Although the United

States rejected this reasoning, the questions of reparations and war debts were closely related throughout the 1920s.

Total Bill.   In 1921, the League's Reparations Commission had calculated that Germany would be required to pay $33 billion. The first $1 billion was to be paid within twenty-five days. Additional annual payments included a fixed amount of $500 million and variable payments constituting a 26 percent tax on German imports. In spite of German protests, the payments in money and goods that Germany had already made were not subtracted from the reparations total; instead, they were considered subsidies to cover the expenses already incurred by the Allied occupation armies and control commissions. Threatened with Allied occupation of the Ruhr if it demurred, the German government accepted the Reparations Commission's proposals in May 1921.

German Default.   An unfavorable balance of trade made it impossible for Germany to meet reparations payments. With expenditures outdistancing receipts fourfold during the period from 1919 to 1923, the German government borrowed and printed money to sustain itself and pay its debts. In the ensuing inflation, the value of the mark steadily deteriorated. The attitude of top German industrialists aggravated the problem. Fearful of tax policies that would penalize the wealthy, many transferred their capital to foreign banks. During 1921 and 1922, a government headed by Catholic Center party leader Joseph Wirth, with Walter Rathenau as minister of reconstruction and later foreign minister, led two cabinets that attempted to fulfill Germany's reparations obligations, but the payments made only served to spread the inflation. Having received a partial moratorium for 1922, the German government requested a total suspension of cash payments for the next several years, but the Allied governments refused to grant additional time. Accordingly, focusing on past-due deliveries of timber and coal, the Reparations Commission formally declared Germany in default in January 1923.

Ruhr Crisis.   Notwithstanding British refusals to participate, French and Belgian troops, supported by Italy, occupied the Ruhr industrial district of Germany as far east as Dortmund within a few days after the Reparations Commission's decision. The French and Belgian governments calculated that this action would force Germany to yield to their terms or that they would secure firsthand the payments required. Speaking with a single voice, the disparate political groups in Germany expressed bitter opposition to this punitive move. Antagonisms in Germany and France reached a postwar high as each nation unleashed a flood of propaganda in efforts to discredit the other. Confident that the French could operate the Ruhr industries only with German labor, the German government met the occupation with *passive resistance*. Reparations payments were stopped completely, and the Ruhr's inhabitants were ordered to avoid actions that would assist the occupation. The German government subsidized striking workers with money and goods. With the critical area of the Ruhr largely isolated, economic conditions in Germany worsened precipitously. By September 1923, the policy of passive resistance was recognized as a failure. The government was forced to resign, and a new cabinet was organized under the leadership of Gustav Stresemann. The French were also disenchanted because their actions had resulted in the termination of voluntary payments and they had been unable to confiscate the wealth anticipated. As an aftermath of the Franco-German confrontation in the Ruhr, antagonistic policies were temporarily discredited, thus laying the basis for a greater degree of cooperation between the two governments.

Dawes Plan.   The Ruhr debacle forced the Allies to reassess the reparations question. Two committees were appointed to reexamine Germany's financial status: one to analyze methods of balancing the budget and stabilizing the economy, the other to evaluate problems related to Germany's exported capital. The first and most influential committee was headed by Charles Dawes, an American financier. The report of this committee was completed by April 1924 and became effective the following September. In addition to calling for an Allied evacuation of the Ruhr, the Dawes Plan recommended the following steps: Reparations payments were to be temporarily reduced to $250 million; after four years, these rates would be stabilized at $650 million, to vary with the level of German prosperity; Germany was to be extended a $200 million loan to promote financial stability and economic recovery; and finally, a central German bank would be established. The total obligation of $33 billion imposed upon Germany in 1921 remained in effect. The execution of this plan succeeded in producing reparations payments and reviving German industry. In the summer of 1925, therefore, French and Belgian troops were withdrawn from the Ruhr.

Young Plan.   Sentiments were prevalent among both the Allies and the Germans that a limit should be placed on the total number of years Germany would be required to pay and that downward revisions in the sum assessed were required. The Dawes committee had not assumed the responsibility for dealing with either of these problems. Instead, these tasks were delegated to another committee of experts, also headed by an American, Owen D. Young. This committee issued its report in June 1929, and its recommendations became effective that September. The Young Plan reduced Germany's total bill to $9 billion to be extended over a fifty-nine-year period. By creating the Bank for International Settlements and empowering it to handle the transactions involved, the Young Plan considerably lessened political influence over the sensitive reparations dilemma. Although some optimists believed that the major problems had been overcome, the economic dislocations produced by the Great Depression again made the reparations question a burning issue at the beginning of the 1930s.

6
Western Europe, 1918 to 1929

The nation-states of Western Europe included both highly modernized and traditional societies. The leading nations of Western Europe, indeed of the entire Continent, were the parliamentary democracies of Great Britain and France. Liberal institutions were also firmly established in the Low Countries and Switzerland. Aristocratic rule, monarchism, and well-entrenched Catholicism were the outstanding social and religious legacies of Portugal and Spain. Conditions immediately following the war seemed favorable to liberal regimes in Western Europe and elsewhere. Although the strains of battle had produced the collapse or defeat of prominent autocratic empires, the cradles of parliamentary rule, Great Britain and France, were among the victorious Allies. Nevertheless, governments had manipulated natural and human resources in an uncompromising fashion during the four years of struggle; understandably, the resulting impressions proved indelible. There were prominent spokesmen in all countries who contended that the aggravated domestic problems could best be met by continuing war socialism during peacetime. Liberal values in the West were further challenged by the evolution of authoritarian governments in Central and Eastern Europe. The most influential models were fascism in Italy and communism in Russia. Despite these challenges from within and without, the major democracies maintained their liberal institutions.

GREAT BRITAIN

There were several dominant themes in British society during the 1920s: a continuing economic depression, the Irish problem, and

accommodations in foreign affairs. In the economic realm, a revival
in trade and industry during the early postwar period brought prosperity to most segments of society. By the end of 1920, however, the basic
trend of the decade had been set: Unemployment rates were high, and
strikes were widespread. The Irish problem had roots dating back to the
seventeenth century. Most of the Irish were Catholic; whereas the
British were predominantly Protestant. Until the late nineteenth century, Ireland was ruled as a British dependency dominated by English
landlords. By the 1880s, Ireland's Catholic majority had united behind
a program of national independence summarized by the cry for home
rule. At the end of World War I, their frustrated demands had
increased in adamancy and virulence. In addition to these domestic
matters, Britain faced major difficulties in international affairs. The
burning issue of free trade versus protection and the readjustment of
relations between Great Britain and other European nations involved
projections of the international conditions required for the revival
of British trade and industry. These problems were handled by
a succession of cabinets headed by David Lloyd George, Andrew
Bonar Law, James Ramsay MacDonald, and Stanley Baldwin.

The Conservative party was the guiding force in British politics during the postwar decade. Conservative victories were greatly aided by
two developments: The Liberal party, its historical rival, was declining;
whereas the emerging Labour party had not yet attained full maturity.

End of the Lloyd George Coalition.   In elections held in December
1918, the Conservatives won an overwhelming two-thirds of the seats
in the House of Commons. The Independent Liberals returned only 28
deputies, and the Labour party, with 63 seats, became the official
opposition for the first time. Because of disagreements over some of
Lloyd George's policies, notably his concessions to Ireland, the Conservative party, led by Bonar Law and Baldwin, declared their independence from this coalition in 1922. Lloyd George had no recourse
except to resign; thereupon, Bonar Law formed a new ministry composed entirely of Conservatives. Parliament was dissolved soon afterward, and elections were scheduled for November 1922. With the
Liberals weakened and badly divided between followers of Lloyd
George and Herbert Henry Asquith, the central contest was between the
Conservatives and Labourites. Primarily because many members of the
British electorate were still fearful of the presumed radical leanings of
the Labour party, Conservatives won over half the parliamentary
seats. Nevertheless, the Labour party, which had elected only 2 deputies in 1900, attained an impressive total of 142 seats.

Challenge to Free Trade. Because of ill health, Bonar Law resigned the premiership after six months. He was succeeded by Stanley Baldwin, a relative unknown who had held several financial offices. Without consulting important segments of his party, Baldwin announced a program of protective tariffs as a solution to Britain's continuing problem of unemployment. Because the Conservative party had pledged itself to maintain Britain's traditional policy of free trade unless it received a voter mandate to do otherwise, Baldwin then called for new elections, which were held in December 1923. With Conservatives challenging their time-honored principle of free trade, Liberals subordinated their differences and closed ranks behind Asquith. The election results clearly indicated that Baldwin's financial program had been rejected outright by the electorate. Although Conservatives remained the largest party, they lost their absolute majority in the Commons. Labour maintained its position as the second largest party, winning 192 seats, and the revived Liberal party returned 158 deputies.

Labour's First Ministry. Leaders of the Liberal party faced a pivotal decision. By forming a coalition, they could provide either the Conservatives or Labourites with a governing majority. Unwilling to distort the Liberal party's identity in a political fusion a second time, Asquith insisted that the Labour party deserved an opportunity to rule alone. Accordingly, in January 1924, Ramsay MacDonald became prime minister and foreign secretary in Britain's first Labour ministry. MacDonald's domestic moves were not striking, partly because he wanted to assure the British of the Labour party's willingness to operate within constitutional boundaries and partly because the enactment of key measures required Liberal support.

In foreign affairs, by contrast, MacDonald's actions were more dramatic. Diplomatic recognition was extended to the Bolshevik regime, and a trade agreement was signed with the Soviets. Policies of conciliation with Germany were pursued. Dismayed over the agreement with Russia and other widening differences, the Liberals decided to withdraw their support, forcing MacDonald to dissolve Parliament and call new elections for October 1924. Labour's confidence among voters was undermined by unfounded rumors that their party was associated with worldwide communism. The most damaging incident was the publication shortly before the elections of a letter purportedly written by Grigori Zinoviev, director of the Third International, urging British Communists to prepare for revolution. The elections gave Conservatives more than 400 seats, their largest majority since the war; Liberal and Labour seats combined totaled less than 200. Labour's first ministry had lasted only ten months.

Baldwin Period. Stanley Baldwin then returned to power and headed a Conservative government that remained in office until 1929. Baldwin's cautious policies inspired confidence but did little to resolve the chronic problems of depression and unemployment. A coal strike in May 1926 assumed overtones of a general strike when half of Britain's 6 million unionists joined the walkout for nine days. In retaliation the following year, the government passed the Trade Union Law, which restricted picketing and outlawed general strikes. In 1928, Baldwin fulfilled a campaign pledge by extending the ballot to women, thus adding 5 million voters to the electorate. In foreign affairs, the trade arrangement that the Labour government had negotiated with Russia was allowed to lapse; and in 1927, the government severed all relations with Russia following charges that a Russian agency was engaged in internal espionage. Unemployment was the dominant issue in the elections of 1929. The Labour party offered the most ambitious program to combat it, including nationalization of the major industries. Voters responded by increasing the number of Labour deputies from 151 to 289; Conservative strength declined from 412 to 259. With the support of 58 Liberal deputies, Ramsay MacDonald was thus able to form Labour's second ministry.

Ireland. After three decades of debate, the first Irish Home Rule Bill was enacted in 1914. This reform was vigorously opposed by Ireland's Protestant minority, who constituted a majority in Ulster, the northeastern section. Because of Ulsterite opposition and the outbreak of hostilities, implementation of the Home Rule Bill was suspended until the end of the war. During the four years of delay, the Irish question acquired a more radical and ominous character. In 1918, Ireland elected 70 members of the new Sinn Fein ("We Ourselves") party to the British Parliament. They no longer demanded home rule within the empire; instead, they called for an independent Irish republic with its own legislature (Dail Eireann) at Dublin. The Sinn Fein representatives organized themselves into a separate parliament, and in 1919, they declared Ireland an independent nation under the presidency of their leader Eamon De Valera. For over a year, undeclared warfare persisted between the Irish Republican Army and British forces, who were supplemented by special volunteers, the Black and Tans. In this guerrilla-type struggle, both sides often dishonored themselves by using barbaric and cruel methods.

In a pacification effort, Parliament enacted another Home Rule Bill in December 1920, providing for the formal partition of Ireland, with one parliament for Ulster and another for the rest of the country. Not surprisingly, the Sinn Feiners rejected this plan. To resolve the impasse, in 1921, David Lloyd George invited the Irish representatives to participate in a series of conferences. By December of that year, an agreement had been laboriously reached providing for the Irish Free State, which would be accorded the same status as the other self-governing dominions. Northern Ireland, which was made up of the six counties of Ulster, could opt to become an autonomous part of the United Kingdom, which it immediately did. Moderate nationalists in the Dail approved the treaty. De Valera and his followers, however, announced their opposition, withdrew from the Dail, and plunged Ireland into a civil war that lasted until the insurgents were defeated in 1923. Nevertheless, De Valera was still to be heard from. In 1927, he returned to politics as leader of the Fianna Fail party, which was committed to change through constitutional means. Remaining loyal to his objective of creating an independent and united Ireland, by the 1930s, De Valera had again become spokesman for his country.

Economic Predicament.   Britain's industrial and commercial superiority had ceased by the end of World War I. During the war, the British had loss vast segments of their markets in Europe, China, India, and Latin America to the United States and Japan. Declining trade inflicted hardships upon Britain's shipping industry. Accelerating competition from countries on the Continent and the expanding uses of oil and electricity undermined the traditionally important coal industry. Moreover, inflated currencies in most European countries forced British industrialists to compete in foreign markets with goods produced by cheaper labor. There were additional strains on the economy resulting from the large debts owed the United States from the expanding government expenditures for social services. As stagnation set in during 1920 and 1921, unemployment mounted to over 2 million out of a population of 42 million and hovered around that figure for the next decade. Beginning in 1921, the government resorted to a dole of approximately twenty shillings a week for the unemployed. The chronic economic crisis was the overriding concern of successive British cabinets during the postwar decade. All dealt with the problem unsuccessfully, partly because of the slow and uneven revival of world trade that was necessary for Britain's economic recovery.

Commonwealth.   The British Empire was transformed during the postwar years. Britain retained its older colonial possessions, including India, and, in addition, received League of Nations mandates. Altogether, various forms of British rule affected one-fourth of the world's population. Particularly notable were the evolving relationships between Great Britain and the dominions of Canada, Australia, New Zealand, and the Union of South Africa. During the nineteenth century, these areas had won considerable autonomy in their internal affairs. An imperial conference called during the war recommended that the self-governing dominions be accorded the status of autonomous nations within the Commonwealth. This principle was enunciated by an imperial conference of 1926 and spelled out by the Statute of Westminster in 1931. Great Britain and the dominions were made equal partners "in no way subordinate one to another in any aspect of their domestic or internal affairs, though united by a common allegiance to the Crown, and freely associated as members of the British Commonwealth of Nations." Each dominion chose its own government and enacted its own laws. Acts by the British Parliament could become applicable to a dominion only if the dominion gave its consent. Notwithstanding the loosening of imperial ties, economic, political, and linguistic bonds between the mother country and the dominions remained strong, and the crown was an effective symbol of Commonwealth unity.

FRANCE

France occupied a more impressive position on the world stage following World War I than it had during the prewar period. French overseas possessions, like those of Great Britain, were scattered over the globe. At the war's end, the mandates of Syria in the Near East and Togo and Cameroun in Africa were added to the older dependencies. In Europe, French supremacy was undisputed. With Germany defeated, Britain withdrawn, and Russia isolated, the French assumed the major responsibility for directing European affairs. Although France had suffered more physical damage during the war than any other Western state, it also made the most imposing recovery. The widespread devastation of some areas required programs of complete reconstruction. In the industrial realm, these conditions facilitated the introduction of advanced techniques and equipment. Nevertheless, France's relative advantages were more apparent than real. Four years of fighting on French soil had produced an enormous drain of economic, human, and psychological resources; and Germany's prostrate condition, the prerequisite to French hegemony, was unlikely to endure indefinitely.

France's political structure emerged intact from the war, and so did the salient characteristic of the Third Republic's parliamentary politics. The Chamber of Deputies, the popularly elected lower house of the National Assembly, continued to include numerous political groups. Because none possessed a working majority, ministries were invariably formed by party coalitions. These combinations usually proved unstable, resulting in a short life span for most cabinets.

Economy. The northeastern parts of France, including the areas of greatest industrial and mining concentrations, had been ravaged by the war. Over half a million homes and buildings were demolished; railroad systems had been destroyed; and 5 million acres of farmland had to be restored for cultivation. The French government directly assumed the responsibility for rebuilding devastated areas and repaying its citizens for the losses they had incurred. A budget of *recoverable expenditures* was created to implement these plans. The government floated bonds to borrow large sums of money from its citizens with the expectation that sizable reparations payments from Germany would help liquidate the bill. When combined with an inefficient system of taxation and the principal and interest on the 150 billion francs borrowed during the war, these expenditures created a national debt of enormous proportions.

Foreign Affairs. The principal postwar goal of French statesmen was to ensure the nation's future security against Germany. Dissatisfied with the restrictive guarantees of the Versailles treaty and the abortive mutual security arrangements with Britain and the United States, French leaders decided to construct alliances with secondary European powers whose self-interest would also be promoted through maintenance of the status quo. In 1920, a military convention was signed with Belgium, whose strategic position and acquisition of some key German areas afforded it sufficient reason to fear a revival of Teutonic militarism. The Poles were even more apprehensive of German retribution because they had acquired Upper Silesia, Posen, and West Prussia from Germany through the Paris settlements. According to a Franco-Polish alliance signed in 1921, each signatory pledged to support the other in case of a German attack. This system of alliances and friendships was extended to Czechoslovakia (1924), Romania (1926), and Yugoslavia (1927). The Locarno treaties of 1925 added Britain and Italy as allies in case of a German attack. Aristide Briand, minister of foreign affairs, engineered most of these diplomatic agreements. Through collective arrangements with lesser states, France thus responded to the postwar failure of its principal allies to devise effective machinery for the preservation of the peace settlements.

Bloc National.   France was governed during the last two years of World War I by the Bloc National, a coalition of center and right-wing parties that won a decisive victory in the first postwar elections. The Bloc's most prominent spokesmen were Georges Clemenceau, Raymond Poincaré, Alexandre Millerand, and Aristide Briand. Supported by business, church, and army interests, these men sought to achieve economic and social stability while maintaining a hard line against Germany. Concurrently, they were unalterably opposed to the radical programs advanced by the Socialist and Communist parties. Divisions among these two groups had widened at the war's end. The Socialists remained committed to policies of legal reform; whereas the Communists advocated more orthodox Marxist policies of revolution. Beginning in 1921, the adaptable Briand and the intransigent Poincaré were the leading conservative figures in the French cabinets. A ministry headed by Briand in 1921 failed by 1922 because of disagreements over financial difficulties aggravated by Germany's failure to make reparations payments. Briand was succeeded in 1922 by Poincaré, who formed a nationalist ministry dedicated to enforcing reparations terms against Germany. Poincaré's policies, highlighted by the Ruhr invasion of 1923, were discredited by 1924 because they had failed to promote French recovery and had created apprehensions of militancy that might lead to another war.

Cartel des Gauches.   In the elections of 1924, the Bloc National was defeated by a left-wing coalition, the Cartel des Gauches. The ability of Radicals and Socialists to cooperate during the campaign was the key to this alliance. Both parties were anticlerical and supported the republic, but they disagreed sharply over economic and foreign policy questions. The Radical-Socialist party, led by Edouard Herriot, was the largest single party in the Chamber of Deputies; the Socialist party, which had separated from the Moscow-oriented Communists in 1920, was directed by Léon Blum. With Herriot as premier, the ministry that was formed after the election was dominated by Radicals. Although the Socialists refused to accept any portfolios, the government depended upon their support. Herriot was heir to France's proliferating financial difficulties, marked by runaway inflation and huge budgetary deficits, problems upon which Radicals and Socialists held strongly differing views. As the leftist parties quarreled over how the burdens of taxation would be allocated, the value of the franc plunged; by 1926, it was worth only one-tenth of its prewar value.

Successful Years of Poincaré.   Within fifteen months after Herriot's resignation in 1925, six cabinets were formed and fell. Radicals were faced with the choice of accepting Socialist proposals for high progressive taxes on the wealthy or abdicating power and transferring their support to the moderate conservatives. Their decision to adopt the latter course in 1926 returned Raymond Poincaré to the premiership for three years, a longer span than any since the war. Aristide Briand, who had reentered the cabinet as minister of foreign affairs in 1925, held that position until 1932, providing an unusual period of continuity in the foreign office. Domestically, these years were highlighted by Poincaré's ability to save the franc and promote economic recovery by bolstering confidence in the government. In 1926, for the first time in thirteen years, the budget was balanced. Policies of increased taxation and reduced expenditures eased the inflationary spiral and encouraged a return of capital from abroad. Foreign affairs were dominated by Briand's efforts to seek reconciliation with Germany and to be assured through various defensive pacts that French security would be protected in case these efforts failed.

IBERIAN PENINSULA

Portugal and Spain, the two nations of the Iberian Peninsula, had taken the lead in overseas expansion during the fifteenth and sixteenth centuries. However, by the end of the sixteenth century, the center of expansionist activity had shifted to northwestern Europe, with the Dutch, the French, and the British eclipsing the Iberian countries in the race for markets and colonies. Since the seventeenth century, Spain and Portugal have played a subordinate role in world affairs. The reasons for this decline were far-ranging and complex. Religious persecution of Jews and Muslims discouraged productive efforts of the peninsula's most energetic industrial and agricultural groups. At the same time, the Spanish aristocracy, immune from taxation although they owned most of the country's wealth, frowned upon careers in commerce and industry as base and dishonorable. During the sixteenth century, inflationary prices, which encouraged an unfavorable balance of trade, further hampered Spain's economic development, and the nobility's predisposition to favor sheep raising over crop production retarded agricultural advancement.

Spain.   During the 1920s, Spain faced recurring national dilemmas. Labor unrest, added to regional and separatist movements, particularly in Catalonia, sparked widespread social turbulence. The resulting ministerial instability was worsened by the interference of army officers in politics. The constitutional monarchy headed by Alfonso XIII (r. 1886–1931) aggravated its problems through attempts to broaden its rule over Spanish Morocco. In 1921, efforts to subjugate that area produced a military disaster in which 12,000 Spanish soldiers were killed. Hoping to stem the rising tide of popular discontent, General Miguel Primo de Rivera y Orbaneja, with the king's encouragement, established a military dictatorship in 1923. Rivera imposed stringent censorship, dissolved national and provincial legislatures, and exiled some republican leaders. Within a few years, there was general dissatisfaction with his authoritarian methods and the government's failure to resolve major problems. As confidence in Rivera's rule was lost, the monarchy that supported him was also discredited. Resistance took the form of army mutinies, strikes, and student riots, which became so generalized that by 1929 they had created revolutionary conditions.

Portugal. Portugal was ruled by a succession of dynasties until 1910, when Manuel II was overthrown; a republican regime governed until 1926. The years of republican rule were extremely unstable, and the inability of the government to unify the nation or resolve its financial problems endangered the very survival of the republican form of government. Portugal's army, traditionally a key force in domestic politics (as was the case in Spain), executed a coup in 1926. Power eventually gravitated into the hands of General Antonio Oscar de Fragoso Carmona, who was elected president in 1928 and held that position until 1951. During 1928, in an attempt to deal with critical financial problems, control over economic policies was placed in the hands of Professor Antonio de Oliveira Salazar, who served as minister of finance. Within a few years, Salazar was to become political dictator as well.

LOW COUNTRIES

The area known as the *Low Countries* comprises modern Belgium, the Netherlands, and Luxembourg. Although geographically small in comparison with the major nations that surround them, these states have played important roles in European history. Their strategic location has made them both crossroads of trade and objects of invasion. Not surprisingly, Great Britain at times waged war when other nations threatened to dominate these areas. The Low Countries demonstrated commercial prowess by the seventeenth century and still share a respectable portion of the world's traffic in goods. In religious and cultural areas, the impact of the Low Countries has been similarly striking.

From 1815 to 1830, the three political units were merged into the United Kingdom of the Netherlands. A revolution in 1830 dissolved this union and led to the independence of Belgium; this was followed by Dutch and Belgian acquisition of Luxembourgian territory that left the principality considerably reduced in size.

Belgium. Having endured four years of occupation, Belgium had problems of reconstruction exceeding even those of France. Because the government was also determined to implement a social welfare program, the tax burden of Belgian citizens rose astronomically. The nation's traditional constitutional monarchy was preserved after the war largely because of the popularity of Albert I, the wartime king, who remained on the throne until 1934. Parliament was dominated by three major parties: Catholics, Liberals, and Socialists. A coalition that had governed during the war ended after Socialists withdrew their support. The new basis of cabinet support was a coalition of Catholics and Socialists, which was maintained from 1925 to 1939.

Several critical domestic problems, antedating the war, continued to plague the nation throughout the 1920s. There was conflict between Catholics and Liberals over the amount of religious instruction to be permitted in secondary schools and a related controversy of religious versus secular control over education. A growing Socialist movement demanded broader programs of social legislation and greater state control over public services. There was continued division between two ethnic groups: Flemings (who identified with the Dutch) and Walloons (who were oriented toward the French). Although a minority of the population, Walloons held the most privileged positions and had made French the national language until a 1921 law established the parity of French and Dutch. Radical Walloons continued to agitate for the complete administrative separation of Belgium into Flemish and Walloon regimes.

The Netherlands. The Netherlands were able to maintain neutrality during World War I because of German and British desires to maintain the area's autonomy. Constitutional monarchy and domestic progress continued during the reign of Queen Wilhelmina (1890–1948). Despite a multiple-party system that by 1926 totaled twenty-seven political groups, the nation enjoyed unusually stable coalition governments. The most enduring alliances were those between two Protestant parties (the Anti-Revolutionary and the Christian Historical) and the Catholic People's party, which was the largest single force in parliament. Although the Socialist party was potent politically, no Socialists held ministerial positions during the postwar decade. In response to broadening liberal sentiments, steps were taken to extend political and social democracy. Universal suffrage was granted to men in 1917 and extended to women in 1919. Legislation providing health insurance, assistance to the aged, and improvements in labor conditions was enacted. Although the home front remained calm under the moderately conservative governments, there was growing unrest in the Dutch colonies, particularly Java and Sumatra.

Luxembourg. When the German armies swerved westward in 1914, the neutrality of Luxembourg was violated along with that of Belgium. Common problems and experiences persuaded the two countries to establish a closer economic union after the war. Luxembourg's constitutional duchy, although challenged by Socialists in November 1918, was quickly restored to power and popularity. Major domestic developments paralleled those in the sister kingdoms. Suffrage was broadened to include women in 1919; and labor legislation, including the eight-hour day and protection of trade-union rights, was implemented.

SWITZERLAND

Under the 1874 reforms of the Federal Constitution of 1848, Switzerland was a confederation of twenty-two cantons, each possessing considerable local autonomy. Political diversity resulted from the area's geographic, religious, and cultural variety. Communities isolated from each other by the mountainous terrain naturally developed separately. Because they share common borders with France, Germany, Italy, and Austria, the Swiss have been heavily influenced by many cultures. German, French, and Italian were coequal official languages. Primarily because both sides profited from the export of Swiss consumer and war goods, the federation was able to maintain its neutrality throughout World War I. As the war ended, labor agitation erupted in a general strike, which was dissipated after the Federal Council promised political and social reforms; these promises were later faithfully implemented. Switzerland altered its traditional policy of avoiding all alliances by entering the League of Nations in 1920 and by signing the Kellogg-Briand Pact of 1928. Swiss policies within the League included participation in nonpolitical activities and the advocacy of universal League membership.

7

Central and Eastern Europe, 1918 to 1929

At the war's close, partly to secure more favorable peace terms, and partly because their traditional regimes had been discredited, most Central and Eastern European nations adopted systems of representative government similar to those of the major Western states. Constitutions were formulated proclaiming the rights of man and providing for universal suffrage and popular elections. Yet, the forces of the Old Regime remained well entrenched. Central and Eastern Europe had traditionally been dominated by agrarian aristocrats possessing huge estates, and the masses had been relegated to the role of landless rural workers. It was only during the nineteenth century that large numbers of the population had been freed from serfdom. A line running roughly from the mouth of the Elbe River through central Germany to Trieste separated this tradition-bound society from the more diversified cultures of the West. This division had profound social as well as economic implications. In the West, literacy rates were higher, and parliamentary institutions and values had their deepest roots. The adoption of liberal regimes by nations in Central and Eastern Europe therefore had an artificial quality. As the democratic governments proved weak and ineffectual, they were replaced with authoritarian systems. Fascism in Italy was their most influential model.

GERMANY

Following Germany's military collapse, the emperor and the army's high command yielded power to provisional governments that were dominated first by Majority Socialists, Progressives, and Centrists, and then by Social Democrats. In 1919, the National Assembly approved a constitution for the Weimar Republic, which ruled Germany until Hitler's advent in 1933. This same body sanctioned the humiliating Versailles treaty, thus associating the Weimar government in the minds of many nationalists with defeat and antipatriotism. Because of Germany's central position in Europe and the potential of its revived power, the fate of the Weimar Republic was fraught with both international and domestic significance. Six parties held sway over Germany's political life during this period: Social Democrats, Democrats, Centrists, Nationalists, the People's party, and Communists. However, no group possessed an absolute majority in parliament, and coalition politics became a way of life.

Fall of the Empire.   Ludendorff and Hindenburg, leaders of the German high command, had dictated military and civilian policies during the final years of the war. With the nation's collapse imminent, the liberal Prince Max of Baden was appointed chancellor in October 1918. On November 9, the emperor abdicated, and the German republic was proclaimed. The interim government that assumed power was headed by Friedrich Ebert and dominated by Majority and Independent Socialists. Having organized and crusaded for over half a century, Socialists formed their first ministry under unusually adverse circumstances because revolutionary conditions then existed in Germany. Leading the insurgency were the Spartacists, most extreme of all the Socialists, who campaigned vigorously for a proletarian takeover. Although the Spartacists were aided by the Russian Bolsheviks, the Ebert ministry defeated them by welcoming aid from vigilante groups and returning army officers. The most successful Communist insurgency, which occurred in Bavaria during April 1919, was overcome within a month.

Weimar Republic.   Elections to the National Assembly, held in January 1919, awarded the largest number of deputies (163) to Majority Socialists. The Centrists won 88 seats, and the Democrats won 75. These three groups from the political Center and Left then formed a coalition ministry headed by Philipp Scheidemann, a Majority Socialist, and Friedrich Ebert became the first president of the republic. The Weimar Constitution, adopted on July 31, 1919, was highly democratic in principle. It created a state based upon the theory of popular sovereignty. The national legislature included two houses: the Reichstag, made up of representatives chosen by universal suffrage for a term of four years, and the less powerful Reichsrat, representing the various states and exercising only a suspensory veto over legislation. The president was chosen by popular vote for a seven-year term. Under normal circumstances, the chief executive exercised little power; yet, Article 48 of the Weimar Constitution allowed him to prescribe emergency measures during periods of national crisis. Responsibility for formulating and implementing general policy was vested in a chancellor and his ministry, who were accountable to the Reichstag. Although the empire remained federal in structure, the state was more centralized than it had been during the imperial regime.

Economy. Economic conditions in the Weimar Republic were characterized by severe inflation from the end of the war to 1923 and a period of recovery from 1923 to the Great Depression. As a result of the imperial government's reliance on internal borrowing and its reluctance to impose heavy direct taxes during the war, by 1919, the German mark was worth less than half its prewar value. Continued exorbitant expenditures were necessitated by reparations payments and peacetime readjustments. Because the Weimar government was unwilling to levy needed taxes, larger budgetary deficits were created, which only heightened the inflation. By 1923, the mark's value as a medium of exchange had vanished completely. Before the war, 4.2 marks had equaled the value of 1 dollar; now, over 4 million marks were required to purchase a dollar's worth of goods. Farmers and merchants were reluctant to sell their products for worthless currency, and the barter of real goods replaced the use of money among large segments of the population. Particularly hard hit were workers whose wage increases lagged far behind soaring prices and members of the middle class who lived on fixed incomes, savings, and pensions. Life savings were wiped out, and many bourgeois families were relegated to the status of demoralized and embittered proletarians. Simultaneously, some businessmen built huge fortunes by taking advantage of cheap labor and low interest rates to accumulate sizable empires in real property and goods.

Drastic measures to achieve economic stabilization had become imperative. In November 1923, a new currency, the rentenmark, was stabilized at the level of the prewar mark (4.2 to the dollar). Concurrently, the government decided to end its passive resistance in the Ruhr and to request renegotiation of the reparations question. The Dawes Plan (see p. 105) encouraged foreign investments in Germany while easing the economic and political turmoil over reparations. Public confidence was further restored through the successful efforts of Finance Minister Hans Luther to balance the budget. Economic recovery proceeded at a rapid rate. Following the American example, the

German government made mass production and standardization premier industrial goals. Major construction was undertaken in housing, merchant vessels, and capital goods. Consequently, by 1929, Germany's industrial output exceeded its prewar level.

Politics.   The Social Democratic, Catholic Center, and Democratic parties were architects of the Weimar Republic. Social Democrats favored socialization through parliamentary means rather than revolution and were therefore considered by Independent Socialists and Communists heretics from the cause of socialism. The Catholic Center party, also an established prewar force, included a spectrum of political views. Centrists usually combined dedication to the republican idea with strong opposition to radical social reform. The newly organized Democratic party included members of the former Progressive party and left-wing adherents of the prewar National Liberal party. Favoring welfare measures and progressive taxation, the leaders of this group campaigned against monarchism and militarism. Prominent groups on the Right were the Nationalists and the German People's party. These organizations were generally antirepublican, militarist, and monarchist. Nevertheless, Gustav Stresemann, leader of the German People's party, became the Weimar government's most prominent leader.

During the 1920s, the weight of political power in Germany shifted from Left-Center to Right-Center. Until 1923, a coalition of Social Democrats, Centrists, and Democrats held the reins of power. Beginning in that year, the coalition was broadened to include members of the People's party. The evolving role of the Center party also illustrates this conservative trend. The single most important group throughout the history of the Weimar Republic, the Center party was represented in every cabinet until 1932. During the early 1920s, Centrist ministers belonged to the party's left wing; later, they were spokesmen primarily for its right wing. In addition to its other severe problems, the Weimar government faced repeated attacks from groups on the extremes of Left and Right. During 1918 and 1919, Communists sponsored the first serious efforts to overthrow the republic. As their threats abated, attacks from reactionaries increased. During March 1920, General Walther von Lüttwitz and Wolfgang Kapp executed a putsch, capturing Berlin, but the uprising collapsed after one week. Another plot, devised by General Ludendorff and Adolf Hitler in November 1923, was aborted before a grave threat to the republic materialized.

Foreign Policy.   The direction of Germany's foreign policy was determined by the nation's postwar circumstances. Along with its allies, Germany shared the humiliation of military defeat. The terms of the peace transferred all Germany's colonies and about one-tenth of its European population and territory. The common desire of all parties was to revise the Versailles treaty's hated provisions and restore Germany to its prewar eminence. Some German statesmen believed that recovery could best be promoted through friendly relations with Eastern powers, notably Russia. The signing of the Rapallo treaty (April 1922) was the most dramatic move in this direction. Under its terms, both nations mutually canceled war claims, and Germany extended de jure recognition to the Bolshevik regime. Other spokesmen contended that Germany could best modify the Versailles settlement through policies of cooperation with the victorious Western nations. Begun in 1921 and resumed when passive resistance in the Ruhr ended, this program of *fulfillment* as it was called became Germany's dominant and most constructive foreign policy toward the end of the 1920s. Gustav Stresemann, foreign minister from 1923 until his death in 1929, was the leading advocate of moves designed to achieve Germany's reconciliation with the West. Downward revisions in the initial reparations demands, the Locarno treaties, economic recovery, and Germany's admission to the United Nations were all products of this course.

ITALY

Liberalism suffered its most dramatic defeat during the 1920s with the rise of fascism in Italy. Like communism, fascism had as its ultimate goal the establishment of governmental mastery over all institutions of society. Fascism and communism were also similar in their predispositions to use brutal and violent tactics to achieve and maintain power. In the economic sphere, Italian fascism stood midway between communism and capitalism. Although institutions of private property were maintained, pervasive governmental controls were established over them. Those who were attracted to this monopoly of power by the political Right viewed it as a way of regaining the nation's honor and as a corrective to the problems of unstable government and labor-capital conflicts that plagued many parliamentary democracies. At the same time, socialists, republicans, and liberals everywhere viewed with alarm the lower status to which Fascists relegated the rights of labor and the rights of man. By effectively replacing Italy's established parliamentary regime, Benito Mussolini's experiment succeeded not only in dominating Italian society but also in providing an example that affected the politics of many other countries.

Background of Fascism.   Italians were profoundly disillusioned with the failure of the Paris peace conference to fulfill their territorial ambitions in Europe and overseas. They blamed government leaders for betraying the conditions under which Italy entered the war and for the nation's wartime sacrifices. Meanwhile, Italy shared with other countries the postwar problems of unemployment and inflation, which traditional Italian poverty and economic backwardness only intensified. In the elections of November 1919, Italians vented their disillusion by deserting the well-established Liberal and Radical parties and flocking to the Socialist party, which had denounced the war from its inception. In 1919 and 1920, labor militancy, culminating in the seizure of numerous factories, created threats of a leftist takeover. Italy's faction-ridden Chamber of Deputies was paralyzed in the face of these national crises. Under these circumstances, Mussolini and his Fascist followers, promising both order and reform, broadened their support among conservatives and the masses.

Rise of Mussolini. Before World War I, Mussolini had established himself as a left-wing Socialist who had been heavily influenced by *Reflections on Violence,* Georges Sorel's study of revolutionary syndicalism. He opposed government efforts to establish control over Libya in 1911 on the grounds that it would mean exploitation of backward people. For this, he was sentenced to five years' imprisonment (he served only five months). Mussolini used journalism as a tool of protest and in 1912 was promoted to the editorship of *Avanti,* the Socialist party's official newspaper. Soon after hostilities began, he violated the Socialist doctrine of nonintervention and, along with the poet Gabriele D'Annunzio, agitated for Italy's entrance into the war on the side of the Allies. Forced to resign as editor of *Avanti,* he founded another newspaper, *Il Popolo d'Italia.* He entered active service in 1915 and was wounded in 1917. Mussolini spent the rest of the war using *Il Popolo d'Italia* to help sustain Italian war efforts.

After the war, Mussolini gathered around him the Fascio di Combattimento, a small band comprising principally former soldiers and Socialists. The organization's initial efforts were unimpressive, and in the parliamentary elections of 1919, Mussolini was defeated. The disorders of 1920 and 1921 provided the setting for his ascent. At first, he supported militant labor agitation as a way of weakening capitalism and punishing war profiteers. Then, sensing the popular mood, he shifted his tactics to attacks on communism as a way of attracting middle-class and conservative support. Although his rhetoric remained revolutionary, his message emphasized order and national glory, goals that had a broad appeal to the established classes. His following increased in size and militancy with the addition of many of D'Annunzio's legionnaires, who had been dislodged from the mutinous but popular control that they had established over Fiume in 1919. *Squadristi* of Black Shirts aroused popular enthusiasm by attacking real and imagined Communists with guns, bludgeons, and heavy doses of castor oil. By the elections of 1921, which the reform parties dominated, Fascists succeeded in winning 22 of the roughly 500 seats.

Fascist Takeover. By the autumn of 1922, Mussolini considered conditions ripe for seizing power. The Fascist party had achieved widespread popularity as the nation's protector from the Communist left. In the outlying provinces, local Socialist and Communist officials were being driven from office and replaced by Fascist loyalists. To ease the doubts of his conservative adherents, the previously anticlerical and republican Mussolini announced his support of the monarchy and the Catholic church. He repeatedly called for the dissolution of parliament or the resignation of Luigi Facta's ministry, then in power. When the government declined to do either, Mussolini and his followers staged their March on Rome. After the king denied Facta's request for a proclamation of martial law to repel this challenge, the cabinet resigned. The king immediately summoned Mussolini to form a new government, which was established with the support of the Nationalist and Popular parties on October 31. After receiving virtually dictatorial powers until the end of 1923, Mussolini forced a bill through parliament assigning two-thirds of all legislative seats to the party winning the largest number of votes in a general election. In the elections of 1924, which were characterized by governmental rigging and *squadristi* intimidation, Fascists received well over half of the popular vote, making them masters of the Chamber of Deputies.

Assassination of Matteotti. To assure victory in the 1924 elections, Fascists engaged in widespread fraud, intimidation, and violence. Giacomo Matteotti, a Socialist deputy, charged governmental involvement during a chamber speech condemning these acts. Subsequently, Matteotti disappeared and was later found brutally murdered. Most observers correctly assumed that Fascists were responsible for the assassination, and Mussolini's ministry was faced with a profound sense of popular outrage that threatened to topple him from power. Many deputies from the Socialist, Popular, and Liberal parties withdrew from the Chamber in protest. At first, Mussolini acted defensively, removing from office those involved in the plot; but by 1926, he felt strong enough to assume responsibility for Matteotti's death without endangering his power. Confident of his popular support, he permanently deprived of their seats those deputies who had seceded from the Chamber and ordered the parties they represented dissolved.

Corporative State. From the inception of his rule, Mussolini expressed only contempt for theories of popular sovereignty and the practices of parliamentary government. He castigated democracy for encouraging class conflict and minority politics. As a substitute, he promoted the theory of a *corporative* state, under the direction of the Fascist party and led by a vigorous and visionary leader (*Il Duce*), in which the usually embittered relations between capital and labor would be harmonized. In reality, Mussolini's policies led to the creation of an omnipotent state in which industry was privileged and labor and the professions were subjugated. After 1924, the Fascist party eliminated the Italian parliament's freedom of operation. Patriotic and well-disciplined youth organizations were created; the press was censored; universities were purged; and government regimentation of labor unions was effected. In return for support of Mussolini's policies, large employers in industry, commerce, and agriculture were organized into semigovernmental bodies and given authority to manage the economy.

Lateran Treaty. Before 1870, popes were temporal rulers of the Papal States, including Rome, in central Italy. During that year, the recently united Italian state seized Rome as its capital. In an effort to pacify the papacy, the Italian government in 1871 passed the Law of Guarantees, which ensured the pope's sovereignty over a reduced area of land that included Saint Peter's, the Vatican, and the Lateran Palace. Successive popes refused to recognize the legitimacy of this unilateral act and accordingly rejected the annual subsidies offered by the government. Mussolini inherited this predicament, which had created problems of loyalty among Italy's predominantly Catholic population. Although he was an atheist, he recognized the popular value of resolving the so-called Roman question. Accordingly, he initiated negotiations with the Vatican that culminated in the Lateran treaty (1929). Under its terms, the papacy finally agreed to recognize the Italian state, and the Italian government assured papal sovereignty over Vatican City, an area of about one square mile. Recognizing Catholicism as the state religion, the government bound itself to enforce religious instruction in the public schools and canon law throughout the nation. As a result of this settlement, Mussolini's prestige in Italy and abroad rose rapidly.

NEW NATIONS

Between Germany and Italy to the west and Russia to the east, there were thirteen states, small to moderate in size, that had been newly created or significantly altered by the peace settlements. All had profited by the dissolution or weakening of the Austro-Hungarian, German, and Russian empires. Austria, Czechoslovakia, Hungary, and Yugoslavia were successor states to the Austro-Hungarian Empire. Romania, which had obtained independence from Turkey in 1878, gained Danubian territory that doubled its size. Poland and Lithuania, partitioned out of existence during the eighteenth century, were revived as independent states. Albania's independence from Turkey was similarly restored. Latvia, Estonia, and Finland attained sovereignty after enduring several centuries of German, Swedish, and Russian domination. Although Bulgaria and Greece had maintained their prewar sovereignty intact, both nations were altered politically through boundary adjustments and massive transfers of dislocated populations.

Economy. The secondary states in Central and Eastern Europe, with the exceptions of Czechoslovakia, Austria, and Greece, were preindustrial societies in which agricultural production continued to predominate. In some states, including Serbia and Bulgaria, agriculture was characterized by dispersed and small proprietorships; whereas in most of the former territories of the Austro-Hungarian Empire, large estates were the rule. In all areas, land reform was planned during and immediately following World War I. Wholesale redistributions were effectively implemented in Romania, Czechoslovakia, and Yugoslavia with momentous social and political consequences. Land reform was frequently used to destroy the economic power of nonnationals. For example, the Czechs dissolved the agricultural holdings of German and Hungarian nobles, and the Yugoslavs dealt in a corresponding manner with Turkish and Hungarian estates. A similar situation prevailed in the Balkan countries and in Estonia, Latvia, and Lithuania, where land redistribution was used to break the power of the traditional German, Swedish, and Russian aristocracies. In Hungary and Poland, however, redistributions were relatively minor because the native aristocracies still dominated the public life of the two countries.

But land reform failed to fulfill even its most moderate promises. Where the large estates were divided, agricultural production was placed in the hands of peasants who usually lacked necessary capital and expertise. Economic stability in all areas required either industrial development as a complement of agriculture or a greater degree of economic cooperation among states. Tariff barriers thwarted the flow of goods, and the middle class remained weak and numerically small in most countries. Only Czechoslovakia, which had an established factory and mining structure, approached balance among the various sectors of its economy. Other successor states of the Hapsburg empire suffered adverse economic effects from its disintegration because the Dual Monarchy, despite its political problems, had constituted a diversified and stable economic entity with a common tariff. Some areas, including Poland, possessed the resources for industrialization but lacked the necessary technical skills; others, such as Albania and Bulgaria, had neither. Underdeveloped economies meant the continuance of miserable living conditions for the masses.

Politics. During and immediately after World War I, these thirteen new political units adopted modern constitutions patterned on Western models and based on the principle of popular sovereignty. With Czechoslovakia again an outstanding exception, the economic conditions and liberal attitudes essential for democratic government were lacking in most places. When these factors were combined with cultural, social, and linguistic heterogeneity, the obstacles to stable government usually proved overwhelming. Efforts by dominant groups to centralize power competed with the varied programs of federalism advanced by minority groups. Without the moderating influence of a large middle class, political parties were dominated by elites of nobles, merchants, the intelligentsia, and occasionally, union leaders. Multiple-party systems were the rule, leading to coalition ministries that usually proved transient and ineffectual. Thus, during the postwar decade, these practices encouraged a trend toward the replacement of parliamentary governments with illiberal regimes.

RUSSIA

Several years elapsed between the Bolshevik seizure of power and the stabilization of Communist rule in Russia. From 1918 to 1921, Bolshevik leaders were preoccupied with the struggle to survive efforts of domestic and foreign enemies to overthrow their regime. This period of War Communism was characterized by civil warfare, stringent police measures, and radical social reforms. By 1921, their opponents had been defeated or discouraged, but the domestic turmoil left Russia's economy in shambles. To accelerate recovery, the New Economic Policy (NEP), which represented a compromise between capitalist and Communist principles, was enforced. Meanwhile, a struggle for power developed among Bolshevik leaders. The eventual victor, who left his peculiar and indelible imprint on Russian and world communism, was Joseph Stalin. Concurrently with Stalin's success, the principle of placing priority on the development of socialism in Russia won out over the idea of concentrating first on the achievement of a worldwide Socialist revolution. This choice of policy had far-reaching consequences.

War Communism. The Bolshevik party attained power under chaotic conditions that generated varied forms of resistance by opponents of the revolution. Encouraged by independence movements, non-Russian nationalities, beginning in 1917, started to withdraw from the empire and establish governments of their own. In the summer of 1918, after the Constituent Assembly had been disbanded and the hated Treaty of Brest Litovsk signed, a civil war erupted as the forces of counterrevolution (Whites) attempted to destroy the Bolshevik government and its supporters (Reds). Led by former army officers, Whites elicited support from groups of diverse political complexions, including Cossacks, Czech troops, Socialist Revolutionaries, and national groups seeking independence. Furthermore, Allied forces landing at the ports of Murmansk, Arkhangelsk, and Vladivostok made troops and supplies available to the anti-Bolshevik forces. To complicate its problems further, the Soviet government fought a war during 1920 with newly independent Poland over the boundaries between the two countries.

Bolsheviks responded to the independence movements, civil war, and acts of foreign resistance with policies of terror, propaganda, and military resistance. Counterrevolutionaries were depicted as army officers, landlords, capitalists, and their sympathizers who wanted to restore their prerevolutionary prerogatives. Domestic and foreign opposition was countered with a ruthless secret police force (Cheka) and the Red Army, which by 1919 totaled over 100,000. Domestic resistance was silenced as Bolsheviks suppressed rival parties, censored the press, and established firm controls over the soviets and trade unions. Nationalization of industry and agriculture was highlighted by the forcible requisitioning of agricultural produce from the peasantry. Except in Finland, the Baltic states (Estonia, Lativa, and Lithuania), and Poland, the Bolsheviks were able by 1921 to suppress nationalist uprisings through alliances established with local Communists. The war with Poland was terminated by the Treaty of Riga (March 1921), which awarded Poland most of the lands it desired, including areas inhabited by Ukrainians. By the end of 1920, the White armies had been defeated, and the policies of War Communism had achieved the principal objective of preserving Bolshevik rule.

New Economic Policy. By 1921, Russia had endured seven years of continuous war, revolution, and civil strife. As a consequence, the nation was approaching almost total economic disorganization. Industrial production had declined to less than one-third of its prewar level; many factories were idle; shortages of food and fuel had reached epidemic proportions. Many early Bolshevik supporters had also grown disenchanted with the stringent policies implemented during the period of War Communism. These measures clearly violated Bolshevik promises of a freely elected constituent assembly and protection of the freedoms of speech, press, and assembly. Evidence of the dissension that dictatorial controls had created within Communist ranks was a rebellion in March 1921 at the Kronshtadt naval base, which had been a key source of Bolshevik strength. The rebels, including sailors, soldiers, and workers, demanded the elimination of Bolshevik domination within the soviets and the convening of a constituent assembly to draft a new constitution. Bolshevik leaders responded mercilessly, labeling their former comrades *counterrevolutionaries* and using the Cheka and Red Army to suppress them in bloody fighting.

Recognizing the country's profound and widespread distress, Lenin persuaded the Tenth Party Congress (1921) to approve a series of measures that became known as the *New Economic Policy (NEP)*. The NEP was designed to protect the revolution by stabilizing the economy while pacifying peasants and industrial workers. This would be achieved by reestablishing semicapitalist market conditions to end or moderate the most restrictive features of War Communism. Forced government requisitioning of farm produce was abandoned, and peasants were permitted to sell on the open market after they paid taxes in money and kind. The government maintained its dominance of large- and medium-sized industries (described by Lenin as the "commanding heights"), but private operation was permitted in small plants and retail businesses. These changes encouraged an economic revival, allowing Russian agricultural and industrial production to reach or exceed prewar levels by 1928. The reforms also permitted small capitalists in business (nepmen) and agriculture (kulaks) to thrive, causing severe arguments among Bolsheviks over the length of time that compromises with free enterprise could be tolerated.

From Lenin to Stalin. Lenin's long illness, which lasted from May 1922 until his death in January 1924, measurably weakened his active control of party affairs. The struggle for succession that had developed during his illness intensified after his death. Because a small, self-perpetuating oligarchy dominated the Bolshevik organization and the government, neither the party's rank and file nor the Russian masses participated in the choice of Lenin's successor. Although the annual congress was theoretically the Bolshevik party's supreme governing organ, this body habitually acquiesced in the dictates of three select agencies of the Central Committee: the Politburo, a governing body made up of party leaders; the Orgburo, which managed the party's organizational tasks; and the Secretariat, which assisted the endeavors of other bodies. Prominent figures in the struggle for power included Leon Trotsky, second in command, an illustrious writer and orator who served as the first commissar of foreign affairs and later as organizer of the Red Army; Joseph Stalin, general secretary of the party, commissar of nationalities, and member of both the Orgburo and the Politburo; Grigori Zinoviev, head of the party organization in Leningrad and leader of the Third International; Lev Kamenev, party leader in Moscow; and Nikolai Bukharin, theoretician and leader among Bolshevik conservatives.

Most observers conceded that Trotsky was Lenin's logical heir because of his prestige, colorful personality, and intellectual brilliance. But the offices that Stalin held made him the most powerful figure in the party and in the government, positions that he skillfully used to construct a broad base of party support. To counter Trotsky's eminence, Stalin, Zinoviev, and Kamenev formed a troika against him in 1923. By the mid-1920s, they had succeeded in undermining Trotsky's support among the party faithful. Meanwhile, the power balance had shifted toward Stalin; and the troika, whose reason for being had now vanished, disbanded amid factional disputes. Against Zinoviev and Kamenev, who switched positions to join forces with Trotsky, Stalin allied himself with a right-wing faction, including Bukharin, Aleksei Rykov, and Mikhail Tomski. Stalin succeeded in crushing the Trotskyites and then in eliminating rivals within the right-wing faction. His ultimate triumph came at the Fifteenth Party Congress (December 1927). Followers of Trotsky were expelled from the congress, and Trotsky was deported to Central Asia. In 1929, he was banished from Russia.

The ideological dispute that dominated the succession struggle focused on theories of a permanent world revolution versus socialism in one country. According to the former argument, best advanced by Trotsky, efforts to achieve socialism in one country were doomed to failure because of the combined strength of capitalist nations. Hence,

Bolsheviks had no recourse except to concentrate on supporting Social-ist revolutions in other countries while simultaneously developing an industrial and proletarian state within Russia. Stalin emerged after 1924 as the chief spokesman for the view that Bolsheviks should place prior-ity on domestic stabilization. Supporters of this position held that Socialist revolutions in other countries were not imminent and that Bolsheviks should therefore compromise with peasants and encourage the investment of foreign capital in order to assure the gradual success of the Socialist regime in Russia. The two arguments differed primarily in matters of timing and emphasis; all Bolsheviks favored the eventual attainment of socialism both in Russia and in other countries. After Stalin's triumph in 1927, he revised his earlier position, adopting the leftist argument that Russia should move quickly toward a Socialist society by embarking upon a program of rapid industrialization together with large-scale collectivization of agriculture. These were the concepts that guided Russia from 1928 to the end of the 1930s.

8

European Culture
during the 1920s

The twentieth-century cultural revolution had its roots in the intellectual ferment that preceded World War I. Scientists, writers, artists, and social theorists had begun a rebellion that was accelerated by the disintegrating effects of the war. Emphasis on innovation, or *modernism,* was the common basis for diverse cultural trends. To a considerable degree, the antitraditionalist impetus was a reaction against the mechanistic notions of man and nature that had reigned supreme during much of the nineteenth century. In physics, concepts of relativity and mutability replaced deterministic theory; in painting and literature, realism yielded to individualism and abstractionism; in social theory, positivism and rationalism were challenged by assumptions of uncertainty and irrationalism. Architects emphasized the social purpose of design; musicians turned to atonal experiments, challenging the standard harmonies of romanticism. Cultural trends were set by intellectuals who gravitated to a few European cities, notably Berlin and Paris. But the impact of their ideas eventually became worldwide and affected all segments of society.

SCIENCE AND TECHNOLOGY

By promoting revolutionary concepts of the relations and nature of energy, matter, and motion, physics became the dominant natural science during the twentieth century. The implications of Max Planck's quantum theory and Albert Einstein's theory of relativity (see pp. 3–4) assisted Ernest Rutherford and Niels Bohr in formulating a model of an atom in 1913. The atom, which was previously thought to be the irreducible building block of the universe, was found instead to be sub-dividable into positive protons surrounded by negative electrons. The era of nuclear physics was launched in 1919 when Rutherford discovered that atoms could be divided and transformed.

Other celebrated achievements in science included refinements in the genetic theory of Gregor Mendel, which were not widely recognized until the twentieth century, and progress in the understanding of vitamins, hormones, and antibiotics.

Unceasing technological advances, furthered by wartime necessities, continued to transform European society. A variety of new synthetic products came into use, and motor and air travel established superiority over horse-drawn carriages. The use of electricity in lighting, radio, motion pictures, and industry revolutionized both urban and rural societies. Unlike the United States, which permitted private enterprise to broaden its control over these developing industries, most European states operated the new services themselves or placed them in the hands of regulated monopolies. In their quest for more efficient techniques of production, Europeans at the same time copied from American corporations so-called scientific forms of production designed to increase efficiency and output. Class lines became less distinguishable as skilled white-collar workers filled the large gulf that had previously separated owners and laborers. Applications of new technology varied widely within and among European states. The greatest impact was felt in Western and Central Europe; the fewest changes occurred in southern and southeastern countries.

SOCIAL THOUGHT

Prevailing social theories of the 1920s were marked by a rivalry between time-honored ideas and evolving ways of viewing man in society and the universe. World War I had dramatized for many observers the invalidity of the assumption that reason governed the affairs of men. Newer conceptions of man, especially Freudian theories, placed greater emphasis on the irrationality of his nature and condition. Freudians were supported in their arguments by existentialist theories in philosophy and elitist theories in sociology and politics. At the same time, dominant nineteenth-century ideas continued to carry considerable weight. In philosophy, for example, the positivist tradition led to the postwar school of logical positivism; in sociology, anthropology, and other social sciences, continuing emphasis was placed on incorporating the tools of natural science.

Philosophy. Logical positivism, or logical empiricism, has been a dominant trend in contemporary philosophy. The school was formed immediately after the war by a group known as the *Vienna circle*. They were heavily influenced by the earlier writings of Bertrand Russell and his former student Ludwig Wittgenstein, whose book *Tractatus Logico-Philosophicus* (1922) contended that most philosophical theories prove illusory when subjected to logical analysis. Exponents of logical positivism considered the central role of philosophy to be the clarification of the meaning of language. Reflecting their deep admiration for the precision of science and mathematics, logical positivists restricted themselves to manageable problems that could be logically or empirically verified, excluding the traditional philosophic concentrations on the nature of reality and on moral, political, and religious questions. Although logical positivists met considerable resistance on the Continent, where the preoccupations with ethics and metaphysics remained strong, their school became dominant in Great Britain and the United States.

Existentialism was the philosophic expression of irrationalism. The movement emerged in its present form after World War II in the writings of Jean Paul Sartre and Albert Camus. It grew out of the alienation felt by the individual faced with the wreckage of customary values in the wake of two world wars. Martin Heidegger, a German philosopher whose principal book was *Being and Time* (1927), was a founder and leading exponent of existentialism in the 1920s. Unlike logical positivists, existentialists were concerned with traditional questions, focusing on the nature of man's existence on earth. They concluded that the world was essentially absurd, contradictory, and meaningless. Each individual must therefore assume the responsibility for making his own choices and developing his own identity. This philosophy has achieved particularly wide response, pervading virtually every form of contemporary thought and expression.

Psychology. Freud's central statement that man's unconsciousness (id) embodied primitive, primarily sexual drives which his directing consciousness (ego) attempted, often unsuccessfully, to repress was published in *The Interpretation of Dreams* (1900). His theory of psychoanalysis, which attracted widespread attention and controversy, assumed that psychic difficulties created by the id-ego conflict could best be resolved through the patient's discovery of the matters being repressed. Freud's writings during the 1920s attempted to apply to society the implications of earlier theories that developed out of the treatment of individual patients. These views on man in modern society were expressed in *Civilization and Its Discontents* (1930), which argued that man's desires, which community values barely managed to contain, were perpetual threats to social integration on the one hand and to individual happiness on the other.

Among psychiatrists, several major challenges to Freud's ideas were formulated during the postwar decade. The Gestalt school, in Germany, theorized that the psyche could be understood only by studying the entire human being rather than by focusing on certain primitive drives. Other qualifications of Freudian ideas were presented by two of his former disciples. Alfred Adler, a Viennese like Freud, stressed the individual's conscious feelings; Swiss psychiatrist Carl Gustav Jung advanced a broader definition of the unconscious that included common collective images and symbols.

Sociology. Sociologists also employed scientific methods to focus on the irrational aspects of human nature. Max Weber, one of the founding fathers of sociology, continued to rank first in influence even after his death in 1920. Weber popularized the use of social models, or *ideal types,* as a basis for evaluating and comparing social phenomena. He examined the ways in which institutions destroyed spontaneity by requiring that processes become established and organized. Other sociologists whose works were widely read were the Italians Vilfredo Pareto and Gaetano Mosca. Their major works also preceded the war, and their most influential findings were in the area of political sociology. Both Pareto and Mosca concluded that "the people" seldom governed even in democratic regimes, where the tendency toward oligarchy remained and an elected elite replaced the traditional hereditary ruling class.

LITERATURE

The literary revolution, rooted in the prewar symbolist movement, reached maturity during the 1920s. The physical and moral wreckage of the war, indelibly branded on the popular mind, was captured by novels like Henri Barbusse's *Le Feu* (1916) and Erich Maria Remarque's *All Quiet on the Western Front* (1929). The disillusionment they expressed helped to create conditions receptive to the dissemination of radical values. The prevailing trend among writers was a search for hidden and implied meanings in the events they depicted.

The dadaist school, which developed during and immediately after the war, angrily and randomly registered protest against the absurdity of accepted standards. Surrealists went a step farther, attempting to express the nonrational through the Freudian approach of exploring dreams and the subconscious. Politically, dissenting writers turned against the bourgeoisie, whom they held accountable for the ills of modern civilization, and many became members of pacifist and Communist groups.

The works and influence of the most prominent writers of the 1920s bridged the prewar and postwar periods. André Gide, in *The Counterfeiters* (1925), examined the reactions of adolescence to stern and bewildering traditional values. Franz Kafka, in his masterful *The Trial* (1925) and *The Castle* (1926), depicted modern man as a confused wanderer who becomes a pawn of forces beyond his control or understanding. Like Proust (see pp. 29–30), James Joyce, in *Ulysses* (1922), abandoned the customary novel format. Joyce developed the stream-of-consciousness technique to chronicle his protagonist's search for identity in modern Dublin. In Germany, Thomas Mann captured the contemporary disillusion in *The Magic Mountain* (1924), which probed the condition of modern man, symbolized by patients in a tuberculosis sanitorium. The willingness to portray controversial themes in new and daring fashion was exemplified in England by the publication of D. H. Lawrence's *Lady Chatterley's Lover* (1928), which dealt frankly and approvingly with human sexuality.

Poets and dramatists were also preoccupied with social criticism and maintained and expanded the prewar symbolist trends. In England, T. S. Eliot expressed his despairing criticism of modern society in his long poem *The Waste Land* (1922). Eliot later converted to the Anglican faith and portrayed the religious experience in verse and drama. An attitude of doubt arising out of the conditions created by the war was voiced by the French symbolist poet Paul Valéry in *La Jeune Parque* (1917); his verse was characterized by precise phrasing and detached intellectuality. Germany's outstanding and most influential poet during the 1920s was Rainer Maria Rilke, a mystic who sought to achieve peace by absorption in nature. The leading playwrights during the postwar decade were the Irish George Bernard Shaw, whose major satiric works preceded the war, and the Italian Luigi Pirandello, who was famed for the experimental technique he employed in *Six Characters in Search of an Author* (1918); in this play, a family that had experienced tragedy occupies the stage simultaneously with the professional actors chosen to recreate their drama.

PAINTING

The innovative tendencies in painting began before the war were bold applications of color and strokes, as demonstrated by the fauves ("wild beasts"); abstractionism, as evidenced in cubist paintings; and assertion of the primacy of emotions, which motivated works by the expressionists. As the shocks of war made the educated public more tolerant of unconventional aesthetic expressions, these trends became more manifest. Dadaist and surrealist influences encouraged the trend away from representational art. Yet, by the late 1920s, some of the maturing unconventional artists, including Henri Matisse, one of the original fauves, had introduced a greater degree of realism in their works. Pablo Picasso, who launched the cubist movement, continued to emphasize abstraction, passing through a surrealist phase and later experimenting with other forms. Many avant-garde painters, influenced by Freud's focus on dreams and the unconscious, attempted to give visual expression to this subliminal reality. Others relied on the expression of their own emotions as a way of communicating meaningful visions and evoking emotional responses from their viewers.

MUSIC

Postwar musical innovations centered on departures from the traditional major-minor system of tonality, in which compositions were dominated by one of the twelve tones on the chromatic scale. The most radical innovator before the war was Arnold Schönberg, a Viennese composer, who eliminated the concept of a unifying principal key, instead according equal importance to all tones on the scale. A fresh and grating musical effect, sometimes offensive to exponents of traditional music, was usually the result. These radical compositions had little popular appeal in the 1920s. Schönberg's most renowned students were Alban Berg and Anton Webern. Berg employed Schönberg's system to create nightmarish effects in his opera *Wozzeck* (1925). Meanwhile, the works of established masters such as Richard Strauss, Richard Wagner, and Gustav Mahler continued to dominate Austrian and German music.

The most influential new trends in music after the war were centered in France. Maurice Ravel and Albert Roussel led the postimpressionists by adapting Debussy's vague and fluid impressionistic styles to more precise forms. They were closely allied with the Six, a group of young composers. Members of this coterie were consciously anti-impressionistic in their search for a greater degree of musical concise-ness and sharpness and for a more down-to-earth type of music that would embody some of the syncopations of jazz. The leading members of the group were Arthur Honegger, Darius Milhaud, and Francis Poulenc. Honegger's oratorio *King David* and his opera *Antigone* remained close to the tradition of conventional German music; Milhaud, working in a variety of forms, developed a simple lyrical style that was uniquely his own; Poulenc excelled in short piano works and songs.

ARCHITECTURE

Modernism in architecture has concentrated on the marriage of art and technology, with an accompanying de-emphasis of ornamental design. This trend traces its origins to the plain and attractive constructions of William Morris, a nineteenth-century English poet and artist, and to the innovative Chicago school, developed around the turn of the century by Louis Sullivan, an American architect. By the 1920s, stress on adapting construction to purpose had evolved an *international style*, led in Germany by Walter Gropius, in France by Le Corbusier, and in the United States by Frank Lloyd Wright. Although Le Corbusier's major influence was not apparent until the 1930s, Gropius achieved preeminence immediately after the war by organizing in 1919 a school of designers known as the *Bauhaus,* which effectively promoted his ideas. Emphasis was placed on achieving a balanced unity of design by gathering under one roof competent artists, architects, and engineers.

Contemporary developments in architecture have reflected the revolution in building materials that has provided the architect with a wider range of options while requiring of him a greater degree of technical competence. The stress on functionalism was encouraged by the need for cheap, economic, and swiftly constructed buildings in cities.

9
The Americas during the 1920s

The evolving industrial power and world prestige of the United States had become the overwhelming influence on the North and South American continents. European culture continued to exercise a penetrating and enduring effect in all places. Yet, to Canadians to the north and the Latin Americans to the south, the United States had clearly become a Western colossus whose economic and political clout exercised an increasing impact on their lives. By 1919, the demoralizing effects of the First World War had undermined values of the Old World, and even Europeans were looking to Woodrow Wilson (and to developments in Russia) as a lodestar for their own actions. Europe's global hegemony appeared undiminished. The total colonial possessions of European nations, although reshuffled, had actually expanded as a result of the postwar territorial acquisitions in the Middle East. In reality, however, Europe's world position had grown weaker. Nationalist movements were loosening the traditional colonial bonds, and the United States had become the leading industrial and financial power.

UNITED STATES

During the postwar decade, Americans revolted against the spirit of reformism that had dominated politics before the United States entered World War I and also against the moral crusade to "make the world safe for democracy," which had served to justify participation in that war. President Warren G. Harding articulated this mood by calling for a "return to normalcy." In economics, social thought, domestic politics, and foreign affairs, the quest for normalcy made conservatism the reigning philosophy. Accepting uncritically the right of industrial leaders to pursue material profit, the government openly advocated and implemented policies favoring big business. Striving also for the simpler world that antedated America's role as an international leader, the United States turned its back on the affairs of Europe and concentrated instead on exploiting natural resources and expanding wealth at home. Provincialism and intolerance in domestic politics were encouraged by this trend toward isolationism. Concurrently, the 1920s proved a period of unsurpassed prosperity for most Americans, filling them with a sense of security and pride. This complacency endured until 1929, when it was profoundly shaken by the Great Depression.

Red Scare.   The Red scare, which peaked during 1919 and 1920, was a wave of hysteria based on beliefs that social unrest threatened the existing order with a Communist-type revolution. The Bolshevik Revolution and the announced intention of Soviet leaders to promote Communist victories throughout highly industrialized Western countries lent credibility to both real and imagined threats of insurrection in America. The wartime suppression of dissent laid the groundwork for intolerance of radicalism. Business leaders exploited the public's fear of revolution to encourage resistance to the increasingly militant demands of the trade-union movement. Thus, bombings and bomb threats during 1919 produced reprisals not only against socialists and anarchists but also against more conservative labor leaders. The leader of the so-called Red hunt was Woodrow Wilson's attorney general, Alexander Mitchell Palmer, who conducted raids, frequently without warrants, on suspected Communist meeting halls. At the local level, many other public officials and vigilante groups harassed anyone whose unconventional economic or political ideas could be considered un-American. The most famous martyrs of the radical cause were two anarchists, Nicola Sacco and Bartolomeo Vanzetti, who were convicted and executed for a robbery-murder in South Braintree, Massachusetts. Many observers believed that the legal proceedings against Sacco and Vanzetti were prejudiced and based on insufficient evidence.

Persecution of Minorities.   Other minority groups also suffered from the fervent intolerance of the 1920s. Not surprisingly, blacks endured the most systematic and ferocious attacks. Many blacks had migrated northward during the war to obtain jobs in war-related industries. Over 400,000 had served with the armed forces during the war, many of them in Europe. After receiving their discharges, a significant number of black soldiers sought employment in the industrial North as a way of escaping the South's narrow caste system. To keep blacks in their subservient roles and eliminate them as threats for jobs, whites freely used tactics of terrorism and violence in both the North and the South. A series of race riots occurred, the most serious in East Saint Louis, Illinois, where at least thirty-nine blacks and eight whites were killed in 1917, and in Chicago, where twenty-three blacks and fifteen whites were killed in 1919. Intolerance against blacks, Jews, and Catholics was given an organizational base when the Ku Klux Klan was revived. Reaching its peak during the mid-1920s, the new Klan dominated politics in several states, including Indiana, by using tactics of intimidation, torture, and lynching.

Anti-immigration sentiments, growing since the 1880s, also reached a new peak after the war. Opposition to aliens came from many sources. Native labor feared their competition for jobs; many citizens suspected them of being militants; spokesmen for the Protestant Anglo-Saxon majority resisted the influx of Italians, Catholics, Jews, and Slavs, who might destroy the American way of life. Reacting to these pressures, Congress passed the Immigration Act of 1921, which was designed primarily to limit newcomers from southern and eastern Europe. Each nation was assigned an annual quota of immigrants, which was limited to 3 percent of its nationals who resided in the United States during the base year 1910. This formula, which allowed an annual total of approximately 350,000 immigrants, favored the peoples of northwestern Europe, notably Great Britain, whose nationals constituted the dominant part of America's population. The Immigration Act of 1924 reduced quotas to 2 percent and changed the base year to 1890, when the proportion of southern and eastern Europeans in the U.S. population was even lower. Although the stream of immigrants from Europe was thus severely reduced, over a million Canadians and a half million Mexicans, mostly Catholic, came to the United States during the 1920s.

Economy. Postwar economic trends passed through three phases: a boom period from 1918 to 1921, a depression from 1921 to 1923, and a period of unusual prosperity from 1923 to the Great Depression. Intense economic activity immediately after the war was sparked by an expansion of bank loans to private speculators and by acceleration of production in the construction and automotive industries. The brief but acute depression that followed was a normal readjustment after the wartime expansion. Government spending at home and abroad had declined, and European nations, staggering under economic burdens, were forced to curtail their purchases of U.S. goods. Predictably, exports and imports declined radically during 1921 and 1922. By 1923, widespread industrial expansion generated a recovery that ushered in a period of intense economic activity lasting until the Great Depression of 1929. In addition to the spectacular development of the automotive and construction industries, there were other conspicuous advances in the manufacture of electrical machines and appliances. Largely as a result of improvements in techniques and efficiency, combined with expansion, industrial production almost doubled, with the national income rising from $59 billion in 1921 to $78 billion by 1929.

Warren G. Harding. Disenchanted with the politics of foreign entanglements under the Democratic administration of Woodrow Wilson, American voters overwhelmingly chose Ohio Senator Warren G. Harding, the Republican nominee, over the Democratic candidate, James M. Cox, in the 1920 election. Harding carried thirty-seven states, winning over 61 percent of the popular vote and amassing 404 electoral votes to 127 for Cox. Harding's years in office were notable for the absence of definite policies and specific programs. His administration did include some able men: Charles Evans Hughes, secretary of state; Herbert Hoover, secretary of commerce; Henry A. Wallace, secretary of agriculture; and Andrew Mellon, secretary of the treasury. However, Harding was plagued by poor judgment in the selection of his subordinates, many of whom betrayed the public trust. Scandals followed in the Justice Department, in the Veterans' Bureau, and most spectacularly, in the Interior Department, when Secretary Albert Fall fraudulently leased naval oil reserves at Teapot Dome, Wyoming, to private businessmen. Depressed and overwhelmed by the responsibilities of the presidency, Harding died of a heart attack in August 1923. He was succeeded by Vice-President Calvin Coolidge.

Calvin Coolidge. Coolidge shared Harding's negative concept of the presidency. An abiding conservative and a man who projected keen personal integrity, he frowned upon dynamic and unsettling policies that would have a divisive effect in the country. His presidency was characterized by a wave of economic prosperity that made it comfortable for the nation to "keep cool with Coolidge." Business maintained its preeminent and privileged place. Andrew Mellon, secretary of the treasury throughout the Coolidge years, proposed a series of tax cuts designed to encourage the wealthy to make business investments. At the same time, Secretary of Commerce Herbert Hoover championed the cause of smaller businessmen. But most laborers and farmers shared unequally in the huge profits amassed during the "Coolidge prosperity." Although higher tariffs protected industrial prices, farmers lost government price supports in 1920 and campaigned unsuccessfully throughout the decade for parity plans designed to secure government guarantees that the prices of stable crops would be maintained at a prewar level. Legislation incorporating this idea was passed by Congress in 1927 and 1928. But President Coolidge, an outspoken advocate of concessions to business interests, vetoed both measures as preferential legislation.

Herbert Hoover. When Calvin Coolidge let it be known that he did not "choose to run" in 1928, leaders of the Republican party turned to Herbert Hoover as the Republican nominee. The Democrats chose Alfred E. Smith, the popular and progressive governor of New York. However, Smith was Catholic and opposed to Prohibition, thereby alienating many rural and small-town Americans. Although Smith's popular vote was double that of John W. Davis, the previous Democratic nominee, Hoover won a popular majority that exceeded 6 million votes. He took office on March 4, 1929, as the euphoria of the 1920s was waning. Eight months later, a stock-market collapse signaled the beginning of the Great Depression, for which his presidency is best remembered.

Culture. In the United States, the 1920s (which were preceded by the physical and spiritual disciplines of wartime and which would be followed by the more somber mood of the depression-laden thirties) were a period of cultural and industrial vitality. Labels for the period, including the *Roaring Twenties,* the *Jazz Age,* and the *Era of Wonderful Nonsense,* described significant alterations in fashions, values, and attitudes. The impact of the war produced in the United States (as it did in Europe) the so-called Lost Generation that questioned traditional values. The effects of rapid industrialization and urbanization further accounted for the quickening pace and diversity of change. The 1920 census revealed that, for the first time, more Americans lived in cities than on farms, a trend that increased during the decade. Much of the cultural ferment centered on the novelty and experimentation inherent in urban life, as contrasted with the traditional rural tendencies toward conformity.

Social Trends. Changing social patterns in American life included the Prohibition era, steps toward the emancipation of women, and dramatic changes in popular uses of leisure. Prohibition of the sale, manufacture, or transportation of intoxicating beverages became effective in January 1920, following ratification of the Eighteenth Amendment and passage of the enforcing Volstead Act. This law was widely disobeyed, particularly in urban areas, with the consequent emergence of bootleggers and speakeasies dominated by gangs such as the Al Capone mob in Chicago. By the decade's close, the futility of enforcement was widely recognized, resulting in the adoption of the Twenty-first Amendment (1933), which ended Prohibition.

Rights for women were expanded to include a guarantee of the right to vote under the Nineteenth Amendment, expanding job and educational opportunities, and a revolt against conventional fashions in dress, highlighted by short skirts and bobbed hair. In popular entertainment, the movie industry was undergoing distinct changes. Hollywood was establishing its preeminence; Cecil B. De Mille became the foremost producer with extravaganzas like *The King of Kings* (1927). Also in 1927, *The Jazz Singer,* with Al Jolson, ushered in the era of the talkies. Spectator sports such as tennis, boxing, football, and baseball and the participant sports of hunting and fishing were increasingly popular as the five-day workweek gave Americans unparalleled opportunities for leisure activities.

Literature. In *This Side of Paradise* (1920) and *The Great Gatsby* (1925), F. Scott Fitzgerald symbolized the cynicism and sense of betrayal common to many writers of the Jazz Age. Among the most important writers of the period were Ernest Hemingway, who voiced his disenchantment with the war in *A Farewell to Arms* (1929), and William Faulkner, who in *The Sound and the Fury* (1929) began the in-depth analysis of his southern homeland that established his reputation. Assaults against what they considered the hypocritical standards of contemporary society were launched by Sinclair Lewis, in *Main Street* (1920) and *Babbitt* (1922), and by John Dos Passos in *Manhattan Transfer* (1925). Eugene O'Neill, America's foremost playwright, had turned away from experimentation to produce *The Emperor Jones* (1921), *Anna Christie* (1922), and *Strange Interlude* (1927), all popular successes. Among poets, two outstanding figures became expatriates: T. S. Eliot (see p. 137), who moved to London, and Ezra Pound, who moved to France and began writing the series titled *Cantos* (1925–1940). Black writers in the Harlem renaissance, including James Weldon Johnson, Claude McKay, Langston Hughes, and Countee Cullen, revolted against what they considered the sterile middle-class standards of their parents by concentrating on black culture and their African heritage.

Art. Modernism in art was signaled by a revolt against genteel tradition. Influenced by European cubists, dadaists, and expressionists, American experimentation with color and design affected advertising, furniture construction, and interior decoration, as well as painting and sculpture. European influences were evident in the canvases of Rockwell Kent, Maurice Sterne, and Max Weber. The dominant style was still naturalism and realism in the tradition of the prewar Ashcan school. Among the painters influenced by Parisian abstractionism were John Marin, Charles Demuth, and Preston Dickinson. William Zorach and Gaston Lachaise led American sculpture in the direction of more abstract forms. Yet, some of the better-known sculptures were those of the realist Daniel Chester French, whose works include the statues of Abraham Lincoln at the Lincoln Memorial (Washington, D.C.), John Harvard (Cambridge, Massachusetts), and *The Minute Man of Concord* and Ralph Waldo Emerson (Concord, Massachusetts).

Music. The United States became a center of musical activity following World War I. A number of European composers, including Igor Stravinsky, Béla Bartók, Arnold Schönberg, and Paul Hindemith, migrated to America's shores. At the same time, the young American composers Aaron Copland, Roy Harris, and Charles Ives were experimenting with modern trends in classical styles and were also developing native themes. The widest popularity was enjoyed by the operettas of Victor Herbert and Sigmund Romberg and by the popular ballads of Irving Berlin. The 1920s were further noted for the rise of jazz, a distinctively American music characterized by improvisation and a highly syncopated beat. Borrowing from the Negro music of West Africa and the West Indies and from the spirituals, minstrels, and marching bands of the American Negro, jazz developed in the South, particularly in New Orleans. Jazz pioneers included the guitarist Huddie "Leadbelly" Ledbetter; William C. Handy, the "Father of the Blues"; and the trumpeter Louis ("Satchmo") Armstrong. Jazz was made acceptable and popularized among whites by Paul Whiteman's band and by George Gershwin's compositions, which included *Rhapsody in Blue, An American in Paris,* and *Porgy and Bess.*

CANADA

Canadian history has been shaped both by its European ties and its geographic proximity to the United States. Although the country is dominated by people of British ancestry, one-third of its population has consisted of a French minority intent on preserving its separate identity. French language and culture have thus exerted a measurable influence on Canadian development. Canada both preserved and relaxed its imperial ties with Great Britain and in 1931 became a member of the British Commonwealth. A greater degree of economic independence paralleled Canada's expanding control over its own political affairs. Although most of its exports were still shipped to Great Britain, during the interwar years Canada imported more goods from the United States than from any other country. News, music, novels, and movies accompanied the flow of products northward, making American culture, along with British and French, one of Canada's molding social forces.

Canada's sense of national identity has been affected by the internal and external competition of these cultures and allegiances. After their political ties with France were broken in 1763, the French Canadians found it difficult to adjust to their role as a Catholic minority on a continent dominated by Protestant Anglo-Saxons. Many were further concerned that the independence won from Great Britain would be replaced by the economic and cultural domination of their southern neighbor. Like the dominions of Australia and New Zealand, Canada maintained close relations with Great Britain based on traditional ties, common citizenship, and allegiance to the British crown. At the same time, Canadian policies reflected a close identity and common interest with the United States. Affected by America's democratic creed, for example, the Canadian House of Commons in 1918 voiced its objection to a local aristocracy by voting to abolish titles of nobility. A fishing treaty between the two countries (1923) was followed by other agreements and the exchange of ministers (1927). In the League of Nations, Canada voiced isolationist sentiments similar to those prevalent in the United States.

LATIN AMERICA

In the traditional societies of Latin America, the governing elite came from the landed aristocracy, whose prestige and security were based upon control of large estates, careers in civilian or military service, or membership in the priesthood. Rival factions of the aristocracy usually competed for the rewards of officeholding, and the army frequently intervened, becoming the decisive force in domestic politics. The industrial and democratic revolutions, two transforming forces with origins and roots in Europe, were challenging these historical patterns during the interwar years. The masses in Latin America joined those in other lands in demanding a higher standard of living and a lessening of social inequities. Among and within the numerous states of Latin America, the impact of these forces varied widely.

Geographically, Latin America constitutes over 15 percent of the world's inhabited space. Brazil alone is larger than the continental United States excluding Alaska. In western South America, the Andes, extending from the Caribbean Sea to Cape Horn, is the world's longest continuous mountain range. Latin America is especially rich in natural resources: nitrate in northern Chile, iron ore in Brazil, and tropical forests in the Amazon basin. The peoples of Latin America are scattered; areas of heavy population concentration are separated by semipopulated areas. With few restrictions against racial mixing, Latin Americans developed a wide variety of racial and cultural combinations. The principal racial stocks, each of which embraces a diversity of types, are Indian, Negro, and European. The mestizo, a mixture of Indian and European, is the most common racial type. The states of Latin America are frequently divided into Middle America (consisting of Mexico, the states of Central America, the Antilles, and Panama) and South America (comprising the areas from Venezuela, Colombia, and the Guianas in the north to Chile and Argentina in the south).

Mexico. Largest of the Middle American states, Mexico has a population consisting overwhelmingly of Indians and mestizos, for whom poverty has been the normal condition of existence. From 1876 to 1911, the country was ruled by Porfirio Díaz, one of the most successful Latin American dictators. Díaz was overthrown by the Mexican Revolution (1910–1915), and the politicians who succeeded him all pledged their support to the social transformation of the nation. To most Mexicans, *la revolución* came to mean the expectation that widespread illiteracy and poverty would be eliminated and that economic development would ensure a higher standard of living for the masses. The constitution adopted in 1917 was designed to abolish dominance of the nation's wealth by less than 1 percent of the population; it proclaimed that the right of ownership, including land, could be justified only if the property served a social purpose. During Díaz's regime, most of the land had been divided into haciendas, large feudal estates controlled by a minority of private owners. The redistribution of land after the revolution gradually transformed the form of tenure from haciendas to peasant communities, which in most cases were parceled out to farmers in individual lots.

Venezuela. Located in the northwestern part of South America, Venezuela is heavily populated by Indians, Negroes, and mixed-bloods. Its independence was gained in 1830 under the leadership of José Antonio Páez following the creation of Great Colombia by Simón Bolívar. At the beginning of the twentieth century, Venezuela was an impoverished tropical country with a virtually inaccessible interior. As a

LATIN AMERICA TODAY

San Francisco

Los Angeles

CANADA

Ottawa

UNITED STATES

Chicago

Washington · New York

MEXICO

New Orleans

20

México

Havana · Miami

CUBA

BR. HONDURAS

DOMINICAN REPUBLIC

Belize

HAITI

Ciudad Trujillo

GUATEMALA

HONDURAS

Guatemala

Tegucigalpa

Port-au-Prince

San Salvador

EL SALVADOR

NICARAGUA

10

Managua

COSTA RICA

San Jose · Panama

PANAMA

Caracas

VENEZUELA

BRITISH GUIANA

COLOMBIA

DUTCH GUIANA

FRENCH GUIANA

Bogotá

0

Quito

ECUADOR

Manáos

PERU

BRAZIL

Natal

10

Lima

La Paz

BOLIVIA

Paraguay

CHILE

Asunción

São Paulo

Rio de Janeiro

30

Santiago

URUGUAY

Rosario · Montevideo

Buenos Aires

ARGENTINA

Legend

MEXICO	
DOMINICAN REP.	
HAITI	
CUBA	
GUATEMALA	
EL SALVADOR	
HONDURAS	
NICARAGUA	
COSTA RICA	
PANAMA	
COLOMBIA	
VENEZUELA	
ECUADOR	
PERU	
BOLIVIA	
CHILE	
ARGENTINA	
URUGUAY	
PARAGUAY	
BRAZIL	

0 MILES 800

ALLEN K. PHILBRICK

From *The Growth and Culture of Latin America*, 2d ed., Vol. II by Donald E. Worchester and Wendell G. Schaeffer. Copyright © 1956, 1971 by Oxford University Press, Inc. Reprinted by permission.

result of the discovery of oil and accelerating American investments, particularly after World War I, production and national wealth increased significantly. But the profits were not equitably distributed. Educational facilities remained limited, and most of the population continued to be illiterate and impoverished. From 1909 to 1935, the country was ruled by Juan Vincente Gómez, one of a series of despots. Son of a mestizo father and an Indian mother, Gómez was a ruthless and ambitious leader who filled the country's treasury by oil-producing arrangements with American companies. Along with Argentina and Uruguay, Venezuela achieved a fast rate of economic progress in comparison with other Latin American countries. During the interwar years, the per capita income in these three countries was more than three times the average income in the others.

Brazil. Occupying almost half the South American continent, Brazil has a population that includes a mixture of Portuguese, Indians, and Negroes, combined with other Europeans and Asians. The population settled mostly along the eastern coast, and the interior areas remained sparsely inhabited. Coffee has been Brazil's most profitable product and leading export during the nineteenth and twentieth centuries. Brazil produced over 75 percent of the world's coffee before World War I and about 60 percent during the interwar period. Political trends were strongly influenced by these economic developments. The coffee-growing and industrial states, including São Paulo, Minas Gerais, and Rio Grande do Sul, were located in the south. Competition among these states for control of the federal government was a continuing and significant element in Brazilian politics. Of the fourteen presidents between the establishment of the republic in 1889 and the outbreak of World War II, ten came from the southern states.

Argentina. Largely because of the influx of capital investment from Great Britain, Argentina has had one of the highest levels of economic development in Latin America for over a century. During the interwar period, it remained the most urbanized nation, was the leader in per capita income, and had the lowest rate of illiteracy. Unlike other Latin American areas, Argentina was populated primarily by peoples of unmixed European ancestry, although many mestizos lived in border sections of the country. The national life and most of the population were concentrated near Buenos Aires in the Humid Pampa region. The standard landholding unit remained the estancia, which ranged from 5,000 to over 200,000 acres. With the rise of middle and laboring classes to political prominence during the nineteenth century, demands were made for alterations in the social structure. The Union

Civica Radical, organized to end the preeminence of the estancieros, succeeded in electing its candidate, Hipólito Irigoyen, to the presidency (1916–1922). However, although Irigoyen and his successor, Marcelo Torcuato de Alvear (1922–1928) promised reforms, no efforts were made to radically redistribute the land.

10

Japan, China, and India between the Wars

Reactions to the forces of Western imperialism have been a determining feature of Asian life during the twentieth century. Along with political and economic penetration, Western doctrines of social progress and national self-determination infiltrated many Asian areas in the nineteenth century. Included among these were the dominant Asian nations of Japan, China, and India. Imperialist advances were most successful in India and China, where the incursions of Western power coincided with the weakness and decay of traditional regimes. At least theoretically, India was ruled as a single unit by one outside power, Great Britain. Parts of China, on the other hand, were parceled out among a number of external powers, both Western and Asian. Political disunity became a way of life in China after the Manchu dynasty was overthrown in 1912. Of the three major Asian nations, Western penetration was least successful in Japan, whose institutions had been adapted to meet the West's challenge through political, technological, commercial, and military reforms.

JAPAN

The Japanese emerged from World War I economically prosperous and politically disenchanted. Industrial productivity and trade had expanded as Japan became a principal wartime supplier to the Western Allies. However, opposition from the West, particularly the United States, had prevented Japan from acquiring the domination it desired in Asia. After the war, Japan's parliamentary system came under constant siege by militant nationalists who sought to pursue more aggressive foreign policies. This continuing struggle dominated domestic politics during the interwar period. From 1918 to the Great Depression, the balance of power was weighted in favor of the forces of liberalism. The attacks upon representative government that occurred in many Western countries because of the economic crisis also had a severe impact in Japan.

Gains in World War I.   World War I, which focused the attention of Western nations on Europe, provided Japan with an excellent opportunity to pursue its goal of domination in Asia. Having declared war on Germany (see pp. 60–61), Japan took Kiaochow in November 1914, after a two-month siege and acquired German-held rights in China's Shantung Peninsula. Japanese ambitions for further control in China were dramatized in the so-called Twenty-one Demands, which were submitted to the Chinese government in 1915. They included special rights in Shantung and Manchuria and the appointment of Japanese advisers for China's internal and military affairs. Despite American protests, China yielded to most of these demands, but not to those requiring foreign advisers. Japan's assistance to the Allied cause later made the American mood more conciliatory, and in the Lansing-Ishii Treaty (November 1917), the United States recognized Japan's "special rights" in China.

Promise of Democratic Government.   The attractiveness of parliamentary government was strengthened in Japan by the wartime victories of Western democracies. During most of this period, premiers and their cabinets were chosen as popularly elected representatives of the Seiyūkai and Kenseikai parties, which dominated the parliament. A movement to enlarge the franchise and make national leaders more representative of the masses enjoyed considerable success. A 1919 law broadened the franchise from 1.5 million to 3 million, and in 1925, the electorate was increased to 14 million by a statute granting manhood suffrage. These domestic changes were accompanied by a less aggressive mood in international affairs. Japan joined the League of Nations as a permanent member of the Council and signed treaties at the Washington Conference (1921–1922) that promised to maintain peace in the Pacific, lessen the naval arms race, and preserve the territorial integrity of China.

Authoritarian Dominance during the 1930s.   Reactionary sentiments were prominent in Japanese political life even during the period of liberal ascendancy. They frequently found expression in extralegal groups that extolled military rule and territorial conquest. These feelings intensified as world trade declined during the Great Depression and many nations raised their protective tariff rates, thereby reducing the market for Japanese goods. This situation seemed to vindicate the claim by ultranationalists that Japan should resume its colonial expansion in order to control the sources of needed raw materials. Ambitious army officers used this argument to justify openly wielding the power that they had been manipulating behind the scenes. Peasants, who were the dominant element in the army, aided their cause by supporting military officers against urban middle-class political leaders. These rightist forces directed frequent threats and terrorist acts against national leaders. The conquest of Manchuria, which began in 1931, had profound repercussions in international politics (see pp. 217–218) and marked the turning point in Japan's shift from liberalism to authoritarianism in both domestic and foreign affairs. As popular support increased for their action, Japanese militants felt less need to disguise their quest for power. Military and naval officers, rather than elected civilians, began to dominate the cabinets. In this manner, by the early 1930s, representative government in Japan was destroyed.

CHINA

China was without an effective central government at the end of World War I. The Manchu dynasty, overthrown in 1912, proved easier to topple than to replace. In the absence of centralized authority, China's political life was dominated for most of the period from 1912 to 1926 by rivalries among strong warlords, whose private armies were financed by taxes collected from occupied territories. Gradually, during the late 1920s and 1930s, Chinese politics achieved a greater degree of unity and coherence. The Kuomintang (Nationalist) party expanded to become the most powerful force in China. Under the leadership of Mao Tse-tung, the Communist party developed into the Kuomintang's most potent domestic rival for power. All these events influenced, and in turn were influenced by, the continuing threat of Japanese aggression.

Kuomintang-Communist Alliance.   Bolshevik successes in the Soviet Union were naturally attractive to Chinese revolutionaries. Although both nations were Asian, agrarian, and tradition-oriented, Bolsheviks had achieved much greater success following their revolution than Chinese insurgents enjoyed after theirs. Soviet leaders encouraged this affinity by making a concerted effort to harness and direct the forces of change in China. Their strategy was to win local support by presenting themselves on the world stage as China's staunch ally. Accordingly, they vowed to relinquish the special prerogatives in China that had been obtained by Russian czars and to aid the Chinese in eliminating the special rights accumulated by other nations.

These efforts were rewarded by a 1923 agreement between the Soviet government and the Kuomintang. Soviets would give domestic support to China's nationalist movement by upholding Dr. Sun Yat-sen's leadership; in the area of foreign affairs, Soviet support would take the form of resistance to the forces of Western imperialism. This understanding led to notable changes in the Kuomintang. Under the direction of Mikhail Borodin, Soviet advisers reorganized the party according to the Soviet model. Supreme authority was vested in the Central Executive Committee, which in turn was responsible to the National Party Congress.

Changing Leadership and Policies. The death of Sun Yat-sen in 1925 removed the Kuomintang's most prestigious figure and immediately unleashed latent party conflicts. The most divisive controversy by far was over the role that Soviet Communists should play in the Kuomintang. Kuomintang members split over this issue into a leftist faction, which supported collaboration with Russia, and a rightist faction, headed by Chiang Kai-shek, which feared foreign domination of the party. Chiang and his followers engineered a decisive blow against the Communists in March 1927 by a campaign of terror and execution that eradicated Communist control in Shanghai. Under Chiang's direction, Kuomintang forces then conducted a successful campaign that extended their military and political domination from southern into northern China. During this campaign, the chasm between Communists and Kuomintang members widened irreparably. In addition to the recurring question of domestic versus foreign control, Communists desired more extreme actions against landlords and foreigners than Kuomintang members were willing to tolerate. Non-Communists on the Left therefore joined with the Kuomintang's Right to establish a new national government in 1928. Chiang Kai-shek was recognized as the political leader, and the national capital was transferred from Peking to Nanking.

Domestic Politics and Japanese Aggression. Two interacting forces dominated China during the 1930s: the Kuomintang-Communist conflict and the Japanese advance. After breaking with Chiang Kai-shek, Chinese communism passed through the Kiangsi period (1927–1934), characterized by bitter struggles with Kuomintang armies. Accords reached after the Japanese invaded Manchuria proved only a tempo-

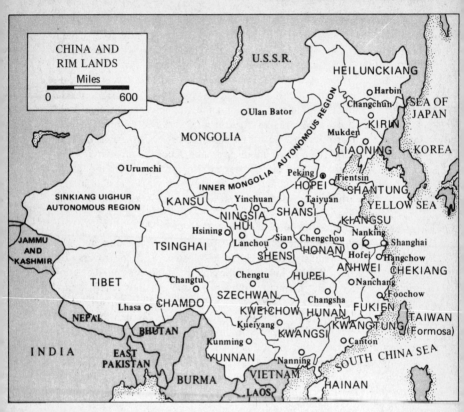

rary lull in the continuing struggle. Driven from the cities, Communists began their fateful dependence upon, and leadership of, the more numerous peasantry. This period ended in 1934 with the Communists' Long March northward, during which many were exterminated by Kuomintang armies. The survivors settled in the Shensi province of northwestern China, establishing their capital at Yenan.

During the Yenan period (1937–1945), a greater degree of unity was achieved, and the party's agrarian base was expanded. As the result of several significant developments, a basis for Communist-Kuomintang cooperation was also established. First, the Soviet Union formulated the Communist policy of organizing *united fronts* with other anti-Fascist groups in 1935; second, Communists cooperated in mediating a dispute between Chiang Kai-shek and some mutinous Kuomintang troops at Sian in 1936; and third, the resumption of the Sino-Japanese War in 1937 threatened to engulf both protagonists unless they combined forces. This uneasy alliance endured until the end of World War II.

INDIA

By the twentieth century, the British government directly ruled about two-thirds of India. Administrative powers were centered in the hands of the executive council and the governor-general; each was responsible to the British Parliament through the secretary of state for India. Native princes ruled the remaining states, subject to the principle of *paramountcy* exercised by the British viceroy. This arrangement ensured British control of foreign affairs and dominance over critical areas of domestic life. Along with political control, British administrators introduced their own language, legal system, and cultural standards, thus deeply altering India's traditional patterns of life.

National Congress. The National Congress party, the organization that led the fight for Indian independence, was created in 1885 to coordinate hitherto dispersed local efforts to win political rights from Great Britain. During its early years, the party was controlled by middle-class professionals whose policy was to obtain political concessions in installments from the British government. Their moderate position centered on requests that Indians be admitted to higher branches of the civil service and that Britain end economic policies which drained India's wealth. Parliamentary institutions gradually took root, and the Indian intelligentsia gained valuable administrative experience as the result of the party's willingness to cooperate with British officials.

Impact of World War I. The uncompromising character of the National Congress party's demands for self-government evolved during World War I as a greater degree of political assertiveness was combined with expressions of loyalty to the British crown. Indians dutifully purchased war bonds and more than 1 million Indian soldiers fought alongside their British comrades; in return, Indians expected expanded domestic political power. In 1915, the National Congress party requested increased autonomy for provincial councils at the war's end. The following year, the party urged the British Parliament to define publicly its intentions regarding India. The British government, aware of impending unrest if no positive response was made, and as a display of gratitude for the Indian war effort, announced in August

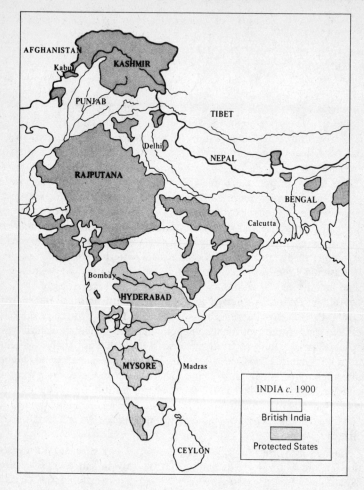

INDIA *c.* 1900

British India

Protected States

1917 that self-governing institutions would be developed for India.

Repression and Reform.   Some parts of India, particularly Bengal, were plagued by anarchistic activities during the unrest that followed the war. The British government reacted by passing the Rowlatt Acts of March 1919, which permitted trial without a jury for persons charged with certain political crimes. In April 1919, national leaders assembled a large, militant gathering at Amritsar to protest this legislation. Troops were called to maintain order, and 379 people were

killed when the local military commander ordered indiscriminate fir-
ing into the crowd. Soon after this incident, in December 1919, the
British government fulfilled its promise to establish a greater degree of
self-government by passing the Government of India Act. Under this
dyarchic reform, ministers chosen by the provincial legislatures controlled certain governmental departments, including education, public
health, agriculture, and local self-government; other departments, including law and order, land revenue, and famine relief, were regulated by the central government. Largely as a result of the bitterness
that followed the Amritsar massacre, militants in the National Congress party dissociated themselves from this reform and voiced demands for complete independence.

Gandhian Revolution.   Mohandas Karamchand Gandhi's life of
poverty and austerity was symbolized by the loincloth he wore. His political tactics, which brought him to leadership of the National Congress
during the 1920s, grew out of a philosophical conviction that campaigns of passive resistance could force Great Britain to grant self-rule
to India. Gandhi achieved national prominence by organizing agitation against the Rowlatt Acts and by leading a campaign of nonco-
operation after the Amritsar massacre. Although he was deeply revered
during his lifetime, Gandhi's influence, within and outside the Congress,
ebbed and flowed with changing circumstances. His popularity declined during his imprisonment from 1922 to 1924, after his campaign
of civil disobedience led to an incident in which nationalists attacked a
police station, killing twenty-two policemen. Other campaigns of passive resistance, resulting in additional periods of imprisonment for
Gandhi, occurred during the 1930s. Gandhi's tactics and personal de-
meanor attracted support from Indians of diverse classes and faiths. As
a result, the base in the National Congress was broadened, and the
independence movement became more representative of diverse national groups. This achievement and his emphasis on nonviolence were
Gandhi's most distinctive contributions to India's campaign for self-
government.

Divisions within the National Congress.   The crusade for Indian
independence was obstructed not only by opposition from British governing officials and from local rajas and maharajas who profited from
British rule but also by dissension within the independence movement.
As the dominant political organization in India, the National Congress
professed to represent all shades of opinion that promoted national
unity and self-government; yet, doctrinal and tactical disagreements
plagued it throughout the 1920s and 1930s. The major division was

between the moderates, who withdrew from the Congress in 1921 and formed a new party called the National Liberal Federation, and the extremists, who then dominated the Congress. Both groups favored self-government; their principal differences were over strategy. Moderates believed that political participation under the 1919 act could serve as a stepping-stone to dominion status within the Commonwealth; extremists concluded that the same goal could be won more quickly through an accentuated campaign of resistance.

Hindus and Muslims.   Religious dissension further complicated the prospects for independence. Muslims and Hindus frequently cooperated during the 1920s to achieve common goals of unity and self-government. Many Muslims were members of the Hindu-dominated National Congress party, and representatives of the All-India Muslim League, created in 1906, occasionally coordinated their anti-British strategies with leaders of the party. However, disagreements between the two religions and cultures were never far below the surface and caused recurring clashes between Hindu and Muslim extremists. After 1935, bitterness was aggravated, and conciliation proved impossible when the All-India Muslim League came under the able and militant leadership of Mohammed Ali Jinnah. Muslims of many persuasions were increasingly inclined to the view that an independent and democratic India would eventually be dominated by an autocratic Hindu majority. Mohammed Ali's leadership thus laid the basis for independence with separation, resulting in the eventual creation of the Muslim state of Pakistan.

Renewal of Civil Disobedience.   Gandhi's second nonviolent campaign was inaugurated in 1930. His famous march to Delhi in western India and his extraction of salt from seawater as a protest against the government's salt monopoly were symbolic acts of this passive resistance. British officials reacted vigorously to ensuing economic boycotts, mass strikes, and terrorist attacks against government officials. Efforts at conciliation soon followed. During 1930 and 1931, two round-table conferences, convened by Britain to deal with the crisis, recommended federation and a greater degree of self-government for the Indian states. Although these concessions pacified moderates, extremists persisted in their demands for complete independence.

Government of India Act of 1935.   The second Government of India Act, resulting from the round-table agreements, made radical transformations in India's governing system. Its distinctive feature was the greater independence accorded to provincial governments. Elected legislatures and appointed governors would rule almost autonomously in each of the eleven British provinces. On the national level, the provinces were represented in a bicameral legislature, consisting of the Council of State and the Legislative Assembly. The ultimate objective of this reform, which was not effected before the war, was the establishment of an all-India federation that would include both the British provinces and the princely states.

Reactions of the National Congress. Considerable anticipation accompanied the approaching April 1, 1937, date set for the act's implementation. Leaders of the National Congress debated whether to contest the provincial elections or deny themselves governmental power by boycotting the elections as they had done in 1921. In 1936, Gandhi persuaded Jawaharlal Nehru, then serving as president of the Congress, to support the organization's participation. Predictably, in elections held early in 1937, the dominant National Congress won overwhelmingly, accumulating either a majority or a plurality of the seats in seven of the eleven provincial legislatures. From 1937 to the outbreak of World War II, the provincial governments enjoyed a moderate degree of success. Cooperation ended when the National Congress voted to refuse participation in a war "conducted on imperialist lines" and all Congress ministers resigned their positions in late 1939.

11

Africa between the Wars

World War I had considerable influence upon developments in Africa. The League's mandate system awarded former German colonies to Britain, France, and Belgium as a "sacred trust of Civilization," thereby making the colonial powers more responsible to world opinion for the way they governed in Africa. There were, in addition, movements among the colonial powers to formulate uniform policies for their African territories instead of treating each unit separately. In most of the British colonies, a system of indirect rule evolved, encouraging emphasis on the use and maintenance of traditional African institutions. In French and Portuguese Africa, economic and administrative integration were immediate goals; cultural assimilation remained a long-range objective. The Belgian colonial administrative system, like the French, was highly centralized. However, Belgium adopted the British policy of subsidizing mission schools rather than the French policy of creating state systems. In contrast with Britain, which encouraged the development of some secondary schools, both France and Belgium concentrated primarily on broadening education at the primary level.

Africa's racial, geographic, and historical variety significantly shaped the policies adopted in London, Paris, Gent, and Lisbon. Climatic and topographical conditions ranged from snowcapped mountain peaks to arid deserts, from temperate zones to tropical jungles. Geographic diversity was paralleled by cultural and racial variety. Northern Africa had always maintained closer contacts with Europe and the Muslim world than other parts of the continent. In the heart of black Africa, including the west coast and Congo regions, there were several thousand blacks to each white; this ratio declined in parts of eastern Africa, where more Europeans and Asians had migrated, to

5 or 6 to 1. White supremacy was most firmly established in the Union of South Africa, which had developed into the richest country on the continent. Despite the considerable differences among indigenous Africans, the importance of kinship ties, tribal attachments to land and religion, and a low per capita income were features shared by all. Most of Africa remained rural, but an accelerating trend toward urbanization was noticeable during the interwar years. In Africa, as in the West, the townsmen were to prove the most energetic force for social and political change.

EGYPT AND THE SUDAN

Possessing the region's largest population and the most advanced industry and commerce, Egypt was the most influential North African state. The country's history continued to be shaped by the relationship of its people to the Nile River, which determined the areas of cultivation and settlement. Egypt's rapidly growing population was concentrated in Cairo and Alexandria, but there were also many oversized village settlements. Despite racial diversity, the Arab language and Muslim faith provided an unusual degree of linguistic and religious unity. There were wide disparities in social structure. The bedouin tribesmen, organized into autonomous clans until the twentieth century, lived a nomadic existence in the less productive areas. In rural village communities, family organization played a more significant part. Western influence was greater in urban centers, and it was from these areas that Egypt's governing elite was drawn. The masses lived miserable existences. Only 5 percent of the land was habitable, and these areas were dominated by an elitist ruling class that showed little interest in the widespread squalor.

Although Turkey still claimed nominal sovereignty over Egypt, the British occupied Cairo for strategic reasons in 1882. British control spread rapidly throughout the Nile valley region, thereby severely weakening Egypt's already tenuous political relationship with Turkey. Britain's interests were recognized in the Anglo-Egyptian Condominium of 1899, which brought the Sudan under joint control. Nevertheless, British status in Egypt remained ill-defined because Egypt was formally neither a colony nor a dominion. During the latter stages of the war, Woodrow Wilson's doctrine of national self-determination had a considerable impact in Egypt, as it did in other places. As the war ended, a group of national leaders (Wafdists), headed by Saad Zaghlul Pasha, presented the British high commissioner with a list of de-

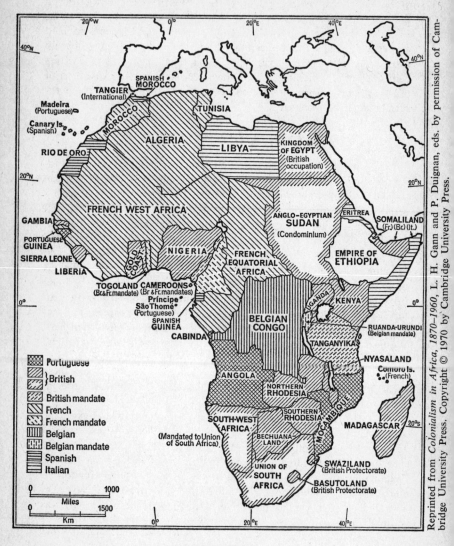

Key:

- Portuguese
- British
- British mandate
- French
- French mandate
- Belgian
- Belgian mandate
- Spanish
- Italian

SPANISH MOROCCO
TANGIER (International)
Madeira (Portuguese)
Canary Is. (Spanish)
RIO DE ORO
MOROCCO
TUNISIA
ALGERIA
LIBYA
KINGDOM OF EGYPT (British occupation)
GAMBIA
PORTUGUESE GUINEA
SIERRA LEONE
LIBERIA
FRENCH WEST AFRICA
GOLD COAST
NIGERIA
FRENCH EQUATORIAL AFRICA
ANGLO-EGYPTIAN SUDAN (Condominium)
ERITREA
SOMALILAND (Fr.) (Br.) (It.)
EMPIRE OF ETHIOPIA
TOGOLAND (Br.&Fr. mandate)
CAMEROONS (Br.&Fr. mandates)
Príncipe
São Thomé (Portuguese)
SPANISH GUINEA
CABINDA
UGANDA
KENYA
BELGIAN CONGO
RUANDA-URUNDI (Belgian mandate)
TANGANYIKA
NYASALAND
Comoro Is. (French)
ANGOLA
NORTHERN RHODESIA
SOUTH-WEST AFRICA
(Mandated to Union of South Africa)
SOUTHERN RHODESIA
MOÇAMBIQUE
MADAGASCAR
BECHUANA-LAND
SWAZILAND (British Protectorate)
UNION OF SOUTH AFRICA
BASUTOLAND (British Protectorate)

0   1000
Miles
0   1500
Km

Reprinted from *Colonialism in Africa, 1870–1960*, L. H. Gann and P. Duignan, eds. by permission of Cambridge University Press. Copyright © 1970 by Cambridge University Press.

Africa 1919

mands. The British retaliated by exiling Zaghlul and his comrades, and a series of rebellions ensued from 1919 to 1924. By the end of that troubled period, the British had decided to diminish and mask their involvement in Egypt's internal affairs and to concentrate on protecting their strategic interests, particularly in the Suez Canal and Sudan regions.

Formal adjustments in Anglo-Egyptian relations were made in 1922 and 1936. Unable to reach an agreement with Wafdist leaders, who had become highly suspicious of its intentions, the British government in 1922 unilaterally declared Egypt independent, recognizing the khedive as king and permitting a parliament chosen under a system of universal male franchise. At the same time, the British reserved control over defense and foreign affairs and retained mastery over the Sudan and imperial communication lifelines. After years of unproductive negotiations, the two parties, influenced by the growing Axis threat in the Middle East and Africa as well as in Europe, signed a compromise treaty in 1936. A British garrison of 10,000 men was to be stationed in the Suez Canal zone, and joint administration of the Sudan was to be continued, with the proviso that the Sudanese would eventually be given a choice between national independence and allegiance to either Egypt or Britain. Egypt's position was strengthened because it achieved greater control over its own diplomatic affairs and representation on the Suez Canal Company's board of directors and because the basis was laid for nationalist gains in education and administration. Although controversies continued to rage among domestic groups, on the eve of World War II, these measures had eased some of the Anglo-Egyptian bitterness.

ETHIOPIA

The process of changing Ethiopia from a traditional to a modernized society was accelerated by Emperor Menelik II (r. 1889–1910) and Haile Selassie I (r. 1916–1936, 1941–1974). Menelik's conquering armies expanded Ethiopia's borders to roughly their present locations. They also succeeded in defeating Italian forces at Aduwa in 1896, an uncommonly decisive defeat of a European army by African forces. As a result of Menelik's incapacitating illness and his death in 1910, Ethiopia was ruled for three years by his grandson Lij Yasu, whose public conversion to Islam created widespread dissension within the predominantly Christian kingdom. After the nobility, army, and church pooled their strength to overthrow Yasu in 1916, Ethiopia was governed by a regent, Ras Taffari. He gradually succeeded in extending his powers until he overcame the rival influences of the Empress Zauditu and powerful army figures. He was crowned king in 1928 and proclaimed Emperor Haile Selassie I in 1930. Haile Selassie's rule was highlighted by Ethiopia's admission to the League of Nations in 1923, the abolition of slavery in 1924, and a flow of foreign advisers and administrative reforms designed to make Ethiopia a more productive and efficient state.

Ethiopia's affairs became a matter of absorbing international interest during the 1930s. Bordered by Eritrea and Somalia, two colonies of Fascist Italy, Ethiopia began to import arms during the 1930s as part of its efforts to build a modern state. These pursuits were aborted by a crisis with Italy at Walwal late in 1934, which led to Italy's invasion of Ethiopia (October 1935). Lacking effective European allies, and facing the might of Italian airplanes, arms, and poison gas, Ethiopia was overrun by May 1936. Soon afterward, Italian East Africa, comprising Eritrea, Ethiopia, and Somaliland, was formed. This act of naked aggression again subjected the League's peace-keeping machinery to a severe test. Emperor Haile Selassie made a memorable speech before the League of Nations Assembly (see pp. 221–222), in which he pleaded for enforcement of the principle of collective security to protect his nation. Failing in these efforts, the emperor sought exile in England while his kingdom was ruled by Italy from 1936 to 1940.

NORTHWEST AFRICA

Europe's occupation of the African north began with French expansion into Algeria during 1830, under the pretext that this was required to end piracy among the Barbary States. The loss of Tunisian independence to France occurred in 1881. European expansion eastward was continued in 1911 with the Italian invasion of Libya, justified by Italy as the liberation of Libyans from Turkish control. Following a series of international crises and as the result of a diplomatic agreement, in 1912, Morocco was jointly occupied by Spain and France. Thus, on the eve of World War I, the network of imperial control was completed, with the French, Italians, and Spanish having assumed mastery in the northwest. The predominance of the Islamic faith and cultural traditions in these areas set northern Africa apart from tropical Africa. These deeply rooted institutions affected the form of European administration and provided an earlier basis for resistance to colonial control than was the case in other areas of Africa. The Muslims' historic enmity for European Christians served only to intensify their bitterness toward their colonial masters. Revolts that were sporadic and disorganized during the early 1900s had become more sophisticated and structured by the 1930s.

Tunisia. Ironically, French control in North Africa exposed native intellectuals to the egalitarian philosophies of the French Revolution at the same time that the subject areas were suffering the effects of discriminatory treatment. Organized efforts to achieve reforms began in Tunisia, where nationalist stirrings were evident during the decade preceding World War I. In 1907, a student-led group, the Young Tunisians, used newspapers and self-improvement societies to promote the modernization of their nation. In 1920, Sheikh Taalbi organized Tunisia's first political party, the Destour ("Constitution") party. Taalbi campaigned for a constitution that would guarantee certain fundamental rights, including the freedoms of press and assembly and a government responsible to a legislature elected on the basis of universal suffrage. Although opposing this program, the French in 1923 offered French citizenship to "qualified" Tunisians, a move that served only to antagonize the sensibilities of Tunisian Muslims. In 1927, the Destour party attracted the membership of Habib Bourguiba, who had recently returned from studies in Paris and who was to become the leading nationalist statesman in North Africa. At a party congress in 1934, Bourguiba and his followers defeated the Destour's old guard and formed the more militant Neo-Destour party, which sought to inform and recruit the masses. For its agitation, the Neo-Destour party was periodically repressed by the French government; on the eve of World War II, most of its leaders were imprisoned, and the party was driven underground.

Morocco. From 1912, when French rule began, until 1925, Morocco's affairs were administered by a single resident-general, Marshal Louis Lyautey. Demonstrating unusual understanding and respect for traditional customs and institutions, Lyautey devised colonial policies to promote the political and economic welfare of the Moroccans. Not surprisingly, his efforts incurred the wrath of fortune-seeking businessmen and land-hungry colons from France. Toward the end of Lyautey's regime, Moroccan nationalists organized. By 1926, intellectuals were forming small clubs to discuss grievances against France. Discontent coalesced in 1930 after the French government sponsored a reform that removed Berbers from the jurisdiction of Islamic law. During the late 1920s, nationalist leaders succeeded, through flattery and persuasion, in encouraging Morocco's Sultan Mohammed V, the temporal and spiritual ruler of his people, to become the symbolic leader of Moroccan nationalism as well. In 1934, Nationalists formed the Comité d'Action Marocaine (CAM). Their program included an end to the French policy of divide and rule, the protection of basic individual rights, and the popular election of a national council. The CAM was forced to dissolve in 1937, and on the eve of World War II, unity within the nationalist movement was still an elusive goal.

Algeria.   Assimilation in all areas except religion remained the aim of Algeria's moderate nationalists during the 1920s and 1930s. A leading spokesman for this view was Ferhat Abbas, a Muslim educated in French schools. In 1930, Abbas formed a French-oriented group of local officeholders, called the Federation of Elected Muslims. By that time, Abbas's objectives were opposed by more militant organizations, notably the Association of Algerian Ulema (teachers of religion and law), which favored a stronger brand of Arab nationalism. The goals of both assimilationists and nationalists were effectively resisted by the colons, Algeria's privileged European minority. With roots in Algeria that for some went back four generations, the colons recognized that their elitist status could be upheld only by keeping native Algerians subjugated. They unsuccessfully opposed the granting of French citizenship to natives who had distinguished themselves in fighting for France during World War I, and they helped abort a 1937 government proposal to extend political rights to a limited number of Algerians. Thus, Algerians were divided into two social categories: the 1 million Europeans, who were jealously guarding their prerogatives, and the 8 million native Algerians, whose national consciousness was not fully awakened until World War II.

Libya.   After the fall of Tunis to France in 1881, Italian policy focused on Tripoli as the area of North Africa that was destined for Italian conquest. This dream was realized during the Italo-Turkish War of 1911–1912, which was sparked by Italy's desire to compensate for the recent French advance in Morocco. Although only a few coastal towns were conquered, Italy proclaimed the annexation of the provinces of Tripolitania and Cyrenaica. The subjugation of interior areas proved extremely difficult and was not completed until 1931. A system of self-government, established in 1919, was revoked in 1927. In 1934, Mussolini's Fascist regime divided Libya into four provinces. Italy's rule in North Africa was ended during World War II, after which Libya acquired its independence.

WEST AFRICA

The term *West Africa* refers to that region of the continent bounded to the north by the Sahara Desert, to the west and south by the Atlantic Ocean, and to the east by a line running roughly from the Cameroons in the south to Lake Chad in the north. At the beginning of the twentieth century, European powers claimed control over the entire area with the exception of Liberia (an independent state colonized by freed slaves from the United States). France had accumulated the largest empire, including Mauretania, Senegal, Sudan, Niger, the Ivory Coast, Upper Volta, and Dahomey. The British were next, claiming over 475,000 square miles of territory divided into four colonies: the Gold Coast, Gambia, Sierra Leone, and Nigeria. British and French influence expanded at the end of World War I when they were awarded mandates over Germany's two former possessions, Togoland and the Cameroons, totaling about 240,000 square miles of territory. Portugal, which had led the way in the exploration of the coastal areas of West Africa, had been reduced to the colony of Portuguese Guinea, consisting of 13,000 square miles. Occupation and effective control were much more restricted than these extended areas suggest because European power and presence were still nonexistent in many parts of West Africa.

French West Africa. The peoples of French West Africa included Berber nomads in the north, who had heavily intermixed with Negroes, and communal dwellers, consisting almost entirely of thirteen Negro tribes. Some religious unity was imposed upon these divisions because most French West Africans were Moslems and fetishists. During the interwar years, the dominant imperial trend was toward direct administration. Since 1904, French West Africa had been organized on a federation basis, with each colony assigned a governor and a separate budget and all responsible to a governor-general who resided at Dakar. The governor-general ultimately was responsible to the minister of colonies and to the French parliament. Equipped with his own corps of officials and possessing ambiguous powers, the governor-general undermined the authority of both the minister of colonies in France and the local governors through his close supervision of administrative matters. Within each colony, the historical political formations were replaced by territorial divisions that for the most part prevented Africans from being represented by their traditional leaders. Chiefs were stripped of economic and political power and often reduced to the status of tax collectors or labor recruiters. An elite class, recruited largely from the sons of former ruling families, was educated in French schools to fill secondary administrative positions. Although many West Africans chafed under French rule, regional and tribal divisions remained strong enough to hamper the development of nationalist movements prior to World War II.

British West Africa. Systems of indirect rule were implemented in most parts of British West Africa during the interwar years. This trend was encouraged by Lord Frederick Lugard, whose reputation as a colonial administrator was established before World War I. Lugard decided to administer Northern Nigeria indirectly, through the Fulani emirs, customary rulers who already possessed a system for collecting taxes and dispensing justice. After he was elevated to governor-general of all Nigeria in 1914, Lugard attempted to apply his principle of indirect rule to Southern Nigeria; but he discovered that there, the existence of large towns in which tribal authority had been weakened necessitated the use of more European officials. Lugard's colonial theories were expounded in his book *The Dual Mandate* (1922), which became required reading for British politicians and colonial administrators. The British had a double responsibility, he argued, both to the African natives and to other parts of the world. On the one hand, Africans should be prepared for eventual self-government; on the other, Africa's natural resources should be developed for the world market. According to Lugard's thinking, both objectives were attainable through systems of indirect rule. The persuasiveness of his practical experience, combined with the reasoning expressed in his book, encouraged extension of indirect rule from Nigeria to other British colonies (the Gold Coast, Sierra Leone, and Gambia).

CONGO REGION

European explorations of the Congo basin were begun by the Portuguese during the latter part of the fifteenth century. From the sixteenth to the eighteenth centuries, economic activity focused on the slave trade. Although the Portuguese accounted for a considerable share of this human traffic, French, Dutch, and English trading companies had also become regular participants. Not until the second quarter of the nineteenth century did European powers suppress the slave trade. The interior areas of central Africa remained largely unexplored and unknown to Europeans until the 1870s, when explorations were conducted by Savorgnan de Brazza for France and by Henry Stanley for Belgium. International disputes over the Congo led to the convening of the Berlin Conference (1884–1885), which decided the assignment of the Congo Free State area to Belgium and the northern area of the Congo to France. Although boundaries in this area continued to fluctuate as political fortunes changed, major divisions had become stabilized by the eve of World War I. France controlled French Equatorial Africa, the northern Congo region; Belgian authority was paramount in the south; and Portugal maintained its control over Angola along the coast.

French Equatorial Africa.   During the 1880s, the French government established the rudiments of an administrative structure for the French Congo. Brazza was appointed commissioner of the colony, and an internal administration was formalized with the creation of a native hierarchy. In the 1890s, these arrangements were dramatically undermined as the Congo region was exploited by large concessionary companies that were awarded virtually sovereign control over immense areas. This economic aggrandizement was opposed by Brazza, whose humanitarian campaign led to his dismissal in 1898. Revelations of widespread cruelties by the concessionary companies after 1905 were accompanied by a decline in their power and the creation of a new administrative structure, French Equatorial Africa (AEF), which governed the region from 1910 to 1959. AEF incorporated principles of both federalism and centralism. A governor-general, appointed by the French government, resided at Brazzaville. In addition to a secretary-general and an advisory council that he appointed, the governor-general was assisted by lieutenant governors for each of the territory's sub-divisions: Middle Congo, Gabon, Ubangi-Shari, and Chad. In spite of these changes, which pointed up the French government's direct responsibility for administering the area, the revelation of cruelties in the Congo was a recurring theme in the French press during the interwar years.

Belgian Congo.   The extension of Belgian power into the Congo, an area almost as large as Europe, was the personal accomplishment of King Leopold II, who by 1885 had persuaded other European nations to recognize his sovereignty over the Congo Free State. Leopold's governance of the Congo, which centered on exploitation of the region's rubber resources, was characterized by atrocities on a wide scale. As news of these conditions spread around the turn of the century, a domestic and international scandal developed. As a result, in 1908, control of the Congo was transferred from Leopold's personal rule to the Belgian government. An administrative reorganization completed by the end of World War I divided the region into four areas:

Kasai, Equator, Oriental, and Katanga. Although constitutionally the Congo's administration was headed by a governor-general, business leaders and officials of the Roman Catholic church also exercised a guiding influence over the colony's development. In theory, equality between the races was guaranteed; but in fact, paternalist policies based upon attitudes of white supremacy permeated all areas of Congolese society. For the natives, education during the years between the wars focused almost entirely upon primary and vocational schooling. Congolese students were not allowed to pursue their studies overseas, and no college was established in the Congo before World War II. These unenlightened practices laid the groundwork for the Congo's problems during the period following the Second World War.

Portuguese Angola.   Despite over 300 years of involvement with Angola, Portugal's effective occupation in the early 1900s was still limited to coastal areas, notably Luanda (the capital city) and Benguela. Efforts to broaden Lisbon's control were encountering serious African resistance on the eve of World War I, notably from the Mbundu, Ovimbundu, and Guanhama peoples. By 1930, however, the Portuguese government had succeeded in extending its mastery over all Angola. As in neighboring French Equatorial Africa and the Belgian Congo, primary administrative responsibility was vested in a governor-general, who was assisted by several secretaries and a legislative council. In addition, the colony was divided into administrative districts, each headed by a district governor. Key Portuguese policies separated the natives into *assimilado* and *indigena* groupings. *Assimilados* were Europeanized or "civilized" natives, distinguished primarily by their ability to speak Portuguese and their "good character." Natives who achieved this status were subjected to fewer restrictions on their travel, were exempted from the head tax, were allowed to participate in national referenda, and were paid for government work on a par with Europeans. The *indigena,* who remained unassimilated, were denied political and civil rights and occupied the lower level of the social strata. By 1940, of the more than 3.5 million natives, less than 1 percent had achieved *assimilado* status.

EAST AFRICA

The geographic position of eastern Africa has exposed the region to crosscurrents of Asian and European influences. The continent's east coast had long attracted merchants from India and southern Arabia. Beginning early in the sixteenth century, coastal commercial settlements were conquered by Portugal, the first European nation to extend its influence into the area. However, led by the country of Oman, the Arabs expelled the Portuguese from most coastal areas during the early eighteenth century. In 1840, Saiyid Said, the ruler of Oman, transferred his throne to the East African coast, choosing Zanzibar as his capital. Said's kingdom conducted a brisk trade in slaves, and its authority became recognized over most of the coastal towns. Committed to the abolition of the slave trade, and interested in the region's commercial possibilities, other European powers, including France, Holland, Britain, and Germany, challenged Arab and Portuguese claims during the later nineteenth century. By World War I, Britain and Germany had become the dominant imperial powers in East Africa. The British sphere of influence included Uganda and Kenya; German paramountcy was recognized in Tanganyika.

Immediately after World War I, Great Britain was placed in control of most of East Africa. The former German colony of Tanganyika was added to the prewar territories of Kenya and Uganda as a mandate of the League of Nations. *Trusteeship* and *indirect rule* were the reigning British doctrines, implying that imperial rule was to be exercised in the best interests of the subject peoples. This objective was enunciated by the British government in 1923 in a policy statement that proclaimed the principle of trusteeship for all the East African territories under its control. A favorite way to honor this obligation was through the implementation of systems of indirect rule (patterned after those developed in British West Africa) that encouraged the preservation of native institutions and the development of local leaders. Efforts were also made during the interwar years to achieve a closer union of the East African colonies. The movement was sponsored by the European settlers in each area, particularly Kenya, who professed interest in the goals of economic and administrative cooperation. They were primarily interested, however, in creating a federation that the European settlers could dominate. Opposed to these schemes were the Africans, Asians, and some leading British officials who considered European domination incompatible with the pursuance of trusteeship policies. This resistance was sufficiently strong to defeat federative schemes prior to World War II.

Tanganyika. Covering over 360,000 square miles, Tanganyika is the largest area in East Africa and is much more extensive than any nation in Western Europe. Of its 4 million people in 1921, approximately 1 percent were non-Africans, including Indians, Arabs, and Europeans. Reflecting this racial diversity, both Islam and Christianity have been important nonindigenous religions. After the British mandate in Tanganyika became operative in 1920, provisions were made for civil administration. Wide-ranging executive authority was placed in the hands of a governor and an executive council responsible to the foreign office in London. The British system of indirect administration was begun in 1923 and completed during the governorship of Sir Donald Cameron (1925–1931). Chiefs of tribes and subtribes were made local agents of administration and were provided with annual stipends to replace the tribute and services traditionally rendered by their subjects. The range of responsibilities assigned to native authorities included administrative, judicial, and financial matters. This British system won warm approval from the Permanent Mandates Commission of the League and considerable support from local African leaders.

Kenya. The history of Kenya (British East Africa) was shaped largely by the British government's conscious and successful efforts beginning around the turn of the twentieth century to encourage European settlement. The numerous European estates thus established were surrounded by native reserves in which Africans were prohibited from growing cash crops such as tea and coffee. At the same time, through special legislation, African workers were compelled to labor on the so-called White Highlands. Efforts to make Kenya a white preserve also created the Indian question. The white settlers adamantly opposed political rights for Indian immigrants. Nevertheless, supported by their own government and receiving considerable sympathy in Great Britain, Indians demanded a common electoral roll with Europeans and the right to acquire land in the White Highlands. In an attempt to resolve these questions, the British government in 1923 issued a white paper that declared Kenya an "African country," guaranteed the rights of minorities, and dealt ambiguously with Indian claims. These matters were not resolved before World War II, and they caused the bitter racial feelings that dominated Kenyan politics during the postwar period.

Uganda. British mastery in Uganda, spreading outward from the country's southern kingdom of Buganda, led to the proclamation of a protectorate in 1894. By World War I, British control had been extended northward and eastward to include all Uganda. An administrative system had also been established, placing district commissioners and native authorities under the direction of the protectorate government. Forms of native administration varied; the province of Buganda, which maintained a special relationship with the British, was awarded the greatest degree of autonomy. After the war, there was a debate over land policy that carried considerable import for Uganda's political and social development. One segment of opinion favored the creation of a plantation economy geared to cash farming. The inevitable result of such a course would be the influx of politically ambitious European settlers and an increase in the number of landless Africans. Others contended that peasant farming, which was less harmful to native institutions, should be accorded priority. By 1923, the policy of peasant farming had emerged victorious as the basis for Uganda's development during the interwar years.

SOUTHERN AFRICA

Southern Africa has been most heavily populated during recent centuries by Bantu tribes. The first permanent European settlement was established at the Cape of Good Hope in 1652 by the Dutch East India Company. With the adoption of cattle farming, the numbers of whites and the amount of land under their control accelerated rapidly. The introduction of slaves after 1716 eliminated the need for a white laboring class and resulted in the development of sharp social stratification along racial lines. British occupation of the cape, first between 1795 and 1803 and then continuously after 1806, permanently ended the Dutch East India Company's control. As a result of the activities of British missionaries and philanthropists, greater concern was evidenced than formerly for the manner in which natives were treated. Angered by the abolition of slavery throughout the British Empire in 1834, and determined to seek land to the north where they could maintain unquestioned white supremacy, the Dutch (Boer) cattlemen and farmers made the Great Trek between 1835 and 1837, founding new colonies in southeastern Africa at Natal, the Orange Free State, and the South African Republic (Transvaal) by the middle of the nineteenth century. Natal was made a British crown colony in 1843, but the independence of the Orange Free State and the South African Republic was maintained throughout the nineteenth century.

From 1890 to 1896, Cecil Rhodes was both prime minister of the Cape Colony and director of the British South African Company, which was given the responsibility for controlling the region between Bechuanaland and the Zambezi River. In honor of Rhodes, this territory, after 1895, became known as Southern Rhodesia. To the north of the Zambezi, the territories constituting Northern Rhodesia were united in 1911. Rhodes's ambition was to combine most of this territory with the two Dutch republics into a single South African union under

British control. Paul Kruger, who served as president of the Transvaal from 1883 to 1900, had the opposite goal: a South Africa in which the Boers (Afrikaners) would be dominant. A series of clashes between these two men produced the Boer War (1899–1902), which pitted the forces of Great Britain against those of the Orange Free State and the Transvaal. Although it began with a series of British defeats, the war ended with complete British control over all South Africa. The way was thus paved for the creation in 1910 of the Union of South Africa, which united the Cape Colony, Natal, the Orange Free State, and the Transvaal. Southwest Africa, formerly a German colony, was made a mandate of this union after World War I.

South Africa.   The interwar years witnessed the continuing growth of various forms of African nationalism. By far the most uncompromising of these movements was led by the Boers, who considered it their divine mission to bring "civilization" to the African "savages" and who called for a society based on white supremacy that they rather than the British descendants would direct. Following unification in 1910, the British settlers developed an overriding loyalty to the colony of South Africa and, despite bitter antagonism toward the Boers, united with them on questions involving white versus African rule. Nationalism among native Africans prior to World War II was relatively tolerant. The South African Native Congress, formed in 1912 and renamed the African National Congress in 1935, campaigned for a multiracial society in which the Bantu peoples could share the voting, working, and traveling privileges of the whites. However, neither the African National Congress nor the Industrial and Commercial Workers Union, which was formed in the 1920s, succeeded in halting the imposition of legal discrimination over most areas of African life. Severe restrictions were placed on native voting and landownership. Natives were forbidden by law to travel without a permit or passbook, and if they were servants, they were not allowed to leave their white masters while under contract. Throughout the Union of South Africa, two separate societies were developed along racial lines.

The Rhodesias and Nyasaland.   Prior to World War I, Southern and Northern Rhodesia were ruled by a company under a royal charter. Efforts to unite Southern Rhodesia with the Union of South Africa failed in a 1922 referendum because of the widespread distrust of the Boers by the English settlers of Rhodesia. Instead, London took direct control by establishing crown colonies in Southern Rhodesia (1923) and Northern Rhodesia (1924). In Nyasaland, a British protectorate had been established in 1893. Southern Rhodesia was granted responsible government, including an appointed governor and a legislature chosen by British subjects of any race who had an annual income of at least £2,000. As in South Africa, the dominance of white settlers prevented the system of indirect rule that was introduced in Northern Rhodesia, Nyasaland, and most other British colonies. Southern Rhodesia developed a rigid system of land segregation similar to that of South Africa. Under the Constitution of 1923, although special Native Reserves had been traditionally set aside for Africans, they maintained the theoretical right to occupy land in European areas. The Land Apportionment Act of 1930 ended this prerogative by designating most lands outside existing reserves as either a Native Area, which was closed to European occupation, or a European Area, in which Africans were prohibited from acquiring land rights. Northern Rhodesia and Nyasaland principally followed the administrative models of the British East and West African dependencies; whereas Southern Rhodesia followed more closely the governmental tradition of South Africa. However, both Northern Rhodesia and Nyasaland adopted the pass system used by South Africa and Southern Rhodesia to restrict native travel.

12

The Great Depression and Its Consequences

Unlike this century's two world wars, the economic collapse of 1929 began in the United States and then spread to Europe. Like the wars, the Great Depression was a profoundly traumatic experience that rocked the economic, political, and psychological moorings of modern man. Economic interdependence among nations, combined with a widespread boom preceding the collapse, was responsible for the pervasiveness and intensity of the depression's effects. Since 1925, stabilized political conditions, highlighted by the détente between France and Germany, had encouraged an industrial revival in the West that some optimistic observers considered limitless. Production, trade, and income increased dramatically in the leading countries. Furthermore, by 1926, all major nations had returned to the gold standard, prewar symbol of business confidence and prosperity. A stable franc in France, an economic revival in Germany, and unprecedented prosperity in the United States all seemed clear signs that the political and economic order disrupted by the war had been at least partially restored.

Yet, critical elements of economic instability remained. In all places, prosperity rested on the accelerated production and trade of manufactured items; a contrasting agricultural decline produced pockets of misery in the midst of unparalleled affluence. Declining prices of agricultural goods, accompanied by an international surplus of farm commodities, limited the ability of rural dwellers to buy available manufactured products. Consumer purchasing power was further lessened as a consequence of technological innovations that simultaneously quickened the production of manufactured goods and raised the rates of unemployment. Within the world of international finance, the emergence of an isolationist United States as the industrial and banking leader destroyed the unitary financial system that before the war had centered in London. Recurring problems of war debts and reparations were additional clouds on the horizon. Unable to liquidate their liabilities in goods and services, debtor nations were hamstrung by tariff barriers that precluded the excess of exports over imports needed to make payments in gold. Thus, by the late 1920s, the persistence of economic good fortune was based upon precarious foundations. Continued relaxation of political tensions, both domestically and internationally, also rested upon this shaky edifice.

The depression started in the fall of 1929, when stockholders feverishly began to sell their declining securities on the New York Stock Exchange. Pressed American investors withdrew their capital from European countries, thereby undermining confidence in the financial solvency of Central Europe. Declining production and prices, combined with astronomical rises in unemployment, reached crisis proportions in Britain by 1931 and in France and Germany by 1932. Although social and political unrest encouraged governments to experiment with a variety of remedies, rearmament and World War II proved eventually the most potent incentives for an economic revival.

UNITED STATES

The Great Depression was undisputedly the worst economic disaster in U.S. history. The gross national product (GNP) decreased from $104 billion in 1929 to $73 billion in 1933 and by 1938 had climbed back to only $105 billion. Employment figures fell correspondingly. In 1929, only 3 percent of the labor force was unemployed; but during the critical years of 1933 and 1934, an incredible average of 24 percent was without jobs. In 1940, 15 percent of the labor force was still idle. In politics, Franklin D. Roosevelt, a bold and activist Democrat, replaced the temporizing Republican administration of President Hoover. An unprecedented flood of experimentation and legislation followed. The first New Deal of 1933 and 1934 concentrated on measures of immediate social relief and reform. Between 1935 and 1938, another wave of legislation, the second New Deal, focused on long-range economic recovery. The unrivaled peacetime authority exercised by President Roosevelt and the legislation that he sponsored had far-reaching consequences upon American democracy and life. Nonetheless, a return to prosperity was halting and incomplete for most Americans. Not until mid-1941 did the labor force achieve a full-employment level.

Bull Market. During 1928, the American Stock Exchange was possessed by a speculative mania that approached the realm of economic fantasy. In part, the rise of prices on the stock exchange reflected the increasing productivity and efficiency of American industry. A considerable amount of the speculation was financed out of mounting business profits, speculation that was encouraged by the inequitable distribution of these profits. Yet, gambling on the market was a popular sport that affected all classes, whether participants or nonparticipants. Envious of large investors, new and smaller stock purchasers entered the market, following tips in the hope of acquiring quick profits and thus further raising the prices while increasing the demand for securities. By 1927 and 1928, rising prices and expanded trading were only distantly related to economic realities. On March 12, 1928, a record of nearly 4 million shares were traded; by March 27, this figure had exceeded 4.5 million. In June, a new plateau of over 5 million shares sold was reached; and on November 23, 7 million shares changed hands.

The Crash. The bull market, which began to crumble in September 1929, completely collapsed the following month. By mid-October a trend toward liquidation was evident as major investors undertook to transfer their holdings. Amid mad confusion, this movement reached feverish proportions on October 24, when 12,894,650 shares were traded. A banker's pool organized by the House of Morgan failed to halt the selling deluge, and on October 29, a record 16 million shares were sold. Effects of the financial panic spread quickly. Confidence among businessmen evaporated, and the uncritical trust that most Americans had placed in both business and government leaders was severely shaken. Bank failures, unemployment, and levels of income were indexes of the depression's depth and scope. Bank closures totaled 29 in 1929, 2,294 in 1931, and 1,456 in 1932. Unemployment rose to 15 million during the winter of 1932–1933, and most workers who kept their jobs suffered severe salary cuts. The farmers were the hardest hit; total farm income plunged from $7 billion in 1929 to $2 billion in 1932. The key question was controversial: What role should the government play in promoting economic recovery and reform?

Reactions of the Hoover Administration. Hoover's initial response to the Wall Street disaster was an attempt to confine its effects to the liquidation of artificially inflated security prices. As economic problems worsened, he invoked government powers cautiously and reluctantly.

In 1928, he urged business leaders to maintain production and wage rates and began a program of public works on which his administration eventually spent about $3 billion. Nonetheless, the president denied government wheat surpluses to the drought-seared Southwest in 1930; and although government funds were spent for public buildings, harbors, and highways, he rejected a recommendation to include low-cost housing, slum clearance, and rural electrification in the spending. Hoover's philosophy, which disapproved of direct aid to destitute farmers or to families of unemployed workers, was grounded in his belief that government assistance would promote individual reliance upon Washington, thus undermining personal initiative. Concurrently, direct assistance to corporations facing bankruptcy was reluctantly approved because it was believed that their revival ultimately promoted the public good. Accordingly, in January 1932, Congress created the Reconstruction Finance Corporation (RFC) as a lending agency for businesses in financial trouble. In 1932 alone, RFC loaned over $1.8 billion to 7,411 corporations; nevertheless, the decline in business activity, employment, and mass purchasing power was becoming overwhelming.

International Impact. In the early 1930s, the depression eradicated the widespread optimism of the Stresemann-Briand era (see pp. 102–103). A worldwide chain reaction of financial crises, bank holidays, and withdrawn capital persuaded President Hoover during 1931 to negotiate a one-year moratorium on intergovernmental debts. The depression deepened by the following summer, and a conference was called at Lausanne to consider ways of liquidating the obligations outstanding among Western countries. Agreements were reached that virtually terminated Germany's reparations payments. During 1933, most nations decided to settle their debts with the United States by making final token payments or defaulting altogether. Multilateral arrangements designed to revive trade included the Ottawa Agreements of 1932, which lessened tariffs among British Commonwealth countries, and a series of reciprocal trade pacts initiated by the United States in 1934. Nevertheless, the disintegration of international trade and finance generated a mood of fear and defensiveness that led to policies of economic nationalism. Most states relied upon high tariffs and currency regulations to protect their own products and revive domestic stability.

Political Impact. Acute social and political discontent mounted as Hoover's policies failed to check the depression in its early phases. The impression grew that the administration was responsive to the needs of big business but cared little about small businesses or the plight of the hungry. Public disenchantment was demonstrated during the congressional elections of 1930, which severely reduced the Republican majority in the House of Representatives. Even this slim margin disappeared soon thereafter because of the deaths of several Republican legislators. Symptomatic of the distress that plagued the nation was the 1932 Bonus March to Washington by World War I veterans seeking a bonus enacted in 1924 but not payable until 1945. Interpreting the demonstration as an attempt by a mob to coerce the government, President Hoover ordered the march dispersed by the military. Inevitably, the depression was the all-consuming issue in the presidential election of 1932. Rather than admit failure, the Republican party renominated Hoover and defended his policies. Democrats chose Franklin D. Roosevelt, then governor of New York. Roosevelt dramatically flew to Chicago and accepted the nomination in person, pledging a "New Deal" for the American people. Carrying all but six states (Maine, Vermont, New Hampshire, Connecticut, Pennsylvania, and Delaware), Roosevelt won with a popular majority of 7 million votes and a decisive margin in the electoral college of 472 votes to Hoover's 59.

First New Deal. When Roosevelt took the oath of office on March 4, 1933, the gloomiest days of the depression were at hand. Improvising with speed and audacity, the Roosevelt administration executed a series of emergency responses designed to promote economic recovery and extend relief to the impoverished. The executive and legislative actions of Roosevelt's first three months, labeled the *Hundred Days,* were unparalleled during peacetime. They embraced the proclamation of a national banking holiday (March 6), followed by the Emergency Banking Act (March 9), which permitted the reopening of banks that federal inspectors judged solvent; the Agricultural Adjustment Act (May 12), which authorized production controls to restore prices; the Federal Emergency Relief Act (May 12), which awarded federal grants-in-aid to states for relief; the Civilian Conservation Corps Act (March 31), which provided jobs for unemployed young men; the National Industrial Recovery Act (June 16), which was intended to stimulate business revival by government regulation; and establishment of the Tennessee Valley Authority (May 18), which was empowered to develop the resources of a seven-state region. Another major measure enacted during the New Deal's first phase was the Securities Exchange Act (June 1934), which authorized the regulation of transactions on the stock exchange.

Second New Deal. Although the worst of the depression was over by 1935, the nation was still suffering from economic stagnation. Over

10 million people remained unemployed, and the national income was approximately $40 billion less than it had been during the predepression years. Furthermore, the constitutionality of some New Deal measures, including the National Recovery Administration, was being successfully challenged in the courts. Responding to a mood of bitterness that encouraged ambitious proposals from the extremes of left and right, Roosevelt sponsored a series of reforms that permanently altered the character of American life. The Works Progress Administration (April 1935), headed by Harry L. Hopkins, established a work relief program to improve roads, schools, hospitals, and public parks. Subsidies to musicians and artists were also initiated. A landmark piece of legislation, the Social Security Act (August 1935), provided for old-age pensions and unemployment compensation. Partly to counteract Huey Long's radical Share-the-Wealth movement, Roosevelt sponsored the Revenue Act (August 1935), which elevated tax rates on gifts, stocks, personal income, and estates. The New Deal's controversial view that the government, through its lending and spending policies, should actively maintain and promote the economic welfare of its citizenry was soon to become the new orthodoxy. But the experiments of the New Deal were unable to sustain the economy's revival; by 1939, on the eve of World War II, 9 million Americans remained unemployed.

GREAT BRITAIN

The second Labour ministry of Ramsay MacDonald assumed power in May 1929. The Labourites won 288 seats, the Conservatives won 260, and the Liberals won 58. Lacking a parliamentary majority, the Labourites were captives of the Liberals, as they had been in 1924. Labour's victory coincided with the advent of the world depression, whose worst effects were being felt by 1931. A severe crisis developed that summer after gold payments were suspended by the Credit-Anstalt, Austria's central bank, which held deposits for other financial institutions in Austria and southern Germany. The soundness of British finances was also questioned because the Bank of England had extended large loans to some of the banks in Central Europe. By August, the financial plight had produced political repercussions, bringing Labour's second ministry to an inglorious end. The coalition National Government ruled Britain through the worst depression years.

May Committee. In 1931, Labourites and Conservatives accepted a Liberal proposal to establish an independent committee to consider ways of reducing the national expenditures. The committee was chaired by Sir George May, a leading insurance expert. Before the committee completed its report, effects of the depression were being sharply felt. Unemployment was on the way to a total of more than 2.5 million during the year, and revenues began a precipitous decline as industries and shipping firms lost their customers. Because of the accelerating withdrawal of gold, and in spite of loans rushed from financiers in New York and Paris, the Bank of England was threatened with collapse. As tax receipts declined and the dole expanded, it was clear that severe economies were required to balance the government's budget. Estimating a deficit of £132 million for fiscal year 1932 if existing trends continued, the May committee proposed a general reduction in salaries combined with cuts in unemployment benefits. An irreparable break occurred within MacDonald's cabinet over these proposals. Both Labour members of the May committee had dissented from them, and adamant opposition also came from officials of the Trades Union Congress. With withdrawals from the Bank of England continuing and national bankruptcy impending, some changes in the administration became imperative.

Formation of the National Government.   Although some Labourites were willing to concede minor cuts in salaries and welfare payments, a substantial group, led by Arthur Henderson, rejected all concessions on the ground that no genuine national crisis existed. On August 23, 1931, New York investors indicated that they were unwilling to extend new loans unless some of the May committee's recommendations were enacted. The second Labour cabinet held its last meeting on August 24. That evening, the prime minister announced to the country and startled members of his party that he would remain at the head of a coalition National Government. Most of the Labour ministers declined to enter this ministry; Chancellor of the Exchequer Lord Snowden was a notable exception. For their heresy, the Labour party formally expelled MacDonald, Snowden, and twelve others. Arthur Henderson was chosen as the new Labour leader.

National Government: *Ramsay MacDonald*.   Immediate economies were achieved along the lines recommended by the May committee. In addition to salary cuts, unemployment insurance rates were reduced by 10 percent. Supplemental revenue was obtained through a 25 percent increase of the income tax, along with increased levies on gasoline, beer, tobacco, and amusements. These actions succeeded in balancing the budget, but they did not stem the flow of gold from the Bank of England. To avoid bankruptcy, therefore, the government, in

September 1931, abandoned the gold standard, which had obligated the Bank of England to redeem paper money with gold upon demand. Parliamentary elections were then called to secure approval of this drastic step and also to ratify the cabinet changes. Conservatives, who had predicted national catastrophe in the event of a Labour victory, were overwhelmingly successful. Of the 556 seats won by deputies of the national coalition, 472 went to Conservatives, and a total of 74 went to National Liberals and National Labourites. Only 52 Labour and 4 Liberal deputies were returned to constitute the opposition.

In the following years, the National Government faced recurring problems of balancing the budget, remedying the nation's unfavorable balance of trade, and alleviating unemployment. Solutions were sought in an atmosphere of economic nationalism, as each nation desperately attempted to rely on its own resources. Long the bulwark of free trade, Britain adopted a program of tariff protection combined with preferential trade agreements with the dominions. Meanwhile, economic recovery was proceeding slowly. Incomes were increased by virtue of a building boom, government subsidies to industry, and rearmament programs. Imports were limited by the 10 percent tariff levied on a variety of items. Simultaneously, exports were increased through reciprocal commercial agreements with other countries. The budgetary and employment pictures also brightened. From 1931 to 1936, all budgets closed with surpluses. Unemployment peaked at 3 million in 1933; thereafter, the rate lessened progressively until, by 1937, it had leveled out at 1.5 million.

National Government: Stanley Baldwin. In 1935, a reconstruction of the coalition cabinet brought Conservative leader Stanley Baldwin to the helm of the National Government. Opposition to the protective tariffs had led Liberal members of the cabinet to depart in 1932, and the coalition, which had always been a facade for Conservative rule, now appeared more clearly as the partisan ministry it was. Baldwin scheduled elections for November 1935 and campaigned in support of the popular issue of internationalism. The National Government again achieved an easy victory, with the Conservatives winning a majority of 150 seats over the combined total of all other parties. However, a strengthened Labour party added 100 seats to its previous total. Baldwin survived a royal and national crisis when King Edward VIII, who had succeeded to the throne in January 1936, decided in December of that year to abdicate in order to marry an American divorcée. Baldwin's ministry marked a transition to an era of unbalanced budgets resulting from the costs of rearmament programs, which were considered essential because collective security measures were failing to contain the aggressive energies of Japan, Germany, and Italy. In 1937, a new depression reversed the downward trend in unemployment. This situation continued until the threats and then the outbreak of war absorbed idle manpower into war industries and larger armies.

FRANCE

France enjoyed an economic boom beginning in 1926 and continuing until 1931, in spite of the worldwide economic crisis affecting other countries. The self-sufficiency of many small farms, a balance between industry and agriculture, and the continuing stability of the franc combined to postpone the effects of the depression until 1932. Even at its worst, the depression produced an unemployment level of fewer than 1 million. Hardest hit were commercial farmers; like farmers elsewhere, they encountered a world market glutted with agricultural surpluses. Convinced that the nation's problems resulted from the unhealthy international conditions generated by the less stable economies of other nations, French leaders attempted to shelter France behind a barrier of protective tariffs. The political pendulum swung first to the Left, then to the Right, and back to the Left again.

End of Moderate Rule. After parties on the Right emerged triumphant in the 1928 elections, Poincaré, who had headed the National Union government since 1926, retained the premiership until 1929, when he retired because of illness. The momentum of Poincaré's popularity and achievements allowed the Moderates to retain power until 1932. During this period, André Tardieu, who served as premier in three ministries, was the dominant figure. Tardieu was confident that political stability was the prerequisite to economic prosperity. He therefore proposed eliminating the requirement of a runoff if no candidate received a majority of the votes cast and instead electing representatives by a simple plurality. Unable to gain sufficient support for his program in the Chamber of Deputies, Tardieu took his case to the people in the 1932 elections. Moderates were opposed by the Cartel des Gauches, made up of Radicals and Socialists. The Radical and Socialist parties had profited from popular disenchantment with the government's depression policies, and the Cartel won a decisive victory, with Radicals returning more deputies than Socialists, although Socialists amassed more popular votes.

From Herriot to Daladier. Remaining loyal to their traditional doctrine of refusing participation in a cabinet whose policies they could not control, Socialists supported the Radical cabinet while refusing to accept any ministerial portfolios. Reminiscent of the divisions that paralyzed their coalition from 1924 to 1926, the moderately reformist Radicals and the more radically oriented Socialists were again unable to agree on a program of economic recovery. Resulting cabinet instability produced six Radical ministries between June 1932 and February 1934. In 1934, an infamous financial scandal, the Stavisky affair, focused national discontent on charges that the government lacked honesty and integrity. Serge Alexandre Stavisky was a repeatedly convicted swindler who managed to elude justice through his contacts in high places until January 1934, when he either committed suicide or was murdered by the police. Popular frustrations manifested themselves in riots climaxed on February 6 by a demonstration on the Place de la Concorde opposite the Chamber of Deputies. Troops fired on militants attempting to penetrate its cordons, killing fifteen people. The bloodshed discredited Edouard Daladier's new ministry, forcing him to resign the following day. The Daladier cabinet was replaced by a National Union government headed by Gaston Doumergue and including some Radicals but based upon a preponderance of Moderate ministers.

From the National Union Ministry to the Popular Front. Doumergue's premiership was far less successful than Poincaré's. His efforts to achieve economic stability failed, and his ministry lasted only nine months. The next decisive figure was Pierre Laval, prime minister from June 1935 to January 1936. An adroit parliamentary tactician, Laval had completed a political circle from Left to Right. In an atmosphere of domestic problems, declining foreign trade, and rising unemployment, he implemented a deflationary program that reduced state expenditures and helped to lower prices. Laval's critics, however, contended that his measures not only placed the burden of recovery on the masses but also had little effect in sparking the economy. As resentment grew, some Radicals withdrew their support from Laval's ministry and joined with Socialists and Communists to form the Popular Front, which governed France during two tumultuous years, from 1936 to 1938.

Popular Front. The parties of the Left (Radicals, Socialists, and Communists) feared that after the 1934 riots, right-wing groups presented a dire threat to the republic. Several Fascist-oriented movements had become prominent opponents of democracy by the 1930s. Attracting the largest following was the strongly nationalistic Croix de Feu, led by Colonel François de la Rocque. Although these groups had never coordinated their efforts, all had participated in the riots and demonstrations of 1934. The rise of fascism in Europe, including its open advocacy in France, persuaded Communists, who were also inveterate enemies of the republic, to seek closer cooperation with Socialists and Radicals. Their reorientation was paralleled by a Radical decision to stop supporting Moderate ministries and to seek again an alliance on the Left. This was the final ingredient that made the Popular Front possible. In 1936, leaders of the leftist parties agreed upon a platform which they carried into that year's hotly contested parliamentary elections. The Popular Front parties won an undisputed victory. Socialists emerged as the largest party in the chamber, with 146 deputies, followed by the Radicals, who won 116 seats. Communists dramatically elevated their total from 10 to 71 deputies.

Because Socialists were the most numerous element in the coalition, their leader, Léon Blum, who came from a wealthy Jewish family, received the premiership. Communists, like the Socialists before them, supported the government while refusing to join it. Blum assumed office under unusually trying circumstances. From the Left, a wave of sit-down strikes had accompanied the election and paralyzed many industries. Meanwhile, extremists on the Right mounted a scurrilous antigovernment campaign that was maintained with unbridled ferocity throughout the Blum years. Significant reforms were rushed through parliament, including wage increases, the forty-hour week, compulsory arbitration of labor disputes, and nationalization of war industries. Yet, the hopes that accompanied Blum's premiership were soon shattered. "Rather Hitler than Blum" became a popular anti-Communist and anti-Jewish slogan. Blum's policies, undermined in part by a flight of capital out of the country, failed to stem the rising government deficits or lessen the high rates of unemployment. In 1937, his ministry was overthrown by Radicals in the Senate. After the Senate also defeated a second Blum ministry, which survived for only a month in 1938, Popular Front politics in France came to an end. Radicals again shifted their support to the Right, producing a new ministry in which the Radical leader Edouard Daladier served as premier and Paul Reynaud, a Moderate, exercised a directing role in domestic politics. The experiments of Daladier's ministry failed to revive the economy before the outbreak of World War II.

GERMANY

The depression years marked the transition from the Weimar Republic to Hitler; thus, their effects were more ominous in Germany than in any other country. Following the broadening effects of the economic collapse in the United States, which coincided with Stresemann's death in 1929, the Weimar Republic entered what proved to be its final phase. Economic frustrations soon unleashed the political and social tensions that the years of prosperity had only thinly cloaked. From 1930 to 1933, Germany's political life was characterized by sharp polarizations and naked class conflicts. In four Reichstag elections held during these years, moderate parties lost power to extremists on the Left and the Right, until, in January 1933, the chancellorship was finally and fatefully entrusted to Adolf Hitler.

Advent of the Depression. Germany's industrial output reached new heights during 1928 and 1929, exceeding prewar levels of productivity. The depression's impact was dramatic. Because German prosperity was based largely on short-term loans, industrialists were forced to limit operations and discharge workers within a few weeks after the October crash. A precipitous fall in wages was paralleled by rising unemployment, which exceeded 3 million in 1930, 5 million in 1931, and 6 million in 1932. A system of unemployment insurance, enacted in 1927, proved inadequate to meet the crisis because too little time had elapsed for sufficient reserves to accumulate. Since 1928, the Reichstag had been ruled by a coalition that included the Center party, Socialists, the Democratic party, and the People's party, with the Socialist leader Hermann Müller as chancellor. A proposal to replenish the state's unemployment insurance fund by increasing the level of contributions exposed fundamental antagonisms between Socialists and the People's party. Socialists supported the measure, but the conservative People's party rejected the increased rates, which would have imposed additional burdens upon employers, advocating instead that unemployment benefits be reduced. Representatives of the two parties failed to compromise on the unemployment question, forcing Müller to resign in March 1930. The coalition was thus dissolved, and a significant step was taken toward the downfall of the Weimar Republic.

End of Parliamentary Government. Following Müller's resignation, President Hindenburg appointed Heinrich Brüning, a leader of the Center party, chancellor. An orthodox economist, Brüning formulated programs of retrenchment designed to rescue Germany from its economic straits. His cabinet, weighted toward the Right, included no Social Democrats. Brüning's majority in the Reichstag was precarious, depending on support from either Socialists or Nationalists, both of whom were disenchanted with his economic measures. Socialists opposed some budgetary cuts, claiming they weighed too heavily upon the laboring classes; whereas Nationalists argued that the proposed taxes imposed undue burdens upon the upper classes. Brüning, supported by President Hindenburg, threatened to use emergency executive powers if the Reichstag failed to enact his proposals. Despite this warning, the combined votes of Social Democrats, Nationalists, Nazis, and Communists defeated several of his measures on July 16, 1930. That evening, the government decreed its program on an emergency basis. When the same parties that had earlier thwarted his wishes also passed a vote of no confidence in his ministry, Brüning dissolved the Reichstag on September 14, 1930.

Republic Ruled by Decrees. From Heinrich Brüning to General Kurt von Schleicher, each ministry received the approval of an aging and senile President Hindenburg to bypass parliament and rule by fiat. Results of elections held in September 1930 reflected a crisis of broadening proportions for the government and the republic. Although the Socialists and Centrists maintained their dominant positions, sizable increases in the number of Communist and National Socialist deputies made the Reichstag virtually unmanageable. At the same time, street fights involving Communists and National Socialists, with particular violence directed against Jews and Social Democrats, were becoming regular occurrences. In the presidential elections held in the spring of 1932, the major opponents were Hindenburg and Hitler. Hindenburg won the runoff election after republicans rallied behind him as a more suitable candidate than either Hitler or Ernst Thälmann, the Communist candidate. A few weeks later, Brüning was forced to resign after his plans to reform the Prussian voting system alienated Hindenburg. He was replaced by the reactionary Franz von Papen. Meanwhile, unemployment had grown to over 6 million. Seeking more extreme solutions to their problems, voters in the July elections made the National Socialists the largest party in the Reichstag. During November, General Kurt von Schleicher replaced Papen as chancellor, the last government change before Hitler assumed power the following month.

13
Stalinist Russia

During the 1930s, the Communist party extended and solidified its pervasive control over Russian society. In contradiction to Marxist theory, the Russian state, like other totalitarian nations, developed into an all-powerful societal institution. The complete party domination of government machinery and policies had already been established during the 1920s. The 1930s were further distinguished by Joseph Stalin's personal consolidation and exercise of dictatorial authority. In the process, Stalin (like Lenin before him) ignored or distorted the party's announced safeguards designed to circumvent overcentralization of power. The most notable result of Stalin's ruthless drive was the unprecedented economic transformation of Soviet society that made Russia one of the foremost industrial nations by the eve of World War II.

ECONOMIC TRANSFORMATION

Although Marxism assumed a high level of industrialization, Soviet leaders realized that the Russian economy remained backward and inferior in comparison with those of industrialized Western countries. The New Economic Policy (see p. 130) had rescued Russia from a disastrous economic collapse; nevertheless, by 1928, production in industry and agriculture had not exceeded prewar levels. With his victory within the party and the government secured, Stalin embarked upon an economic revolution whose principal objective was the development of heavy industry and munitions. Between 1928 and World War II, three comprehensive and intricate five-year plans were launched, each administered by the Gosplan, an all-powerful government agency. Aims of the first plan were fulfilled by 1932; the second plan completed its full course between 1933 and 1937; a third plan, begun in 1938, was aborted by World War II. These plans envisioned a critical role for rural Russia. The enlarged urban population had to be fed, and at the same time, grain reserves had to be exported in order to pay for required imports. There were two choices: a moderate plan of industrialization that would also encourage the production of consumer goods which could be exchanged for peasant produce or a program of accelerated industrialization in which consumer production would be de-emphasized and the peasant surplus confiscated. Soviet leaders chose the second course.

Collectivization. Adopting the reasoning of Trotsky, Stalin concluded that a dispersed system of agricultural holdings perpetuated archaic methods and was inconsistent with the desired widespread conversion to industrialized farming methods. Hence, a campaign to replace small farms by merging them into either sovkhozy or kolkhozy was begun in 1928 and intensified during 1929. Each system was directed in large measure by the state. The *sovkhoz,* a state-owned and state-operated enterprise, was used principally for experimental purposes and in undeveloped regions. The more widely used *kolkhoz,* after being leased to its participating members by the state, was obligated to return to the government a significant portion of its profits in the form of taxes or deliveries in kind. As this system evolved, other shares were divided among participants based on the number of workdays each contributed or placed into a common fund to be used for general social purposes. At the same time, each participant was entitled to work a small private plot whose produce he could claim as his own.

To launch this agrarian revolution, the government first dispatched propaganda agents and organizers to the countryside in efforts to achieve its goals through persuasion. As resistance mounted among the peasants, the confiscation of land and equipment was ordered. These measures crystallized opposition, particularly among kulaks, who had the most to lose if agriculture was collectivized. In many cases, entire villages rebelled by killing livestock, smashing equipment, and burning their crops. When added to a crop failure in 1932, these reactions produced widespread conditions of famine and starvation. The government surmounted this insurgency by ordering military and police agencies to enforce obedience through mass executions and deportations. Meanwhile, in 1930, Stalin published a statement (titled "Dizzy with Success") that attempted to halt the excesses of collectivization while shifting the blame to his subordinates. The pace slackened only temporarily, and by 1932, with victory against the kulaks nearly complete, the campaign for collectivization was resumed. By the eve of World War II, as a result largely of the inhuman methods employed, Soviet agriculture had undergone an impressive transformation. Over 90 percent of the land was collectivized. In the process, agricultural production was made more efficient, and unemployed farmhands were driven to the cities, where they became urban laborers and joined the movement for industrialization.

Industrialization. The first Five-Year Plan (1928–1932) anticipated the overall doubling of production: 136 percent in industry and 55 percent in agriculture. During the early phases, virtually every sector made claims that assigned quotas were being exceeded. However, severe problems eventually became manifest: Quantity was often emphasized at the expense of quality; there was a shortage of technical labor; transportation facilities lagged behind needs; and shortages of consumer goods resulted in enforced rationing. Despite these problems, the intended goals were accomplished in less than five years; and in 1933, the second Five-Year Plan was inaugurated. The new plan placed greater emphasis on the construction of transportation facilities, the quality of production, and meeting consumer needs. By the end of the 1930s, the strides toward socializing production were singularly impressive. Private enterprise in industry and agriculture was virtually eliminated, and Russia had outdistanced Britain, becoming the world's third-ranking industrial power (after the United States and Germany).

Political and Social Changes. Economic transformations generated political and social changes. Centralized controls extended government power beyond the economic realm and into all areas of society. The growing need for skilled personnel encouraged the construction of technical and scientific schools. The intelligentsia, formerly relegated to subordinate roles by party theorists, became a privileged elite accorded higher material rewards. Capitalist incentives in the form of unequal wages and salaries were also extended to industrial and agricultural laborers. Serving as models for other workers were the highly publicized Stakhanovites, named after Aleksei Stakhanov, a coal miner who reportedly exceeded his daily quota by unbelievable amounts. In some respects, the rapidity of Russia's economic advance telescoped the social agonies that economic change spread over generations in other places. Living and working conditions became insufferable in the newly created or overcrowded cities. Besides the pacification and extermination of the kulaks, millions of other citizens were sent to forced labor camps.

GREAT PURGE

Between 1935 and 1939, the Soviet government decreed that thousands of people from all levels of society be executed, deported, or sent to forced labor camps. Principal victims were party members, including prominent Old Bolsheviks, who had already been discredited in earlier struggles against Stalin. As the purge gained momentum, lesser party leaders, bureaucrats, those accused of foreign conspiracies, officers of the armed forces, members of the secret police (NKVD), and even former supporters of Stalin became its victims. The purge was generated by Stalin's paranoid fear that former rivals endangered his life and the security of his regime. The chain reaction of events, which ravaged Russian society, began when Sergei Kirov, Stalin's deputy as Communist party leader in Leningrad, was assassinated in December 1934. It remains unclear whether the assassin actually belonged, as charged, to a remnant of the Left Opposition or whether Stalin ordered Kirov killed for his own reasons.

In any case, within a month, the Soviet regime had secretly tried and executed the alleged assassin, Nikolaiev, along with his accused accomplices. Zinoviev and Kamenev, leading Bolsheviks associated with opposition to Stalin, were tried for treason in 1935 and sentenced to long prison terms. The dramatic Moscow trials began the following year. Unlike the other proceedings, which were secret, the Moscow trials of prominent party leaders were highly publicized. In the first Moscow trials, in August 1936, Zinoviev and Kamenev were retried, along with fifty-two other defendants, and both were executed. Seventeen additional Communist leaders, including Karl Bernardovich Radek and Grigori L. Pyatakov, were listed as defendants in the second Moscow trials held during January 1937. Leaders of the Right Opposition, including Bukharin and Rykov, were among the twenty-one defendants in the final trials of March 1938. Obviously under heavy psychological pressure, most confessed to charges of having conspired with Trotsky, and some pleaded guilty to conspiracies with foreign powers or even to having assassinated Soviet leaders. The great purge eliminated undesirables from within the party, discouraged all resistance to the Stalinist dictatorship, and created opposition to potential foreign aggressors by arousing patriotic sentiments among the Russian masses.

CONSTITUTION OF 1936

On Stalin's order, the Eighth Congress of Soviets adopted a new constitution in December 1936. By Western standards, the document, as written, was unusually democratic. Legislative power was vested in the Supreme Soviet, which was divided into two chambers, the Soviet of the Union and the Soviet of Nationalities. Both chambers were elected on a representative basis through universal suffrage. The Supreme Soviet in turn chose a permanent Presidium, which exercised legislative power between chamber sessions, and a cabinet, the Council of People's Commissars. The federal character of the Soviet state that had been established under the Constitution of 1924 was maintained, and the number of republics increased from seven to eleven. There was considerable debate over the motives for this development, particularly because the document was never implemented. Domestically, the new consitution promised concessions to liberality that would relax the tensions that had developed as the harsh plans of collectivization and industrialization were carried out. In foreign affairs, the constitution was intended to lessen differences between the Soviet government and Western democracies in the hope that Russia would not be forced to deal alone with the increasingly aggressive tendencies of Italy, Germany, and Japan.

Unlike constitutions in most Western countries, which actually set the permissible boundaries of government activity, the Soviet Constitution in operation was subordinated to the whims of Communist party leaders. In theory, all authority in Soviet society was vested in the proletarian dictatorship. This principle was used to justify centralized one-party control, the Soviet state's distinguishing feature as it evolved during the 1930s. On all levels, power gravitated to small executive bodies composed of party leaders. For practical purposes, the Presidium assumed the legislative functions assigned to the Supreme Soviet; federal principles, although implemented in some cultural areas, were largely ignored on political and economic questions.

CULTURE

Authoritarian regimes, including communism in Russia and fascism in Italy and Germany, were inclined by nature toward the imposition of conformity in cultural areas. In order to inculcate widespread acceptance of a single ideology and to create a disciplined tribe of millions who would respond to anticipated situations in a mechanical fashion, systematic conditioning of thought patterns was required. To a considerable degree, these controls were perfected in Russia during the 1930s. Justification for pervasive constraints was provided by the presumably infallible character of the Marxist-Leninist creed. The vehicles of control were diverse. Party leaders monopolized the management of mass communications media, including newspapers, radio, publishing houses, and libraries. Activities of social, recreational, and youth groups were also directed by the party. Through evolving combinations of coercive and persuasive techniques, Soviet leaders attempted to create a body politic that would enthusiastically support the government. The impact of these state controls was heavily felt in literature, education, the arts, and religion.

Education.   Educational policies were shaped by the objectives of indoctrinating youth with Communist ideology and of supplying trained personnel for the nation's expanding technical needs. The responsibilities of teachers reflected these goals; classrooms were devoted both to conveying knowledge and to serving as propaganda agencies for the regime. The first Five-Year Plan recognized the need for a vastly expanded Soviet educational system. By the end of this plan, largely as a result of a compulsory education law of 1930, the number of pupils in elementary and secondary schools had increased from around 14 million to 24 million; by 1938, the number had increased to 33 million. In rural areas, students completed a four-year course that emphasized reading, writing, and arithmetic. In addition to these subjects, urban students, who were required to complete seven years of schooling, studied a foreign language, literature, history, science, and military training. In higher education, the major emphasis during the 1930s, in both the ordinary universities and the new higher technical institutions, was on the training of specialists. On all levels, political education was widespread. In addition to inculcating strong patriotic sentiments, Soviet schools conveyed the obligation of all citizens to be productive through disciplined labor for collective purposes.

Arts.   New attitudes toward artists paralleled the political and economic thrusts to achieve collectivization and industrialization. Since 1924, a policy announced by the party's Central Executive Committee that permitted diversity in the varied artistic fields had coincided with the New Economic Policy, which represented a compromise in the political and economic arenas. Beginning with the first Five-Year Plan, however, Soviet leaders insisted that artistic talents of all kinds be used to elicit support for the Socialist state. The supreme goal became that of *socialist realism,* the view that artists should compose, paint, and write in a practical and comprehensible manner designed to convey the values of the new order to the masses. This yardstick of social utility was applied to the selection and treatment of artistic themes. Not surprisingly, highly acceptable topics during the 1930s included uncritical praise for collectivization, industrialization, and the Stakhanovites. Held up for condemnation and abuse were the kulaks, private merchants, and inefficiency in all forms. Above all, artists were expected to keep Marxist-Leninist thinking uppermost in their minds, thereby emphasizing proletarian over capitalist values, optimistic rather than pessimistic outlooks, and realism over romanticism.

Religion. Communist hostility toward the churches was grounded in the Marxist view that organized religion served the ruling capitalist class as an "opium of the masses." Historically, the churches with the widest support among the Russian peoples were the Russian Orthodox and the Roman Catholic. Soon after the October Revolution of 1917, Bolsheviks attempted to abolish these and other organized religions by nationalizing church property and decreeing separation of church and state; many bishops and priests were imprisoned or executed as counterrevolutionaries. Although attacks were lessened after 1921, they were immediately renewed with the first Five-Year Plan on the basis that organized religion had no place in the Socialist society being created. By 1935, church authority had been dramatically weakened; many churches were closed, and most religious leaders were either imprisoned or executed. Because these excesses further alienated the peasantry and complicated the problems of collectivization, a greater degree of religious toleration was permitted during 1935, and the Constitution of 1936 restored some civil rights to the clergy. Nevertheless, the campaign against religions never really ceased; and during 1937 and 1938, many clergymen were among those tried for sabotage and espionage.

NATIONALITIES

Russia is a land of many nationalities. Great Russians were dominant among the Slavs, who constituted over 70 percent of the population. Other racial groups, in the order of their numerical strength, included Finno-Ugrian peoples, Turkic peoples, Mongolians, Tungus, Paleo-Asiatics, Caucasian peoples, Iranians, and Jews. During the turbulent years following the 1917 Revolution, Bolshevik leaders made concessions to ethnic groups in order to secure their shaky grip on the reins of power. Thus, the Constitution of 1918 recognized the equality of all races and nationalities; and in 1921, party leaders launched an educational program designed to elevate the diverse nationalities to the political and cultural level of the Great Russians. Major strides in this direction had been taken by the end of the 1930s. At the same time, the imposition of uniformity in other areas adversely affected the ability of nationalities to maintain their separate institutions. Efforts to develop a transcendent Soviet patriotism encouraged the rewriting of history in order to emphasize unity in the development of the Soviet peoples. Frequent purges, particularly in the Ukraine, were conducted in order to replace separatist leaders with Russian nationalists. Although the Constitution of 1936 was based upon federal principles that permitted direct representation of nationalities, the centralized structure of the state was maintained in practice. Communist parties in ethnic areas were only subordinate regional agencies of the Central Executive Committee and the Politburo.

FOREIGN AFFAIRS

Relations between Soviet Russia and other nations were aggravated from the outset by the refusal of Bolsheviks to honor czarist debts and by Russia's sponsorship of the Third International (Comintern), which had the avowed purpose of assisting in the overthrow of bourgeois governments everywhere. Nevertheless, most nations, with the notable exception of the United States, had extended diplomatic recognition to Russia by the end of the 1920s. These moves to end the Communist regime's isolation were largely due to the efforts of Grigori Chicherin, commissar of foreign affairs from 1918 to 1930. During the 1930s, Maksim Litvinov headed the foreign office. These years coincided with the increasing aggressiveness exhibited by Japan, Germany, and Italy. Because of the ominous threats that these developments posed for Russia, Litvinov's mandate from party leaders was to improve the nation's relationships with other countries opposed to fascism. Accordingly, considerable efforts were undertaken to create a meaningful system of collective security.

Shifting Relations. The shift toward more amicable relations with Western powers began before 1933 and quickened after the Nazis came to power. During 1932, treaties of nonaggression were signed with Poland, Latvia, Finland, and France. In 1933, the United States became the last major nation to extend diplomatic recognition to the Soviet regime. As Hitler consolidated his authority within Germany, Russian leaders took closer notice of the passages in *Mein Kampf* that envisioned the extension of German Lebensraum to include Russian territory. The Nazi government's hostile intentions toward the Soviet Union were further demonstrated by its nonaggression pact with Poland in 1934 and by Hitler's public pronouncements. The trend toward more amicable relations with Western countries continued. Two of France's allies, Czechoslovakia and Romania, extended diplomatic recognition to Russia in 1934. In the same year, the Soviet Union entered the League of Nations and received a permanent seat on the League Council.

Popular Fronts. Cooperation with Western powers attained new heights during 1935. The Soviet Union signed defensive pacts with France and Czechoslovakia requiring each signatory to come to the other's aid in case of an attack by a third power. The most dramatic announcement, however, occurred at the Seventh Party Congress, which convened during July and August. In a fundamental reversal of policy, Communist parties in other countries were instructed to form alliances with parties that opposed German and Italian fascism. This policy inaugurated the era of popular fronts, in which Communists in many countries cooperated with leftist parties, including Radicals and Socialists in France and Socialists and Catalans in Spain. When civil war erupted in Spain in the summer of 1936, pitting defenders of the republic against a Fascist military revolt led by General Francisco Franco, Russia became the strongest champion of the republican cause. However, popular front politics did not triumph in either France or Spain. The coalition government in France had lost its energy and spirit by the end of 1937, and the civil war in Spain was eventually won by the military insurgents.

Collaboration with Germany. From the mid-1930s to the eve of World War II, the ineffectiveness of Soviet and Western efforts to establish common action against fascism was clearly demonstrated. Western states acquiesced in Hitler's renunciation of the Versailles treaty's disarmament clauses, Italy's conquest of Ethiopia, and Germany's remilitarization of the Rhineland. This pattern of appeasement was repeated when Western states failed to effectively oppose Germany's and Italy's active support of Franco in Spain's civil war. The Soviet Union's position was made even more threatening in 1936 when Germany and Japan signed the Anti-Comintern Pact, which Italy joined in 1937 and Spain in 1939. Meanwhile, Russia's relations with Japan further deteriorated, producing military skirmishes along the Manchurian and Mongolian borders. Western appeasement of Hitler was climaxed by the Munich agreement of 1938, which soon led to the complete Nazi subjugation of Czechoslovakia. Convinced that the

intent of Western leaders was to direct Germany's ambitions eastward, Russia astounded the world in August 1939 by signing a nonaggression pact with Germany that demarcated eastern territories
between the two nations and paved the way for Germany's invasion
of Poland.

14

The Rise of Nazism in Germany

From its inception, the Weimar Republic was plagued by a series of crises. Some were caused by the new regime's domestic enemies, including militant groups on the Left and Right. Others were generated by Germany's prostrate postwar condition and its inability or reluctance to meet Allied demands for reparations. After a period of economic recovery and political promise between 1924 and 1929, the depression was to prove the republic's worst and final calamity. Between 1929 and 1933, democratic government ended in Germany the way it had begun, amid revolutionary threats from insurgent Communist and conservative groups. This time, defenders of the republic were unsuccessful in meeting the onslaughts. Government rule by decree, instituted during 1930, transferred authority from the hands of democratic leaders until in 1933 it was placed in the hands of Adolf Hitler, leader of the National Socialist German Workers' party. For the next thirteen years, domestic and world attention was focused on the "thousand-year Reich" that Hitler boasted he would create.

RISE OF HITLER

Son of a customs official, Adolf Hitler was born in 1889 in an Austrian province along the German-Austrian border. He was orphaned during his formative years and drifted to Vienna at the age of nineteen. Semieducated and usually jobless, he became a dreamer who ardently believed in Pan-Germanism. Hitler also developed a passionate hatred for Jews and for the cosmopolitan character of the

Austrian capital. In 1912, he moved to the German state of Bavaria. During World War I, he became a corporal in the German army. Like many veterans after the war, Hitler longed for the discipline, companionship, and sense of mission that the army had given to his life. Returning to the Bavarian capital of Munich, in 1919, he joined the German Workers' party, one of the numerous groups of malcontents that agitated against the republic, and he soon became its leader. This organization, which changed its title in 1920 to the National Socialist German Workers' party, established intimate relations with other Pan-German parties in Germany and also in Austria, Czechoslovakia, and Poland. After forming an alliance with a racist clique led by the elderly General Ludendorff, Hitler staged an unsuccessful *putsch* against the government in 1923 and was sentenced to a short prison term. While in prison, he began writing *Mein Kampf* ("My Struggle"), which became the bible of his movement.

As Germany recovered economically after 1924, the limited attractiveness of National Socialism speedily dissipated. Meanwhile, having completed his prison term, Hitler restyled his movement into a normal political party seeking power through constitutional means. He also imposed greater discipline within party ranks. The Great Depression was Hitler's godsend. Many Germans, having already suffered through the inflationary debacle of 1923, now lost all confidence in their economic and political system. The growing Communist vote, furthermore, caused widespread fears of a Bolshevik-type takeover. National Socialists were able to recruit many frustrated and disillusioned men from the jobless ranks for their brown-shirted army of Storm Troopers. In the 1930 elections, National Socialist strength in the Reichstag increased from 12 to 107; two years later, the Nazis expanded their total to 230, making them the strongest party in the legislature. Powerful conservatives and nationalists among businessmen, the aristocracy, and the army provided funds and public support for Hitler's party in the belief that they could control him for their own purposes. Franz von Papen and General Kurt von Schleicher, the last two chancellors before Hitler, finally persuaded President Hindenburg to make Hitler chancellor of a coalition in which the Nationalists and nonparty deputies shared power with the National Socialists. In this manner, on January 30, 1933, the Nazis came to power in Germany entirely through legal means.

Consolidation of Nazi Authority. Hitler's goal was the complete domination of the German government and nation. His successful efforts to achieve this *Gleichschaltung,* or regimentation of German life, has been described as the *Nazi Revolution*. First, the Reichstag was made the Nazis' pliant tool. Because Hitler's ministry did not command a parliamentary majority, new elections were called in March 1933. One week before the balloting was scheduled, in the midst of a vicious election campaign, Nazi plotters conspired to burn down the Reichstag building and then blame Communists for the deed. Despite terror by the Brownshirts and interference with free speech and the press, Nazis won only 44 percent of the Reichstag seats. Combined with the 8 percent won by the Nationalists, however, their control of a parliamentary majority was now complete. Nevertheless, Hitler proposed a law to transfer legislative power from the Reichstag to the Reich cabinet, which he headed; this authority could be granted only through an amendment to the constitution that required a two-thirds vote. With the Communist deputies excluded, support from the Center party provided the additional support Nazis needed to pass the Enabling Act on March 23, 1933. Hitler was thus allowed to enact ordinary laws by decree. Only the Social Democrats braved Nazi threats and voted against this measure, which was the major step in establishing Hitler's dictatorship.

Ideology of National Socialism. Early statements of Nazi philosophy were included in the party program of 1920 and later in *Mein Kampf*. Sources of Nazi ideas have been variously attributed to the glorification of nationalism, militarism, unity, and authority in German history; to the historical anti-Semitism prevalent in Germany and other countries; and to the Italian and Russian totalitarian examples. National Socialists placed emphasis on building a greater Germany, to be populated only by the superior race of Aryans or Nordics. The German *Volk* (nation) would achieve its deserved glory under the elite leadership of the Nazi party's governing hierarchy. National Socialist ideas, designed to appeal to the heterogeneous groups of dissidents in German society, were dynamic, emotion-packed, and freely adjustable to changing circumstances. In fact, so much was this the case that some observers of the Nazis contend that their leaders had no fixed program except the naked pursuit and acquisition of power.

NATIONAL SOCIALISM IN PRACTICE

The Third Reich, like Mussolini's Italy and Stalin's Russia, soon evolved into an authoritarian state that claimed control over every area of the nation's life. After Hitler had disposed of his political opponents, he turned his wrath upon the Nationalists, his political partners. The series of actions against Jews was begun. Hitler's opposition within the party was purged, and trade unions were brought under government control. Youth organizations were established to inculcate loyalty to the Reich, and educational institutions and all levels of government were cleansed of political unreliables. By 1938, the powerful army (Reichswehr) was also subjected to Hitler's domination. The institutions that resisted Hitler most adamantly were the Christian churches, whose leaders were intimidated and persecuted. Hitler's most spectacular triumphs were in the realm of foreign affairs, where his expansionist goals of *Weltpolitik* eventually led to the outbreak of World War II.

Anti-Semitism. Nazi propaganda made Jews the scapegoats for everything the Nazis despised. In addition to claims that they polluted the purity of the German race, Jews were depicted as internationalists, pacifists, and capitalists who had gained a stranglehold on the German economy. Verbal and physical intimidation of Jews, which had been a galvanizing force in the Nazi rise to power, became the official policy of the Third Reich. Jewish shops were boycotted, and beginning in the summer of 1933, many Jews were removed from their leading positions in Germany's political and cultural life. During 1935, the anti-Semitic measures became more systematic. The infamous Nuremburg Laws enacted in September of that year defined as a Jew anyone with one Jewish grandparent and then proceeded to strip all Jews of their civil rights. In retaliation for the murder of a German diplomat by a Jewish boy, vandalism and violence against Jews were further intensified in 1938. Of the half-million Jews in Germany when Hitler came to power in 1933, nearly half had emigrated by the outbreak of war in September 1939; after that, government restrictions made departures impossible.

Economic Policies. In the process of acquiring power, National Socialists effectively bid for the support of sizable business elements by concluding special arrangements with industrialists, including promises to maintain private property rights. Although government controls over industry were expanded, business leaders sustained and advanced their privileged role in German society. Major industrialists were able to amass huge profits through building and rearmament programs. Many were rewarded with party titles and ranks for their efforts. On the other hand, labor activities were regulated and subjugated by the Nazi-dominated Labor Front. Unions lost their rights as bargaining agents, and employers, subject to government supervision, were made virtual dictators over their factories and businesses. Yet, because

Hitler's policies greatly increased the employment rate, they won support from the working people. Many workers were absorbed through extensive public works programs; others found jobs in industries devoted to the rearmament effort. The Nazis' professed goal was economic independence for Germany, an objective promoted in part through foreign trade strategy to acquire goods Germany needed most in exchange for those it required least.

"Night of the Long Knives." The "Night of the Long Knives" marked a far-ranging and bloody purge conducted by Hitler's elite SS forces. Its principal objective was to destroy the independence of the Storm Troopers (SA), whose brawling participants had constituted the heart of the Nazi movement from its inception. Ernst Röhm, leader of the SA, had alienated himself from Hitler through repeated calls for a leftist revolution to destroy conservative power bases in industry, the aristocracy, and the army. Röhm wanted the Storm Troopers (2.5 million strong by 1934) broadened into a people's army, which along with the regular army (Reichswehr) and the black-shirted SS troops, would form a single defense ministry that he would head. No longer dependent upon vigilante street fighters now that he had acquired power, and unwilling to alienate the Reichswehr, upon whom he depended for the reinvigoration of Germany's military strength, Hitler promised army leaders that, in return for their support, Röhm and the SA would be suppressed. On June 30, 1934, not only SA leaders and other nonparty rivals for Hitler's leadership were eliminated but lesser enemies and accidental victims as well. Estimates of the number killed ranged from 77 to nearly 1,000. In addition to Ernst Röhm, they included Gregor Strasser, a leftist party spokesman, and General Kurt von Schleicher, Hitler's predecessor as chancellor. By Hitler's eliminating both conservatives and radicals who opposed him, the purge proved a major step in the consolidation of Hitler's dictatorship.

Persecution of the Church. Hitler's campaign against the church began on a moderate note. During July 1933, the Nazi government negotiated a contract with the Vatican, guaranteeing the Catholic church freedom of action and autonomy. This agreement gave international prestige to Hitler's regime during its early and formative stages. The combination of nazism and Christianity, however, was impossible to reconcile, and during the following years, Hitler battled with Catholicism on the issues of education and youth organizations. Since Hitler wanted control over these areas in order to inculcate Nazi ideas at an early age, the Catholic Youth League was dissolved, and church schools were either closed or persecuted. To discredit church leaders, trumped-up charges of immorality and smuggling were directed against Catholic priests and nuns. By 1937, Catholics were thoroughly disenchanted by the moral depravity of Hitler's government and by their abortive efforts to cooperate with the Nazi regime. Pope Pius XI castigated Nazi racial policies and the government's hostility to the church in his encyclical *Mit Brennender Sorge* ("With Burning Sorrow"). Although the concordat was maintained and Pius XI's successor, Pius XII, adopted a more conciliatory attitude toward the Nazis during the war, Catholic opposition formed a measurable part of the continuing, though waning, resistance to Hitler inside of Germany.

Protestants constituted a two-thirds majority among German Christians, and to control them, the Nazis proceeded with greater hope and effort. The overwhelming majority of Protestants belonged to Lutheran and Reformed churches, with various independent sects, including Baptists and Methodists, in a minority. As early as 1932, Prussian followers of Hitler who accepted his racial doctrines organized the German Christians' Faith Movement. Around this nucleus, the Nazis attempted to force the Protestant churches to unite into a single Reich church, headed by a Reich bishop. Since most Protestant pastors resisted these measures, the Nazis met with only mixed success. Nazification efforts were most adamantly opposed by a minority group called the *Confessional church,* led by Pastor Martin Niemöller. This denomination, along with the less influential Jehovah's Witnesses, provided the most determined organized Christian resistance to Hitler. In retaliation, during 1937, the Nazis arrested 807 leaders of the Confessional church, including Niemöller, and in the following years, additional ministers were imprisoned. (Niemöller was confined in a concentration camp until the end of the war.)

Cultural Regimentation.   The Nazi government, through the Propaganda Ministry headed by Joseph Goebbels, developed meticulous and unprecedented regulations affecting all areas of German cultural life. The Reich Chamber of Culture, created in 1933, included subagencies to control the fine arts, music, the theater, literature, the press, radio, and films. The governing criterion was that all forms of expression must serve the propaganda ends of the Nazi regime. Those whose creative efforts were considered inimical to these interests were prohibited from practicing their professions. Many internationally renowned books were publicly burned. Most of Germany's prominent writers emigrated; those who remained acquiesced to the government's demands. Except for Jews, fewer musicians left, and a variety of classical music was still performed with excellence, as was classical drama. Conformity was so pervasive that newspapers were daily told what to print and how to arrange their news items. Radio and film content was also effectively censored. In no part of the Western world had the regimentation of culture ever been so comprehensive and effective.

Control of Education.   Government controls were gradually established over all levels of education. As in other totalitarian societies, the Nazis were determined to indoctrinate and control the minds of the young during their formative years. Classroom learning was supplemented by the political and military training of various youth groups. Before Hitler's takeover, public schools and universities had been regulated by localities and the federal states. In 1934, the Reich Ministry of Science, Education, and Popular Culture was created to control these areas. Textbooks and curricula were revised, with Nazi ideology and political expediency becoming the supreme tests of truth. In 1937, a civil service law was enacted requiring all teachers to comply with the dictates of National Socialism. Most teachers, including those on the university level, prostituted themselves by taking an oath to support Hitler and serving as purveyors of distorted Nazi ideas of science, race, and history. Among the notable exceptions were Karl Jaspers, Alfred Weber, and Gerhard Ritter, all of whom opposed Nazi policies and participated in resistance movements.

Foreign Policy.   Nazi foreign policy was distinguished by a dynamic and unlimited expansionism that eventually led to World War II. Hitler's major goals, spelled out in *Mein Kampf,* included revisions of the Versailles treaty, additional space (Lebensraum) in Europe for the German people, fervent opposition to international communism, and avoidance of a two-front war. With uncanny ability, Hitler precipitated international crises that aroused fears in other countries and then persuaded national leaders that his most recent demands would fulfill his utmost ambitions. Understanding the widespread pacifist sentiments and internal divisions of Western nations, he effectively used boldness, deception, and threats to achieve an impressive list of foreign policy objectives short of war. Among these were national rearmament, remilitarization of the Rhineland, Anschluss with Austria, and annexation of the Sudetenland. Hitler's efforts to establish political and economic control over sovereign European states made nazism the preeminent world problem by the late 1930s.

Mastery over the Army.   By 1938, the German Reichswehr, which had a long tradition of autonomy, was the only institution that still possessed the power and means to unseat Hitler. The highest-ranking senior officers were General Werner von Blomberg, the war minister, and General Werner von Fritsch, commander in chief of the army. Two incidents during 1938 destroyed the reputation of both men and cast a shadow over the proud institution they served. Blomberg was forced to resign after the disclosure that his bride of two weeks was a former prostitute. Although Fritsch was the logical successor, his antagonism to the Nazi party and the SS was well known. To discredit him, therefore, the SS leader Heinrich Himmler made available a dossier that purported to prove that Fritsch was a homosexual. Without waiting for the military trial that soon exonerated Fritsch, Hitler forced his resignation and assumed personal command over the armed forces. With military, political, and economic power in Hitler's hands, the Nazi revolution in Germany was completed.

15

Western Civilization at the Crossroads

In most areas of human endeavor, World War I and the depression of the 1930s were watersheds. The economic collapse and its political repercussions destroyed hopes that a return to prewar stability had been achieved. Intellectuals made a zealous effort to understand the origins of these cataclysmic events and to interpret their immediate and long-range consequences. At issue were the traditional values, institutions, and orientations of Western society. The criticism ranged from concentrated attacks on particular hallowed principles (such as those underlying representative government, established religion, and the free market system) to analyses of the directions in which Western civilization was moving. In an era dominated by crises, it was natural that these precepts would be subjected to scrutiny; they had been regarded as cornerstones of Western culture, progress, and prosperity.

Open to particular inquiry was the concept of laissez-faire, which held that undue government intervention in economic affairs would stifle the initiative and creativity that sparked the free market. In the efforts to remedy what many now regarded as defects of modern capitalism, the proposals of John Maynard Keynes's New Economics were most influential.

In politics and philosophy, as well as in economics, Western liberalism's most implacable foes were the totalitarian creeds and regimes on the Left and Right. Fascism presented the greatest threat, and intellectuals reacted to its antiliberal, anti-intellectual, and antimodernist mood by relinquishing their detachment and actively campaigning for programs of social justice. At the same time, Protestant and Catholic leaders, aroused by widespread suffering and by the attractiveness of fascism and communism to the disillusioned and unemployed masses, sought a closer connection between religious faith and social activism.

COSMIC SPECULATION

World War I and the tribulations of the depression years thoroughly demoralized Western man. The theories of German historian Oswald Spengler were among the most popular philosophic attempts to answer the riddle of where Western society was headed. Spengler's major work, *The Decline of the West* (1918–1922), became a best seller. Spengler was a rigid and gloomy systematist who concluded that each civilization was an organism fated to follow an inevitable course of birth (spring), growth (summer), maturity (autumn), and decay (winter). He believed that the winter of Western civilization had begun with the Napoleonic Wars and continued throughout the nineteenth century as manifested by materialistic philosophies and intellectual fluctuations. In the twentieth century, Western man could expect an era of armed conflict; and as in the case of the Roman Empire, a succession of Caesars would attempt to restore peace and stability. Spengler popularized a respectable authoritarianism in politics and thereby helped diminish respect for the republican ideals of the Weimar regime. Although some observers concluded that his ideas were stepping-stones to the rise of National Socialism in Germany, Spengler himself became disenchanted with the excesses of Nazi rule.

Fifteen years after Spengler's work appeared and a year after Hitler came to power, British historian Arnold Toynbee began publishing his interpretations of twenty-one civilizations, collectively titled *Study of History*. The first three volumes appeared in 1934; three were added in 1939; and the final four books were published in 1954. Toynbee rejected the traditional division of Western civilization into ancient, medieval, and modern periods; like Spengler, he accepted the thesis that all civilizations are fated to rise, flourish, and finally, disintegrate. Although they were criticized as superficial by some historians, Toynbee's works were characterized by more deliberate scholarship and less pessimism and dogmatism than Spengler's study. According to Toynbee, although Western civilization was indeed declining, its rapid decay was by no means inevitable. A return to religious faith, which he identified as the distinctive motive force of the West, could revive its creative energies.

In *History as the Story of Liberty* (1938), Benedetto Croce, Italy's leading writer, stated his philosophy of history. He concluded that past tyrannies had been transient episodes, having only a limited effect on the development of civilizations; liberal values and institutions, by contrast, were the directing and unifying forces in human existence and therefore governed the evolution of history.

KEYNESIAN ECONOMICS

During the 1930s, the deepening severity of the depression stimulated economists to reexamine their traditional theories. The most influential study was John Maynard Keynes's *The General Theory of Employment, Interest and Money,* which appeared in 1936. A Cambridge University economics professor, Keynes had gained international prominence through his strictures against the Versailles treaty in *The Economic Consequences of the Peace* (1919) and in *A Revision of the Treaty* (1922). *The General Theory* attacked widely respected assumptions that free-market mechanisms would automatically lead to the best employment of a nation's men and resources. Keynes argued instead that the government should intervene in the economy when competitive markets failed to expand production and employment sufficiently. Careful state manipulation of interest rates, government spending, and public works projects would achieve desired economic goals. Keynes's plea for an activist government role in the economy was based upon his recognition that the orthodox deflationary practices of limiting spending and balancing the budget had failed to end stagnation and depression in Great Britain.

Keynes's *macroeconomics* provided the basis for a middle way between socialism and laissez-faire. The government would neither abolish private property nor treat the economy with reverence. This so-called New Economics first gained wide acceptance in the United States because Keynes's theory provided theoretical justification for the extensive government regulation that New Dealers already accepted. The British economist thus afforded President Roosevelt needed intellectual support for his heretical policies of state intervention and deficit financing. After World War II, Keynes's theories also became the new orthodoxy in Great Britain. In both countries, the government increasingly served as a doctor keeping constant check on the economy's pulse. When business fluctuations created dangers of either severe depression or inflation, state manipulation of interest rates, credit, taxes, and spending frequently followed. Keynesian methods remained less popular on the Continent, where overall economic planning (rather than the management of finances) was emphasized.

WANING INFLUENCE OF THE MIDDLE CLASSES

The decline of liberal economic and political institutions during the 1920s and 1930s coincided with the impoverishment of the middle classes, who had been liberalism's staunchest supporters. Bourgeois individualism was thus one of the major casualties of World War I and the ensuing depression. Soon after the war, increased taxation and rampant inflation drastically reduced middle-class earnings and savings. In Russia, the middle classes were proletarianized through programs of expropriations and collectivization. The middle classes in Germany, ruined by the inflation of 1922 and 1923, were devastated again by the depression of the 1930s. German Jews in particular suffered heavily during the Nazi confiscations. In other nations of Central and Eastern Europe, land reforms and plans to limit landholdings lessened the historical control of property owners. In all areas, the rise of the laboring classes, supported in part by progressive taxation that directly burdened propertied classes, helped precipitate the decline of the bourgeoisie. This trend was paralleled by the expansion of large industrial and financial enterprises that concentrated management in fewer hands, forcing previously independent bourgeois owners to become salaried employees.

Middle-class values in family life and morals also declined. Increasingly, the more liberated and aggressive role of women drastically altered family life. Many women achieved economic independence when they assumed the jobs of men who had departed for the war, a step that permanently opened some hitherto forbidden areas of employment to women. The feminist movement brought the right to vote and greater legal equality to women in most countries. Bourgeois mores in education and employment were undermined by the evolution of the public school system and of large impersonal corporations, developments that diminished family responsibility in these areas. Sexual codes were permanently loosened by the war and the introduction of contraceptive devices. Finally, instability among middle-class families was increased by the adoption of new divorce laws that broadened the legal grounds and simplified the legal procedures for ending a marriage.

TOTALITARIANISM

A word first popularized by Mussolini, *totalitarianism* became basic to the vocabulary of modern man during the 1930s. Prerequisites to the rise of totalitarian regimes were the evolution of mass democracy and modern technology. Both Communist and Fascist ideologies promised types of democratic classless societies in which the embracing interests of the entire community would serve as the mainsprings of policy. The pervasive controls underlying this commitment were made feasible only by modern technology. There were both differences and similarities between the Fascist and the Communist totalitarian systems. A chasm separated the two ideologically. The Communists were committed to attaining a worldwide proletarian revolution; whereas Fascists sought supranational domination by a particular nation or race. A characteristic common to both leftist and rightist systems was rule by a single party under the leadership of one man. This party monopolized societal power, including the government, the economy, mass communications, the armed forces, and cultural activities. An official ideology, demanding total allegiance from all citizens, embraced these disparate yet integrated activities. In all totalitarian countries, a secret terroristic police force was formed to help maintain control both within the party and over society.

The trend toward totalitarian governments, culminating in fully developed systems in Russia, Italy, and Germany and in lesser dictatorships elsewhere, enjoyed particular success in Europe during the 1930s. The major dictatorships often helped finance and organize the international assault on liberal institutions. Totalitarian philosophies were presented as complete alternatives to the liberal way of life. Instead of governing officials being subjected to constitutional restraints, the state was viewed as monolithic and absolutist. In place of protected freedom for each citizen, the individual became valuable only to the extent that he promoted national goals. This view was supported by social theories of the nation as an organism within which men existed only as expendable cells. Totalitarian regimes commonly came to power by exaggerating social conflicts and then by pretending that they were nonexistent once power was solidified. Thus, the Bolsheviks emphasized rivalries between property owners and laborers before 1917, only to proclaim the elimination of social classes following the liquidations of the 1930s. Similarly, Mussolini and Hitler exaggerated the importance of Communists in their midst before acquiring power, then shifted emphasis to undivided loyalty under their leadership when the reins of government had been firmly grasped.

POLITICAL INVOLVEMENT OF INTELLECTUALS

Once the human suffering of the depression became widespread, Western intellectuals ended the detached disillusionment of the postwar decade and revived the traditional liberal sympathies. The Popular Front mentality and the civil war in Spain served as additional catalysts for their involvement. Some intellectuals had shown fascination with Fascist movements in the 1920s, but most were repelled by the revelations of brutality under Hitler's and Mussolini's regimes. Their political orientation was thus generally toward the Left, with communism holding a strong attraction for many. To promote their reformist goals, writers and artists organized societies, frequently publishing their own periodicals. However, by the end of the 1930s, efforts to merge aesthetic efforts with political action had brought profound disillusionment. In France and in Spain, the preeminent Popular Front experiments had been distinguished primarily by their failures. Meanwhile, the terrors of the purges in Russia and the Nazi-Soviet pact of 1939, both following on the heels of Stalin's brutal collectivization campaigns, dispelled the aura that had once surrounded Marxist ideals. On the eve of World War II, perplexed intellectuals were searching for safer harbors.

LITERATURE

Thomas Mann, a German who sought refuge from nazism in the United States, wrote a series of books (1933–1943) in which he placed the biblical story of Joseph in a contemporary setting. Through Joseph, Mann depicted the humane virtues that the Nazi regime was crushing. Meanwhile, Erich Maria Remarque's *All Quiet on the Western Front* (1929) maintained its reputation as the major German anti-war novel. In France, Jules Romains wrote *Men of Good Will* (1932–1946), a series of interrelated novels depicting the diversity of society and exalting the common bond uniting all men. *Les Thibaults* (1921–1946), Roger Martin Du Gard's series focusing on a French bourgeois family, was profoundly pacifist and socialist, expressing in the final volumes a Spenglerian despair both for France and for the future of the West. In America, the most widely read depression novel, John Steinbeck's *The Grapes of Wrath* (1939), chronicled the miseries of an Oklahoma (Okie) farm family that migrates to California after being forced off their dust-bowl land. Other writers, reacting to widespread human suffering, focused their attention on the deplorable conditions in urban areas. James T. Farrell's trilogy *Studs Lonigan* (1935) linked the collapse of lower-middle-class morality in Chicago to individual helplessness in the face of social and economic pressures. For those who wanted a romantic escape from commitment, Margaret Mitchell offered her novel of the Civil War, *Gone With the Wind* (1936).

THE DEPRESSION AND THE ARTS

In Europe and America, the depression and ideological polarization affected many art forms. Totalitarian regimes subjected all forms of cultural expression to their new orthodoxy. Fascists and Communists agreed that abstract and modernist tendencies should be replaced by their own brand of realism, which placed a premium on traditional styles and, in the case of the Soviet Union, on expressions of socialist realism. Broadened popular involvement in the arts was characteristic of the decade. This trend was partly due to continuing technological and industrial advances that brought increasing numbers of people within the range of movies, radios, newspapers, and novels. Popular exposure to the arts was also advanced deliberately as a matter of government policy. Fascist regimes incorporated their favored artistic styles into their propaganda messages; in the United States, New Dealers sponsored art classes, art museums, and stage productions to provide employment and relieve depression doldrums.

RELIGIOUS ACTIVISM

The crisis-laden 1930s undermined confidence in the reigning political philosophies of conservatism and liberalism. Although many gave vent to their disillusionment by flocking to communism and fascism, others sought comfort by returning to religious faith. Church spokesmen themselves promoted this trend by more consciously relating theology to efforts to alleviate human suffering. The most influential statement was *Quadragesimo Anno,* an encyclical issued by Pope Pius XI in 1931 dealing with the character of contemporary industrial society. (Catholic doctrine on this question had previously been established in *Rerum Novarum,* an encyclical issued in 1891.) Although again condemning the inhuman conditions spawned by the capitalist order, *Quadragesimo Anno* advocated forms of social cooperation which were stated so broadly that they found support among both extreme conservatives and extreme leftists. Liberalized and updated interpretations of the biblical message absorbed the interests of many Catholic theologians, notably Jacques Maritain and Emmanuel Mounier, both from France. Karl Barth, from Switzerland, one of the most prominent neoorthodox Protestant theologians, rejected modernization of dogma and saw no contradictions between traditional tenets of Christian charity and contemporary involvement in social reform.

16

International Affairs during the 1930s

In international affairs, the 1930s were dominated by the aggressive acts of three totalitarian powers: Germany, Italy, and Japan. In response, Western governments pursued cautious and divided policies that were heavily influenced by moods of pacifism and isolationism. Widespread disillusionment following the holocaust of World War I had generated an attitude that peace at any price was preferable to an even more horrible world war. Japan launched the decade of belligerence by invading Manchuria in 1931. Italy's conquest of Ethiopia, begun in 1935, was completed in 1936. Meanwhile, in 1935, Hitler proclaimed Germany's intention to rearm, and in 1936, he remilitarized the Rhineland. Also during 1936, the two Fascist powers began a fateful coordination of their policies through the Rome-Berlin Axis. The Spanish civil war (1936–1939) was a testing ground for totalitarian policies and weapons. Germany and Italy intervened in behalf of the Nationalists; Russia assisted the Loyalist regime. The final crises preceding general warfare were precipitated by Adolf Hitler, who had become the greatest menace to world peace. Germany's annexation of Austria and acquisition of the Sudetenland in 1938 served as a prelude to the dismemberment of Czechoslovakia the following year. When German forces invaded Poland in September 1939, Western appeasement ended, and World War II began.

MANCHURIAN CRISIS AND THE LEAGUE OF NATIONS

In 1931, Manchuria consisted of three eastern provinces of China. The area, which had abundant mineral resources, had long been viewed by imperial powers as a valuable prize. Under a Russo-Japanese agreement of 1907, strengthened by concessions obtained in 1915, the Japanese had already succeeded in acquiring extensive rights in southern Manchuria. These included administration of the territory of Kwantung and other areas associated with the 700-mile South Manchurian Railway, which Japan managed. Intent on exploiting Manchuria's rich mineral resources, Japan became progressively more imperialistic in the exercise of its authority. Heightened friction between the two powers was inevitable. Their resulting conflict produced the first challenge to world peace during the 1930s.

Japanese Conquest of Manchuria.   Two incidents in 1931 served as a pretext for armed hostilities by Japan: the murder of a Japanese army captain and an explosion on the South Manchurian Railway. Without notifying the civil government in Tokyo, military leaders rapidly extended their occupation over all southern Manchuria between September 1931 and January 1932. This policy of conquest continued the following month when the Japanese created the puppet state of Manchukuo, which was declared independent of China and was nominally headed by Henry P'u-yi, the last of the Manchu emperors.

Lytton Commission.   The Manchurian crisis was a supreme test of the League of Nations ability to resolve international disputes because Japan's treaty obligations and the Covenant of the League of Nations were clearly violated by the invasion of China's soil. China therefore appealed to the League for support. Reacting to proposals from both China and Japan, the League created a five-member commission containing one representative each from France, England, Italy, Germany, and the United States. Before the Lytton commission made its report, Henry Stimson, secretary of state in the Roosevelt administration, acted unilaterally in announcing that the United States would not recognize the legality of actions taken in violation of the Nine-Power Treaty (1922) and the Kellogg-Briand Pact (1928). While other powers withheld formal responses to this declaration, the Lytton commission presented its findings in October 1932. Cautiously attempting to avoid offending Japan, the report condemned Japanese aggression while recommending direct negotiations between China and Japan. But Japan remained adamant, and the implementation of League sanctions was required to uphold the Lytton commission's recommendations, which necessitated at least the nominal restoration of Manchuria to China. However, divisions among Western powers precluded punitive actions.

JAPAN AND CHINA TO WORLD WAR II

Although they were losing diplomatic battles, the Japanese continued their military advance. By 1933, they had further broadened their base of operations into northern China after being antagonized by a nationwide Chinese boycott of Japanese goods. In order to block further incursions, the Chinese agreed in 1934 to a truce that acknowledged Japanese conquests in Manchuria and northern China. The determination of Japanese leaders to maintain their triumphs in disregard of world opinion precipitated their withdrawal from the League in March 1935. By permitting aggression against one of its member states without taking effective action, the League had seriously weakened its world prestige and authority. These were ominous signs for those who believed that the arbitration of disputes and adherence to the League Covenant were the only ways to preserve world peace.

Between 1934 and 1937, the Japanese continued to consolidate their gains in Manchuria and make gradual incursions into northern China. In 1937, another incident, this one real but exaggerated, served as Japan's excuse to resume large-scale hostilities. On July 7, Japanese and Chinese forces exchanged shots at the Marco Polo Bridge near Peking. By the end of July, Japanese troops had occupied Peking. Once more, the Japanese used the device of a puppet regime to give legitimacy to their control. A satellite government under Japanese control, led by a Chinese figurehead, was created for the area around Peking. Thereafter, an undeclared state of war existed between China and Japan. Their clashes continued and later merged into the worldwide conflict that began in 1939.

JAPAN AND THE UNITED STATES

Japan's aggression during the 1930s severely tested America's policy of protecting its own interests while attempting to maintain stability in Asia. Following the Manchurian crisis, President Hoover and Secretary of State Henry Stimson disagreed over the degree of pressure to be brought upon Japan. Stimson was willing to cooperate with League members in imposing economic sanctions. Aware of America's isolationist mood and Britain's and France's opposition to coercive measures, Hoover suggested instead a policy of refusing to recognize territorial changes that violated treaty obligations. In January 1932, Stimson enunciated this policy (the Stimson Doctrine) in identical notes sent to Japan and China. When Japan created the puppet state of Manchukuo, the Hoover administration's limited policy of moral persuasion continued. Largely as a result of American pressure, the League refused recognition to Japan's conquests. Furthermore, the United States supported League approval of the Lytton commission's report, which reaffirmed the Stimson Doctrine.

Japan's advances into China's northern provinces occurred while worldwide attention was focused on the belligerent words and acts of Mussolini and Hitler. After initially hesitating, the Roosevelt administration in 1937 adopted a firm position. The United States supported the League's condemnation of Japan and participated in the Brussels Conference (November 1937) to consider the Asian crisis. Participants included signatories of the Nine-Power Treaty and other nations that had special interests in China. Meanwhile, President Roosevelt made a dramatic speech, calling upon the international community to protect its health by "quarantining" aggressor nations. Isolationists condemned the speech's provocative language, discouraging Roosevelt from executing his forceful formula with economic and military sanctions. This combination of moral suasion and a reluctance to adopt constraining actions characterized America's response to Japanese aggression until World War II.

GERMAN REARMAMENT

The timidity shown by Western powers in the face of Japan's acquisition of Manchuria encouraged Hitler in his aggressive designs. These plans were dramatized by Nazi policies toward disarmament and the League. After years of planning by the League's Preparatory Commission, the World Disarmament Conference was convened in Geneva in February 1932. From the outset, several disruptive problems confronted delegates from the sixty nations represented. Considering the various conscription and reserve systems, what methods should be used to calculate the number of effective soldiers? Should steps to provide increased security precede any disarmament plans? How were any agreements to be supervised? Even after Hitler's accession to power, Germany demonstrated that all hopes of compromise were not lost, accepting in principle a proposal, offered by Prime Minister Ramsay MacDonald, that provided for a uniform system of conscription.

With difficulties over the steps to general disarmament still unresolved, the conference adjourned in June; it was to reconvene in October 1933. During this period, the Nazi attitude hardened considerably. A few days before the October conference session, Germany shook world opinion by proclaiming its intention to withdraw from both the Geneva disarmament conference and the League of Nations.

Reactions: Russia, France, and Italy. Hitler's action produced shock waves that caused a flurry of activity in European capitals, most dramatically in Russia, where Nazi ambitions of eastward expansion were profoundly feared. To gain Eastern allies, Russia completed agreements with Romania and Poland guaranteeing existing frontiers (June 1934). Three months later, Russia joined the ranks of moderate powers by becoming a member of the League of Nations. France also took bolder steps on the world stage under the direction of Jean Louis Barthou, who became foreign minister in February 1934. Abortive efforts were made to prevent German aggression eastward through the adoption of mutual-assistance and arbitration agreements patterned after the Locarno Pact of 1925. The French government further attempted to woo Italy away from a German alliance by a series of agreements (January 1935) that granted Italy concessions in Africa and promised joint consultation in case Austria's independence was threatened. Converging French and Soviet fears culminated in a mutual-assistance pact (May 1935) in which each power promised to aid the other in case of unprovoked aggression by a third power.

Final Steps. Early in 1935, Germany freed itself from two restraints imposed by the Versailles treaty. The peace settlement had provided that after fifteen years of administration by a League commission, the people of the Saar basin would choose annexation with either France or Germany. Following fervent Nazi agitation, results of the plebiscite, which was taken in January 1935, overwhelmingly awarded the region to Germany. Two months later, Hitler achieved another triumph by taking a step that explicitly violated the Versailles treaty. He boldly proclaimed German rearmament on the grounds that the failure of Allied powers to implement their promised reductions in arms necessitated extraordinary measures for Germany's self-defense. Although Germany had been secretly rearming long before Hitler came to power, this meant that regular conscription would again be introduced. The League Council formally condemned this unilateral action, but no effective steps were taken to negate it. France, Britain, and Italy did form the so-called Stresa Front and agreed to take common action, but this measure proved both transitory and illusory. Britain even indicated its acceptance of Hitler's move by concluding a naval agreement with Germany in 1935 permitting the Nazi state to build a fleet 35 percent as large as that of Great Britain.

ITALIAN CONQUEST OF ETHIOPIA

Before Mussolini assumed power, Italy had failed miserably in its efforts to achieve great-power status. Prior to World War I, it had acquired only modest colonial holdings and had suffered a humiliating defeat by Ethiopia at Aduwa (1896). Italy had endured further disillusionments at the end of World War I. Some European territories that Italy passionately desired, notably Fiume, were denied it at the Paris peace conference, and all the German colonies were distributed among other states. Since he gained power, Mussolini had repeatedly proclaimed the imperial destiny of Italy. By the 1930s, Ethiopia was the only African nation besides Liberia that was under black rule; thus, it was a logical object of Mussolini's ambitions. Italian expansionists justified imperial conquest by arguing that the nation's growing population had created undue pressures on living space and resources and that Italy shared the "civilizing mission" that other states claimed for themselves in Africa. In addition, a foreign policy venture that would simultaneously extend imperial holdings and avenge the defeat at Aduwa would serve Mussolini's purpose of distracting attention from domestic problems while galvanizing the nation behind his regime.

Beginning of the Crisis. Late in 1934, several border clashes were reported between Ethiopia and Italian Somaliland, notably at Walwal, a disputed border area. Italian threats led Ethiopia to appeal for the League to arbitrate the dispute. The arbitration commission's report, delivered in September 1935, eliminated the incident as a pretext for military action. Concurrently, Great Britain and France were negotiating directly with the two protagonists in an effort to resolve the crisis. After Mussolini rejected an Anglo-French proposal that Italy be granted a League mandate over Ethiopia, Great Britain decided to support collective sanctions if Italy's imminent invasion of Ethiopia occurred. Although the French agreed to support the British decision, they did so reluctantly because rising German militancy had encouraged them to make overtures of friendship to Italy.

Invasion and Conquest. After announcing that actions of the League had failed to take the rights and vital interests of Italy into consideration, Mussolini's forces began their invasion of Ethiopia on

October 3, 1935. A committee appointed by the League Council a few days later expressly branded Italy the aggressor in the conflict. This decision was approved both by the Council and by the League Assembly, which also endorsed the use of sanctions against Italy. These included an embargo on arms, credit, and raw materials and a boycott of Italian imports. But all efforts failed to extend the embargo to oil, which was essential for the movement of Italy's armies. Thus unchecked, Italy's seven-month military campaign climaxed on May 5, 1936, when Italian troops entered the capital of Addis Ababa. Four days later, Ethiopia was formally annexed. When the League voted to end its ineffectual sanctions in July, the concept of collective security had suffered another crushing blow.

REMILITARIZATION OF THE RHINELAND

According to terms of the Versailles treaty, Allied occupation of the left bank of the Rhine was to be accompanied by the indefinite demilitarization of an area thirty miles wide on the right bank. This settlement, along with Germany's other territorial adjustments in the West, were further guaranteed by the Locarno treaties, which Britain and Italy were bound to uphold. Therefore, Hitler again startled the world when he announced on March 7, 1936, that German troops would be sent into the Rhineland. The French armies were still clearly superior to those of Germany, and Hitler's advisers had forewarned him of the need to withdraw if the Allies chose to resist this move militarily. Despite all odds, the audacious gamble worked. A divided France was hesitant to act without support from Great Britain, and British public opinion would not back a war to resist Germany's reoccupation of a German region. Italy was already alienated from Western powers as the result of their opposition to its moves in Ethiopia. In the end, both France and the League registered protests, but no effective actions were taken, either individually or collectively.

SPANISH CIVIL WAR

During the 1920s, Spain was governed by military leaders with the support of King Alfonso XIII. By the end of the decade, Republican parties, whose strength had steadily increased, were successfully challenging this authoritarian rule. Following a demonstration of republican strength in local elections in April 1931, Alfonso XIII was persuaded to go into exile, permitting proclamation of the Spanish republic. In July, a constituent assembly convened, with the divided

Republican parties holding a majority. For the next two years, the government implemented a moderate program of social reform that alienated spokesmen for extremes of Left and Right. Legislation was enacted to curb military and clerical authority, and concessions were made to the disruptive independence movement in Catalonia. Land redistribution, which many reformers perceived as their most significant goal, proceeded at a slow pace. In 1933, the first regular elections returned to power a conservative and clerical majority that began steering Spain in Fascist directions. Before the next scheduled elections in February 1936, parties of the Left (including Republicans, Socialists, Syndicalists, and Communists) banded together in a Popular Front to resist the militarist and clerical reaction. After the Popular Front won a decisive victory, extremists of the Left promoted revolutionary strikes and land confiscations, along with acts of vandalism and intimidation against churches and the clergy. Thus provoked, Nationalist insurgents led by General Francisco Franco began an insurrection against the government in July 1936. This was the opening act of the Spanish civil war.

Alignment of Forces. Over two-thirds of Spain's regular military forces sided with the insurgent Nationalists. Supporting the government were the remaining portion of the army and a speedily organized popular militia. Because of its own newly formed Popular Front, the French government seemed predisposed to assist the Loyalist cause. But the Popular Front parties in France were badly divided among themselves, and the French political scene in general was polarized into Left and Right factions. Only the totalitarian regimes were free from the divisiveness that hampered democracies. Foreign intervention in the Spanish conflict thus assumed the character of an international struggle between extreme ideologies. The Fascist nations of Italy and Germany extended aid to the Nationalists, and the Soviet Union became the major supporter of the Loyalist government.

Both Hitler and Mussolini obviously considered attractive the possibility of establishing another Fascist state on the border of France. Using the ruse of permitting involvement by volunteers, Mussolini committed to Franco's cause sizable numbers of Italy's regular ground forces (over 100,000 by 1937). Hitler added aviation and tank units and other specialized support, allowing his military leaders to experiment with tactics and equipment. At the urgings of Britain and France, Italy and Germany early in 1937 joined a nonintervention agreement that provided for a cordon of ships around the coast of Spain to halt the flow of foreign volunteers. However, Italy and Germany withdrew

from this pact after a warship from each nation was bombed by Loyalist airplanes during May. Although later agreements were reached
ending submarine attacks in the Mediterranean, foreign involvement
in the war was never effectively controlled. Soviet influence, meanwhile, had grown along with that of the Fascist powers and by 1937
was being felt on all levels in Spain. Under Russian direction, Communists occupied key positions among Loyalists in the government,
army, and police, pursuing moderate policies in order to capture middle-class support. Soviet leaders calculated that this course would attract support for the Loyalist cause from other Western nations. But
the bankruptcy of these efforts became evident by the summer of 1938,
and Russia diminished its assistance to the Loyalist regime.

Triumph of Franco.   The tide of victory began turning in Franco's
favor during the fall of 1937, when threats that Nationalist forces
might separate the republican strongholds of Madrid and Valencia
from Catalonia persuaded the Loyalists to transfer their capital to Barcelona. These fears were substantiated in the summer of 1938 when
Nationalists succeeded in intersecting the road connecting Barcelona
with republican cities to the west. A stalemate lasted until December,
when a powerful Nationalist army advanced toward Barcelona. Loyalist armies were compelled to surrender the city in January 1939. The
key industries, armament plants, and shipping facilities in the area were
soon brought under Nationalist control. Loyalist supporters, now recognizing the futility of their cause, began fleeing by the thousands
across the French border. Unable to obtain a negotiated peace,
Loyalist leaders withdrew from Madrid shortly before Franco's armies
entered the city on March 28, 1939. In this manner, another state in
Western Europe was transferred from the democratic to the Fascist
camp—not because Franco's forces had won the hearts of a majority
of Spaniards, but rather because the Fascist powers had stood united
behind him while the democratic states had temporized in their assistance to the Loyalist regime.

GERMAN ANNEXATION OF AUSTRIA

Germany was first tempted to absorb Austria in 1934 when local
Nazis assassinated Engelbert Dollfuss, the Austrian chancellor. Mussolini discouraged this ambition by mobilizing troops along Italy's frontier with Austria. In July 1936, seeking to end the isolation that his
pronouncements and actions had brought upon Germany, Hitler had
recognized the sovereignty of Austria and agreed not to intervene in

its internal affairs. The following October, Hitler and Mussolini concluded a rapprochement that outlined mutual interests, specified areas of collaboration, and included trade agreements. In November 1937, Italy became a signatory of the Anti-Comintern Pact earlier signed by Germany and Japan, thus creating the Rome-Berlin-Tokyo Axis. Hitler further calculated that the other major powers were unlikely to offer military resistance to his efforts to achieve German-Austrian unity. Majority sentiment within Britain's Conservative government favored concessions rather than war, and the French government was paralyzed by ministerial instability and polarized politics. Finally, by early 1938, Hitler had succeeded in bringing the German military establishment under his personal control. There were now no independent institutions within the German government or society with authority to veto the activist foreign'policy he wished to pursue.

The first step toward Anschluss with Austria was the unrelenting pressure that Hitler placed on the Austrian government beginning in February 1938, when he met with Austrian Chancellor Kurt von Schuschnigg at his Berchtesgaden mountain retreat in Bavaria. In response to Hitler's threats, Schuschnigg agreed to free imprisoned Nazis and admit members of the Austrian Nazi party into his cabinet, where they were assigned key portfolios of interior, justice, and foreign affairs. Still hoping to maintain his nation's independence, Schuschnigg sought desperately to limit Nazi power by rallying popular support. He declared that a plebiscite on the question of union would be taken on March 15. Local Nazis responded by rioting against the scheduled vote, and Hitler, after failing to secure a postponement, mobilized German troops along the Austrian border. Under these circumstances, Schuschnigg chose to resign rather than subject the country to civil war and a foreign invasion. Artur von Seyss-Inquart, a Nazi who had been serving as minister of interior, became the head of the new cabinet, which quickly invited German troops to enter Austria. This action was followed by the formal incorporation of Austria into the German Reich. In this venture, Hitler had again realistically assessed the international scene. Although France and Germany lodged formal protests, no state came to Austria's defense.

FALL OF CZECHOSLOVAKIA

By 1938, Czechoslovakia was the only remaining democratic state in Central Europe. Under the leadership of Thomáš G. Masaryk, president from 1918 to 1935, and Eduard Beneš, who succeeded him, the

Czechs maintained modernized industries and enjoyed a standard of living comparable with that of advanced Western countries. In the international arena, the Czechs had entered into defensive alliances with two major powers, France and the Soviet Union, and had formed the Little Entente with Romania and Yugoslavia. Although the nation had a comparatively enlightened policy toward its minorities, widespread disaffection among the subordinate nationalities remained. Among these, the Germans were to create the most difficult problem. Concentrated in the Sudetenland, an area along the margin of Bohemia and Moravia, the Germans of Czechoslovakia had been progressively gripped by the Pan-Germanic goals of National Socialism. By the late 1930s, most Sudeten Germans followed the leadership of Konrad Henlein, whose activities as director of the Sudeten German party were subsidized by the German Foreign Office. After the Anschluss with Austria was consummated, Hitler openly and ardently espoused the complaints of the Sudeten Germans. Using their exaggerated grievances as a pretext, he made union of the Sudetenland with the Third Reich a critical first step in the dismemberment of Czechoslovakia.

Chamberlain's First Meetings with Hitler. During the summer and autumn of 1938, Hitler's orchestrated threats again created panic in European capitals. In May, rumors of an impending German invasion of Czechoslovakia caused the Czechs to mobilize. Following warnings by France, Russia, and Britain, Hitler gave firm assurances that he had no such intentions. Leadership in negotiating with Hitler was assumed by Neville Chamberlain, Britain's Conservative prime minister. In spite of the treaty obligations that France and Russia owed to Czechoslovakia, British policies were to avoid an international war over the Sudetenland at all costs. When a German invasion appeared imminent, Chamberlain decided to attempt personal negotiations with Hitler. His first meeting with the Führer, on September 15, 1938, at Berchtesgaden, produced an agreement that the Sudeten Germans were to be accorded "self-determination," including the right to unite with Germany. After persuading France to accept this formula, which the two Western powers then imposed upon the Czech government, Chamberlain held a second meeting with Hitler on September 22 and 23 at the Rhineland town of Bad Godesberg. By this time, Hitler had increased his demands. Instead of the gradual transfer that had been worked out, he demanded the immediate withdrawal of Czech forces and officers from the Sudetenland, with the area to be immediately occupied by German soldiers. At this point, Czechoslovakia, Britain, and France declared Hitler's terms unacceptable. It seemed that finally a coalition of powers was ready to call the German dictator's bluff.

Munich Crisis.   In a final effort to avoid war, leaders of the Western powers urged Mussolini to use his influence with Hitler to resolve the impasse. Although he was committed to support Germany if a conflagration occurred, Mussolini was reluctant to add participation in a general war to his involvement in Ethiopia and Spain. He therefore recommended a four-power summit conference, consisting of Hitler, Daladier, Chamberlain, and himself, to deal with the Sudeten issue. Leaders of Czechoslovakia and the Soviet Union were conspicuously ignored. This proposal was quickly accepted, and the conference was arranged for September 29, 1938, at Munich.

There, Chamberlain and Daladier accepted what they had previously rejected, the extreme demands that Hitler had insisted upon at Bad Godesberg. Czech evacuation of the Sudetenland was to begin on October 1, to coincide with Germany's progressive occupation of four specified areas. By October 10, all territory of a German character was to be brought under control of the Third Reich. Chamberlain and Daladier then persuaded Czech leaders to accept these harsh terms. By this decision, Western leaders again indicated their willingness to concede to Germany some areas in the East. Hopes of an alliance between Western powers and the Soviet Union against Hitler accordingly grew dimmer. Czechoslovakia itself was left defenseless because the areas to be ceded contained strategic fortifications and mountainous terrain. Nevertheless, Chamberlain confidently returned to England and voiced his judgment that the Munich conference had achieved "peace in our time."

Fall of Czechoslovakia.   Hitler's designs, despite his solemn promises to the contrary, had always embraced the inclusion of Czechoslovakia in the Third Reich. In the months following Munich, the dimensions of his ambitions became more evident. Even as an international commission drew new boundaries, the plebiscites that had been promised for disputed areas were ignored. Immobilized by the German threat, the Czechs suffered additional losses as a result of Poland's seizure of the Teschen region and Hungary's acquisition of nearly 5,000 square miles of Slovak territory. Any remaining illusions were dispelled in March 1939, when Hitler decided to annex Bohemia and Moravia, parts of the besieged republic that were the ancient Czech homelands. His goals were aided as the Slovaks, chafing under Czech rule since 1919, further weakened the Czech position by seizing the opportunity to gain autonomy within the republic. Encouraged by Hitler, Slovakia and Ruthenia declared their independence. These events were shortly followed by Hitler's announcement that Bohemia and Moravia had been made a protectorate of the Third Reich. At this point, Hungary took advantage of the imbroglio and incorporated Ruthenia, an area containing large numbers of Magyars. With the dissolution of Czechoslovakia, the period of appeasement was finally brought to an end. It had become clear to Western leaders that Hitler's demands were insatiable, that his most solemn promises were completely worthless, and that he was determined to annex not only the foreign territories peopled by Germans but also other non-German areas in Central and Eastern Europe.

Diplomatic Consequences. It was widely assumed that Poland would be the next object of Hitler's aggression. That German violations of Polish sovereignty would risk general warfare became evident when, on March 31, 1939, Britain and France announced full support of Poland's resistance to any threats undermining its independence. The British followed this concord in April with a unilateral commitment to Poland that strengthened the existing Franco-Polish treaty of mutual assistance. A week later, after Mussolini's seizure of Albania, similar Anglo-French assurances were given to Greece and Romania; Turkey was added to the anti-German coalition by the end of June. More critical, however, were relations between the Western powers and Soviet Russia. Assessing the unwillingness of democracies to defend Czechoslovakia, Stalin suspected the Western powers of tolerating Nazi expansion eastward in the hope that if war erupted, it would be fought between the totalitarian powers. His mistrust deepened after Czechoslovakia's dismemberment because the Western powers still maintained an air of caution in their negotiations with the Soviets.

A particularly thorny problem, leading to an irresolvable deadlock, was Polish resistance to allowing Russian troops on Polish soil, a provision that Soviet leaders considered the prerequisite for an Anglo-French-Soviet defensive pact. In August 1939, Stalin's Western-oriented policies of the 1930s came to an abrupt end. Negotiations with Western powers were proving nonproductive, but the Bolsheviks had been conducting parallel negotiations with the Nazis, their arch ideological enemies. On August 23, 1939, the Germans and Russians surprised and confounded world opinion by announcing that they had signed a nonaggression pact (which was combined with a secret protocol dividing Eastern Europe into German and Russian spheres). With his major Eastern opponent neutralized, Hitler was certain to strike again.

17

World War II

The second world conflict of the twentieth century naturally invites comparisons with the preceding conflagration. Although the responsibility for World War I was diffused among several states, the origins of World War II were clearer. Its architect was Adolf Hitler, unquestioned master of the German state, who risked an invasion of Poland on the calculation that his nonaggression pact with the Soviet Union would again persuade Western powers to yield to his terms. The Second World War was also more truly global, produced more formidable weapons of destruction, and involved a more decisive role by nations of the East.

World War II may be seen as four parallel and intersecting wars, involving (1) the Western Allies against Germany and Italy, (2) Russia against Germany, (3) a Pacific war, and (4) a war for the Far East. In addition to the unprecedented numbers of soldiers in arms, never in history had civilian populations been so deeply involved as targets for bombs and rockets or as participants on the domestic front. Furthermore, decisive roles were played by technological achievements and the ability of industrial organizations to mass-produce vast volumes of goods and to transport them with millions of men over extended distances.

WAR IN EUROPE TO 1941

World War II began when Nazi troops crossed the Polish frontier during the dawn hours of September 1, 1939, thus beginning a blitzkrieg ("lightning war") that resulted in the speedy conquest of Poland. Allied and German armies did little fighting during the winter of 1939–1940, as they faced each other across the supposedly impenetrable Maginot Line constructed by the French along their border with

Germany and the Siegfried Line erected by the Germans along the Rhine frontier. Areas of military activity during this "phony war" included Russia's attack on Finland and Hitler's invasions of Denmark and Norway. In May 1940, German assaults on Holland and Belgium ended the deceptive calm. French resistance crumbled quickly following the fall of Holland and Belgium, and before the end of June, the Nazis had occupied northern France, including Paris, thus bringing the Third Republic to an inglorious end. The Nazis then directed their arsenal against Great Britain. Throughout the winter of 1940–1941, German aviators attempted to destroy Britain's will to fight by daring day and nighttime bombing. Meanwhile, Hitler's armies were making puppets out of the Balkan states. By the spring of 1941, most of Europe had been brought under the domination of the Third Reich.

German Invasion of Poland.   Nazi pressures on Poland intensified in March 1939, when the German press began denouncing alleged brutalities against Poland's German minority. During the following month, using the Anglo-Polish mutual-security agreement as an excuse, Hitler withdrew from both the German-Polish nonaggression pact of 1934 and the Anglo-German naval agreement of 1935. These actions were combined with rising Nazi demands that Danzig and the Polish Corridor be returned to Germany. After the Nazi-Soviet nonaggression treaty (see pp. 199–200) became known, both Britain and France warned Hitler that their commitments to Poland had not altered. Last-minute negotiations failed because Hitler had already decided on the invasion of Poland, which began on September 1. Two days later, Britain and France honored their treaty obligations by declaring war on Germany. In a flaunting display of mechanized speed, German armies penetrated all the way to Warsaw within ten days. In two weeks, Nazi forces had overrun all of Poland's western provinces, forcing Polish troops to retreat southward and eastward in hopes of establishing a more stable front. This goal was crushed after Soviet armies, acting under a secret protocol in the German-Soviet pact, began advancing into Poland's eastern provinces on September 17. By the end of the month, Germany had subdued all military resistance and quickly incorporated its new conquests into the Third Reich.

Russia and the Baltic States.   Under provisions of the Nazi-Soviet treaty, the Baltic states, along with eastern Poland, were defined as Soviet spheres of influence. To implement these terms, the Soviet government by the end of October had pressured Estonia, Latvia, and Lithuania into granting Russia rights to maintain military bases and armed forces within their territory. Similar demands were then made upon the more stubborn Finns. After negotiations reached an impasse, the Soviet government demanded the withdrawal of Finnish troops along its border, and when this demand was not met, Russian troops invaded Finland on November 30, 1939. Western sympathies clearly supported the Finns, whose heroic resistance halted the Russian advance in December and January. Britain, France, and the United States shipped supplies to the beleaguered nation, and Britain and France supported the expulsion of Russia from the League of Nations for its aggressive actions. But by the end of February, the overwhelming weight of Soviet manpower had broken Finnish resistance. The government of Finland had no choice except to sue for peace and accept the terms that Russia dictated. Not surprisingly, these were more stringent than the Soviet proposals that preceded the war. Finland was required to cede over 16,000 square miles of territory, including the city of Vyborg and a naval base at Hangö.

"Phony War." During the winter months following the fall of Poland, only limited military engagements were conducted on the Western front. Supreme control over Allied forces was placed in the hands of French General Maurice Gamelin. Convinced that the Maginot Line could not be penetrated, and remembering the advantages held by defensive troops during World War I, Gamelin decided on a strategy of defense and attrition. No efforts were made to attack Germany's Siegfried Line, despite the fact that Hitler had reduced his strength in the west in order to launch his invasion of Poland. An unofficial truce prevailed both on land and in the air as the Nazis and Allies refrained from assaults upon the other. Meanwhile, the security of Britain seemed guaranteed by British mastery of the seas. Demonstrating again the supremacy that it maintained in World War I, the British navy forced German ships, except those operating in the Baltic Sea, into their home or neutral ports. Optimists in the West placed hope in the possibility that somehow mass destruction within their countries could still be averted. Developments in the Baltic and Scandinavian countries, however, were more accurate auguries.

Nazi Conquest of Norway and Denmark. In addition to providing invaluable submarine and air bases against the British, control of Norway and Denmark would assure Germany of vital imports of Swedish iron ore. With these goals in mind, Germany launched attacks against these two neutral nations on April 9, 1940. Striking before dawn, German warships, which were well protected by air support, made coordinated landings at the principal Norwegian seaports. Concurrently, a swift land and air invasion of Denmark was executed. With little time to react, the Danish government quickly yielded to the Nazi invaders, allowing Denmark to become a German protectorate. Germany's occupation of Norway was potentially troublesome because some Norwegian coastal defenses were virtually impregnable and also because a British-French expeditionary force came to Norway's aid from April 16 to 19. Nazi strategy, however, offset these advantages. In addition, the Nazis were aided in Norway by well-placed sympathizers, notably Major Vidkun Quisling. Pushing northward from Oslo and southward from Trondheim, German units forced the evacuation of Allied troops from central and southern Norway by May 3. Resistance in the north, which was based at the seaport of Narvik, continued throughout May. By early June, however, the German invasion had succeeded. Norway's regular government became an exiled regime in London, and Quisling was designated the Nazis' puppet ruler.

Nazi Conquest of the Low Countries. Since rumors of an impending German invasion of the Low Countries were widespread in Europe during the winter of 1939–1940, the British and French had attempted to coordinate defensive policies with the Belgians and Dutch. All was to no avail; prevailing opinion in the Low Countries supported the tenuous hope that declarations of neutrality might avert war with Hitler. This speculation and the period of "phony war" ended on May 10, 1940, when Nazi troops crossed the borders of the Netherlands, Belgium, and Luxembourg. Within five days, the Dutch armies had been forced to capitulate; and in the process, Germany had inaugurated the policy of bombing cities, killing 40,000 civilians in Rotterdam. On May 12, the critical Belgian fortress of Eben Emael, which controlled access to the Meuse River and the Albert Canal, was overrun by German soldiers. The next day, before the British and French could assume their planned defensive positions, Germany's mechanized forces had penetrated the French lines at Sedan. About a week later, these armies had advanced westward across northern France to Abbeville, thus isolating the Allied forces in Belgium from the principal French armies and producing extensive disorganization and chaos in the Allied rear. Subjected to constant pounding, the Belgian army surrendered on May 26, leaving an Anglo-British force exposed to seemingly certain German annihilation on the beaches of Dunkirk. Because the Germans hesitated before they attacked, however, the British, by utilizing naval vessels of all types, were able to evacuate 350,000 British and French soldiers.

Fall of France. The 1940 German strategy was a modification of the Schlieffen Plan, which had nearly defeated France at the beginning of World War I. The German right flank would again strike the crucial blow, in this case through the Ardennes forest just north of the Maginot Line. By the end of May, this strategy had enjoyed remarkable success. The breakthrough at Sedan had neutralized the Maginot Line, compelling the French to organize a new defensive perimeter roughly along the lines of the Somme and Aisne rivers. Heavily outnumbering the French in planes, tanks, and troops, the German armies on June 5 began their drive south and west toward Paris. This advance forced the French government to flee Paris for Tours on June 11, and it soon fell back again to Bordeaux.

Seeking to participate in the promised glory and spoils, Mussolini finally declared war against France on June 10. In a desperate attempt to hearten French leaders, the British government proposed the merger of Britain and France into a single state with a common citizenry. Premier Paul Reynaud, who had succeeded Daladier in March 1940, was intent on continuing French resistance with British support, even if the French government was compelled to flee to North Africa. His hopes and those of the British were dashed on June 16, when the French cabinet voted to ask the Germans for armistice terms. After Reynaud's resignation, the government was headed by eighty-four-year-old Marshal Henri Philippe Pétain, a World War I hero. On June 22, delegates of the French government signed peace terms with Hitler in the same railway car at Compiègne where in 1918 the Germans had been forced to accept armistice terms.

The Western world was incredulous at the speed of Germany's defeat of France, and Frenchmen were left numbed and demoralized. Under terms of the armistice, Nazi troops were to occupy and administer more than half of France, including all its Atlantic ports. Except for the minimal forces required to maintain order, the French armies and air force were compelled to disarm. The Third Republic crumbled along with the nation's armed forces. Naturally, the political system that had permitted the debacle was itself discredited. Meeting at Vichy outside the area of German occupation, the French Assembly on July 10, 1940, voted Pétain full powers to formulate a new regime. Pétain quickly established dictatorial control of the Vichy government, assuming for himself unbridled legislative and executive powers and requiring all top officials to take an oath of loyalty to him. He named as vice-premier Pierre Laval, a former premier who favored cooperation with the Nazis. Meanwhile, a government-in-exile was already forming to challenge the legitimacy of the Vichy government. It was headed by Reynaud's former undersecretary of war, General Charles de Gaulle, who called for continued French resistance with British support. Patriotic and stubborn, de Gaulle had unsuccessfully campaigned in France during the interwar years for acceptance of the mechanized type of warfare that was making German armies irresistible. The Free French movement had its headquarters first in London and then in Algiers.

Battle of Britain.   The defeat of France left Britain alone against the seemingly unstoppable German armies. With millions in Europe already made his subjects, and with the military odds weighing heavily in his favor, Hitler expected British leaders to acquiesce to his terms. But Britain's parliamentary system produced a dynamic leader in Winston Churchill, who had replaced Neville Chamberlain as prime minister in May 1940, after the fall of Norway brought to a head Parliament's disenchantment with Chamberlain's leadership. A political maverick who had switched from the Conservative to the Liberal party and then back to the Conservatives again, Churchill during the 1930s had repeatedly warned the Baldwin and Chamberlain governments that their policies of appeasement and slow military preparations were inadequate to meet the threat of Hitler. Churchill's cabinet included representatives of all three parties, with Clement Attlee, the Labour party's leader, designated deputy prime minister in 1942. Faced with German attacks, Churchill galvanized his countrymen to resistance in a series of speeches warning of the "blood, toil, tears, and sweat" that lay ahead, and by adamantly pledging that ". . . we shall fight on the beaches . . . on the landing ground . . . in the streets and in the hills; we shall never surrender."

The plan for the invasion of Britain, code-named *Operation Sea Lion,* envisioned the assembling of thousands of landing craft by September 1940 for amphibious operations across the English Channel. In the meantime, persistent bombing by the German air force (Luftwaffe) would weaken British defenses. Marshal Hermann Göring, commander of the Luftwaffe, was certain that air power alone could win the Battle of Britain, calculating that four days of attacks would destroy British air defenses and another month of generalized bombing would bring Britain to its knees. These estimates seemed credible because the German conquests provided them with air bases close to Britain; also, despite the accelerated British rearmament, the Luftwaffe still possessed almost twice as many planes as the Royal Air Force (RAF). In an attempt to execute Göring's plans, there were four days of intensive bombing in mid-August. They failed to demolish .

British air defenses, first, because the Nazis diffused their strength on a variety of targets and, second, because the British did not commit all their fighters to the struggle. An ensuing effort to knock out RAF planes and bases nearly succeeded but eventually failed because the attacks were not sustained long enough. A change in Hitler's strategy further aided Britain. Seeking revenge after the RAF retaliated against the accidental bombing of London on the night of August 24–25 by raiding Berlin, the Nazis attempted to destroy London, thereby diverting attacks from principal targets. London survived, and by the end of September, Hitler was forced to cancel Operation Sea Lion. Britain was saved by the heavy losses RAF pilots were inflicting upon the Luftwaffe, inspiring Churchill's memorable assessment of the struggle: "Never in the field of human conflict was so much owed by so many to so few."

Nazi Domination of the Balkans.   After the fall of France, there was an inevitable reorganization of the smaller Eastern European powers whose autonomy had depended upon French support. Acting first, the Soviets in June 1940 forced Romania to cede Bessarabia and northern Bucovina to Russia. During the fall and winter of 1941–1942, the Nazis brought Romania, Hungary, and Bulgaria into their orbit and in the process forced Romania to cede territory to Hungary and Bulgaria.

Seeking to overcome the subordinate position to which German superiority on the battlefield had relegated Italy, Mussolini ordered his troops in Albania to invade Greece on October 28, 1940. The Greeks immediately halted this assault and retaliated with an offensive that put Mussolini's inept forces on the defensive. Italy's debacle in Greece was eventually transformed into triumph by the Germans, who had decided to bring the Balkans under their control as the prelude to an invasion of Russia. In the spring of 1941, Nazi pressure was brought to bear upon Yugoslavia to force its adherence to the Axis pact to which Bulgaria, Romania, and Hungary had already assented. The Yugoslavs, who were deeply divided internally by the continuing struggle between the dominant Serbs and the minority Croats, signed the pact on March 25, 1941. But bitterness among Serbian patriots sparked a coup d'etat two days later, which substituted a nationalist government that speedily repudiated this German alliance. Thus provoked, on April 6, Hitler launched an attack that culminated in conquest of Yugoslavia within ten days and conquest of Greece in about two weeks. By the end of April, despite British reinforcements, the island of Crete was also brought under German control. The masters of Western Europe and Scandinavia had now become the rulers of the Balkans as well.

BROADENING SCOPE OF THE WAR FROM 1941 TO 1942

World War II achieved its global character during 1941. The war expanded eastward in June 1941 after Germany ended the formality of Nazi-Soviet friendship with a large-scale invasion of Russia. From the beginning, Stalin and Hitler had few illusions about their friendship. Both knew that ideological and territorial differences precluded a stable relationship. Seven months later, Japan's attack on Pearl Harbor (December 7, 1941) ended America's ambiguous role, directly and fully bringing the United States into the war.

German Invasion of Russia. After the fall of France, Soviet-German relations steadily deteriorated as both Hitler and Stalin attempted to define their spheres of influence in the Balkans. Like Napoleon before him, Hitler decided upon the conquest of Russia after his plans for a cross-Channel invasion of England had been shelved. In November 1940, he first proposed that Russia direct its territorial aggrandizement toward the Indian Ocean. Soviet leaders indicated their acceptance of the pact only if their historic claims in the Balkans were upheld. Sensing that Russia would never yield to his terms peaceably, Hitler decided upon Operation Barbarossa for invasion of Russia. Suspecting German intentions, Stalin accelerated military preparations and moved to avoid a two-front war by signing a nonaggression pact with Japan in April 1941. Despite friendly warnings, though, the Soviet leader still refused to accept the imminence of the German attack. With deep apprehensions among his generals, and as usual without warning, Hitler launched his massive invasion on June 22, 1941.

Fruits of the Invasion. Buttressed by forces from Italy, Romania, Slovakia, and Hungary, the German army made coordinated advances that eventually covered the entire western frontier of Russia. According to Hitler's designs, the war would be won within three months through a series of mass spearheads in which encircling movements by mechanized forces would destroy Russian resistance. Internal discontent would then incite the overthrow of the Bolshevik regime. At first, German armies swept everything before them. In the north, the Germans were at Smolensk, two-thirds of the way to Moscow, by mid-July. Hitler's generals then argued for a concentrated campaign against the capital city 200 miles to the east. Instead, Hitler ordered armored divisions diverted north toward Leningrad and south toward the

Ukraine. By the end of September, the Baltic states had been conquered, and the northern armies were on the outskirts of Leningrad; in the south, the Ukrainian capital of Kiev had fallen, and 600,000 Soviet troops had been captured.

Battle of Moscow.   After the fall of Kiev in September, preparations were made for the final German assault on Moscow. Earlier miscalculations became evident during this campaign. Hitler's conquest of the Balkans and his failure to attack Moscow when the opportunity first presented itself had given Soviet leaders the time to reorganize and mass their forces. At this point, German armies were faced with problems similar to those that had confronted Napoleon in 1812. The long advance had severely strained supply lines, and the harsh Russian winter would soon descend. The initial stage of the Nazi assault on Moscow brought German forces so close to the city that Soviet leaders moved the capital east to Kuibyshev. However, fierce Russian resistance, aided by heavy rains and snow, halted the German advance by late October. Ignoring the advice of some military commanders to delay the Moscow campaign until the spring, Hitler ordered a final effort during the first week of December. This time, Soviet defenders, strengthened by fresh divisions arriving from Siberia, held firm and turned the tide of battle. Taking advantage of temperatures reaching 30 degrees below, Stalin ordered a counteroffensive, and on December 8, Hitler was compelled to suspend the Moscow invasion. Disenchanted with what he considered the ineptness and hesitancy on the part of army leaders, Hitler dismissed his commander in chief, Field Marshal Walther von Brauchitsch and assumed personal command of the army.

Entry of the United States.   Although deeply divided over the question of active intervention, the United States had since the beginning of the war moved progressively from isolation to involvement. In the words of President Franklin D. Roosevelt, the role of the United States was that of "the arsenal of democracy." In 1939, neutrality laws were amended to allow the sale of arms to Britain; in exchange for overseas bases, fifty destroyers were sent to Britain in June 1940; and in 1941, the Lend-Lease Act committed the United States to supplying those nations fighting the Axis powers. Despite ideological differences between the United States and Russia, this pledge was fulfilled when the United States joined with Britain to ship aid to the Soviets after Hitler's attack on Russia. Roosevelt further united with Churchill in August 1941 to draft the Atlantic Charter, which defined the war aims of Western nations. The hope was expressed that after the "Nazi tyranny" was destroyed, a peace might be established so that people everywhere could be free from "fear and want."

Meanwhile, tension between Japan and the United States had progressively intensified following Japan's occupation of northern China in 1937. The United States shipped supplies to the forces of Generalissimo Chiang Kai-shek and in concert with Britain imposed an embargo on trade with Japan. Increasingly, a warmongering faction in Tokyo insisted on a showdown with the United States. After last-minute negotiations during November 1941 failed to produce agreement on the status of China, Japanese leaders ordered a surprise attack on Pearl Harbor, the principal U.S. base in the Pacific. Their strategy was to destroy American air and naval power in the Pacific while conducting coordinated landings in the Philippines and other eastern areas. On December 7, 1941, the attack at Pearl Harbor achieved its objective by completely crippling America's Pacific Fleet. A day later, domestic divisions over participation in the war ended, and Congress voted (with only one dissent) a declaration of war on Japan. Because Germany and Italy indicated immediately that they would honor their pact with Japan, the United States became fully committed to a war against all three Axis powers. Roosevelt and his advisers soon decided to coordinate their efforts with other Allied leaders to achieve first the destruction of Nazi power in Europe.

In the meantime, Japan speedily extended the perimeters of its power, invading Malaya (December 8), the Philippines (December 10), and Sarawak (December 17). Two British battleships were sunk three days after Pearl Harbor as they attempted to attack a Japanese convoy. By the spring of 1942, the Japanese had conducted a blitzkrieg in the East that matched the speed of Germany's successes. Guam, Wake Island, and Hong Kong had been conquered; Indochina and Thailand were occupied; Singapore had fallen; the Allies had been forced to retreat from Burma; key areas were controlled in the Netherlands East Indies. In May 1942, defenders of the Philippines surrendered. President Roosevelt ordered General Douglas MacArthur, who had directed the Filipino defense, to reestablish his headquarters in Australia. Having achieved mastery on the sea and in the air, the Japanese were free to strike where they pleased. During the months immediately following Pearl Harbor, neither the United States nor Great Britain could challenge Japan's military superiority in the Pacific.

North Africa. The Axis campaign in North Africa proceeded in September 1940 with an Italian offensive from Libya into Egypt that threatened control of the Suez Canal and the Mediterranean. But in December 1940, counterattacking British forces forced the Italians out of Egypt. Taking the offensive, the British succeeded in invading both Libya and Ethiopia by the end of February 1941. The fortunes of battle continued to alternate after the Italians were reinforced by German armies led by General Erwin Rommel, who drove the British out of Libya in April 1941, only to have the British march into Libya again later that year. With his armies strengthened by the arrival of an air corps from the Russian front, Rommel returned to the attack in May 1942. As British resistance crumbled, he pursued a relentless campaign designed to capture Cairo, Alexandria, and the Suez Canal. The British retreated into Egypt until they were at El Alamein, sixty miles from Alexandria. Here they withstood Rommel's assaults during July and August. Under a new commander, General Bernard Montgomery, the British launched a series of counterattacks during late October that compelled Rommel's troops to retreat. At this point, the British had won the war for Egypt, ensuring that the Suez and the Mediterranean would remain under Allied control.

OCCUPIED EUROPE

By the end of 1941, Hitler had become the most powerful conqueror in European history. Some regions along Germany's eastern and western borders had been annexed outright. Most of the overrun areas, however, were conquered states under Germany's direct administration. They included those parts of Poland that neither Germany nor Russia had annexed, Norway, the Netherlands, and occupied France. In the east, German administration extended to the Baltic states and included the areas conquered in Russia. Over those states where they wished to maintain the illusion of national independence, the Nazis extended indirect rule. Included in this category were Czechoslovakia, Greece, Slovakia, Vichy France, and Denmark. Other states, including Finland, Hungary, Romania and Bulgaria, were dependent territories, although they remained technically independent. For the Continent, Hitler pledged a "new European order" in which all nations and peoples would be assigned their just roles. At first, these promises encouraged widening collaboration with the Nazi conquerors. But as the bitter realities of Nazi rule became evident, the overwhelming majority of the subjugated populations turned against Hitler, with sizable numbers organizing into local resistance movements dedicated to undermining the Nazi system from within.

Resistance Movements. Resistance fighters were motivated by patriotic, ideological, and reformist goals. Most favored the ending of Nazi rule as the first step to a general housecleaning that would sweep away the prewar economic and social system and substitute a reformed society based on democratic and Socialist principles. After Hitler's attack on Russia, Communists became particularly prominent in the European underground, causing rifts in many instances with non-Communists who were suspicious of their motives. Guerrilla warfare, combining various methods of sabotage, was a common feature of resistance campaigns. Toward the end of the war, as the tide of battle turned against Germany, the resistance movements achieved their greatest strength and significance. Harsh Nazi treatment of Slavs and the mountainous Balkan terrain, which served as suitable bases of operations, prompted the first effective underground organizations in Poland and Yugoslavia; weaker organizations developed in Belgium, Denmark, and the Netherlands. In France, resistance sentiment blossomed as disenchantment with Vichy collaboration grew; in Italy, strong resistance organizations took shape after Mussolini was overthrown in 1943. Marshal Tito of Yugoslavia and General Charles de Gaulle of France emerged as the most prominent resistance leaders.

Genocide for Jews.   Nazi rule in Europe was conditioned by savage and repressive racial doctrines. Those peoples who were viewed as fellow Aryans, including the Danes, Flemings, and Scandinavians, were accorded the most bearable forms of treatment. Subjected to much harsher forms of rule, including their widespread use as slave labor, were the Poles, Greeks, and Russians, whom the Germans considered racially inferior. Nazis relegated Jews to the lowest rung on the social scale. Their repression during the war occurred in several stages. In 1940 and 1941, Polish Jews and others were forced to reside in ghettos formed within Polish cities. Late in 1941, following the invasion of Russia, Hitler decided upon the "final solution": extermination of Jews in Europe. Because persecution had forced many Jews to leave Germany by 1939, this policy applied principally to conquered areas. Organized throughout by Himmler's SS, Jews were first gathered into ditches and shot. Later, they were herded into vans and gassed. Finally, five large extermination camps were formed. The most infamous of these was at Auschwitz in Silesia; at the peak of its operation, an estimated 12,000 Jews were killed daily with Zyklon B gas. The Nazis exterminated over 5 million Jews during World War II, giving birth to the concept of *genocide*, that is, the obliteration of a race of people for political or ideological reasons.

DEFEAT OF THE AXIS

For the first three years of warfare, the armies of Germany seemed unconquerable. But by the end of 1942, a resurgence among Allied nations began reversing the tide. Germany's defeat at Stalingrad was a significant omen of other defeats to come. While the Western Allies postponed opening the second front in Western Europe that the Russians adamantly demanded, British and American forces were turning the tide of battle in North Africa. Following the Battle of Stalingrad, as the Russians were launching successful counteroffensives, the Allies were concentrating their principal efforts on restoring mastery in the Mediterranean and establishing another front in Italy. In 1943, Mussolini's regime was overthrown. The second front in the west was finally inaugurated in June 1944. Within a few months, France and Belgium were liberated, placing Germany in a vise between Allied forces advancing from both the east and the west. While the war in Europe was ending, the tide of Japanese triumphs in the East was also being reversed.

Battle of Stalingrad. Having failed to conquer Leningrad and Moscow, Hitler decided in 1942 to shift his major efforts to the south. His goal was the extension of German control from the Ukraine to the Caucasus, thereby disrupting Soviet communications along the Volga and transferring an area rich in oil reserves to German hands. Once more, the German advance seemed irresistible. During July 1942, Sevastopol in the Crimea and Rostov on the Don were captured. By late August, Panzer divisions had reached the suburbs of Stalingrad, the next major objective. An industrial center, Stalingrad commanded access to both the Volga and the Don rivers and to the southeastern areas of Russia. With its defenders ordered to hold ground at all costs, the Battle of Stalingrad began on August 22. Commencing their siege with a heavy fusillade of artillery and bombs, German troops penetrated the perimeters of Stalingrad early in September and by the middle of the month had conquered most of the city in hand-to-hand combat. But surprisingly, Soviet troops, under the leadership of General Georgi Zhukov, on September 21 began executing an effective counterattack that trapped German forces between Soviet armies advancing from the north and from the south. Over 300,000 German soldiers were eventually lost because Hitler refused to allow the twenty-two threatened German divisions to retreat. The remnants of these divisions surrendered in February 1943. On the heels of this victory, Stalin ordered a westward counteroffensive that eventually forced a general German retreat along the entire Russian front.

North Africa. Early in 1943, Axis forces in Africa were wedged between two Allied armies advancing from the east and west. After General Montgomery's troops forced Rommel's armies to retreat from Egypt and Libya, the Axis powers made their last stand in Tunisia. Meanwhile, in November 1942, American and British troops commanded by General Dwight D. Eisenhower landed in French-controlled Morocco and Algeria. On the order of General Pétain, French forces greeted the Allied invaders with bitter resistance. Within a few days, however, Eisenhower had signed a controversial agreement with Admiral Jean François Darlan, a major figure in the Vichy regime. Darlan was made provisional ruler of French North Africa, and in return, the French forces there were committed to fighting alongside the British and American troops. (Darlan was assassinated in December 1942; he was succeeded by General Henri Giraud.) In retaliation, the Germans completed their occupation of France while strengthening Axis forces in Tunisia in order to resist the Allied threat. From Algeria and Libya, the armies directed by Eisenhower and Montgomery began a series of coordinated attacks against the Axis forces during March 1943. In May, the Allied mastery of North Africa was completed, the remaining Axis troops were captured, and the way was paved for an Allied invasion of Italy.

Invasions of Sicily and Italy. At meetings held in Casablanca (January 1943) and Washington (May 1943), Roosevelt and Churchill decided to make Sicily and Italy their next primary objectives. The prospect of foreign assistance to help overthrow Mussolini encouraged secret societies within Italy to collaborate with the foes of il Duce inside the government. The assault on Sicily began in July with British and American landings and was completed by mid-August. With Hitler at this point refusing further aid for the defense of Italy, dissidents in the government forced the resignation of Mussolini on July 25, 1943. Mussolini was succeeded as premier by Marshal Pietro Badoglio, who after some delay agreed to Allied terms of unconditional surrender on September 3, 1943. The armistice coincided with two Allied invasions of the Italian mainland. A British force under General Montgomery landed at Italy's southern tip on September 2, and six days later, British and American forces commanded by General Mark Clark disembarked at Salerno.

Within three months, southern Italy, including Naples, had fallen to Allied forces. Meanwhile, German reinforcements had come across

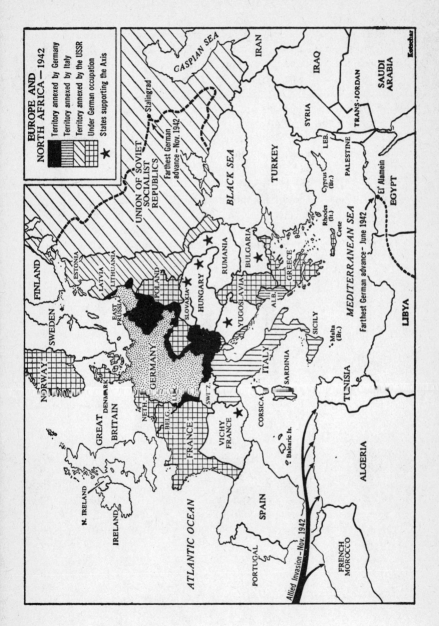

EUROPE AND
NORTH AFRICA—1942

■ Territory annexed by Germany
▨ Territory annexed by Italy
▥ Territory annexed by the USSR
▦ Under German occupation
★ States supporting the Axis

the Brenner pass and were securing mastery of the north. They quickly seized Rome, forcing the Badoglio government to flee southward, and freed Mussolini, who became a puppet of the Nazi rulers. Bitter fighting continued throughout the winter, but the deadlock remained until the spring of 1944, when British and American forces finally succeeded in breaking out of their Anzio beachhead. As Allied armies advanced toward Rome, the Germans proposed that it be declared an open city. Therefore, Allied forces entered Rome on June 4 without fighting, making it the first European capital to be liberated from Hitler's grip. In the fighting that remained in northern Italy, the Allies were supported by the powerful Italian resistance movement.

Normandy Invasion. In November and December of 1943, at Teheran, Roosevelt and Churchill held the first of their two meetings with Stalin and decided to begin the long-awaited invasions in the West. Under Eisenhower's command, elaborate preparations were made in England for the seaborne attacks that were scheduled to begin in May 1944 with landings on the beaches of Normandy. Although Churchill expressed serious reservations about this plan, favoring instead campaigns in the Adriatic and eastern Mediterranean, he yielded to Stalin and Roosevelt, who believed that the war could be ended more quickly by directly confronting the strongest German armies. Delays in completing preparations, difficulties in coordinating the Normandy invasion with a Soviet summer offensive, and harsh weather resulted in postponement of the Normandy invasion until June 6. Despite heavy casualties, more than 150,000 Allied troops were landed in Normandy before the end of the day. Two artificial ports were hastily constructed through which more than a million men passed within a month. The second front was finally launched.

Plot to Kill Hitler. By July 1944, it was clear that the invasions at Normandy had succeeded and also that the German war efforts in Italy and Russia were on the verge of collapse. With Hitler refusing to recognize the imminence of national disaster, a small group of high army officers and conservative politicians decided that Germany could be saved from destruction only through the assassination of its deranged leader. Colonel Klaus von Stauffenberg, who was convinced that Hitler represented evil incarnate, was the key figure in this plot. His task was to kill Hitler by planting a bomb during a staff conference. News of the event would then be flashed to co-conspirators in Berlin who would assume control of the government. Although the bomb exploded and some officers were killed, the Führer was only slightly injured. Predictably, all suspects in the conspiracy paid with their lives. Thus, the already weak resistance to Hitler within Germany was eradicated, and it was apparent that Germany would surrender only when military destruction brought the nation to its knees.

Liberation of France and Belgium. After Normandy, the initiatives lay clearly with the Allies. By the end of July, American forces commanded by General George Patton had broken out of their beachheads. Patton's troops raced south toward Orléans and then east toward the Seine, allowing Paris to be liberated by resistance fighters on August 25. To the north, advancing Canadian and British forces commanded by General Montgomery, supported by the U.S. First Army under General Courtney H. Hodges, forced the German armies into a full retreat. In mid-August, Allied troops established a beachhead on the Riviera and in a matter of days, with the help of resistance leaders, were liberating southern France. By the end of August, virtually all of France had been freed from German control; in the process, German armies had lost over 500,000 men, and a continuous front had been formed by Allied forces advancing from Normandy and the south. In early September, Montgomery's troops forced the Germans out of Belgium and began their advance into the Netherlands. At this point, Montgomery undertook the bold gamble of parachuting men across the Rhine at Arnhem in the Netherlands to launch an invasion of Germany. Paratroopers succeeded in establishing the base, but German resistance forced cancellation of the operation within a week. It was clear that the conquest of Germany would be delayed until the following year.

Russian Advance. During the autumn and winter of 1943–1944, Soviet armies recaptured much of the territory that they had lost to German forces. A spring offensive in 1944 freed the Crimea and the Ukraine. During the following months, Soviet armies maintained their momentum and continued marching west, bringing large areas of Central and Eastern Europe under Russian domination. Campaigns coordinated with the Normandy invasion ended resistance in Finland and brought Russian troops to the borders of East Prussia. During August and September, Soviet armies extended their control in Poland, and Romania and Bulgaria sued for peace. During September and October, Tito's Partisans in Yugoslavia, requiring only moderate assistance from the Red Army, expelled the retreating Germans and dealt harshly with their local sympathizers. Although the principal battles for Hungary, Austria, and Germany remained, in the East and in the West, the ultimate outcome of the war was no longer in doubt by the end of 1944.

Battle of the Bulge. Forced on the defensive along both fronts,

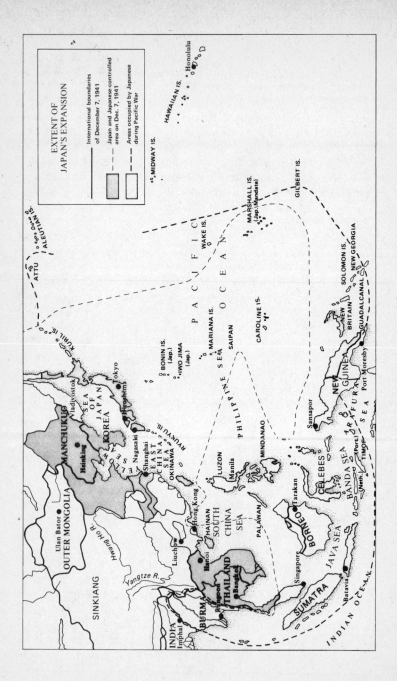

EXTENT OF
JAPAN'S EXPANSION

International boundaries
of December 7, 1941

Japan and Japanese-controlled
area on Dec. 7, 1941

Areas occupied by Japanese
during Pacific War

ALEUTIAN IS.
ATTU
KURIL IS.

SINKIANG

OUTER MONGOLIA
Ulan Bator

MANCHUKUO
Hsinking

Vladivostok
SEA OF JAPAN
KOREA
Tokyo
Hiroshima
Nagasaki
Shanghai
EAST CHINA SEA
RYUKYUS
OKINAWA
YELLOW SEA

CHINA

Hwang Ho
Yangtze R.

INDIA
Imphal
BURMA
Rangoon
THAILAND
Bangkok
Hanoi
Liuchow
Hong Kong
HAINAN
SOUTH CHINA SEA
PALAWAN

SUMATRA
Singapore
Batavia
JAVA SEA
BORNEO
Tarakan
CELEBES
BANDA SEA
TIMOR
(Neth.) (Port.)
ARAFURA SEA
Port Moresby

MIDWAY IS.

BONIN IS.
(Jap.)
IWO JIMA
(Jap.)

MARIANA IS.
SAIPAN

PHILIPPINE SEA

LUZON
Manila

MINDANAO

Sansapor

NEW GUINEA

CAROLINE IS.

WAKE IS.

MARSHALL IS.
(Jap. Mandate)

GILBERT IS.

PACIFIC OCEAN

NEW BRITAIN
SOLOMON IS.
NEW GEORGIA
GUADALCANAL

HAWAIIAN IS.
Honolulu

INDIAN OCEAN

Hitler decided in December 1944 to attempt to divide the U.S. First and Third armies by striking at their point of least resistance through the Ardennes forest. If the bold plan succeeded, the Allies would be deprived of access to the key port of Antwerp, their rear would be disorganized, and as many as twenty-five divisions would be destroyed. Informed by their meteorologists that predicted bad weather would obstruct the use of Allied air power, the Germans began their assault on the night of December 15. Catching the Allies completely by surprise, German forces scored significant breakthroughs, compelling a speedy Allied retreat in Belgium and Luxembourg. It was from the bulge into Allied lines that this battle received its name. Not until mid-January did the reserves that Eisenhower transferred from the south succeed in repelling the German advance. Nevertheless, this offensive, like the daring one of 1918, depleted the resources of an already weakened Germany, thereby simplifying subsequent Allied penetrations in the west.

Closing of the Vise. In February 1945, Allied leaders met at Yalta in the Crimea to make decisions regarding the future of Germany, the reorganization of Eastern Europe, the creation of a world organization, and the war in the Pacific (see pp. 238, 248). Meanwhile, the eighty-five divisions under Eisenhower's command were making preparations to cross the Rhine. In early March, Allied troops spanned the Rhine at Remagen and before the end of the month had bridged the Lower Rhine on their way into the North German plain and the Ruhr. Russian armies captured Budapest in mid-February and Vienna in mid-April. On April 25, as the Allies were converging on Berlin, advancing Russian and American troops first met on the Elbe at Torgau. Five days later, as Russian troops were entering the rubble-strewn capital, a mentally deteriorating Hitler and his mistress committed suicide in a Berlin bunker. On May 7, the Second World War in Europe was brought to a close when the German high command surrendered unconditionally at Eisenhower's headquarters in Reims.

Victory in the Pacific. Toward the end of 1943, American forces began reducing the outer defenses of the Japanese empire; and in 1944, they made significant strides toward the heartland of Japan. From the Solomon islands, Guadalcanal, the reconquest of the Philippines, and a variety of islands and atolls in the mid-Pacific, the bitterly fought war proceeded. In October 1944, the American navy won a critical battle at Leyte Gulf; and by the time of Germany's surrender, Allied troops were in possession of Iwo Jima and Okinawa, placing them only 300 miles from Japan itself. Considering the fanatical resistance demonstrated by the Japanese in defense of Saipan and Iwo Jima and the suicide missions of Japanese pilots at Okinawa, Allied commanders calculated that an invasion of Japan would cost at least 1 million casualties. To avoid the predicted high price in American and Allied lives, President Harry S. Truman ordered that new and devastating atomic bombs, worked on secretly since 1942, be used against Japanese cities. The first bomb, dropped on Hiroshima (August 6), destroyed the city and killed 75,000 people; the second, dropped on Nagasaki (August 9), wreaked similar destruction and killed 40,000. The Japanese immediately laid down their arms and later signed a formal surrender on September 2, 1945. After over 30 million civilian and military deaths, with cities in Europe and Asia in ruins, with overwhelming shifts in international power balances, the Second World War had finally ended.

18

The Cold War

Bipolar relations between the United States and the Soviet Union have dominated international affairs since World War II. European nations, including the once dominant states of Great Britain, France, and Germany, became satellites or junior partners in opposing Eastern and Western alliance systems led by the two superpowers. Evolutions have occurred in both alliances, largely from the conflict between nationalistic ambitions and considerations of mutual interest. Between the East and West, there have been limited military clashes and extensive political and economic struggles. The nuclear capacities of both sides, however, have cautioned against running the risks of a general war. Relations between East and West have thus constituted a cold war, consisting of clashes more limited than total, yet far too extensive and ominous to be considered peaceful.

YALTA AND POTSDAM

As victory over Germany approached, the requirements of wartime cooperation were gradually replaced with widening differences among Allied leaders over reconstruction in Europe. These conflicts, which were never far below the surface during the war, were compromised at the Yalta and Potsdam conferences held just before and soon after Germany was defeated. Agreements included pledges at Yalta (February 1945) to eliminate militarism and nazism in Germany, to support the formation of an international organization to maintain world peace and security, and to hold free elections in the liberated countries of Eastern Europe. The Soviet Union also consented secretly to enter the war against Japan within sixty days after Germany's defeat; in return, the United States agreed to harbor and railway privileges for Russia in Manchuria. Accords at Potsdam (July and

August 1945) included a promise to integrate the economic policies of a zoned and divided Germany and granted permission for the Polish government to administer the areas of eastern Germany up to the Oder and western Neisse rivers.

SOVIET PROVOCATIONS

Repeated Soviet refusals to implement important terms of the Yalta and Potsdam agreements raised growing suspicions in the West. The two most serious areas of disagreement were political rule in Poland and economic reconstruction in Germany. Democratic elements were not permitted to participate in the coalition Polish government as promised. Positions hardened as Soviet designs to make satellite areas out of most countries in Eastern Europe became undeniably clear. The basis of this control was established during the final years of World War II, as Soviet troops captured territories that had been overrun by Hitler's forces. It was extended as Hungary in May 1947 and then Czechoslovakia in February 1948 succumbed to Soviet pressures. At the same time, the Soviet Union refused to cooperate with the other Allies in treating Germany as a single economic unit. At the end of the war, Germany was divided into British, French, U.S., and Soviet zones; Berlin was similarly partitioned. Each power ruled in its own zone, and supreme authority for all of Germany was vested in the Allied Control Council composed of representatives from all four nations. Disagreements over currency reforms and the collection of reparations created a deadlock between the three Western states and the Soviet Union. From July 1948 through September 1949, Soviets stopped all rail and road traffic between the Western zones and Berlin. Only a determined and dramatic airlift by the Western powers maintained the flow of vital supplies into Berlin's Western sectors.

MUTUAL RESISTANCE

In 1947, the United States adopted a policy of containment, which was designed to prevent the spread of communism by extending aid to threatened areas. The Truman Doctrine thus justified economic and military assistance to Greece and Turkey, and the Marshall Plan provided massive economic assistance to Western Europe. Russia countered these moves in 1949 by organizing its satellites into an economic union, the Council for Mutual Economic Assistance (COMECON). During 1948 and 1949, the Western powers merged their zones into the Federal Republic of Germany, and the German Democratic Republic (GDR) was established in East Germany as a puppet under Russian domination. Meanwhile, the United States was building a network of alliances, which included NATO (1949); the Soviets responded with the Warsaw Pact (1955), their own military organization. Earlier assumptions that the wartime coalition could be maintained to preserve the peace proved to be invalid. Important terms of the peace arrangements lost much of their meaning as new power alignments emphasized ideological and geographical divisions between East and West, instead of the Allied and Axis combinations that had fought the war.

KOREAN WAR

In June 1950, the Communist state of North Korea moved its armies across the 38th parallel to invade the Western-supported nation of South Korea, thus severely testing the American policy of containing Communist aggression. Viewing it as part of a general Communist assault on the free world, Western leaders promptly blamed the Kremlin for the attack. President Harry S. Truman responded first by strengthening American forces in Southeast Asia and later by committing ground forces to action under the command of General Douglas MacArthur. Although the United States provided the bulk of South Korea's aid throughout the conflict, the war was officially transformed into a struggle between U.N. and North Korean forces by a Security Council decision of June 27, 1950, taken during the Soviet Union's absence.

The Korean War may be divided into several stages. North Korean armies were initially successful in capturing Seoul and driving South Korean forces to the tip of the peninsula. After a U.N. landing (September 1950), the North Korean armies were driven back to their home territory with heavy losses. U.N. armies then pursued North Korean forces on their own ground, preventing their armies from regrouping and making a defeat of North Korea imminent (October 1950). Refusing to permit the establishment of an unfriendly regime on the frontiers of Manchuria, Communist China decided to intervene with its regular armies disguised as volunteers (October–November 1950). U.N. armies were subsequently forced to retreat and resume positions south of the 38th parallel (December 1950). Negotiations for an armistice to end the stalemate began in July 1951 and continued for two years before peace was finally obtained in July 1953.

The Korean War has been the only direct military collision involving the great powers since World War II. American involvement was based on the premise that Communist aggressors would be less likely to start a general war if they were defeated in localized conflicts. After the Chinese invasion, President Truman refused to risk a world holocaust by allowing General MacArthur to direct sea and air power against China's territory. Instead, he took the politically unattractive step of removing the popular general. The Soviet Union also proceeded with caution as Stalin declined to counter U.N. support of South Korea with Soviet troop support of North Korea. Calculated movements both East and West thus avoided the missteps that could have transformed the limited conflict into a global war.

VIETNAM WAR

The post-World War II conflict in Vietnam began as a contest for power among the French, the Vietnamese Nationalists, and the Communist Viet Minh under the direction of their Russian-trained leader, Ho Chi Minh. Despite military aid from the United States, the French and Nationalists were no match for the well-trained and highly motivated Viet Minh forces. Vietnamese Communists were also aided by the 1949 Communist victory in neighboring China that made massive military assistance available to them. French resistance finally collapsed in the spring of 1954 after a decisive defeat by Communist forces at Dien Bien Phu. In the meantime, an international conference consisting of American, Soviet, British, and Chinese foreign ministers, in addition to French and Vietnamese representatives, met at Geneva to negotiate conditions for a cease-fire. The accords that emerged from this conference temporarily divided Vietnam at the 17th parallel, giving control of the north to the Communists and the south to the Nationalists. The Viet Minh were required to leave South Vietnam, whose government from 1954 to 1963 was headed first by Bao Dai and then by Ngo Dinh Diem. At the same time, the French were required to evacuate North Vietnam, allowing that state to be ruled by Ho Chi Minh and the Viet Minh. Elections to achieve reunification were scheduled for 1956, but because of intensifying north-south disagreements they never materialized.

U.S. involvement in Vietnam progressed as more and more Communist insurgents from the north infiltrated into the south. The premise of American assistance was that South Vietnam, like South Korea or West Germany, could become a frontier against Communist aggression. This assumption was repeatedly challenged throughout the 1960s. On the one hand, successive South Vietnamese regimes ineffectively coped with rising social discontent; on the other, Communists broadened the war by moving men and supplies in ever-increasing amounts, reaching the south through supply routes in Laos, Cambodia, or from the sea. The Viet Cong, or National Liberation Front, as Communists called their operations in the south, wrested control from the government in many areas by their campaigns of terror and guerrilla warfare.

In response, U.S. military assistance increased dramatically by 1962. American pilots were flying aircraft in support of South Vietnamese land troops, and American officers were accompanying and assisting these units on military operations. The 1964–1965 years were even more decisive turning points. In August 1964, two U.S. destroyers were attacked by North Vietnamese torpedo boats in the Gulf of Tonkin. Backed by a resolution of support from the Senate, President Lyndon B. Johnson retaliated by ordering selected bombing of North Vietnam's naval installations. These air attacks became massive early in 1965 when the United States expanded its targets in the north. More ominously, in spring 1965, two marine battalions became the first U.S. combat units sent to South Vietnam. By the end of President Johnson's administration in 1968, America's involvement totaled more than 500,000 men. This figure was successively decreased by President Nixon (1968–1974) as efforts were made in the Vietnamization of the conflict (see pp. 340–342).

The Vietnam War, like the Korean War, demonstrated that mutual nuclear deterrents have a limiting effect on wars involving the interests of the United States and the Soviet Union. Each superpower has been careful to avoid any action that would provoke a military attack by the other. At the same time, however, both conflicts demonstrated that warfare as a way of resolving international disputes has not been eliminated. Less powerful states—first Korea and China, then North Vietnam supported by China with its recently acquired and limited nuclear capacity—have challenged and bitterly fought the world's leading nuclear power in stalemated wars. American leaders were reluctant to employ their nuclear arsenals in these conflicts, not only because of widespread domestic and international opposition to their use but also because nuclear weapons directed against a lesser Communist state might broaden the war and provoke a confrontation with the Soviet Union. The balance of terror has thus permitted and sometimes encouraged limited wars, while simultaneously ensuring their localized character.

THE MIDDLE EAST AND THE COLD WAR

Soviet-American rivalry in the Middle East developed after World War II, as British and French power in the area declined. Predictably, competition between the United States and the Soviet Union involved the two superpowers in the Middle East's most historic and dangerous conflicts. The most explosive problem by far was the struggle between Arab nations and Israel. Between 1922 and 1948, the affairs of Palestine were supervised by Great Britain under a mandate granted by the League of Nations in 1922. Britain's announced policy of making Palestine a national home for the Jews and its approval of immigration policies that allowed the Jewish population to mount steadily led to recurring violence between Palestinian Arabs and Jews during the interwar years. The tragic suffering that Jews endured during World War II convinced world, and particularly Western, opinion that the British policy should be implemented. The U.N. General Assembly reflected this mood in November 1947 by voting to partition the then predominantly Arab state of Palestine into Jewish and Arab states. In May 1948, the state of Israel was proclaimed under a provisional government headed by David Ben-Gurion. Since then, Israel adamantly defended its right to exist, and Arab states vigorously denied the legitimacy of the U.N. decision. These seeds of bitterness produced innumerable border incidents that erupted into wars in 1948–1949, 1955–1956, 1967, and 1973.

America's policy has been to maintain a foothold in both camps while recognizing Israel's right to exist. Efforts to pursue this course during the Suez crisis of 1956 made a turning point in America's enlarging Middle East role. In July 1956, President Nasser nationalized the Suez Canal and announced that profits would be used to help build the Aswan Dam. At first, American aid had been promised for this gigantic project on the Nile River, but it was later withdrawn after Washington became disenchanted with Nasser because of his flirtations with the Soviet Union. Assisted by Israel's invasion of Egypt, British and French planes bombed the Suez Canal zone as part of their plan to seize the critical waterway by force. While upholding the principle of free transit for all nations, the Eisenhower administration successfully pressured England and France to abandon their military operations. Shortly thereafter, the Eisenhower Doctrine, announced in 1957, asserted America's willingness to defend the sovereignty of Middle East countries threatened by Communist aggression. During the Arab-Israeli War (October 1973) and afterwards, American efforts to support Israeli interests were severely tested by the new diplomacy of Arab oil-producing countries, who were skillfully manipulating the flow and price of this essential product in efforts to obtain a Mideast settlement on their own terms.

The Soviet Union attempted to increase its influence in the Middle East by polarizing Arab opinion against the United States and Israel. Soviet representatives contended that their assistance was directed to progressive nationalist governments, with no political or economic strings attached, and they denounced American aid to the traditional regimes in Jordan and Saudi Arabia as reactionary and imperialistic. In addition, the Soviet Union firmly opposed the Israeli-British-French invasion of Egypt in 1956 and consistently used its veto in the U.N. Security Council to support the Arab cause. Initially, Israel's defeat of the Arabs in the Six-Day War of June 1967 adversely affected the Soviet Union's prestige, since it was the foremost supplier of military aid to the defeated nations. However, the Soviet government later increased its sway in Arab countries, reequipping Egyptian armies and significantly increasing the number of Soviet advisers and instructors. Meanwhile, Soviet leaders urged the United Nations to condemn Israel and compel it to withdraw unconditionally from occupied Arab territories. A further rise in Soviet prestige resulted from the buildup of a formidable Russian naval force in the Mediterranean as a rival to America's Sixth Fleet. Continued Soviet assistance to Arab states remained an influential consideration in Mideast and world politics.

THE THIRD WORLD

The third world, meaning states unaligned with either power bloc, comprises nearly all of Africa and more than half of non-Communist Asia. Despite their disparate histories, these states have in common their status as underprivileged countries that have been subjected to imperialist penetrations. Both the United States and the Soviet Union have attempted to enlist them as allies and stake them out as spheres of influence. Consequently, third world nations have often exercised diplomatic power disproportionate to their economic and military strength. States that played this game most successfully usually enjoyed two advantages: First, both superpowers considered their support desirable for political and/or economic reasons, and second, skillful leaders were able to use their bargaining positions to attract aid from both sides simultaneously.

Egypt and India, under the respective regimes of Gamal Abdel Nasser (1952–1970) and Jawaharlal Nehru (1947–1964), were examples of third world nations that successfully engaged in this practice. In response to their biddings, the great powers even occasionally pursued courses that clashed with the policies of their friends and allies. For example, the ill-fated efforts of the United States to maintain friendly relations with Nasser and the Arabs conflicted with the Mideast policies of Britain and France; similarly, the Soviet Union supported Nasser in spite of his repressive actions against local Communists. Comparable conflicts between superpowers and their allies applied to India. Although Pakistan pursued more Western-oriented policies, the United States frequently supported India in disputes between the two, while the Soviet Union sided with India in its quarrels with Communist China.

UNITED NATIONS

Created in San Francisco in 1945, the United Nations had as its principal aim the peaceful resolution of international conflicts. Its major organ, the General Assembly, comprises all participating states; each nation is assigned one vote and a maximum of five representatives. The Assembly was empowered to consider any questions related to world peace or security that did not involve purely internal affairs of nations or matters under consideration by the Security Council. The chief administrative officer, the Secretary-General, is recommended by the Security Council and formally appointed by the General Assembly. The Security Council's membership was established at eleven: five permanent members (China, France, the United Kingdom, the United States, and the Soviet Union) and six nonpermanent members chosen for two-year terms. Decisions on procedural matters in the Council require the votes of any seven members; substantive questions, however, require the inclusion of all permanent members in the majority of seven. Each great power was thereby given a veto over all crucial decisions, an obstructive power the Soviet Union frequently used on issues that divide East and West.

Though devoted to the principle of international cooperation, the United Nations was launched principally as a Western organization. Its home was in the United States; its procedures were borrowed from

Western parliaments; and it was dominated by Western diplomats and staff members. The overwhelming majority of the first delegates came from Latin America, Western Europe, and the British Commonwealth; by contrast, only a few Asian and African countries were represented. In the postwar years, most Asian and African areas freed themselves from colonial rule and became independent states. Their resulting membership in the United Nations gave unaligned states a controlling voice in the General Assembly. In addition to the Afro-Asian group, neutralist or unaligned members of the United Nations include Ireland, Sweden, Finland, Austria, Yugoslavia, Cyprus, and Israel.

EUROPEAN INTEGRATION

Support for the movement to cross traditional national boundaries and integrate the major institutions of Europe came from diverse sources. After World War II, many Europeans feared a reversion to the prewar competitive state system. They realized that European nations would automatically be weaker on the world scale as the result of wartime disasters combined with the growth of the two superpowers, the Soviet Union and the United States. In a traditional setting, states would be encouraged to pursue nationalistic policies in order to resolve their overwhelming economic problems. These policies would not only retard Europe's economic growth but would also create national antagonisms that could lead to another world war. Western statesmen additionally favored a closer economic and political involvement of West Germany with other Western nations in order to move German energies in peaceful directions. As the leader of the Western alliance, the United States viewed integration as a way of strengthening Europe and thereby improving the Western position in its rivalries with Communist countries.

In 1947, the U.S. government took an important initial step in this direction by requiring European countries to cooperate in allocating their resources as a condition for receiving Marshall Plan aid (see pp. 263–264, 326). The Organization for European Economic Cooperation (OEEC) was created in 1948 to administer this assistance. In the same year, representatives of most nations in Western Europe gathered at the Brussels Congress to discuss prospects for European federation. The Council of Europe, an organization providing a continuous forum for discussion, was created the following year. Some European statesmen, considering OEEC and the Council of Europe significant but halting steps, acted more decisively to encourage the movement towards supranational cooperation. French Foreign Minister Robert Schuman was a leader of this group. In 1950, he proposed the establishment of an international authority for coal and steel that would include six continental countries (Belgium, France, Italy, Luxembourg, the Netherlands, and West Germany). Productivity in the key industries would thus be pooled, making it virtually impossible for participating nations to organize secretly for military purposes. The European Coal and Steel Community (ECSC) was successfully launched in 1952.

Ensuing efforts toward integration produced first disheartening defeat and later notable success. In the midst of the international tensions that accompanied the Korean War, American leaders decided that a rearmed Germany was essential to European defense. In order to avoid the specter of renewed German militarism, the French government proposed in 1950 to establish a European army under international control in which German soldiers would participate. Despite this radical challenge to traditional notions of national sovereignty, five of the six governments in the ECSC approved this European Defense Community (EDC). By 1954, however, the fears generated by the Korean War had subsided, and nationalists in the French Assembly voted to abandon the plan. The decision was then made to continue efforts toward union in the economic realm. The Treaty of Rome (March 1957) broadened to all products existing agreements applying to coal and steel, thus creating a single free market among the six ECSC countries. This Common Market, officially called the European Economic Community (EEC), was established on January 1, 1958. Its immediate objective was to establish a customs union among participating nations. Barriers to trade would be reduced gradually, and uniform tariffs would be levied on imports from nonmember countries. Great Britain refused initially to join the Common Market because of its reservations about supranational continental authorities and its economic commitments to Commonwealth countries. Instead, Great Britain exerted leadership in formation of the rival European Free Trade Association (EFTA), which included seven nations (Great Britain, Austria, Denmark, Norway, Portugal, Sweden, and Switzerland). This more loosely organized group never enjoyed the Common Market's prominence and success. It was further weakened when Great Britain, Ireland, and Denmark joined the Common Market in 1973.

EAST-WEST POLITICAL TRENDS

Decentralization of power was the dominant political tendency in both Eastern and Western coalitions following World War II. Persuasion and consultation normally characterized all decision making in the Western alliance, since member nations maintained their national independence. The Soviet Union imposed greater uniformity in the East by exercising extensive control over the domestic and foreign policies of Communist parties in other countries. Within each alliance, however, principally as a result of the force of nationalism, the degree of domination by the Soviet Union and the United States was less in the 1960s than in the 1950s.

The Western Alliance. Policy differences between France, on the one hand, and the United States and Great Britain, on the other, produced the most dramatic antagonisms in the West. Charles de Gaulle, French president from 1958 to 1969, believed that France and Western Europe should be self-reliant. A strong nationalist, he opposed British-American plans in 1962 to create a multilateral nuclear force under the auspices of NATO and demanded instead separate nuclear weapons for France. He further pursued an independent course by extending a hand of friendship to some Communist-bloc nations. Distrusting the intentions of Britain and the United States, he vetoed Britain's application for membership in the Common Market, which he considered a pipeline for furthering British and American influence in Europe.

Policies of West Germany further challenged cold war assumptions that Europe would remain in divided campo, Willy Brandt, chancellor of Western Germany from 1969 to 1974, made a determined effort to achieve reconciliation with Communist nations, especially East Germany. This policy proved difficult to implement since East Germany imposed stiff preconditions for closer relations: first, that West Germany accept East Germany as a foreign nation by extending diplomatic recognition to it, and second, that West Germany accept the legality of Poland's control over territories east of the Oder and Neisse rivers, which Poland has governed since the end of World War II.

Status of Japan. Japan's imperial dreams for a new order in Asia ended with its crushing defeat in World War II. Following the war, the Japanese emperor and government were placed under the control of General Douglas MacArthur, the Supreme Commander of the Allied Powers (SCAP). For nearly seven years, Japan was dominated by American occupation authorities, who focused successively on programs of demilitarization, democratization, and social reform. The

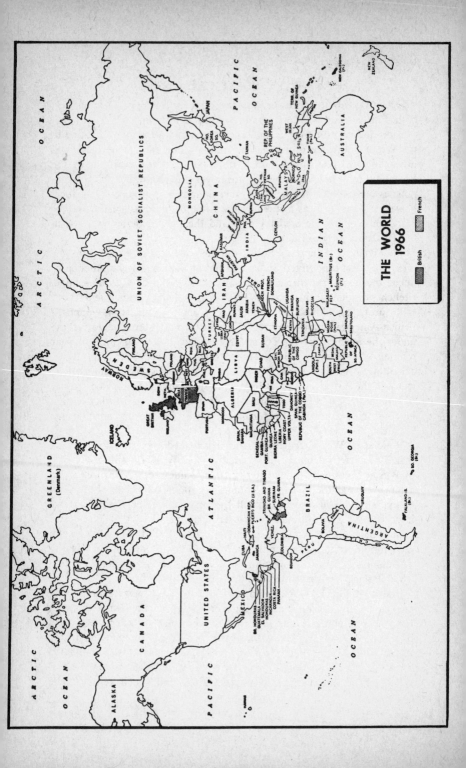

THE WORLD
1966

British French

armed services and the military bureaucracy were dismantled. A new constitution (May 1967) made the Diet representative of the popular will and transformed the emperor into a constitutional monarch. Land ownership was broadened, women were accorded legal equality with men, and compulsory education requirements were lengthened from six to nine years. Because of its dependent status, Japan maintained a low profile in foreign affairs.

With the Communist triumph in the Chinese Civil War (1949) and the outbreak of the Korean War (1950), internal reforms ceased to be the principal concern of American authorities. Instead, Japan became vital to U.S. strategic interests in Asia as a potential ally. With American encouragement, Japanese officials placed tighter controls on leftist movements; some previously purged conservatives were given back their political rights, and a security force was created under a plan of limited rearmament. A peace treaty of 1951 was accompanied by a United States–Japan security treaty that allowed the United States to maintain military bases in Japan for an indefinite period. Within the government, opposition Socialists, who were both anti-American and antimilitarist, resisted rearmament efforts and prospects that atomic bombs would be placed on Japanese soil.

Meanwhile, a sustained economic revival bred confidence in Japanese leaders. By the 1970s, Japan was producing as much as the rest of Asia combined, and its gross national product was the world's third largest, behind the United States and the Soviet Union. Newer markets were found in Africa and the Middle East as Western countries limited their Japanese imports. Compared with advanced Western countries, the Japanese standard of living became the highest in the East. Deep divisions remained regarding the use of this national power on the world stage. Most Japanese supported the continuance of the American alliance, but others, reluctant to remain closely identified with a cold war leader, favored participation in a neutralist Afro-Asian bloc. Socialists, Communists, and Nationalists supported a weakening of the American alliance and cited U.S. efforts to forge closer relationships with China and Russia as indications that Japan should chart a more independent course in foreign affairs.

The Eastern Alliance. Stalin's death in 1953 had a decisive impact on evolving relations among Communist-bloc countries. His policies of internal tyranny both in the Soviet Union and in satellite areas produced widespread, though repressed, bitterness against Communist rule. At Stalin's death, the Soviet Union was left isolated by his antagonistic foreign policies toward non-Communist countries. To improve the situation, Stalin's successors instituted a program of destalinization by emphasizing greater intellectual freedom and consumer production at home. They made Soviet foreign policies more flexible by stressing that Communist goals could be achieved through peaceful coexistence. Liberalization of Soviet policies and the desire for additional reform led to disunity within the Communist bloc. Major but unsuccessful uprisings occurred in East Germany (1953), Poland and Hungary (1956), and Czechoslovakia (1968).

The most far-reaching rift in the East was the one that developed between the Soviet Union and China, the two giants of the Communist world. Territorial disputes have affected relations between the two since the eighteenth century. The Chinese Communists have always been more independent of the Soviet Union than have the European satellites, since they led and controlled the movement that brought them to power in 1949. Stalin's death, moreover, removed the only Soviet leader to whom Mao Tse-tung was willing to defer. Arguments over destalinization were the catalysts that led to the break. Feeling the need to maintain rigid political and economic controls, the Chinese Communists opposed liberalization of domestic policies by the Soviet leaders who succeeded Stalin. They also rejected the policy of coexistence, interpreting growing Soviet military parity with the West as a basis for accelerated aggression instead. Sino-Soviet rivalry for allegiances of other Communist parties and nations and for support of aligned countries produced two major centers within the Communist world. Accordingly, the simplicity and totality of Marxist ideology seems to have been permanently impaired. Furthermore, Chinese militancy often forced the Soviets to take more aggressive positions, thus increasing world tensions and instability.

19

Major Powers of Western Europe since World War II

In 1945, large segments of Europe were desolate, mutilated wastelands. Except for Britain and several neutral states, all countries had endured the traumas of invasion and occupation. Many cities were in ruins, and immense tracts of previously arable land lay barren in the countryside. With bridges destroyed and railways and roads impassable, transportation and communications networks were in disarray. Industry was paralyzed, since most factories had either been destroyed or damaged. Machinery, raw materials, and fuel were in short supply. Hunger was widespread, with starvations occurring in some places. Surviving populations included disproportionate numbers of the sick, the crippled, the aged, women, and children. Over 30 million people had been killed in the war, including the 6 million who died in concentration camps; more than 15 million of these were Europeans. Millions more had been uprooted from their homes, many as refugees, others as forced laborers for the Nazis. Massive population shifts continued after the war, as displaced groups returned to their own or friendly countries. Governments were thus faced with monumental tasks requiring astronomical expenditures that far exceeded their incomes.

Initial steps to cope with these overwhelming problems were taken by the United Nations Relief and Rehabilitation Administration (UNRRA), which distributed food and supplies, and the European governments themselves, who added to their wartime indebtedness by negotiating additional loans from the United States. Recognizing the inadequacy of these piecemeal and uncoordinated efforts, the United States in 1947 launched the Marshall Plan, a long-range recovery program designed to restore Europe's economic health. Between 1948 and 1952, the United States supplied European nations with goods and credit totaling more than 17 billion dollars. At the same time, Europeans combined American aid with their own political and economic inventiveness. Their concern about European states being placed in a secondary role was heightened in 1949 by announcements that the Soviet Union had joined the United States as an atomic power by detonating its first atomic bomb. A campaign for European integration led first to the European Coal and Steel Community (1952) and later to the more ambitious Common Market (1957). Population increases further sparked economic recovery. By 1955, all nations participating in the Marshall Plan were exceeding their prewar levels of production. Government spending in education and social services, combined with rising employment and health standards, were added supports to the unprecedented prosperity. In the quarter of a century after World War II, therefore, the states of Western Europe experienced a remarkable revival. While the economic growth of any single European country was dwarfed in comparison with production in either the United States or the Soviet Union, Europe as a whole more than tripled its imports, industrial production, and wealth compared with 1939 levels.

GREAT BRITAIN

In December 1944, the Labour party, led by Clement Attlee, announced its intentions to dissolve the wartime coalition and urged that a general election be held as soon as the international situation permitted. Following the defeat of Germany, and in deference to Labour's wishes, Prime Minister Winston Churchill scheduled elections for July 1945. By the end of the war, there was a national consensus that the equalitarian programs inaugurated under the trials of battle should be translated into a peacetime social revolution. Both Conservative and Labour parties, therefore, presented platforms advocating social reform. The Labour party was best suited to profit from this sentiment, since it was historically committed to reform above all. Labour leaders had further cultivated widespread popular support by the key domestic positions they held during the war. Nevertheless, the results were surprising. The Labour party won 393 seats to 216 for Churchill's Conservatives, and the Liberal party returned 12 deputies.

ICELAND

NORWEGIAN SEA

Faeroe Is.

Shetland Is.

Orkney Is.

N. IRELAND

IRELAND

GREAT BRITAIN

NORTH SEA

ATLANTIC OCEAN

NORWAY

SWEDEN

FINLAND

G. of Bothnia

DENMARK

Baltic Sea

NETH.

FED.

BELG.

LUX.

REP.

GER.

GER. DEM. REP.

POLAND

CZECHOSLOVAKIA

UNION OF SOVIET

SOCIALIST REPUBLICS

FRANCE

SWITZ.

AUSTRIA

HUNGARY

RUMANIA

YUGOSLAVIA

BULGARIA

BLACK SEA

PORTUGAL

SPAIN

Corsica

ITALY

Adriatic Sea

ALB.

GREECE

TURKEY

Sicily

Malta

Crete

Rhodes

Cyprus

MEDITERRANEAN SEA

Kotschar

EUROPE—1955

NATO Countries   Soviet Satellites

Clement Attlee became the new prime minister. For the first time, Labourites had received a decisive majority in the House of Commons, allowing them to assume office and implement their popular mandate without being obstructed by commitments to another party. At the beginning of Labour's rule, the enthusiasm for reform pushed economic problems into the background. However, from the beginning of 1947 until the end of the Labour ministry in 1951, the overwhelming economic problems made austerity measures the first priority.

Social Reform. In 1946 and 1947, the Labour government enacted unparalleled social and economic legislation, including three revolutionary nationalization bills. The Bank of England was nationalized in February 1946. Soon thereafter, the Coal Industry Nationalization Bill transferred ownership of coal production from private to public ownership. The Inland Transport Act, a third landmark measure, extended governmental management over all forms of inland transportation, including railroads, roads, canals, and harbor facilities. Additional legislation increased state control over industries the government already regulated in part, including aviation, overseas communications, and electric power. These extensions of the public realm placed nearly one-fourth of British workers on the public payroll by 1948. The Labour party also kept its promise to reform and extend the nation's welfare system. Attlee's cabinet formulated programs that made state assistance a reality from birth to death. The crowning achievement of the system was a single national insurance scheme that combined different employment, pension, and sickness insurance plans. The government also inaugurated a single state-directed fund to provide compulsory insurance against industrial accidents. In 1948, another important step was taken when two particularly controversial measures were enacted. The National Assistance Act ensured minimum standards of living for all citizens; the National Health Service Act nationalized hospitals and substituted government compensation for the private sale of medical services.

Economic and Financial Problems. During World War II, the lend-lease program was a central factor in the maintenance of Britain's war effort. In August 1945, one week after the surrender of Japan, the American government's abrupt termination of this program precipitated an immediate financial crisis. Although Lord Keynes, the treasury's chief adviser, was able to negotiate a 4-million-dollar loan from the United States, severe conditions were attached. Britain could not use the funds to reduce its debts to other countries. In addition, Britain was required to end its trade preferences and eliminate all currency restrictions on the movement of trade. Because of Britain's weakened trade position, its heavy foreign debt was difficult to liquidate. With the flow of international trade disrupted and many of its former customers lost, Britain was forced into dependence upon an unfavorable trade relationship with the United States in which imports constantly exceeded exports. Domestic problems complicated the picture. During the harsh winter of 1946–1947, coal productivity was far below industrial and public demand. Fuel shortages forced the closing of many industries, creating widespread unemployment. Persisting shortages of food, clothing, building materials, and other items compelled the government to maintain the wartime system of rationing.

In the meantime, financial woes were becoming overwhelming. Continued excesses of imports over exports confronted the government with a dollar deficit that undermined international confidence in Britain's solvency. Attempting to fulfill the terms of the 1945 American loan, the United Kingdom, beginning in July 1947, made the pound freely convertible into dollars. British creditors immediately opted for the sounder dollar, thus deepening the existing British deficit. To avert a catastrophe, the government reduced imports and tourist spending, made rationing more restrictive, encouraged increased domestic production, and in August 1947, suspended the convertibility of British currency into dollars even though this act required a suspension of the American loan. Combined with the beginning of Marshall Plan assistance in 1948, these moves brightened the picture temporarily. But by 1949, trade conditions had worsened, reducing gold and dollar reserves to dangerous levels. To expand the market for British exports, Sir Stafford Cripps, chancellor of the exchequer, announced a devaluation in the pound from $4.03 to $2.80. This measure, along with recovery in other countries, produced a sudden growth in British exports. Nevertheless, economic problems had seriously impaired the early optimism among Labour leaders and public confidence in Labour rule, and by the summer of 1948, the most fertile period of Attlee's stewardship had passed.

End of Labour Rule. The last major reform of Attlee's administration was a bill introduced in 1948 to nationalize the steel industry. Compared with the coal industry, which had been nationalized earlier, steel enterprises operated much more profitably and efficiently, and Conservatives therefore were moved to launch a full-scale attack upon the Labour proposal. Having anticipated rejection of the measure by the House of Lords, Labour leaders had already introduced a bill designed to lessen further the upper chamber's constitutional power over legislation. Effective in December 1949, the House of Lord's two-year suspensory power over all acts except money bills, established by the Parliament Act of 1911, was reduced to one. Meanwhile, Labour leaders agreed to postpone the effective date for the transfer of the steel industry until 1951 if the Lords would approve the measure. Under this compromise, the Steel Nationalization Bill became law in November 1949. At the same time, Conservatives promised to reverse the legislation if they were returned to office. Growing disillusionment with a divided Labour party eventually gave the Conservatives their chance. First, Labour's majority was reduced to six in the elections of 1950. A year and a half later, with economic and foreign problems mounting, Attlee decided to seek a new mandate from voters. In the elections of October 1951, Conservatives won 321 seats to 295 for the Labourites. Churchill once again became prime minister as Conservatives began their tenure of thirteen years in power.

Churchill's Second Administration. The second Churchill era (1951–1955) was highlighted by years of peace and a return to prosperity. Since Conservatives accepted in principle the need for increased state control and social planning, they made no effort to overthrow the Labour party's reforms. The government moved only to fulfill its limited objectives of denationalizing steel and inland transport. An economic crisis of 1951–1952, brought about by rising inflation and balance of payment problems, was met with reductions in imports, restrictions on credit, government economies, and incentives for production. By 1953, a period of prolonged economic prosperity had arrived, characterized by improvements in trade, rising employment, and record levels of production and consumption. These favorable conditions allowed the government to end the rationing of food as well as many other wartime controls over the economy. By 1955, Conservatives had recovered their self-confidence while regaining large numbers of middle-class supporters who had previously deserted them for the Labour party. In this setting, an aging Winston Churchill announced his retirement. He was replaced as Conservative leader and premier by Sir Anthony Eden. Hoping to expand his slim majority and rule as his own master, Eden scheduled new parliamentary elections for the following month. Voters were obviously attracted by the ability of Conservatives to identify themselves with economic prosperity, which was achieved simultaneously with the loosening of wartime and postwar regimentation. Election results secured the Conservative party's rule by augmenting its parliamentary total to 345, while Labour's representation was reduced to 277.

Eden, Suez, and Macmillan. During the summer of 1955, Eden's cabinet was faced with a deficit in the balance of payments. To restore confidence in the British economy, R. A. Butler, who continued as chancellor of the exchequer, adopted measures to encourage savings and private investment, limit capital expenditures by the government, and raise some taxation levels. In the summer and fall of 1956, Eden was faced with the Suez crisis (see pp. 254–255, 314), one of the most difficult episodes in Britain's postwar foreign relations. Since the canal served as a route to India and Australia and also as a growing avenue for oil, the British strongly resisted Nasser's attempt to nationalize it. They were supported by the French, who wanted to protect the rights of the French-controlled Canal Company and also to overthrow Nasser, whom they blamed for the 1954 revolt in Algeria. After coordinating military policies with Israel, Britain and France moved in the last week of October to eliminate Egypt's control of the canal. By November, the plan had been thwarted as a result of opposition from the United Nations and the United States, combined with resistance in the British Parliament by both Labourites and some Conservatives. Eden's health weakened as the crisis lengthened, forcing him to retire in 1957. Although Butler made determined efforts to buttress his claims to party leadership, the Conservative majority made Harold Macmillan premier.

The Macmillan Years. Britain's domestic development and foreign relations during Macmillan's tenure (1957–1963) were heavily influenced by its ambivalent attitude toward the European Common Market (see pp. 257–258, 272, 277–278). With strong links to Commonwealth countries, and suspicious of the political unity that some supporters of the Common Market envisaged, Macmillan decided not to apply for membership when the Market was inaugurated. But while the nations of Western Europe prospered during the late 1950s, Britain's economic growth lagged behind that of other industrial countries. Thus, in 1961, Macmillan announced Britain's application for membership in the Market, only to have his request denied in 1963 by French President Charles de Gaulle. This blow, when added to President Kennedy's decision to cancel plans for the Skybolt missiles, upon which Britain was working to develop a nuclear striking capacity, considerably undermined Britain's international prestige. Having undergone a major operation, Macmillan decided to resign the premiership in October 1963. After an internal struggle within the party, Sir Alec Douglas-Home renounced his peerage and became the new premier.

Conservative Problems. The new prime minister inherited a party that had led Britain away from postwar austerities to rising standards of living and fuller employment; yet, troublesome problems remained. The growth rate for British industry continued to be one of the lowest in Western Europe. A widening trade gap was again threatening the nation with its persistent balance of payments problems. In 1963, Conservative leaders also faced a scandal that rocked both the party and the government. John Profumo, the war minister in Macmillan's cabinet, became involved with a call girl who had also associated with a Soviet naval attaché suspected of being a spy. Although an investigation into the matter concluded that no classified information had been leaked, the admission of misconduct by a Conservative cabinet minister damaged the party during the next elections.

Election Trends: 1964, 1966, 1970, and 1974.   In the elections of 1964, British voters showed their ambivalence toward either removing the Conservatives from power or returning the reins of leadership to the Labourites. Harold Wilson, a professional economist and successor to Hugh Gaitskell as Labour's spokesman, led the opposition to Conservative rule. With 630 seats at stake, the Labour party emerged with 317 seats in the House of Commons, providing them with a paper-thin majority of four. Conservatives returned 304 deputies, down 56 from their previous total, and the Liberal party's candidates won in nine constituencies. After serving seventeen months with this precarious majority, which required him to pursue cautious programs, Wilson scheduled new elections for March 1966. Conservatives were led in the election campaign by Edward Heath, who had replaced Sir Alec Douglas-Home at the party helm. Voters chose between Wilson's adept handling of the government under difficult circumstances and Heath's unsuccessful efforts to discredit the Labour ministry on major issues. Wilson was victorious, increasing Labour's majority to a commanding margin of 97 seats. Labourites were thus able to act decisively on the country's pressing economic problems. The pound sterling was under periodic speculative attack; the large deficit in the nation's balance of payments continued; and wages and prices were rising disproportionately to levels of production.

In attacking these problems, the Wilson cabinet adopted severe measures of retrenchment, including wage and price freezes, devaluation of the pound, and heavy taxes. These policies reversed the nation's balance of payments deficit, producing a surplus of $1.45 billion in 1969–1970. Inflationary pressures were also loosened, encouraging the government to make the popular decision of relaxing curbs on wages. Heartened by these trends and by polls indicating that a large majority of the electorate favored Labourites over Conservatives, Prime Minister Wilson scheduled parliamentary elections for June 1970. During the campaign, the issue of nonwhite immigration was raised by Conservative deputy Enoch Powell, who predicted high levels of violence unless more restrictive immigration laws were adopted. Previous acts had reversed Britain's traditional policy of uncontrolled entry by requiring immigrants to have labor permits (1962) and substantial connections with Britain (1968). Dissatisfied with the continuing immigration from the West Indies, India, Pakistan, and also by Asians from Kenya, Powell recommended the extreme step of repatriating immigrants. Conservatives refused to publicly disown Powell's statements for fear of provoking a split within their party. The election results were the most surprising in modern British history, comparable with Truman's 1948 victory in the United States. Despite all predictions to the contrary, the Conservative party under Heath accumulated a margin of 43 seats over Labourites. To a considerable degree, Labour lost the election because many of its supporters were too certain of victory and simply decided to stay home.

During the winter of 1973–1974, the Heath ministry was undermined by the twin pressures of the Arab oil boycott and successive work slowdowns of electrical engineers, coal miners, and electrical workers who bidded for wage boosts higher than the 13 percent permitted by the government. Over 750,000 people were placed on the dole as dwindling coal reserves led to widespread unemployment and a three-day workweek. A strike by militant coal miners (February 1974) intensified political and economic pressures. Elections held later in the month failed to provide either Wilson's Labour party or Heath's incumbent Tories with a majority in Parliament. Harold Wilson, who returned as leader of a minority government, was compelled to pursue cautious policies since Labour won only 301 of the Commons's 635 seats, with the Tories returning 296 deputies, a revived Liberal party 14, and other parties 21. With new elections (October 1974) giving the Wilson ministry a majority of only 3, the nation's intractable economic problems were posing serious threats to its democratic traditions. The prime minister promised to fulfill Labour's campaign promises of nationalizing the shipbuilding and aircraft industries, placing potential sites for housing under government control, and purchasing 51 percent of the stock in companies drilling for oil in Britain's offshore reserves. Labour's narrow mandate was a major barrier to the enactment of these pledges.

Britain's Declining World Role. Under the Labour governments headed by Harold Wilson and the Conservative ministry of Edward

Heath, Britain's secondary role in world affairs became dramatically evident. While France was opting for world leadership, Britain was adjusting to a small-power status that assumed greater dependence upon the United States. The overriding problems were economic, as a chronic trade deficit was accompanied by high levels of inflation and unemployment, and recurring financial crises. Austerity measures sponsored by the first Wilson cabinet, including devaluation of the pound, retrenchments, and higher taxes, were more effective as palliatives than cures. Britain's Conservative government placed primary emphasis on another approach: reshaping the cradle-to-grave concept of Britain's welfare system by reducing the role of government and enlarging individual initiative in economic matters. Tax cuts for businesses and families were combined with rent increases in low-cost housing and reductions in the amounts spent for health services, school meals, and other social measures. In January 1973, Britain entered the European Common Market.

FRANCE

From August 25, 1944, when General Charles de Gaulle arrived in Paris, until the election of the Constituent Assembly in October 1945, France was ruled by a provisional government in which de Gaulle, by popular consent, exercised dictatorial authority. Elections to the Assembly demonstrated the predominantly reformist sentiment in politics. Two-thirds of the ballots favored parties on the Left. The Communist party, profiting from its role in the resistance, gathered 27 percent of the votes. The newly organized and reform-minded *Mouvement Republicain Populaire* (MRP), formed around Georges Bidault, a resistance leader, captured 25 percent. In third place with 24 percent was the revived Socialist party, led by Léon Blum. The Constituent Assembly immediately confirmed de Gaulle in power as it began deliberations over a permanent constitutional structure. Although representatives of all major parties were passionately committed to change, the shape of the projected regime became a matter of sharp controversy. Some spokesmen, including de Gaulle, favored a strong executive, while others, notably Communists, advocated the maximum power of a one-house assembly. The first constitutional draft, which concentrated considerable power in the National Legislature, was defeated by voters in May 1946 after MRP leaders had campaigned against it. In the second Constituent Assembly chosen in June, MRP delegates emerged as the largest party. Voters ratified the draft of this Assembly at a referendum held in October 1946. The new constitution provided for two popularly elected chambers of parliament with most power concentrated in the lower house, the National Assembly. Both houses were responsible for choosing a president to serve for a seven-year term.

From Tripartism to the Third Force. During elections to the two constituent assemblies and the first regular elections held under the new constitution, the Communists, the MRP, and the Socialists continued to be the dominant governing forces. The more conservative Radicals and Catholic Moderates organized in opposition to this tripartite rule. Despite all efforts to reform French politics, old habits and practices soon returned. The Fourth Republic, like the Third, was dominated by a shifting multiparty system that produced the usual cabinet instability. The political trend was toward the Right. After Communists were ejected from the governing coalition in 1947 and the Socialists departed in 1951, the Radicals, the MRP, and the Moderates constituted the governing majority, which became known as the third force in French politics. Socialists and Communists remained strong on the Left, and Gaullists and Poujadists were periodically influential on the Right. The trend toward the Right continued during the early 1950s among the third force parties, allowing the Moderates to exercise a more significant role. Although Socialists returned as a fourth member of the coalition after the elections of 1956, the balance of power remained in the hands of Conservatives.

Gaullism. De Gaulle's provisional powers as head of government were confirmed by the first Constituent Assembly when it met in December 1945. He was unable, however, to persuade the Assembly's majority that the cabinet should govern without legislative interference. For this reason, de Gaulle abruptly resigned and announced his retirement from politics in January 1946. He emerged from retirement briefly in June 1946 to denounce the second constitutional draft and by spring of 1947 had decided to reenter political life. In that year, he formed the *Rassemblement du Peuple Français* (RPF), designed to appeal to Frenchmen of diverse political leanings. Since Socialists and MRP leaders quickly adopted a negative attitude toward the RPF's antiparliamentary overtones, de Gaulle's new organization attracted adherents almost exclusively from the right. Although the RPF returned more than 100 seats in the election of 1951, the movement soon waned in influence due to divisions among its deputies. Discouraged with its results, de Gaulle disowned the RPF in 1953. In or out of office, de Gaulle remained a factor in French politics. A small minority in the government continued to identify themselves as Gaullists, while large numbers of Frenchmen were naturally attracted to his strong leadership in times of crisis.

Mendès-France and Poujadism.   Pierre Poujade was a small shopkeeper who gained prominence by organizing merchants to evade government taxes. These successes encouraged him to enter the political arena. Holding that the ruling parties of the Fourth Republic cared little for the lower middle class, the Poujadists also opposed the efforts of Pierre Mendès-France, a leader of the Radical party, to reform both the French Empire and the domestic economy. Mendès-France had acquired power after France lost the battle of Dien Bien Phu in 1954. By negotiating an armistice, he helped to end France's disastrous involvement in Indochina (see pp. 252, 313). By granting the initial steps leading to statehood, he also helped obviate wars of independence in Tunisia and Morocco. However, his efforts to follow his foreign successes with economic reform were met with a storm of opposition that overthrew his ministry early in 1955. In this setting, the Poujadists formed a national party and campaigned in the 1956 elections. Although they won a surprising total of fifty seats, Poujade's ineffectual leadership and the internal squabbling among his followers produced a rapid decline in the movement. Poujade's right-wing protest movement against republican politics was formed as de Gaulle's RPF faded. Like Gaullism before it, Poujadism provided an outlet for persisting authoritarian sentiments in France.

Algeria and the Return of de Gaulle.   The crisis that eventually sounded the death knell of the Fourth Republic and returned de Gaulle to power had its roots in Algeria. Unlike Tunisia and Morocco, which had been granted a large degree of independence in 1955, Algeria was hindered in its path to independence by the presence of a million colons, European settlers many of whose families had lived in Algeria for several generations. Determined to achieve complete independence, native nationalists formed a small guerrilla army, whose acts of terrorism and violence beginning in 1954 were countered by the presence of sizable French forces. Matters were brought to a climax in 1958, when diverse groups of discontented Europeans in Algeria heard rumors that Pierre Pflimlin, an MRP deputy chosen as the new premier, favored concessions to the nationalists. Determined to keep Algeria French, right-wing colons and army leaders staged a massive and riotous demonstration in Algiers on May 13. After occupying government offices, insurgents organized the revolutionary Committee of Public Safety, but their leaders were badly divided. Some were anti-Gaullists who favored steps to carry the revolution to France proper;

others were devoted Gaullists interested in transforming the Fourth Republic by securing de Gaulle's return to power. This latter group acquired control within the Committee of Public Safety and pressed for a peaceful transfer of power. With France threatened by civil war, de Gaulle's return as premier was recommended by President René Coty and approved by the National Assembly, allowing him to assume office in June 1958.

The Fifth Republic. After voting de Gaulle full legislative and constituent powers for six months, the National Assembly disbanded. Within two months, de Gaulle and his advisers completed their draft of a constitution for the proposed Fifth Republic. Based on republican principles, the document provided for popular election of the Senate and Assembly and for an independent judiciary. At the same time, the Gaullist constitution established a powerful new executive branch that dominated the government. To choose the president of the republic, who possessed wide discretionary powers, a special electoral college was created, consisting of parliamentary deputies in addition to other governmental representatives in metropolitan and overseas areas. To reduce the legislative role in policymaking as well as ministerial instability, the prime minister and his cabinet were given a higher degree of autonomy. By referendum, voters in France, Algeria, and all parts of the French Union except Guinea and West Africa overwhelmingly approved the new constitution. Upon assuming office as president, de Gaulle's most urgent problem was to find a settlement for the Algerian imbroglio. In 1959, he offered a program of independence to Algerian nationalists, a step that provoked extremists to make several attempts on his life. Algerian independence was finally achieved in 1962.

Consolidation of de Gaulle's Power. Much of the opposition to de Gaulle waned after his settlement of the Algerian dilemma. His position was further strengthened by a referendum approving his proposal to change the mode of presidential succession (October 1962) and in new legislative elections held the following month. By now, de Gaulle had become concerned that the electoral college might not in the future select a president who was divorced from politics as usual. Deciding that direct popular election of the president was a more suitable alternative, he directed Prime Minister Georges Pompidou to propose a constitutional amendment incorporating this change. Deputies in the National Assembly were shocked both by the proposal and by Pompidou's tactic of submitting the matter to a direct popular vote, which violated the amending procedure indicated in the constitution. When dissidents in the Assembly united to overthrow Pompidou, de Gaulle responded by dissolving the legislature and scheduling new elections. The electorate was then allowed to cast two ballots in rapid succession, both indicating their assessment of de Gaulle's leadership. In the referendum held on the constitutional amendment, voters approved the proposed change, though only by a slight majority. In the legislative elections, however, de Gaulle's party, *Union pour la Nouvelle République* (UNR), scored an impressive triumph that made it master of the assembly.

Shifting Political Alliances.   In the 1958 legislative elections, de Gaulle's personality and the new constitutional system produced significant changes in the alignment of parties. A descendant of the Gaullist Fourth Republic organization, the newly organized UNR won an impressive number of popular votes and returned 212 deputies. Since de Gaulle disavowed active control of the party, attempting to remain as an arbiter above politics, the UNR's leadership was divided on the one hand between a moderate faction headed by Albin Chalandon and Jacques Chaban-Delmas, and on the other by an extreme nationalist group whose spokesmen were Jacques Soustelle and Léon Delbecque. Profiting from the conservative trend, an enlarged Independent party returned 117 deputies. Led by Roger Duchet, a former Radical, Independents closely allied themselves with the UNR, providing some cohesion among the conservative forces in parliament.

Heavily identified with the discredited Fourth Republic, the Left meanwhile was seriously weakened and fragmented. Suffering severely was the once powerful Radical party whose strength was decreased by half to forty. Representation of Socialists was similarly reduced, but their future was brighter, primarily because of the astute leadership of Guy Mollet, who identified French socialism with the rising nationalist tide. Like Socialists, the Christian Democrats (MRP), under the direction of Pierre Pflimlin, supported de Gaulle. They returned fifty-six deputies while maintaining their usual 10 percent of the popular vote. The most dramatic defeat was that of the unusually strong Communist party headed by Maurice Thorez. Adamantly resisting de Gaulle's return to power, the Communists lost 95 percent of their legislative seats, reducing their total from 145 to 10. However, the Communists remained well organized and regained their usual 25 percent of the popular vote in municipal elections held during 1959.

Economy.   France experienced notable economic growth after World War II. The vision of renovation that the resistance movement encouraged proved a springboard of change in economic matters as in other areas. Rising productivity in France was further promoted by the economic revival throughout Western Europe. The massive infusion of Marshall Plan and the steps taken toward European integration were the forces that sparked this recovery. Buttressed by a population increase that governmental tax policies stimulated, the rate of industrial growth during the 1950s exceeded all prewar levels. Unprecedented peacetime innovations of governmental planning, which encouraged modernist trends, reduced considerably the range of private decision making in economic matters. Influenced by wartime necessities and the Soviet example, a planning commission, headed by economist Jean Monnet, was created in 1946. This group formulated four-year plans, which directed investment funds and resources into priority areas. In the private sector, meanwhile, many businessmen departed from their traditional ways and joined the quest for the higher levels of productivity that Marshall Plan advisers were encouraging. The most dynamic regions of France were located in the northeast, whereas many areas in the south remained more traditional and less enterprising. As a result of progressive trends throughout the Fourth and Fifth Republics, the gulf between traditional and modernized France widened considerably.

De Gaulle's Third Force.   De Gaulle's principal ambition on the postwar world stage was to alter the balance of power held between the United States and the Soviet Union. More specifically, his goal was to transform Europe into a third force that could deal independently with the Soviets and serve as arbiter between East and West. The French leader's forceful enunciation of these views beginning in 1963 had an unsettling effect in Western capitals. De Gaulle simultaneously blocked British bids to enter the Common Market, rejected American offers to share Polaris missiles with France, and obstructed efforts to pool Western Europe's nuclear strength in NATO. In support of his actions, he argued that because of close Anglo-American ties, Britain's participation in the Common Market would open the Continent to domination by the United States and that Europe needed its own atomic deterrent because in a showdown, the United States could not be trusted to risk its cities if Paris or Bonn were threatened. To further dramatize his rejection of American influence in France and leadership of Europe, de Gaulle ordered restrictions on the influx of American capital and the withdrawal of France from NATO's integrated military command.

The Gaullist Era.   General Charles de Gaulle served as president of France for ten years (1959–1969). Among his momentous decisions were the granting of independence to Algeria; constitutional reform, in particular popular election of the president; the development of a French nuclear deterrent; withdrawal of France from NATO; and consistent rejections of Britain's application for entrance into the Common Market. De Gaulle managed to survive a succession of perilous crises, including student riots and strikes that came close to overthrowing his regime during the spring of 1968. Not only did de Gaulle endure; after the disorders, he also led his party to the largest parliamentary majority of any party in French history. Following the victory, the authoritarian and towering president committed several critical political blunders. First, without explanation, he fired Georges Pompidou, premier since 1962, whose cool handling of the upheavals in 1968 had convinced many Frenchmen of his ability to succeed de Gaulle as president. Then in April 1969, de Gaulle arbitrarily based his political future on a minor referendum, which he lost. In an anticlimatic exit, de Gaulle kept his promise by resigning the presidency of France and retiring from politics. He died the following year.

Georges Pompidou. Georges Pompidou, a former teacher and banker, succeeded de Gaulle as president of France (1969–1974). Lacking de Gaulle's imperial style, he provided France with a decidedly lower and more conciliatory profile on the world stage. France ended its resistance to Britain's entrance into the Common Market. Close collaboration with West Germany and a more compromising spirit toward the United States further served to renew hopes of a strengthened Atlantic community. In contrast with de Gaulle, Pompidou's foreign policies precluded major pronouncements on burning international questions, such as Vietnam, or involvement in areas where French interests were peripheral, such as Latin America or Canada. A greater degree of neutrality pervaded French support to Arabs in their rivalry with Israel. Domestic priorities included preserving unity within the large Gaullist majority and resisting the revived Communist party. Following Pompidou's death, Finance Minister Valéry Giscard d'Estaing won the presidency by a narrow margin over François Mitterand, candidate of the united Left (May 1974). With a clear mandate for social and economic reform, d'Estaing fashioned a so-called new majority in the National Assembly, consisting of his own Independent Republicans, Centrists, and Liberal Gaullists.

WEST GERMANY

By the end of 1945, based on Allied agreements at Potsdam, the Soviet Union was transferring to Poland administration of those German areas to the east of a line formed by the Oder and western Neisse rivers. Other concords, formulated during 1944 and 1945, were applied to the rest of Germany as the war ended. The victorious powers—Britain, France, the United States, and the Soviet Union—separated Germany into four occupation zones; Berlin, located deep within the Soviet zone, was similarly divided. Supreme authority was placed in the Allied Control Council located in Berlin and composed of the four commanders in chief of the occupying powers. All decisions of the council required a unanimous vote. The purposes of occupation as defined at Potsdam were denazification, demilitarization, and democratization of the German people and state. It soon became evident that the powers interpreted the occupation agreements differently. Principal discords produced two trends: steps by the United States, Britain, and France to integrate the Western zones into a single economic and political unit and measures by the Soviet Union to place East Germany entirely under its domination. In 1949, the creation of the German Federal Republic (West Germany) and the German Democratic Republic (East Germany) resulted from these diverging trends.

Nuremberg Trials. An international military tribunal was authorized to bring Germany's wartime leaders to trial on several counts: conspiring to wage wars of aggression, planning or engaging in wars of aggression, violations of the rules and customs of war, and crimes against humanity. The court, which met from November 1945 to October 1946, was composed of jurists from the Allied powers. Several top Nazi leaders were absent. Hitler, Goebbels, and Himmler had committed suicide, and Martin Bormann, who could not be found, was tried in absentia. Among the twenty-one defendants were Hermann Göring, Joachim von Ribbentrop, Generals Wilhelm Keitel and Alfred Jodl, Hjalmar Schacht, and Albert Speer. Three were acquitted, three sentenced to life imprisonment, four to lesser terms of imprisonment, and eleven to death by hanging. Also adjudged criminal were several Nazi organizations: the Nazi party, the SS, the SD (security police), and the Gestapo. Controversial since their inception, the trials have been praised as constructive steps of denazification and warnings to potential aggressors; they have also been condemned as the vindictive retribution of victors over the vanquished.

Structure of the West German Government. In 1945, the British and Americans began organizing local and state governments within their zones. Under the supervision of military authorities, minister-presidents and parliaments for the individual states were chosen. Within the British-American bizone, a general government, consisting of the Council of States, was formed. In 1948, the French subdued their fears of a German revival and added their region to this zone. Thereafter, representatives of the state legislatures from the Western zones met in Bonn to formulate a Basic Law for West Germany. The authority of the Bonn government was limited by an Occupation Statute, allowing the Allies to maintain control over disarmament, demilitarization of the Ruhr, enforcement of the Basic Law, foreign affairs, and reparations. The Basic Law, approved in May 1949, created two houses of parliament: The Bundesrat (upper house) represented the states, and the Bundestag (lower house) was popularly elected. The authority of the chancellor and his cabinet depended upon a majority vote of the Bundestag. To avoid the danger of a powerful executive, the Basic Law provided for a ceremonial president chosen indirectly by the legislature.

Political Parties. With nazism dishonored by the war and communism discredited by Russia's intransigence, Social Democrats and Christian Democrats emerged as the reigning parties in West Germany. Kurt Schumacher, who had spent twelve years in a concentration camp, was the Socialist spokesman. Christian Democrats were led by Konrad Adenauer, who after serving sixteen years as mayor of Cologne, had retired from political life when the Nazis came to power. Seventy-three years old in 1949, Adenauer was still energetic enough to dominate Germany's political life into the 1960s. In an election during August 1949, Christian Democrats won 139 seats to 131 for the Social Democrats. The Free Democrats, led by Theodor Heuss, returned 52 deputies. With no party possessing an absolute majority, Christian Democrats and Free Democrats formed a conservative coalition government. Adenauer was chosen chancellor by the bare margin of 202–201, and Heuss became the first president of the republic. Adenauer's position was strengthened by the 1953 and 1957 elections, which gave the Christian Democrats a majority of the legislative seats. Election results were again close in 1961, however, forcing Adenauer to reestablish his alliance with the Free Democrats.

Adenauer. Adenauer's position as chancellor represented a victory for the traditional and clerical forces in German society. Business barons, along with conservative Catholic and Protestant churchmen, combined with some liberals to constitute the prevailing force of the Christian Democrats. Although in theory his office was about the same as that of a premier in the French Fourth Republic, in practice Adenauer completely dominated the West German government. Within the cabinet, his arrogant and intimidating rule made most of his cabinet ministers highly positioned bureaucrats. Adenauer's position was aided by the fact that he was a Catholic in a state from which the principal Protestant territories had been separated and placed in the Russian sphere. He was also a clever negotiator, whose patience, persistence, and moderation helped restore Germany's world position. Realizing that conditions of the cold war made West Germany attractive as a partner of the Allies and in turn that Allied support was essential to the preservation of West Germany, Adenauer calculated that friendship with the West would eventually lead to a partnership on equal terms. His hostility to communism was buttressed both by his knowledge of Russian activities in East Germany and by his devout Catholic convictions.

Independence of the Federal Republic. Adenauer's success in establishing an attitude of mutual trust with Allied leaders soon bore fruit. In 1949, Allied commissioners permitted Germany to reestablish consulates in other countries, eliminated the limits on German industrial production, and ended the scuttling of German factories. To obtain these concessions, Adenauer, in a decision that was highly controversial at home, yielded to the creation of an International Ruhr Authority, thus removing the nation's strongest industrial region from German control. Domestic opposition waned, however, after the Schuman Plan in 1950 placed German and French coal and steel production under a single authority. Two years later, this arrangement was broadened through the European Coal and Steel Community to include Italy and the Benelux countries. A further step toward German independence was encouraged in 1950 when the outbreak of Korean hostilities (see pp. 251–252, 330) seemed to make German rearmament essential to the defense of Western Europe. Despite intense misgivings both in Germany and other places, by 1954, Adenauer and Western leaders had agreed upon a formula for Germany's remilitarization. A national army, prohibited from using atomic, bacteriological, or chemical weapons, was created under NATO command. Defense Minister Franz Joseph Strauss was an architect of this thoroughly democratized force. In 1955, the Saar basin issue was settled. Following a referendum in which the peoples of the region voted overwhelmingly to remain a part of Germany, France ended its control of the area, paving the way for its reunion with Germany.

Berlin. Disputes over Berlin culminated in recurring flare-ups in the cold war. Since the former capital was located entirely within the German Democratic Republic, Soviet leaders could instigate a crisis at any moment by obstructing Western access lines. Allied leaders, recognizing Berlin's role as an outpost of the East-West struggle, were determined to defend the city at high costs, even at the risk of war. Allied leaders resolved the first serious crisis, the blockade of 1948–1949, through an airlift of supplies to the Western zones of the city (see p. 250). Another serious situation developed during the summer of 1961. Confronted with a persisting and rising exodus of refugees from East to West Germany via Berlin, the Russians and the East Germans decided to erect a wall separating East and West Berlin. With few options except to risk general warfare, President Kennedy's administration decided against military action, while reasserting that the status of West Berlin would not be altered. More than twenty-five years after World War II, Willy Brandt's efforts to improve relations with the Communist states of Eastern Europe *(Ostpolitik)* finally provided the most encouraging sign for a resolution of recurring East-West problems over Berlin. In 1971, East Germany agreed to guarantee Western access rights and travel between West Berlin and East Germany. Implementation of these accords became effective with the Bundestag's approval of nonaggression pacts with Russia and Poland (see pp. 284–285).

Economy.   Despite the postwar chaos and the remaining German territorial divisions, the Federal Republic made unusual economic progress. The German qualities of efficiency and technical dexterity, which had placed the country in the forefront of industrialization before the war, speedily reasserted themselves. By the 1950s, the gross national product was exceeding prewar levels for all of Germany. An artificially bloated population, resulting from the migration of displaced persons east of the Oder-Niesse rivers, the Sudetenland, and other areas, provided West Germany with an abundance of skilled labor. Domestic and foreign demands sparked dramatic rises in consumption. Accelerated trade with the United States and the creation of the European Common Market expanded significantly the export of German goods as well as the sources of Germany's imports. In this trade, Germany enjoyed sizable surpluses, produced primarily by the attractiveness of its manufactured items abroad. Economics Minister Ludwig Erhard, Adenauer's rival for party leadership, was an engineer of this revival. Although Erhard was strongly devoted to principles of laissez-faire, large cartels continued to dominate Germany's economic life. In addition to financing a comprehensive welfare state, the widespread prosperity reduced class conflicts in the nation's political life. A notable result of this trend was the broadening of the Socialist party's appeal beyond the laboring classes.

Adenauer's Departure.   The Spiegel affair was the catalyst that led to

Adenauer's resignation. In 1962, *Der Spiegel* newsmagazine published an article blaming Defense Minister Strauss for the low ratings received by German troops in recent NATO exercises. The police thereupon raided *Der Spiegel* offices, attempting to uncover evidence to support a shallow and strange charge of treason against some of the magazine's editors. Confronted with a debacle of their own making, government officers persisted in compounding their errors. Strauss strongly denied his obvious involvement in the proceedings, and Adenauer boldly castigated the editor of the magazine. There was a vehement public reaction, particularly from the press and university professors and students. These pressures forced Strauss's dismissal from the defense ministry. Meanwhile, Adenauer's own party persuaded him to retire within a year under threats by the Free Democratic party to leave the governing coalition unless he did so. In October 1963, Ludwig Erhard replaced him as chancellor.

Ludwig Erhard. Erhard's accession brought no sudden policy changes for the West German government. Both Adenauer and Erhard were members of the Christian Democratic party; both favored close relations with the West and opposition to communism. However, significant new directions did evolve. Erhard was a stronger advocate of German-U.S. partnership at the partial expense of the close Franco-German unity that Adenauer and de Gaulle had forged. He was also friendlier to strengthening the European Common Market. On both questions he had to move cautiously to avoid offending both de Gaulle and the Adenauer wing of the Christian Democratic party. As economics minister, Erhard had been the major architect of the free market economy under which West Germany prospered, and continued prosperity proved to be the bulwark of his strength in the 1965 elections. The Christian Democrats returned an impressive total of 245 deputies to the Bundestag; the Social Democrats, led by West Berlin Mayor Willy Brandt, elected 202 deputies; and the Free Democrats won 49 seats.

Despite this triumph, serious challenges to Erhard's leadership soon developed as a split occurred between the Christian Democrats and the Free Democrats regarding ways to overcome a deficit in the federal budget. Erhard favored increased tax rates, whereas the Free Democrats, largely a party of big business, supported cuts in welfare programs instead. When Erhard refused to compromise, the Free Democrats withdrew their support from the governing coalition. Erhard was also hurt by rifts within his party and charges that he had been indecisive on major questions. (Konrad Adenauer coined Erhard's nickname, "rubber lion.") Under these circumstances, in October 1966, the Christian Democrats unceremoniously withdrew their support from Erhard. Kurt Georg Kiesinger, minister-president of the state of Baden-Württemberg, was chosen to replace him as chancellor. Kiesinger profited by strong support from Franz Joseph Strauss, leader of the Bavarian branch of the Christian Democratic party known as the Christian Social Union. Strauss became his economic minister.

Grand Coalition. Changes in leadership led to dramatic new directions in German politics as Christian Democrats turned toward the Left to form a coalition with the Social Democrats, providing the government with 447 out of 456 Bundestag votes. Willy Brandt became both vice-chancellor and foreign minister in this coalition. Brandt and Kiesinger moved forcefully to rekindle the Franco-German alliance and to extend the hand of friendship to East Germany and other Communist satellite countries. The coalition ended with the 1969 elections, in which a parliamentary majority again eluded both major parties. The Christian Democrats won 242 seats; the Social Democrats, 224; and the Free Democrats, 30. This time the Free Democrats, who had previously entered coalitions only with Christian Democrats, decided to ally themselves instead with the Social Democrats, and Willy Brandt became the new chancellor. For the first time in the Federal Republic, the Christian Democrats were out of power, and Socialists were at the helm of the government.

Willy Brandt. Once in office, Brandt began executing the diplomatic ideas that had evolved during his years as West Berlin's mayor and West Germany's foreign secretary. He attempted to implement a policy of *Ostpolitik,* designed to achieve a détente in Europe by boldly accepting postwar realities and establishing closer relations between the two halves of the Continent. Soon after he became chancellor, Brandt ended West Germany's hesitation and signed the nuclear nonproliferation treaty. Among Common Market countries, he supported moves to settle agricultural differences and pave the way for Great Britain's membership. Principal world attention, however, was focused on his programs of *Ostpolitik*. Renunciation-of-force pacts were signed with Communist countries, their ratification being tied to Soviet guarantees of civilian access by land to West Berlin. In the Treaty of Moscow (August 1970), which West Germany signed with Russia, the Federal Republic accepted the existing borders in Eastern Europe, which were based on Russian hegemony.

The Socialist government also dramatically altered Bonn's previously adamant positions on the Oder-Niesse boundary. The Treaty of

Warsaw (December 1970), in which West Germany renounced claims to 40,000 square miles of previously German territory that Poland controlled, was the first step in normalizing diplomatic relations between the two countries. With East Germany, Brandt agreed to the formula of two German seats within one nation but refused to extend full diplomatic recognition to the Communist regime. Despite these eastward initiatives, which caused some apprehensions among West Germany's allies, Brandt insisted that his policies remained firmly moored in the West.

Implementation of the Moscow and Warsaw treaties required Bundestag approval. During lengthy parliamentary debates and public discussions, the defection of some deputies from the Free Democratic party virtually equalized opposition and government forces and seriously weakened the Brandt coalition. However, after considerable parliamentary maneuvering, with most Christian Democrats abstaining in order to maintain party unity, the Bundestag ratified both treaties by wide margins (May 1972). Although the controversy eroded the government's slim majority, the resolution of boundary disputes remaining from World War II was a major step toward East-West détente. Amid accusations that one of his assistants was an East German spy, Brandt resigned the chancellorship and was succeeded by Finance Minister Helmut Schmidt (May 1974), a Social Democrat who continued the governing coalition with Free Democrats.

ITALY

After the fall of Mussolini, Italy was recognized by Western powers as a cobelligerent, though without Allied status. The last years of warfare provided separate experiences for northern and southern Italy, experiences that accentuated their historic differences. Allied armies had liberated the south by the end of 1943, enabling that area to avoid the struggle that enveloped the north in a bitter civil war between resistance fighters and Nazi partisans during 1944–1945. After the war, American troops remained as occupation forces. At the same time, massive American aid was the prerequisite for Italy's economic revival, because the country was desperately in need of food and raw materials as well as large amounts of capital to sustain long-range reconstruction. Only the United States was prepared and willing to provide large-scale aid for Italy's reconstruction after the war.

Political Revival. The political parties driven underground by Mussolini's regime had begun reassembling before his fall in the summer of 1943. Christian Democrats, Communists, and Socialists evolved as the major parties. The Christian Democratic party was successor to the Popular party, which, along with the Socialists, had dominated Italian politics during the pre-Fascist period. United by their Catholic bond, Christian Democrats, like the Populists before them, remained a heterogeneous grouping whose supporters ranged from left to right. The Communist party had been formed in 1921 by extreme left-wing Socialists. Active in the resistance and well-financed, it had become the largest Communist party in the West within a few years after the war. In elections held for a Constituent Assembly (June 1946), Christian Democrats won 35 percent of the vote; Socialists, 21 percent; and Communists, 19 percent. At the same time, in a referendum to decide if Italy would remain a monarchy or become a republic, supporters of a republic won by a close margin. The new constitution, effective in 1948, established a bicameral parliament consisting of a Chamber of Deputies and a Senate. Both houses chose a weak president of the republic who served for a seven-year term. Real executive power was delegated to the Council of Ministries, which was required to maintain the confidence of both legislative houses.

Period of Alcide De Gasperi.   In the first elections held under the new constitution (April 1948), a bitter contest developed between Christian Democrats and a Communist-Socialist coalition. The fall of Czechoslovakia to Communist rule had a polarizing effect in Italian politics. Fearful of another major Communist victory, the U.S. government applied its clout by threatening to terminate all economic aid if the leftist slate won. The Red scare attracted many moderate voters to the Christian Democratic party, providing it with an absolute majority in parliament. Alcide De Gasperi, leader of the Christian Democrats, remained as prime minister. Although the Vatican urged De Gasperi to organize an all-Catholic ministry, he formed instead a governing coalition based on the centrist parties, including Liberals, Republicans, and Social Democrats. De Gasperi encountered difficulties not only in maintaining this coalition but also in acting as arbiter between the conservatives and liberals within his own party. Included among the Christian Democrats were large landowners in the south and industrialists in the north who opposed the land reform and welfare measures that many rank-and-file members considered essential. Although some limited reforms were achieved under these adverse circumstances, Italy's economic progress remained sluggish. In the election of 1958, the national strength of the Center parties increased at the expense of Monarchists and Neo-Fascists. Although the Christian

Democrats remained the largest single party, the political stalemate continued. This election concluded De Gasperi's political career. Following his failure to form a new government based on the preelection coalition, he retired from politics and died a year later.

Shifting Coalitions.   From 1958 to 1963, Italy was governed by shifting coalitions that were a product of several ingredients. First, there were persisting struggles within the Christian Democratic party between leftist, centrist, and rightist factions. Second, minority parties—Liberals, Monarchists, and the Italian Social Movement—continued to exercise influence under the system of proportional representation Italy adopted in 1948. In 1947, a schism developed within the Socialist party, whose leader, Pietro Nenni, favored cooperation with the Communists. A bloc opposing alliances with the Communists withdrew from the Socialists and formed the Social Democratic party. Although the Nenni Socialists decided to maintain their independence from the Communists after 1953, the two groups of Socialists remained divided.

In the 1958 elections, Amintore Fanfani emerged as the dominant figure of the Christian Democratic party and the Italian government. He led a center-left group in the party that favored implementation of critical domestic reforms and strongly supported the Western alliance and European integration. During his first ministry (1958–1959), Fanfani unsuccessfully attempted to achieve an opening to the Left by establishing good relations with the Socialists. After a period of rule by the party's conservative wing, Fanfani returned as prime minister from 1960 to 1963 and again attempted to forge an alliance with the Socialists. While the Social Democrats supported the government's Western-oriented foreign policy and its plans for domestic reform, negotiations with the Nenni Socialists produced only limited results.

Economy.   Industrial development in Italy has been slow for most of the twentieth century. To a considerable degree, the country remains today what it has been in the past, a land of family craftsmen and peasant farmers. Given this modest base, considerable economic progress occurred in Italy during the 1950s and 1960s, sparked particularly by Marshall Plan aid and the steady prosperity of Common Market countries. The most notable achievements were in the industrialized north. Principal industries where production and employment increased were automobiles, sewing machines, typewriters, electricity, chemicals, and textiles. Though still meager in comparison with other Western countries, Italy's per capita income rose from prewar levels of less than $300 to over $700 during the 1960s. Welfare and health measures undertaken by the government reduced infant mortality and extended life expectancy. However, both socially and geographically the fruits of prosperity were distributed unequally. Middle-class groups and skilled workers profited most, but the income of peasants remained appallingly low. Social problems were endemic in Southern Italy, which remained heavily agricultural and poor despite special developmental programs undertaken by the government.

Center-Left.   Since the elections of 1963 began the long-awaited opening to the Left, Italy has been governed by a succession of cabinets supported by a coalition of four parties: Christian Democrats, Socialists, Social Democrats, and Republicans. The vision and promise of this combination was the enactment of major social reforms that would engender popular support for the Republican coalition and thereby decrease the electoral strength of the Communist party, which was second only to the Christian Democrats and which remained a major threat to Republican rule. The maintenance of Communist popularity is explained by the inability of the Center-Left coalition to fulfill its mandate of implementing strong social programs, principally because of parliamentary paralyses.

By 1970, the Christian Democrats alone could be separated into nine definable subgroups, while Socialists, who split into two parties in 1947 and then temporarily reunited during the late 1960s, again multiplied, this time into three parties: Socialists, Proletarians, and Social Democrats. Faced with intense union pressure for shorter working hours and higher salaries as well as for structural reforms to alleviate Italy's glaring social inequities, Center-Left governments were unable to choose among or to compromise competing demands. By 1974, dependence on high-priced Arab oil contributed to a 17 percent annual inflation rate and a $10.5 billion foreign debt that led, predictably, to new government crises. With thirty-six cabinet changes since World War II, Center-Left politics continued to prove its bankruptcy. Whether repeated failures would spark efforts toward a new opening to the Left embracing the Communist party remained a central question in Italy's future.

20

Postwar Communism: Eastern Europe, China, and Latin America

Before World War II, Russia possessed the only prominent Communist governing system. By 1970, Communist regimes were operating in at least fourteen states, including Eastern Europe, China, North Vietnam, North Korea, and Cuba. In Eastern Europe, Russia's successful military operations against Nazi Germany provided the basis for a postwar consolidation of Communist authority. By 1950, Poland, Hungary, Romania, Bulgaria, Czechoslovakia, and East Germany had been transformed into Russian satellites. Notable Communist victories were also won in Asia. The Red flag was unfurled throughout China in 1949, ending civil warfare and crowning victory by the Communists, led by Mao Tse-tung, over the Nationalists, headed by Chiang Kai-shek. Communist triumphs in North Korea and North Vietnam were recognized by East-West compromises that ended stalemated wars in 1953 and 1954. Fidel Castro's rise to power in Cuba during 1959 heralded the first victory for communism in the Americas. Despite predictions that conditions of poverty and rising expectations presented ideal terrain for Castro's example to be copied elsewhere, Chile was the only other nation in Latin America to adopt a Marxist regime. Ideologically, communism rests on a presumed brotherhood of proletarians that transcends national boundaries; yet, unity within the Communist world has been shaken repeatedly by internal domestic strife and nationalistic deviations. The most dramatic examples of this discontent were revolts by the nations of Eastern Europe, the "national" brand of communism that evolved in Yugoslavia, and the more recent discords between Russia and China.

RUSSIA

Russia emerged from World War II with a monumental problem of rehabilitation. Its cities and many of its villages lay in ruins; approximately 7 million of its people had been killed, and over 25 million were homeless. Reductions in industrial and farm production brought living standards below prewar levels. Depending chiefly on its own resources, the Soviet Union displayed unusual restorative powers. With primary emphasis on heavy industry and military defense, the fourth Five-Year Plan (1946–1950) succeeded in rebuilding the industrial facilities devastated during the war, and the fifth Five-Year Plan (1951–1955), designed to increase investment in industry and total industrial output, achieved or surpassed its objectives in most categories. Economic recuperation was paralleled by the return of rigid political controls. During the war, primarily because of wartime disarrangements and the need to inspire patriotism and unity, party controls were relaxed over many areas of Russian life. Afraid of the erosive impact that war-associated foreign influences might have on the Soviet regime, Stalin reverted successfully to his earlier rigid ideological position. Under the direction of Andrei Zhdanov, Stalin's handpicked agent who before his death in 1948 was expected to succeed him, party discipline was harshly restored over key areas of Russian society.

Death of Stalin. Under circumstances that remain obscure, the death of Stalin was announced in March 1953. Throughout the world, intense speculation focused on his possible successors. Because of the prominent role that he played at the Nineteenth Party Congress in 1952 and afterward, Georgi Malenkov succeeded Zhdanov as Stalin's heir apparent. Malenkov became premier in a collective government that included Lavrenti Beria as head of the secret police, Vyacheslav Molotov as minister of foreign affairs, Nikolai Bulganin as minister of defense, and Nikita Khrushchev in the critical position of Communist party secretary. Beria, who was obviously intent on using his position to advance his political ambitions, was the first to be eliminated; he was arrested and later executed in 1953. As premier, Malenkov advocated significant liberalizations in Stalin's policies. Greater emphasis was placed upon consumer production, and following the East German riots in 1953, the reins of Soviet control over the satellites were relaxed. However, rising opposition by the orthodox faithful discredited these policies, forcing Malenkov's resignation without violence in February 1955. Bulganin replaced him as premier.

Rise of Khrushchev. As first secretary of the Communist party's Central Committee, Khrushchev, like Stalin before him, gradually broadened his support within the Soviet regime while simultaneously strengthening his hand at home by projecting himself as an international figure. By 1955, he had appointed party leaders in the Leningrad, Ukrainian, and Georgian organizations. After the fall of Malenkov, his influence was also widened in the party structure at Moscow. Meanwhile, he used his appointive powers to build essential bases of support among security and military forces. At the Geneva Summit Conference of 1955, it was clear that Khrushchev rather than Bulganin was the leading figure in the Soviet delegation. The following February, at the Twentieth Party Congress, Khrushchev completely dominated the proceedings. In a three-hour speech presented to a closed session of the Congress and later revealed to the outside world, Khrushchev delivered a scalding attack on Stalin, including accusations that he wantonly murdered loyal party leaders and created a "cult of personality" that was an alien curse to the Soviet system. Khrushchev's bid for complete power was challenged in 1957 when a Presidium majority, led by Molotov and Malenkov, voted to oust him as first secretary. Acting quickly, Khrushchev transferred the dispute to the Central Committee, where he possessed a safe majority. By 1958, with his principal rivals all discredited, Khrushchev added the position of head of state to his role as party chief, again establishing a one-man dictatorship in Russia.

Destalinization. Khrushchev's speech at the 1956 Party Congress signaled the beginning of a campaign to demolish the myth of Stalin's infallible wisdom that party propagandists had carefully cultivated for over two decades. Victims of Stalin's trials and purges were restored to honor, many of them posthumously. The former dictator's name and images were removed from positions of public prominence. In the ultimate act of dishonor, in 1961, Soviet leaders removed Stalin's corpse from Lenin's side in Red Square. Simultaneously, political and cultural controls were relaxed. Intellectuals were granted more freedom; some political prisoners were released; and the activities of the secret police were more narrowly circumscribed. Although the essential characteristics of totalitarian rule continued, and liberalized policies were alternated with repressive acts, the most extreme features of Stalin's dictatorship were abandoned.

With the high priests disputing over the meaning of orthodoxy, disillusionment and questioning moods naturally arose among the faithful. In both the East and the West, Communist parties that had faithfully followed Soviet policy lines were in disarray. After Khrushchev's 1956 speech, internal riots broke out in Georgia, and major rebellions developed in Poland and Hungary. At the same time, Chinese leaders favored a continuation of Stalin's hard-line policies and maintained that the discredited autocrat's principles embodied the true spirit of Marxism-Leninism.

Peaceful Coexistence.   Soon after World War II, public pronouncements of Soviet leaders restated the traditional Marxist-Leninist view that socialist states were encircled by hostile capitalist countries. According to this theory, war between socialist and capitalist countries was, at some point, inevitable. The development of first atomic and then hydrogen bombs, the latter by the United States in 1952 and the Soviet Union in 1953, prompted a rethinking of this revered principle. A mutual deterrent had been created that made it unimaginable that rational men in either Moscow or Washington would unleash a general war against the other country. In his historic speech at the Twentieth Party Congress in 1956, Khrushchev therefore enunciated the novel Communist view that conditions of peaceful coexistence had been reached between capitalist and socialist countries. While war was still possible, it was no longer to be considered inevitable. To soothe the ruffled feelings of conservatives and to maintain the image of Communist irresistibility, Khrushchev repeatedly added that the natural supremacy of the Communist system made it certain to prevail throughout the world without war. Although these views lessened the impact of ideological rigor in Soviet foreign policies, they did not eliminate adventuristic schemes designed to test and weaken Western resolve.

Khrushchev's aggressiveness in the foreign arena was strengthened by the consolidation of his personal authority; by the dramatic launching in 1957 of *Sputnik I*, man's first missile, into outer space; and by an uncommonly ample harvest the Soviet Union enjoyed in 1958. Soviet leaders extended ideological and military assistance to national liberation struggles in Egypt, the Congo, and Indochina. In the widely publicized U-2 incident, a scheduled summit meeting with Western leaders planned for May 1960 was canceled as Khrushchev denounced the United States for permitting espionage flights over Russia. In 1958 and again in 1961, the German problem attained crisis dimensions with Khrushchev's demands for a settlement that provided East German control of access routes to Berlin. Tensions over Berlin waned after East Germans and Russians built a wall in 1961 to stem the steady flow of refugees from East to West Berlin.

Khrushchev attempted his most ambitious gamble in Cuba. After years of guerrilla warfare, Fidel Castro overthrew the dictatorship of Fulgencio Batista in 1959. To support Castro's leftist regime and also to extend Russian military might into the Western Hemisphere, Soviet leaders constructed missile sites in Cuba during the summer of 1962. Threats of a nuclear holocaust gripped the world when President Kennedy, in October 1962, imposed a blockade of further military shipments to Cuba. Soviet leaders responded by dismantling the missile bases, and the United States agreed not to invade Cuba. During the final years of Khrushchev's regime, Russia's relationship with the West became more conciliatory. Agreement was reached during 1963 to avoid accidental war by establishing a "hot line" between Moscow and Washington and also to ban all aboveground nuclear tests.

Fall of Khrushchev.   Khrushchev's leadership position in the Soviet hierarchy was gradually undermined by the opposition that his foreign and domestic policies generated. Communist hard-liners in and outside of Russia had opposed efforts of the Soviet government to reach a détente with the West. Despite all threats, the problem of Berlin remained unresolved. The Soviet Union had also met with failure in its efforts to guide the Congo chaos in Communist directions. The Cuban missile crisis was an unconcealed embarrassment for the Soviet Union. Domestically, Khrushchev's efforts to increase the production of consumer goods were resisted by industrialists and military leaders. High hopes had been raised with promises to invigorate the agricultural sector; yet, from 1958 to 1964, the per capita agricultural output had actually declined. In addition, some Soviet leaders viewed with disdain the style of Khrushchev's leadership. His unorthodox manners and unpredictable changes in policy offended ideological purists.

Khrushchev then decided to bring to a head the Sino-Soviet rift that had developed during his stewardship by calling a world conference of Communist leaders in 1964. It was clear by then that a struggle for power was occurring within the Soviet leadership. Before the scheduled world conference met, in October 1964, the Central Committee of the Communist party abruptly removed Khrushchev from his dual positions as Soviet premier and leader of the Communist party. Leonid

I. Brezhnev, who served as president of the Soviet Union, was made first secretary of the party, and Aleksei N. Kosygin, an economics expert and deputy premier, became prime minister.

Brezhnev and Kosygin. Into the 1970s, these two men remained the key figures in the collective leadership governing the Soviet Union. Despite a variety of economic innovations after the fall of Khrushchev, the Soviet economy still did not provide the standard of living that might be anticipated from the nation's resources, the competence of its educated elite, and its industrial, scientific, and technological successes. Severe shortages remained in housing, in ordinary food items such as meat and eggs, in furniture, and in mechanized travel. The deficiencies were products both of conscious Soviet priorities and of the character of the Soviet system. Primacy continued to be placed on technological, military, and scientific programs that would keep the Soviet Union abreast or ahead of the United States. At the same time, a rigid planning apparatus and pervasive party controls have built inflexibility into an enormously complex economy, frequently resulting in inordinate waste, low standards of production, and low levels of production.

As a step toward rectifying these conditions, Brezhnev and Kosygin instituted a reform program called *Libermanism,* after its principal advocate, Evsei Liberman, a professor at Kharkov University. This plan, which enjoyed limited though notable successes, used profit incentives to encourage higher levels of farm and factory production. Nevertheless, as orthodox organization men, Brezhnev and Kosygin maintained the huge imbalance between defense and consumer expenditures. By 1970, Brezhnev had acquired the individual power that has characterized most of the half-century of Soviet rule. Both domestically and on the international scene, he was acting as the supreme Soviet spokesman, and his dramatic trip to the United States in 1973 furthered the goal of East-West détente (see p. 342).

SOVIET SATELLITES

Between 1945 and 1948, Soviet leaders were able to realize imperial ambitions beyond the wildest dreams of the czars. The small Baltic states of Estonia, Latvia, and Lithuania were formally annexed as parts of the Soviet Union. Most other areas of Eastern Europe were transformed into satellites within the Soviet orbit. These included Romania, Bulgaria, and Albania in the Balkans and Hungary, East Germany, Poland, and Czechoslovakia to the north. Immediately after the war, Yugoslavia was the only Communist state to develop a brand of socialism that was not directed by Moscow. Pro-Chinese Albania achieved the status of Yugoslavia in 1961 after its expulsion from the Soviet orbit. In areas east of the Elbe-Trieste line where the Iron Curtain descended, only these Communist states, along with neutralist Austria, Soviet-oriented Finland, and Western-oriented Greece, maintained their national independence.

Soviet rule was gradually extended in Eastern Europe. Communists first held important ministries in coalition governments that included representatives of Agrarian and Socialist parties. The Agrarian opposition was initially eliminated; Socialist resistance was then overcome; and the creation of Soviet-directed puppet states ensued. In Czechoslovakia, there were variations upon this theme. The evolving character of Soviet rule reflected both the persisting spirit of nationalism in satellite areas and related changes in Russia's internal policies. Generally, the Stalinist years were identified with rigid centralized control, whereas a greater liberalization of policies followed Stalin's death. Except for Czechoslovakia, Eastern Europe was primarily agrarian. With leftist regimes in power, a predictable trend after the war was to confiscate the traditionally large private estates. The land was then redistributed to peasants or collectivized.

Bulgaria. In both world wars, Bulgaria supported the German-dominated alliance that opposed Russia. But during World War II, Bulgaria never declared war against the Soviets and further declined to contribute troops to Germany's invasion of Russia. In the autumn of 1944, the Bulgarian regents, ruling during the infancy of Simeon, son of the nation's dead king, deserted the Nazis and requested an armistice with the Soviet Union. Communists, Social Democrats, Agrarians, and the more conservative Zveno National Union formed a coalition government, the Fatherland Front. While the Bulgarian army fought under Soviet command during the final stages of the war, Communists within the government held the central ministries of the interior and justice, allowing them to run the police system and courts. Postwar elections were held in August 1945. Since political reprisals had created an atmosphere of coercion, the Agrarian and Socialist parties refused to participate. Not surprisingly, the single slate run by the Fatherland Front captured 88 percent of the vote. Communists maintained a ruthless campaign to secure unquestioned control. In 1946, a popular referendum abolished the monarchy, and Communist George Dimitrov became premier in the new government. With the Agrarian party dissolved in 1947 and nine Socialist deputies imprisoned in 1948, all organized opposition to Communist control was destroyed.

Bulgaria's political and economic system was radically altered to conform to the Soviet model. Communists constituted the ruling party in a government where the Politburo and the Central Committee were the controlling agencies. Within two decades, virtually all the countryside was divided into collective farms, in some cases totaling 10,000 acres or more. Some of these farms were later merged into even larger agricultural-industrial complexes covering up to 25,000 acres. Nevertheless, there were higher yields per acre, sometimes amounting to three or four times as much, on small private plots comprising less than 10 percent of the land. Recognizing that capitalist incentives would frequently promote efficiency, the government beginning in the mid-1960s made concessions to free enterprise, notably by allowing some profits in the most productive factories to be distributed among the workers. Even by the standards of Eastern Europe, Bulgaria remained an undeveloped country. Most of the native Communist elite had not finished college, and the capital city of Sofia was still dominated by nineteenth-century architecture. Bulgaria continued to be the satellite state having the most intimate relations with Russia. The two countries possess similar languages based on the Cyrillic alphabet, which permits easy communication between them.

Romania. Like Bulgaria, Romania responded to the Russian advance in the fall of 1944 by ending its Axis connections and forming a new coalition government, the National Democratic Front. The major groups in the alliance were the Socialist and Communist parties on the Left and the National Peasant and National Liberal parties on the Right. Inevitable differences over agrarian and financial reform soon forced a dissolution of this coalition, with the leftist parties regrouping into the National Democratic Front (NDF). Soviet leaders were dissatisfied with the divided government's hesitant policies toward social reform and unhappy with Bulgaria's role in the war effort. Under these circumstances, Andrei Vyshinsky, the Russian vice-commissar for foreign affairs, unexpectedly arrived in Bucharest in February 1945. Upon his demands, King Michael was persuaded to appoint a pro-Communist figure, Petru Groza, as the new premier. Groza excluded representatives of the Peasant and Liberal parties from the government until 1946 and included them then only after Britain and France made this step the precondition for their recognizing the regime. This broadened participation was temporary. In the elections of 1946, during which the government terrorized opposition groups, the National

Democratic Front was firmly implanted in office with over 80 percent of the popular vote. The last strongholds of resistance to Communist rule were eliminated in 1947. Leaders of the Peasant and Liberal parties were charged with treason and forced out of the government; the Socialist party fused with the Communists; and King Michael was forced to abdicate. Early in 1948, a Communist-dominated constituent assembly established a Soviet system of government.

Although at one time Romania was one of Russia's most servile satellites, it evolved into one of the most independent. Georghe Gheorghiu-Dej (1952–1965) and Nicolae Ceausescu (1965–) were the prominent Communist rulers of the postwar period. Traditionally a land of agriculture, Romania achieved significant industrialization during the 1950s and 1960s. Largely owing to persisting nationalistic fervor and an unwillingness to become purely a source of farm produce in the Communist world, Romanian leaders successfully resisted the integration of their economy into the Soviet bloc's Council for Mutual Economic Assistance (COMECON). Instead, emphasis was placed on industrial production, notably oil, chemicals, fertilizers, and steel. Consequently, Romania had the highest rate of industrial growth of any satellite state. In foreign affairs, Ceausescu's astute leadership enabled Romania to remain neutral in the Sino-Soviet conflict, to establish diplomatic relations with West Germany, to expand trade with Western countries, to maintain friendly relations with Marshal Tito's revisionist Yugoslavia, and in 1969 to host Richard Nixon, the first American president to visit a Communist country since World War II. Moscow tolerated these aberrations primarily because of Romania's orthodoxy in domestic political and economic matters. The economy remained pervasively collectivized, planned, and controlled, and the Romanian Communist party retained absolute power over the government and society.

Poland. The Polish question was one of the most difficult problems at the end of World War II. During the war, hostility developed between the Soviet Union and a Polish government-in-exile, established in London and headed by Stanislaw Mikolajczyk. Meanwhile, an underground Polish government that the Russians supported was created in Lublin and led by a Polish Communist, Boleslaw Bierut. In January 1945, after the liberation of Warsaw, the government at Lublin was transferred to the capital, where it was quickly recognized by the Soviet Union. At the Yalta Conference, Allied leaders agreed that the Warsaw government would be broadened to embrace democratic elements and also that free elections would be held in Poland. Britain and the United States extended diplomatic recognition to the Warsaw regime after the first condition was met. Scheduled elections, however, were postponed until 1947 and then held in an atmosphere of corruption and terror. The Peasant party, led by Mikolajczyk, refused offers to combine with other parties and form a single slate of candidates. Communists and left-wing Socialists, key groups in the government bloc, won an overwhelming majority, allowing the legislature to choose Bierut as the nation's president. The Peasant party was tamed by October 1947, after Mikolajczyk was forced out of the country. Other independent centers of power were removed through the merger of the Communist and Socialist parties and also through purges of nationalist Communists. However, there was considerable hostility to Soviet rule in this strongly nationalistic and predominantly Catholic country. Peasants resisted the standard measures of collectivization and joined with religious leaders to condemn the anticlerical policies of the Communist government.

With a combined system of state and privately owned enterprises, Poland took major steps toward industrialization under Communist rule. These efforts were greatly aided by the acquisition from Germany of Silesia, a productive industrial center. Heavy industry, including mining and engineering, led the way; the sectors of consumer goods and housing lagged far behind. Although concerted efforts were made toward collectivization, adamant peasant resistance made the process slower and more difficult than in other satellite countries. During 1953, severe rioting occurred in Poland, following the major uprising in East Germany and the arrest of Cardinal Stefan Wyszynski and other Catholic officials. In 1956, discontent over living standards engendered another rebellion that began among the industrial workers of Poznań and spread to other cities. With Hungary also in revolt, Soviet leaders were persuaded to adopt a policy of moderation toward Poland. They therefore approved the accession to power of Wladyslaw Gomulka, a strong nationalist leader who had been imprisoned during the Stalinist years. Gomulka relaxed party discipline by allowing large numbers of peasants to leave collective farms and return to private plots, by decentralizing factory controls to give plant managers greater autonomy, and by allowing religious instruction to be reinstituted in public schools. However, by the late 1950s, the government began restoring traditional controls. In 1970, workers were antagonized by a new five-year plan that threatened to penalize inefficient factory workers and by price rises on food items designed to increase foreign exports by reducing domestic consumption. Gomulka was toppled from power following a week of riots in which 300 people were killed. He was replaced by Edward Gierek, formerly head of the Silesian mining region, who promised new reforms as concessions to popular demands.

Hungary. During the autumn of 1944, Russian troops gained control of eastern Hungary and compelled regent Miklós Horthy to surrender. Horthy's regime was replaced by the Hungarian National Independence Front, comprising Communists and Socialists, the agrarian-oriented Smallholders and National Peasant parties, and the middle-class Bourgeois Democrats. This coalition government, which moved to Budapest in April 1945 after the Soviets had liberated the city, ruled Hungary during the final stages of the war. In November 1945, free general elections were held in which the Smallholders party won a legislative majority. In 1946, Ferenč Nagy became premier in a coalition cabinet that embraced the Communist, Socialist, and National Peasant parties. Communists directed bitter attacks against the Small-holders, who were not only the most powerful but also the most con-servative members of the governing alliance. After the Communists charged some Smallholders with conspiring to overthrow the govern-ment, Nagy resigned in May 1947 and sought refuge abroad. New elections held the following August gave Communists a plurality of the votes, and the government was reorganized. Activities by the conserva-tive parties were banned, and in 1948, Socialists lost their identity through a merger with Communists into the United Workers' party. The Communist victory was completed in 1949 with the dissolution of the last major opposition group, the Democratic People's party. Mátyás Rákosi, a Russian-trained Communist, was the dominant gov-ernment figure.

In a country where before the war one-fourth of the arable land was in the hands of fewer than 400 families, the provisional government and Communist rule brought about fundamental economic reform. By the death of Stalin, one-fourth of the land had been collectivized, and many other confiscated areas were distributed among landless laborers and workers with small holdings. As the nation's largest landholder, the Catholic church became alienated from the government because of state expropriation and also as a result of educational reforms that included nationalization of the schools. In 1949, Cardinal Mindszenty, the leader of Catholic resistance, was charged with treason and impris-oned. Hungarians manifested profound and widespread unhappiness with Communist rule following the death of Stalin. In response, the government moved to broaden its popularity by replacing Rákosi as premier with Imre Nagy, who instituted more liberalized policies. After

Khrushchev's denunciation of Stalin, a major rebellion developed in October 1956, which was suppressed by Russian troops. Nagy was executed, and János Kádár became the new premier with Soviet support.

During Kádár's long regime, Hungary achieved through a quiet revolution what it was denied by Russian tanks in 1956. Trade with Western countries boomed, and the country enjoyed unprecedented cultural and economic freedom. Kádár's ability to cultivate support both in the Kremlin and at home enabled him to bring about surprising reforms. The most momentous innovation was the New Economic Mechanism (NEM), introduced in 1967. Making significant concessions to capitalist practices, this program lessened central planning by promoting industrial responses to market conditions. It further encouraged increases in worker productivity by the incentive of wage bonuses.

Czechoslovakia. Czechoslovakia entered World War II as the only democratic state in Eastern Europe. The promise of democracy after the war lasted longer in Czechoslovakia than in the other Eastern European states except Hungary. The pro-Russian orientation of Czech leaders was dictated by the presence of Soviet troops, Slavic racial ties, and the conviction that national security could not be tied to the same Western powers that had deserted Czechoslovakia at the Munich settlement. As World War II ended, President Eduard Beneš returned to Czechoslovakia and, with Soviet backing, began efforts to reconstruct the republic's constitutional framework. Beneš chose as premier Zdeněk Fierlinger, a socialist sympathetic to Russia. In elections held in May 1946, Communist parties won a plurality of the legislative seats. Their leader, Klement Gottwald, was made premier in a National Front cabinet that also included Social Democrats, National Socialists, the Slovak Democratic party, and the People's party. Communists at first conducted themselves with moderation, holding out the promise that Czechoslovakia could combine an Eastern orientation in foreign affairs with a Western political system. These hopes ended as differences between East and West widened. By late 1947, Communists were resorting to intimidation and lawlessness. Although non-Communist parties resisted these pressures, a key break came when Zdeněk Fierlinger, leader of the Social Democrats, caused a rift in his party by siding with the Communists. In February 1948, representatives of non-Communist parties resigned in an effort to force the resignation of the Communist minister of the interior. Instead, Communists seized the vacated offices and proceeded to consolidate their power.

Under Klement Gottwald's harsh rule, steps were taken to refashion Czechoslovakian society according to the standard Communist models. Industry, including even the small shops of artisans, was pervasively nationalized. Despite delays caused by peasant sabotage, the country-side was completely collectivized. That Communist rule encountered difficulties in eradicating Czechoslovakia's historic spirit of independence and ties to the West was manifested by the continuous stream of purges, trials, and executions of so-called revisionists and traitors. Gottwald died suddenly in 1953, after becoming ill at Stalin's funeral. Succeeding him as party secretary was Antonín Novotný. In a regime almost as inflexible as Gottwald's, Novotný attempted to harness the liberalizing forces that spread throughout Eastern Europe following Stalin's death. Consequently, pressures intensified for reforms to decentralize controls and to introduce more intellectual and cultural freedom.

These forces led to the ouster of Novotný in January 1968 and the accession to power of Alexander Dubček, who immediately inaugurated liberal programs, including provisions for freedom of speech, press, and assembly—all anathema to a closed society. Soviet leaders viewed Dubček innovations as a serious threat to Communist regimes throughout Eastern Europe. Following a series of negotiations and disorders, Kremlin leaders, on August 21, 1968, moved troops into Czechoslovakia to restore Soviet discipline. Dubček was replaced in 1969 by Deputy Premier Gustave Husak, who had first supported then criticized Dubček's reforms. In the tradition of the Good Soldier Schweik, the portly and independent folk hero of Czechoslovakia, the Czech people after 1968 stubbornly resisted Soviet intervention, engaging in work slowdowns and observing August 21 as a day of mourning.

East Germany. The German Democratic Republic (GDR) was officially created in the Soviet zone of occupation during the autumn of 1949 (see pp. 250–251). Bases for Communist rule were laid through the Soviet-manipulated first (December 1947), second (March 1948), and third (May 1949) People's Congresses. Following the third congress, voters were requested to approve a single list of official candidates. From the outset, the Socialist Unity party (SED) served as the instrument through which Russia created a central Communist-dominated government. Although four other parties were allowed to continue a mock existence, all principal leaders came from the SED. They included two figureheads, Wilhelm Pieck as president and Otto Grotewohl as premier. Real power was placed in the hands of Walter Ulbricht, the party's Moscow-trained secretary-general. Both domestically and in foreign affairs, East Germany yielded to Soviet dictates. In 1950, for example, the state became a member of COMECON and agreed upon the Oder-Neisse line as the boundary between Germany and Poland.

In varying ways, however, East Germans manifested profound discontent with their Communist regime. Riots and demonstrations in June 1953 were not quieted until Soviet troops and tanks intervened. Until the Berlin wall was built in 1961 (see p. 234), East Germans regularly voted with their feet, becoming refugees to the West. With the constant presence of Soviet troops buttressing a continuously repressive internal regime, East Germans came to exhibit a greater degree of political resignation. As head of the Communist party and after 1958 chairman of the nation's council of state, Walter Ulbricht was the principal governing official of East Germany. A former acquaintance of Lenin, the sternly ideological Ulbricht enjoyed unrivaled influence with Kremlin leaders and was justifiably proud of the republic's full economic recovery. Its standard of living was the highest in Eastern Europe, and it ranked among the world's leading industrial powers. East Germany became a major supplier of chemicals and machinery to Russia and other satellites. In science and other technical subjects, its educational system was considered superior to West Germany. In 1971, Ulbricht relinquished his post as party first secretary to Erich Honecker, retaining the largely ceremonial office of chief of state. Honecker continued as leader of East Germany following Ulbricht's death (August 1973).

YUGOSLAVIA

Alone among the Communist states of Eastern Europe, Yugoslavia from the beginning was able to defy Kremlin controls and create its own brand of socialist rule. This success was built upon the ability of local resistance fighters, under Marshal Tito, to free the country from Axis rule with little assistance from the Allies and at the same time to liquidate the non-Communist opposition. Recognizing Tito's heretical ways, the Cominform, an international association of Communist parties directed by the Soviets, ejected Yugoslavia from membership in 1948, on the ostensible ground that Tito's government had wavered in its efforts to collectivize agriculture. Immediately thereafter, amidst rising denunciations of Tito, the Soviet bloc organized a trade boycott against the Yugoslavs. This move served only to redirect Yugoslavia's trade relations toward Western countries, further weakening its economic ties with other Communist states. Politically, Tito's regime embodied the standard features of a Communist dictatorship: one-party control, repressive police tactics, and severe restrictions on speech and assembly. Economically, the Yugoslavs created what they called a "socialist market economy." Centralized planning was moderate, allowing the forces of supply and demand to shape industrial activity. Self-management was achieved in nearly 90 percent of the industries through labor participation in worker councils and management boards. After efforts to collectivize agriculture met widespread peasant resistance, the government returned to private farming for about 85 percent of the arable land. Yugoslavia has thus not only been able to maintain its independence from Soviet control but also to establish a socialist system nearer to capitalism than to Marxism.

In foreign affairs, Yugoslavia attempted to maintain a neutralist stance, asserting its Communist credentials while concurrently cultivating friendly relations with the West and nonaligned countries. Soviet leaders after Stalin responded by alternately wooing and attacking Tito, whose continued heresy was the most persistent counterargument to the ideological position that the Kremlin is the sole interpreter of Communist orthodoxy. The increasingly independent role most satellite states have followed, marked occasionally by major rebellions, and the rifts involving China and Albania were influenced by the Yugoslav example. With Tito now in his eighties, a crucial question is whether Yugoslavia can remain united in the face of Soviet pressures once he departs from the scene. During his twenty-seven years of continuous rule since the war, Tito has managed to weld a nation of heterogeneous peoples divided by history, geography, and culture. However, the powerful Croatian minority has never adjusted to its subordinate role in a predominantly Serbian state.

CHINA

Post-World War II rivalries between Nationalists and Communists dated back to the late 1920s. Prewar leaders of the contesting movements, Chiang Kai-shek for the Nationalists and Mao Tse-tung for the Communists, remained the principal antagonists. During World War II, a shaky alliance prevailed between the two camps as they faced common Japanese aggression. This truce quickly dissolved following Japan's defeat, and fighting between Nationalists and Communists broke out again in the autumn of 1945. During 1946, these hostilities grew into a full-scale civil war that lasted until 1949. Although at the war's end Nationalists controlled the major cities, Communists speedily consolidated their power in rural northern China. Despite American mediation and large-scale assistance to Chiang Kai-shek, the reactionary, corrupt-ridden, and authoritarian Nationalists continually lost popular support. Manchuria was the hotly contested area from 1945 to 1947; here the Communists were able to broaden their base of power significantly. Aided by sizable defections, Mao's troops then focused their attention southward and in April 1949 succeeded in occupying the Nationalist capital of Nanking. By the end of 1949, the long and historic struggle had ended. Communists had emerged victorious on the mainland, and the Nationalists withdrew their defeated forces to the island of Taiwan (Formosa).

Government. The People's Republic of China, formally established in September 1949, was the first regime to effectively unite the country since the fall of the Manchu dynasty in 1912. Described in theory as the New Democracy, the regime declared itself to be a dictatorship of the revolutionary classes, embracing the proletariat, the peasantry, and cooperating elements of the bourgeoisie. Key ruling bodies included the Communist party, the government of the People's Republic, and the People's Revolutionary Military Council, which directed the armed services. As was the case in Russia, parallel party and government structures were formed, with party officials administering government organizations at each level. Mao Tse-tung maintained dictatorial control over both party and state. For many years, the chief deputy was Liu Shao-ch'i, who succeeded Mao as chairman of the People's Republic in 1959; Chou En-lai served in the positions of premier and foreign minister. Regional governments were established in six areas, with separate administrations for Mongolia and Tibet. The predominant tendency was the weakening of area governments and a corresponding centralization of authority in Peking. Chinese Communist rulers created a totalitarian regime as effective as that of their Russian counter-parts. Anti-Communist opponents were silenced; government agencies manipulated all means of communications; and deviants from the party line risked arrest, forced labor, and execution. Entire social classes were obliterated, notably the reactionary landlords whom Communists considered enemies of the people.

Economy. In their economic as well as governing policies, Chinese Communists were heavily influenced by the Soviet example. Priorities were placed on comprehensive programs of economic development designed to transform the traditionally agrarian country into a major industrial power. Immediate requirements were to carry out programs of reconstruction necessitated by decades of warfare and aggravated by

Russia's postwar dismantling of factories in the advanced industrial center of Manchuria. In 1953, rehabilitation measures were succeeded by the first Five-Year Plan. Development of the basic industries—coal, iron ore, steel, and electric power—and the creation of entirely new industrial centers were projected. By 1957, the government reported that its goals of capital expansion had been fulfilled or exceeded, bringing the first plan to a successful end.

Programs of land redistribution, implemented earlier in the Communist strongholds of North China and Manchuria, were carried out simultaneously in other parts of the country. Communist strategy in local areas was to become allied with the poor peasants and farm laborers against the landed class. The socialization of agriculture was as destructive of life in China during this period as it had been in Russia during the 1930s, with an estimated 3 million landlords killed. Confiscated land was divided into tiny plots among the peasantry. Although this fragmentation of farming gave the masses direct identification with the new regime, it obstructed the national goals of improved efficiency and higher production. To remedy this problem, the government, beginning in 1953, concentrated on pooling the redistributed land into agricultural cooperatives as the first stage to collectivization.

By the late 1950s, it was evident that the imbalance between industrial and economic expansion was an overriding problem. The second Five-Year Plan, launched in 1958, proposed to achieve a more stable equilibrium between the factory and countryside by maintaining industrial expansion while transforming Chinese agriculture. Called the "great leap forward," this design aimed to remodel the agrarian sector by fusing existing cooperatives and collective farms into communes consisting of as many as 5,000 families each. Private property was eradicated in these all-purpose economic and social units. After concerted efforts throughout the year, the government declared that 98 percent of the agrarian population had been merged into communes. Widespread popular resistance, however, heightened by crop failures and famine, forced the government to abandon the communal idea in 1959 and 1960. Collectives were restored as a way of life, and private property reappeared on a restricted basis. Although the pace remained troublesome and uneven, China's economy has been revolutionized under Communist rule, allowing the People's Republic to rank currently among world industrial powers.

Society and Culture. The Communist regime pervasively transformed traditional Chinese society. Deeper state allegiance was encouraged by the loosening of historically inseparable family bonds. The changed role of women was one of the most conspicuous results. Released from their confining household tasks, and with equality established between the sexes, women began to play critical roles in politics, the professions, and the labor force. The government also made major strides toward the elimination of illiteracy, and technical and higher education were naturally accentuated to spark industrialization campaigns. Activities of scholars, men of letters, and artists were subjected to the inevitable thought control. Social scientists, writers, popular entertainment, and cultural activities were all seen as ways to propagandize socialist ideology. In a system where private ownership was nonexistent and where the government completely dominated the allocation and use of resources, all citizens served in effect as government employees. As the ruling force within the government, the Communist party, at its own discretion, was able to assign individual responsibilities in all walks of life.

The Cultural Revolution.   From 1966 to 1969, China experienced the throes of domestic convulsions that the government labeled the "great proletarian cultural revolution." This represented an attempt by Mao Tse-tung to perpetuate revolutionary purity by purging the army, party, and government of so-called bourgeois or revisionist influences. Instruments of this Communist-approved insurgency were the People's Liberation Army and the Red Guard youth organizations, whose enlistment for the campaign involved the closing of schools. In opposition were many Communist party officials, including Mao's former heir apparent, Liu Shao-ch'i, in addition to factory managers, bureaucrats, and elements of the army. Conditions bordered on civil warfare as pitched battles were fought and counterrevolutionaries were paraded before special courts before suffering public executions. Economic conditions deteriorated ominously during the disorders, with production in coal, steel, and oil, in addition to agrarian output, drastically reduced. China withdrew into virtual isolation at the height of the disruptions, thus profoundly affecting its relations with the outside world. By 1969 and 1970, however, normalization of both domestic and foreign relations was evident. The full meaning and impact of this turbulent period have still not been fully assessed in the West.

Foreign Affairs.   As the end of the cultural revolution signaled a return to normalcy, China began to move more boldly on the world stage under the pragmatic leadership of Premier Chou En-lai. Chinese ambassadors returned to their posts; additional states extended diplomatic recognition; and in October 1971, the People's Republic was admitted to the United Nations, and Nationalist China was expelled. Dramatic Chinese involvement was also evident in the third world. The Peking government extended sizable aid to Tanzania and Zambia, made arms and training available to Arab insurgents in the Middle East, and shipped planes and tanks to Pakistan. Before the cultural revolution, the main thrust of China's policy was to force an international coalition against the United States. At the same time, in the 1960s, differences widened between Chinese and Kremlin leaders. At the beginning of the 1970s, the hardening of Sino-Soviet differences encouraged cautious Chinese overtures toward the West. President Nixon responded by easing trade restrictions in 1970 and then crowned his new China policy by making a historic trip to China in February 1972. As the 1970s evolve, the triangular relations of the United States, China, and the Soviet Union will be crucial forces in world affairs. Given the wide differences that separate each power from the other two, only extraordinary circumstances are likely to produce either a firm Moscow-Washington, Moscow-Peking, or Peking-Washington axis. Nevertheless, a *modus vivendi* worked out between any two of the three powers would have dramatic effects on international relations.

LATIN AMERICA

Two Communist governments were established in Latin America, one on the island of Cuba, the other in Chile.

Cuba.   Communism came to Cuba through a revolutionary movement headed by Fidel Castro, who first led a raid against the repressive dictatorship of President Fulgencio Batista in 1953 for which he was imprisoned and subsequently exiled. In December 1956, Castro returned to Cuba from Mexico as leader of an invasion that included eighty-two men. Only twelve, including Castro, survived this abortive coup. Undaunted, Castro continued to profit from the widespread discontent with Batista's rule. In the hills of Oriente province, he cultivated his small band of followers into a popular crusade, supported by a strong peasant and student army. With this backing, Castro was able to overthrow the Batista government in January 1959.

Castro cloaked his Marxist designs until he had acquired power. But in a matter of months thereafter, his regime was calling for Communist revolutions elsewhere in Latin America, confiscating the property of American businessmen, and edging closer to the Soviet camp. In retaliation, the U. S. government first stopped importing Cuban sugar at a subsidized rate and in 1961 severed all diplomatic relations with

Cuba. Tensions heightened when the U. S. government supported an abortive attempt by Cuban rebels to invade the island at the Bay of Pigs for the purpose of overthrowing Castro (April 1961). A year later, Cuba became the subject of an international crisis when American intelligence sources reported that Russia was installing medium-range ballistic missiles there (see pp. 334–335). After more than a decade in power, Castro's revolutionary zeal had been tempered by realities. Realizing the need to place priority on economic problems, the Cuban government de-emphasized its commitments to Communist revolution throughout Latin America after the death of Castro's revolutionary associate, Ché Guevara, in 1967. All signs indicated that Soviet leaders, whose continued support involved an increasingly important role being played by Russian military and economic advisers, encouraged this mood of coexistence.

Chile.   In contrast with Cuba, Communist rule was established in Chile through constitutional means as the consequence of a popular election in 1970 won by Salvador Allende, an announced Marxist. In a three-man race, Allende was chosen president by a legislative decision even though he received only 36 percent of the vote. He was supported by a leftist coalition of Popular Unity parties that included quarreling Communists and Socialists in addition to four other leftist groups. The Communist party dominated the coalition. Decidedly pro-Soviet, among Communist parties in the West it was third in size to the French and Italian parties. The Allende regime pledged to follow "Chile's road to socialism" through extensive agrarian reform and a comprehensive urban development program. After coming to office, the Marxist president continued to lead the dual life of a constitutionalist and a revolutionary. While attempting to maintain friendly relations with the United States, Allende recognized the Castro regime and entertained the Cuban dictator on a lengthy state visit. Nationalization of the economy proceeded at a rapid rate. Peasants were allowed to seize the estates of absentee landlords, and labor unions were given control over many new plants. A constitutional amendment adopted in 1971 authorized the expropriations of American copper interests under a formula providing compensation over a two-year period.

Chile's middle and upper classes never accepted Allende's so-called democratic road to socialism. Opposition grew as the government's policies resulted in severe economic disruptions. After two years, the nation's foreign reserves totaling $345 million had been spent. Land reforms led to sizable reductions in production, with resulting food shortages. During the first half of 1973, the rate of inflation was 300 percent. These problems were aggravated by a series of bitterly divisive strikes among copper miners, truckers, doctors, shopkeepers, and transportation drivers that plunged the nation into economic chaos. Efforts to make peace with the opposition party, the badly divided Christian Democrats, proved unsuccessful. Allende's appointment of military commanders to cabinet posts encouraged greater political action on the part of Chile's traditionally neutralist generals. They assumed leadership of the rightist opposition and engineered a successful coup in which Allende lost his life (September 1973). Efforts to combine socialism and democracy in Chile thus proved a notable failure.

21

End of Colonialism in Asia and Africa

The movement toward independence in Africa and Asia was the most explosive force in international affairs after World War II. Irresistible pressures against colonial rule had been building up since the beginning of the twentieth century. The Japanese victory over Russia (see pp. 45–46, 49) lessened the prestige of imperial powers by demonstrating that once an Oriental nation adopted the techniques of modernization, it could successfully compete with a Western state. World War I hastened the destruction of colonial rule. Slogans of democracy and self-determination popularized during the conflict raised the nationalistic expectations of subjugated natives. After the war, the termination of German colonial rule suggested the impermanence of empires. Events of World War II provided impetus to the dissolution of empire. During the war, the Japanese leveled added blows at the credibility of Western rule by achieving hegemony in the Pacific and Asia. The weakened condition of European states by the end of the war, paralleled by the rising expectations of subjected natives, turned the halting process of imperial liquidation into an onrushing flood tide. The elimination of Italy as a colonial power reduced the number of European imperial states to five: the major nations of Britain and France, with far-flung empires, and Belgium, Portugal, and Spain, which possessed less impressive holdings.

By the end of the 1960s, most of the pre-World War I colonies in Africa and Asia had been transformed into nation-states. As the process of independence unfolded, two stages of evolution were evident in most places: First, national political leaders formed coalitions to expel the imperial powers, and second, after the advent of political freedom, regional, communal, and tribal differences produced severe fragmentations in the alliance that had made independence a reality. European powers adopted varying attitudes toward independence struggles, largely reflecting policies evolved during the interwar period (see chapter 11). The British sought to extend to the peoples of Asia and Africa the Commonwealth precedent that had proved workable with Europeans in Canada and Australia. French policies centered on the achievement of assimilation, a concept applicable primarily to educated elites and then only if they chose to become Frenchmen. The smaller powers of Belgium, the Netherlands, and Portugal adjusted less willingly to independence demands; their principal objective was the maintenance of traditional colonial rule as long as possible.

ASIA

The British, French, and Dutch were the major imperial powers in Asia. Impoverished and unwilling to bear the high costs of defending its colonial possessions in the face of nationalist demands, Great Britain led the way in relinquishing its colonies not only in the Far East, but also in the Middle East and Africa. India was partitioned and made independent in 1947. Ceylon and Burma gained their freedom in 1948, Malaya in 1957, and Singapore in 1965. With the exception of Burma, all the newly independent states accepted Dominion status within the British Commonwealth. The Dutch and French resisted more strongly the efforts of native nationalists to end imperial control. However, after efforts to reconquer their former colonies failed, the Dutch recognized the independence of Indonesia in 1949. French domination in Indochina ended in 1954, after years of fighting between French armies and Communist-directed nationalist forces.

British Departure.   India was the kernel of the British Empire and the largest colonial area ruled by Europeans. The momentum for Indian independence had gathered steam during World War I, accelerated during the interwar period, and become overpowering by the end of World War II. To encourage support from Indians during the war, the British promised them Dominion status once the war had ended. The major difficulty of keeping this promise resulted from widening differences between the Indian National Congress, spokesman for India's 350 million Hindus, and the militant Muslim League, which represented India's 70 million Muslims. Unable either to reconcile these disputing religious sectors or to postpone demands for independence, in February 1947, British officials announced that their authority in India would cease by June 1948. The bill granting India independence established two sovereign states: the predominantly Hindu nation of India and the predominantly Muslim country of Pakistan, which was itself subdivided into Eastern and Western sections. Both states chose to remain within the Commonwealth. Once India was liberated, the principle of European political dominance was undermined throughout both Asia and Africa.

As anticipated, political freedom further worsened relations between Hindus and Muslims, leading periodically to bloody riots and wars. Perennial problems over Kashmir eventually became secondary to the civil struggle between the two Pakistans until an India-Pakistan war in 1971 resulted in the independence of East Pakistan under the name of Bangladesh.

Independence for the remaining parts of the British empire in Asia logically followed that of India. Ceylon became a self-governing state within the Commonwealth in 1948. Burma's path to independence was more difficult since national consciousness, intensified by the Japanese conquest, was inclined to tolerate fewer ties to the colonial master. However, Burma achieved freedom in 1948 as a neutralist republic with no Commonwealth bonds. After a decade of warfare involving British efforts to subjugate local Communists, Malaya was granted independence within the Commonwealth in 1957. In 1963, Malaya, Singapore, and several remnants of the British empire in Southeast Asia combined to form the Federation of Malaysia, which had as its principal objectives the containment of Chinese influence and the erection of roadblocks to thwart any expansionist efforts by Indonesia.

Dissolution of the Dutch Empire. The East Indies, which provided lucrative careers for many Netherlanders besides a continuous flow of coffee, tea, rubber, and other products, formed the nucleus of Dutch overseas possessions prior to World War II. In 1942, the Japanese forced the Dutch to evacuate the Indonesian archipelago. At the war's end, when the Japanese were also forced to leave, they proclaimed the independence of Indonesia. Already in control were the local nationalists, led by Achmed Sukarno, who had been advocating independence since the end of World War I. Dutch efforts, first to negotiate a limited plan of self-government and then, over a four-year period, to forcibly reassert their control, both ended in failure. Consequently, the Dutch were compelled to grant independence to the sixteen territorial units that comprised the United States of Indonesia in 1949, under a formula that provided for a loose association between the federated republics and the Netherlands. This arrangement was fraught with difficulty, resulting, after a series of negotiations, in its dissolution during 1956. Primarily as a result of President Sukarno's plans for nationalist expansion, Netherlands New Guinea (West Irian) became an object of contention between Indonesia and the Netherlands. In 1962, fighting in New Guinea prompted U.N. negotiations, which resulted in an agreement placing the disputed area under U.N. control as a prelude to its eventual union with Indonesia.

French Expulsion from Indochina. Laos, Cambodia, and Vietnam were principal areas of the French Union in Indochina. Throughout most of the war, Indochina remained neutral and loyal to the Vichy government. Not until March 1945 did the Japanese expel the French and assert their own control. In the meantime, Communists in Vietnam had organized the Viet Minh (Vietnam Independence League) under the leadership of Ho Chi Minh, a Communist trained in Moscow. After the war, the French government attempted to negotiate a large measure of independence with Ho Chi Minh but failed late in 1946 when a local French commander irresponsibly provoked open warfare. For the next seven years, French armies and non-Communists in Vietnam fought against forces of the Viet Minh (see pp. 252, 313). The French received money and supplies from the United States, which, though anticolonialist in its foreign policy pronouncements, feared the consequences of a Communist victory in Vietnam. However, involvement in the Korean War deterred the United States from open intervention on behalf of the French. During 1954, non-Communist South Vietnam and Communist North Vietnam, in addition to Cambodia and Laos, were granted their independence.

AFRICA

Revolts against imperialism occurred in Africa later and more rapidly than in Asia. At the end of World War II, the only independent African states were Ethiopia and Liberia. Nationalist movements among the Arabs in North Africa were the first to achieve dramatic results. The initial European disengagement in Libya (1951) and the Suez Canal (1954) proved to be relatively calm affairs in comparison with later stormy events. Widespread violence was the prelude to the French departure in Tunisia (1956), Morocco (1956), and Algeria (1962). In 1958, those parts of the French Empire south of the Sahara, including French West Africa and French Equatorial Africa, were given the choice by plebiscite of complete independence or attachment to the French Community. British policies also varied. In West Africa, where fewer whites had settled, gradual concessions were made to local self-government, allowing Ghana, Nigeria, and Tanganyika to emerge as self-governing states. Where European settlers formed a higher percentage of the total population, as in Kenya, Rhodesia, and the Union of South Africa, the British government wavered between the competing claims of African natives and white emigrants. By the mid-1960s, the ratio of independent to colonial countries had reversed, as most of the former African colonies had achieved statehood, many under new names. European dominance remained only in Portuguese Guinea and some southern portions of Africa: the Union of South Africa, Southern Rhodesia, and the Portuguese territories of Angola and Mozambique.

Egypt and the Sudan.   During the interwar years, Egyptians had taken significant steps to free themselves from British tutelage. In 1922 and 1936, the British government recognized Egypt's nominal independence, although joint administration of the Suez Canal continued and British occupation troops remained in the canal zone. In 1952, a nationalist group of military officers overthrew King Faruk I, the last king of modern Egypt. Colonel Gamal Abdel Nasser soon emerged as the dominant government figure. (He served as prime minister from 1954 until he was elected president in 1956.) During 1954, Britain agreed to withdraw its troops in stages from the Suez Canal zone and assented to an arrangement that allowed the Sudanese to decide their own political future. After a ballot by the Sudanese parliament in favor of complete liberation, an independent republic of Sudan was proclaimed in January 1956. Later that year, in violation of an international convention of 1888 and more recent Anglo-Egyptian concords, President Nasser nationalized the Suez Canal and ordered his troops to occupy the canal region. This successful challenge to British and French authority (see pp. 254–255, 269) eliminated the last vestiges of British control and helped to project Nasser as a messiah of African nationalism and Arab unity.

Libya.   After World War II, Libya progressed rapidly from a colony to a trust territory to an independent state. During the war, this Italian colony was occupied by French and British forces. According to terms of the Italian peace treaty of 1947, Libya was made a mandate of the United Nations. In response to nationalist pressures, the United Nations promised Libya independence by 1951. Political rivalry then developed involving a Communist group, the National Congress party, which opposed the achievement of independence under a monarchy.

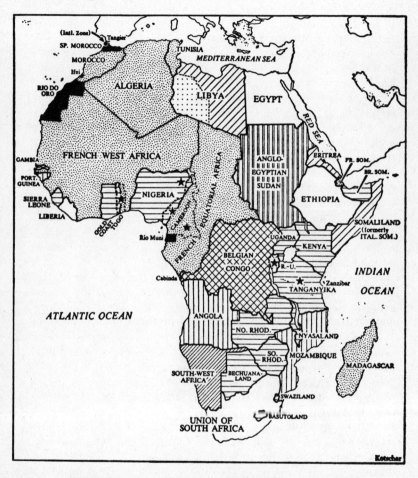

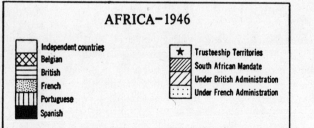

AFRICA—1946

Independent countries
Belgian
British
French
Portuguese
Spanish

★ Trusteeship Territories
South African Mandate
Under British Administration
Under French Administration

Nevertheless, an independent kingdom was created in 1951. At first, Libya was an impoverished state, which depended upon subsidies from abroad; but it evolved as a very wealthy country after the discovery in 1956 of crude oil in its desert led to the development of major oil fields by the United States and other nations. Its geographical location, nearer Europe than other oil-rich areas east of the Suez, provided the country with definite competitive advantages. In return for financial assistance, Libya allowed Western powers to locate major military bases on its soil, despite pressures from its anti-Western Arab neighbors.

Before 1965, Libya was a conservative state that maintained friendly relations with the West. During September of that year, the monarchy headed by King Muhammad Idris al-Sanussi was overthrown by a group of army officers. Under the presidency of Colonel Muammar al-Qaddafi, a socialist republic was proclaimed. The fiery al-Qaddafi soon competed for leadership among the radical Arab states, taking over American and British military bases, confiscating without indemnification large areas of land belonging to Italian Libyans, and nationalizing foreign-owned oil distribution facilities. A further step toward reducing foreign control was taken in 1973 when the government announced that 51 percent of the holdings of all foreign oil companies would be nationalized. In 1970, Libya joined with the United Arab Republic, Syria, and the Sudan in an agreement to work toward federal union of the four countries, leading to a 1973 proclamation that Egypt and Libya had created a new unified Arab state. Actual merger arrangements, however, remained difficult to complete. Premier al-Qaddafi's vigorous efforts to establish an Arab-African alliance, united in opposition to Western supporters of Israel, met with some success. By 1973, in addition to persuading five African nations to sever diplomatic ties with Israel, his radical positions were encouraging the more conservative King Faisal of Saudi Arabia, ruler of the wealthiest oil-producing nation in the Mideast, to threaten reductions in oil exports unless the United States lessened its strong support of Israel.

French North Africa.   French rule in North Africa included the colony of Algeria and the protectorates of Tunisia and Morocco. In all these areas, the problems of independence were aggravated by the presence of sizable colonial settlements. Difficulties were less in Tunisia and Morocco since the European emigrants were fewer in number and more recent arrivals; besides, the Muslims of Tunisia and Morocco, unlike those in Algeria, had always remained subject to their traditional rulers. After 1945, the French government pursued policies of repressing nationalist agitation, led in Tunisia by Habib Bourguiba and in Morocco by Sultan Sidi Mohammed III. Following the independence of Libya and the blow to French prestige caused by the loss of Indochina, nationalist fervor in Tunisia and Morocco became more difficult to manage. France was thus forced to make a series of concessions that led to the independence of both Tunisia and Morocco in 1956. The French were led to yield to pressure in these protectorates in order to concentrate on what they considered a more critical challenge in Algeria, the principal area of French settlement overseas.

Populated by 9 million Muslims and 1 million Europeans (colons), Algeria was not considered a colony but rather a part of metropolitan France. All Algerians were formally declared to be French subjects in 1944 and French citizens in 1947. The 1947 statute also ensured that the Muslim and European populations would have the right to elect equal numbers of deputies to the French parliament. Desiring complete liberation rather than piecemeal concessions, the Algerian independence movement was organized into a revolutionary force known as the National Liberation Front (FLN). Assisted by leaders trained in Egypt and Iraq, this terrorist organization began an armed insurrection in 1954 designed to forcibly wrest Algerian independence from France. They were opposed by the Secret Army Organization (OAS), led by ex-army officers and composed of Frenchmen living in Algeria. The goal of this organization was to maintain rule by the French settlers at all costs. After a long and indecisive war, which had profound domestic repercussions in France (see pp. 274–275), the de Gaulle government recognized Algerian independence in July 1962.

French Colonies South of the Sahara.   Under the Third Republic, the French colonial system, based on a direct hierarchical system of administration, was highly authoritarian and centralized. After the war, steps were taken to introduce representative government by allowing territories to elect deputies both to their local assemblies and to the French National Assembly. Encouraged by many French-trained African politicians and ready to make concessions during the Algerian nightmare, the French government in 1956 adopted a plan based upon the principle of complete autonomy for overseas territories. In the *loi-cadre* that the National Assembly overwhelmingly passed, representative institutions were extended to all twelve of the French sub-Saharan colonies. In 1958, during a referendum held on the proposed Gaullist constitutions, colonies were allowed to vote either for complete independence or for self-governing membership in the French Community. All territories except Guinea, under the leftist leadership of Sékou Touré, opted for the second alternative. However, the French Community proved to be short-lived; within two years, all of these states had obtained complete independence. The new states, most of which joined the United Nations in 1960, included Dahomey, the Ivory Coast, Mali, Senegal, the Central African Republic, and the Republic of Congo. Despite their formal separation, linguistic, cultural, and economic ties between France and the new republics remained strong.

Belgian Congo.   The Belgian possession in the Congo basin was a vast area inhabited by 12 million blacks. White settlements were confined to coastal areas and the enormously rich copper mine region of Katanga in the interior. Until 1959, the Congo remained quiescent under a paternalistic system that raised living standards while permitting a native illiteracy rate of 60 percent. Despite this traditional apathy, the Congo could not stay insulated from the swirling tides of nationalism that surrounded it. The successful efforts of neighboring French territories to move from colonies to independent states was undoubtedly the principal energizing force. The first native rebellions, which occurred in the capital city of Léopoldville in 1959, included four days of rioting, pillage, and rape. Under rising nationalist pressures, and unable to agree on a gradual plan for Congolese statehood, the Belgian government abruptly announced that independence would be granted on June 30, 1960.

Having systematically denied educational and governmental opportunities to Congolese natives, Belgian officials had prevented the emergence of a local elite with administrative experience. Immediately after independence, an amalgam of tribal differences, intense personal rivalries, and anti-Belgian bitterness—all more profound than sentiments of nationalism—led to tribal wars and rising assaults on whites. Three key contestants for power evolved: Premier Patrice Lumumba, Moise Tshombe, leader of the secessionist state of Katanga, and President Joseph Kasavubu.

Faced with an East-West confrontation after the Soviet Union threatened unilateral intervention, the United Nations, under the vigorous leadership of Secretary-General Dag Hammarskjöld, sent to the Congo an international police force of nearly 20,000 men, comprising principally African troops. With assistance from the United Nations, the central government at Léopoldville steadily consolidated its power. Meanwhile, in 1961, Patrice Lumumba was murdered, and Dag Hammarskjöld was killed in an airplane accident in Katanga. Moise Tshombe, whose hand was suspected in both these deaths, decided to exile himself in Spain during 1963 as Katanga was reintegrated into the Republic of Congo. With funds for its operation dwindling in the face of persistent Russian refusals to pay peace-keeping assessments, U.N. intervention in the Congo ended in the summer of 1964. Political and economic scars of the chaos following independence remained.

Portuguese Africa. Undaunted by the predispositions of other European nations to relinquish colonial rule, Portugal, under Antonio Salazar's ruthless dictatorship, staunchly resisted Africa's nationalist tides. Angola and Mozambique, on the west and east coasts of Southern Africa, along with Guinea, were the last surviving colonies of the once far-flung Portuguese Empire. Applying the unitary theory that had characterized French policies, Portugal considered its so-called overseas provinces as integral parts of the fatherland. Paternalistic policies, the *assimilado* system, a common Catholic faith, and governmental repression all combined to thwart nationalist efforts toward independence. In northern Angola, black militants, aided by arms smuggled from Algeria and the Republic of Congo, engaged in an insurrection marked by atrocities against whites in 1961. In retaliation, Portuguese forces indiscriminately destroyed entire villages associated with the insurgency. Assisted by Red China and other Communist countries, banished Angolan rebels then erected a cabinet-in-exile within the Republic of Congo. The Portuguese also used harsh measures when guerrilla warfare erupted in Guinea in 1963. Less politically inclined, the natives of Mozambique were kept under control through harsh police tactics and severe security regulations. Despite widespread censure, including anticolonial resolutions by the United Nations and the Organization of African Unity, Portugal maintained its mastery over Angola, Mozambique, and Guinea. Yet, after a military coup within Portugal (April 1974) overthrew the government of Marcello Caetano, either a loose federation or full independence was envisioned for each of the African colonies.

British West Africa. Britain began its departure from Africa with the termination of its control in Egypt (1954) and the Sudan (1956). Shortly thereafter, Britain set the pattern of liberation for sub-Saharan Africa by granting independence to the Gold Coast, subsequently named Ghana. To implement the gradual program of disengagement, which centered on the transferral of authority and responsibility to local natives, parliamentary institutions were established for the Gold Coast in 1954. The process of liberation was simplified for

West Africa since only a small percentage of Europeans had settled in the region. The British also considered the Gold Coast a suitable prospect for statehood because the country was economically prosperous and possessed a forceful Western-educated leader, Dr. Kwame Nkrumah. After independence was achieved in 1957, Nkrumah fashioned a dictatorial one-party government that, notwithstanding Ghana's membership in the Commonwealth, pursued neutralist policies in foreign affairs. It was only natural that independence for Nigeria, the most populous country on the continent, would soon follow. Although Nigeria was troubled with deep tribal, regional, and religious differences, its path to liberation was traveled peaceably. A federated constitution was adopted in 1954, and in 1960, Nigeria became the second black state to accept Commonwealth status. Britain's remaining West African territories, less impressive in size and wealth, also moved relentlessly toward political freedom.

British East Africa. Largely because of the presence of sizable and influential white populations, independence for the British territories in East Africa occurred later and with greater difficulty than in the West. This was particularly true in Kenya, a multiracial society in which 60,000 whites and 200,000 Asiatics dominated 8 million Africans. Faced with white control over the best farmlands and the reluctance of the British government to make concessions, Jomo Kenyatta, a London-trained anthropologist, returned to Kenya in 1946 and formed the Kenya Africa National Union. Beginning in 1952, rejections of moderate reforms and intensifying bitterness precipitated terroristic activities by a secret organization of militant Kikuyu tribesmen known as the Mau Mau. Dedicated to achieving freedom by campaigns of intimidation, mutilation, and murder against the white population, the Mau Mau engaged in guerrilla warfare that the British could suppress only after four years of brutal fighting. With independence the only realistic option, the British then engaged in negotiations that led to the Kenyan flag's replacing the Union Jack in Nairobi (December 1963). With the new republic retaining membership in the British Commonwealth, an aging Jomo Kenyatta, whose magnetic qualities survived his years of imprisonment between 1953 and 1959, became the first prime minister of independent Kenya.

Faced with adamant Mau Mau resistance in Kenya, Britain was more easily persuaded to accept the independence of Tanganyika, Zanzibar, and Uganda. Although Tanganyika, like Kenya, was a multiracial society, U.N. trusteeship and the moderate leadership of Julius Nyerere smoothed the path to independence. Beginning in the 1950s,

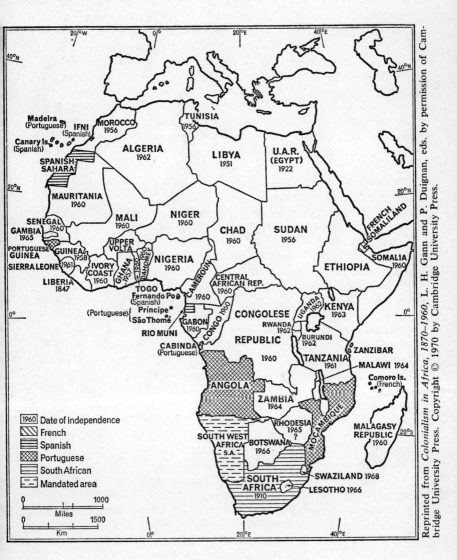

Reprinted from *Colonialism in Africa, 1870–1960*, L. H. Gann and P. Duignan, eds. by permission of Cambridge University Press. Copyright © 1970 by Cambridge University Press.

Africa 1968

membership in the Legislative Council, the principal local organ of administration, was progressively broadened on the basis of racial parity, and in December 1962, Tanganyika achieved independence. The elective principle was also used to broaden native participation in the government of Zanzibar. Despite rivalries between Arabs and Africans, Zanzibar was liberated in December 1963. Uganda, lacking a significant white, Asiatic, or Arab minority, faced different problems, including struggles between the traditional tribal rulers and a more impatient educated class of militants. Rivalries also existed between Buganda, a province that formed one-fourth of the entire colony, and the other peoples of Uganda. In the 1950s, Bugandan nationalists demanded a larger role in the government, as African participation increased the importance of Uganda's Legislative Council. These difficulties were eased by Bugandan representation in the Council, and the transition to full independence was completed in October 1962.

British Central Africa. In their Central African territories of Northern Rhodesia, Southern Rhodesia, and Nyasaland, the British made plans for a multiracial federation during the postwar years. Pressures for amalgamation of the territories were exerted in each country by Europeans who sought closer cooperation to stem the rising tide of African political consciousness. Federation was formally achieved in 1953, under a constitution establishing a government responsible primarily to a white-elected legislature that controlled the areas of external affairs, defense, commerce, and finance. Over one-half the members of the legislature came from Southern Rhodesia, a colony in which for thirty years self-governing white settlers had ruthlessly dominated the black population. Each territory retained its own system of local government, with powers embracing such matters as police functions, education, and welfare. In Southern Rhodesia, the territorial government remained responsible to a legislature chosen exclusively by whites.

From the beginning, African nationalists bitterly opposed this settlement on the ground that it broadened the racist rule of Southern Rhodesia's whites. These grievances were not quieted despite halting efforts toward territorial self-government in Nyasaland and Northern Rhodesia, including expanded African participation in the Legislative Councils. By 1959, there were riots favoring the end of the federation and immediate self-government. In response, during 1962, the British government formulated a plan for the independence of Nyasaland to be achieved in three stages. Having completed these preliminary steps, Nyasaland achieved its independence in July 1964 under the name of

Malawi. Three months later, Northern Rhodesia became a self-governing republic known as Zambia. Both states remained within the British Commonwealth.

Dissolution of the Federation of Rhodesia and Nyasaland combined with the successful strides toward independence by Northern Rhodesia and Nyasaland, accelerated similar demands in Southern Rhodesia. British policy was to withhold self-government for Rhodesia until Africans were permitted greater representation in the legislature and the discriminatory practices against them were eased. In 1964, Ian Smith became prime minister and leader of the opinion among white Rhodesians that Rhodesia should either achieve a negotiated independence or take unilateral steps to eliminate British rule. The British position against minority white rule in Rhodesia was buttressed by a U.N. Security Council resolution of 1965 supporting a democratic constitution and by African prime ministers acting within the Commonwealth's Prime Ministers' Conference.

These moves served only to harden the intransigence among white Rhodesians. Following a U.N. resolution of November 1965 that urged Great Britain to compel majority rule in Rhodesia through force if necessary, Ian Smith's regime rebelled by proclaiming Rhodesian independence. Economic sanctions against Rhodesia were then voted by the House of Commons and later supported by other Commonwealth and foreign countries. However, the problem remained intractable as economic sanctions proved to be ineffective coercive measures against the Rhodesian government and as all efforts to end the deadlock through negotiations have been abortive. During 1971, Ian Smith and Edward Heath, the British prime minister, agreed to a set of principles by which Rhodesian independence would be recognized in return for graduated steps toward political freedom for Africans. Militant African resistance to this settlement, however, prevented its acceptance by the House of Commons.

Britain and South Africa.   After World War II, the Union of South Africa, which provided the example for Southern Rhodesia's unilateral declaration of independence, continued to be the model of intransigent white rule in Africa. Resistance among white settlers mounted as internal interracial tensions and world opinion attempted to force concessions for the native masses. The National party, which dominated South African politics after the war, advocated a program based on principles of white superiority and the inability of whites and blacks to live harmoniously in an integrated community. Accordingly, during the 1950s and 1960s, the party leaders created a rigid racial system of territorial, legal, educational, and political apartheid. The primary architect and spokesman for these measures was Dr. H. F. Verwoerd, who became prime minister in 1958. To lessen differences between British and Boer settlers and thereby strengthen white minority rule, Nationalists were willing to sever all Commonwealth relations. The mechanism that they chose was a referendum among the white voters in 1960, which indicated that a majority favored creation of a republic. This act legally cut the link between the Queen of England and the Union of South Africa, requiring a vote of approval by other members if South Africa's participation in the Commonwealth were to continue. Aware of the strong disapproval by other Commonwealth countries of South Africa's racial policies, Verwoerd decided at the Prime Ministers' Conference of 1961 to withdraw South Africa's application for renewal of membership. Here, as in Rhodesia, the severance of imperial relations hindered instead of promoted native rule.

22

The United States since World War II

By the end of World War II, the United States had established unquestioned economic and military preeminence in the world. The nations of Europe, whether in defeat or victory, faced monumental jobs of reconstruction due to the war's debilitating ravages. In Asia, Japan was vanquished, and China, its natural rival, remained weak and divided. As the Grand Alliance that had won the war degenerated into the cold war between East and West, the United States naturally emerged as the Western leader in efforts to confine the expanding frontiers of Communist influence. Grants to other nations of astronomical sums in economic and military assistance and involvement in the Korean and Vietnam wars reflected the nation's commitment to world leadership. International questions during the postwar years continually competed for attention with domestic issues with which they were frequently interrelated. Among the most significant internal problems were rising inflation, high levels of unemployment, the quest for social justice, and debates over the proper role that the United States should exercise in the world. To deal with these matters, American voters in seven presidential elections since the war have chosen three Democratic and four Republican administrations: Harry S. Truman (Democrat, 1948); Dwight D. Eisenhower (Republican, 1952, 1956); John F. Kennedy (Democrat, 1960); Lyndon B. Johnson (Democrat, 1964); and Richard M. Nixon (Republican, 1968, 1972).

THE TRUMAN ADMINISTRATION

Vice-President Harry S. Truman succeeded to the presidency following the sudden death of President Roosevelt on April 12, 1945. The first president since Grover Cleveland without a college education, Truman was inexperienced in world affairs and had never occupied an executive role, although he had served ten years as senator from Missouri. He had been chosen on the ticket for largely political reasons and as vice-president had been kept ill-informed on many policy questions. Truman gradually adjusted to his new role, however, and during nearly eight years in office, he moved decisively in many areas, particularly in foreign affiars.

President Roosevelt bequeathed to Truman a heterogeneous political coalition comprising organized labor, liberals, blacks in urban areas, farmers in the Midwest, and the so-called Solid South. No longer welded together by Roosevelt's effective role as broker or by the crises of depression and world war, this coalition was soon weakened as its competing interests began to occupy center stage. Southern Democrats, who were embedded by the seniority system in key congressional committee chairmanships, joined with conservative Republicans from rural areas to defeat progressive measures intended primarily for urban areas.

Foreign Affairs. Foreign-policy questions were Truman's immediate preoccupation, and here his ability to act boldly and firmly soon became evident. He unsuccessfully pressured the Soviets to abide by the Yalta agreements regarding Eastern Europe. It was his decision to drop the atomic bombs that ended the war with Japan while taking unprecedented tolls in human lives. After the war, the Truman administration made the crucial decisions that crystallized America's cold war policy of containing Communist aggression. The Truman Doctrine (March 1947) committed large sums of economic and military assistance to the defense of Greece and Turkey. Observing that the economic chaos of Western Europe created a mood of desperation that was also conducive to Communist takeovers, the Truman administration devised and Secretary of State George C. Marshall announced (June 1947) a broad program of economic recovery called the Marshall Plan. Economic progress followed, and none of the major Western states succumbed to the temptation of Communist rule. Military cooperation among Western countries was also stimulated by the Soviet threat. Twelve states signed a charter creating the North Atlantic Treaty Organization (April 1949), which stipulated that an attack on one signatory would be met by resistance from all. The administration's anti-Communist record was less successful in Asia. China succumbed to Communist rule in 1949, and after a bitter fight between Communist North and U.S.-supported South Korea, the two states remained divided at the 38th parallel (see pp. 251–252, 330).

Election of 1948. After sixteen years in power, the Democratic party was in disarray as the 1948 elections approached. Southerners were alienated by President Truman's strong stand in favor of civil rights legislation to aid blacks. Some liberals, including former Secretary of Agriculture and Vice-President Henry A. Wallace, believed that an accommodation with the Soviet Union was the surest path to world peace and were antagonized by the administration's stern cold war positions. Sensing that Truman did not have widespread appeal, some Democrats unsuccessfully tried to deny him the nomination and to attract instead a reluctant General Dwight D. Eisenhower as the party's standard-bearer. When the Democratic party adopted a strong civil rights plank in its platform, Southerners abruptly exited from the gathering and formed their own Dixiecrat party with Governor Strom Thurmond of South Carolina as their candidate. Wallace, meanwhile, ran as the nominee of another splinter group, the Progressive party. Republicans therefore entered the presidential race with high hopes. They again chose as their candidate New York Governor Thomas E. Dewey, the Republican nominee in 1944. Dewey ran an overconfident campaign as political experts and popular opinion polls predicted that he would win by a landslide. Truman conducted a whistle-stop "give 'em hell" crusade against what he described the "do-nothing" Republican Eightieth Congress. His spirited efforts won the affection of many voters, enabling him to carry the West, Midwest, and all but four Southern states in a stunning upset victory.

The Fair Deal. By 1948, very little of President Truman's domestic program had been enacted. Using his startling defeat of Dewey as a mandate, the president in his 1949 State of the Union Address presented to Congress a program labeled the Fair Deal. Intended to further New Deal objectives by bettering conditions of the underprivileged, the Fair Deal embraced plans for broadening social security, raising price supports for farmers, establishing full employment, elevating minimum wage rates, improving housing, creating a fair employment practices commission, and passing antilynching and antipoll tax laws. Extending the Fair Deal abroad, Truman also called for a Point Four program of aid to the underdeveloped areas of Latin America, Asia, and Africa in order to prevent them from falling into Communist hands. Formally established in 1950, the Point Four program was one of Truman's most successful undertakings. Congress also enacted some compromise versions of other administration bills by raising the minimum wage from 40 to 75 cents an hour, passing a moderate housing act, and extending old-age benefits under the Social Security Act. Northern and Southern conservatives combined to defeat other Fair Deal measures, some of which they derided as socialistic. In marked contrast with the Truman administration's achievements in foreign affairs, there were thus few major domestic triumphs. Truman's proposals did help pave the way, however, for later landmark legislation to alleviate conditions of deprived Americans.

The Communist Scare. During the final years of the Truman administration, Americans became gripped with a cold war paranoia based on fears that Communists in high places were undermining the nation's security and governing system. Varied circumstances lent substance to these fears. Despite U.S. assistance, Communists fought the Korean War to a standstill and triumphed in China during 1949. At home, sensational spy cases were repeatedly in the headlines. Alger Hiss, a former State Department employee, was charged by Whittaker Chambers, a writer and admitted former Communist agent, with having made classified State Department secrets available to Moscow agents in 1937 and 1938. Hiss was convicted of perjury in 1949 and sentenced to five years' imprisonment. The next year, Klaus Fuchs, a British-based scientist who had worked on the Los Alamos atomic bomb project, confessed to having supplied Soviet agents with atom bomb secrets. Based on the Fuchs revelations, the FBI arrested Julius and Ethel Rosenberg, who were charged with being his American accomplices. The husband-and wife team was convicted and later executed in June 1953. A national wave of anti-Communist fears inspired repressive legislation and loyalty oaths on both state and national levels. In this atmosphere, Wisconsin Senator Joseph R. McCarthy (Republican) sparked widespread controversy. In a series of speeches beginning in 1950, McCarthy made unsubstantiated charges that within the State Department, there were "card-carrying members of the Communist party." McCarthyism became a code word for militant and irresponsible anticommunism as the senator destroyed public reputations through vilifications and insinuations until, in 1954, he was censured by the Senate for his conduct.

THE EISENHOWER ADMINISTRATION

As the 1952 elections approached, Republican confidence grew with public disapproval over President Truman's handling of the Korean War. This trend was strengthened by the revelations of significant corruption in the Truman administration and by persisting charges that key government officials were "soft on communism." There was also a widespread desire for an escape from commitment and for political change, based on the assumption that the Democrats had simply held power too long. Having decided not to run again, Truman was instrumental in the choice of Illinois Governor Adlai Stevenson as the Democratic candidate. The Republicans chose Dwight D. Eisenhower, unquestionably the most respected figure in American life during the 1950s. Attracted by his distinguished military career and the qualities of sincerity and integrity he projected, voters supported Eisenhower across class, occupational, and party lines. He won the Republican nomination as the spokesman for the party's Eastern internationalist faction after a tenacious struggle with conservative and isolationist Republicans led by Ohio Senator Robert Taft. Eisenhower easily defeated Stevenson by a margin of 442 electoral votes to 89. Internationally and domestically, the Eisenhower years were marked by caution. In foreign affairs, despite his campaign condemnation of abandoning peoples to Communist rule, President Eisenhower continued the Truman policies of containment rather than confrontation. Financially and economically, the government's strongest commitment was to the orthodox policies of reduced taxes and a balanced budget. Eisenhower's critics attacked him for indecisiveness in many domestic matters. He never publicly condemned McCarthy, for example, or spoke forthrightly on the broadening crisis in race relations.

A Cabinet of Businessmen. President Eisenhower's respect for successful businessmen was reflected in his cabinet appointments. John Foster Dulles, a former corporation lawyer who had advised the Truman administration on foreign affairs and negotiated the treaty with Japan, was chosen secretary of state. George M. Humphrey, a fiscal conservative and head of the Hanna Corporation of Cleveland, became secretary of the treasury. For secretary of defense, Eisenhower selected Charles E. Wilson, formerly president of General Motors. Two other business executives, Arthur Summerfield and Douglas McKay, were appointed to the positions of postmaster general and secretary of the interior. Herbert Brownell, Jr., a former political aide to Thomas Dewey, was designated attorney-general. Of the presi-

dent's nine original cabinet appointees, eight had established themselves as millionaires. Throughout his two terms in office, President
Eisenhower borrowed heavily from his military experience, delegating
far-ranging policy decisions to subordinates and relying upon their
recommendations. Under his leadership, cabinet officers in some areas
were able to distinguish themselves to an unusual degree as the real
formulators of policy. This was particularly the case with John Foster
Dulles, whose judgments in foreign affairs the president seldom questioned.

End of the Korean War.   In the presidential campaign, Eisenhower
made his top priority "an early and honorable" end to the Korean
War, pledging to visit Korea after his election for that purpose. Negotiations to end the conflict had begun in July 1951, and when Eisenhower assumed office, agreements had already been reached on methods
of supervising a cease-fire and on a boundary between North and
South Korea. Deliberations had stalemated, however, on the question of repatriating prisoners of war. The United States insisted that
those prisoners who decided against returning to North Korea should
not be compelled to do so, and Dulles threatened a resumption of warfare if North Korea did not alter its stand. The goal of peace was
furthered by the death of Stalin in 1953 and by the conciliatory position of Premier Georgi Malenkov on cold war questions. A truce was
finally signed on June 26, 1953. With continued American support to
the South, an uneasy armed armistice, periodically disrupted by border incidents, remained in effect between North and South Korea.

Defense Policies.   Disillusionment with the outcome of the Korean
War, combined with exorbitant cold war expenditures, significantly
affected America's defense policies. To limit military appropriations
and discourage participation by the United States in local wars, the
Eisenhower administration decided to reduce the conventional forces
of the army and navy. During periods of international crisis, heavy
reliance was to be placed instead on threats of direct and massive retaliation against the Soviet Union and China, the two Communist
giants. To make this planning feasible, the Defense Department
broadened the nuclear bombing capacity of the Strategic Air Command. Some Democrats, notably Dean Acheson, criticized this brinksmanship strategy, contending that the emerging balance of terror undermined its credibility and therefore weakened the Western alliance.
Faced with a test of this policy during the French defeat in Indochina,
President Eisenhower pursued cautious policies by neither sending
in American troops nor playing the game of nuclear brinksmanship.

In its efforts to erect barriers around the edges of the Communist world, the Eisenhower administration clearly built upon the precedents established by President Truman. Military alliances patterned after NATO were created for Southeast Asia and the Middle East. The Southeast Asia Treaty Organization (SEATO), established in 1954, included the United States, France, Britain, Austria, New Zealand, Pakistan, Thailand, and the Philippines. The following year, the United States encouraged but did not join an alliance comprised of Britain, Turkey, Iran, Iraq, and Pakistan, which became known as the Central Treaty Organization (CENTO). The Eisenhower Doctrine of 1957 also promised to countries of the Middle East the same assurances of aid against Communist insurgencies that President Truman had extended to Greece and Turkey.

Economy.   The so-called modern Republicanism espoused by Eisenhower made no efforts to reverse the economic and social revolution the Democratic New Dealers had engineered. Instead, Eisenhower placed primary emphasis on maintaining the stability of prices, thereby protecting the integrity of the dollar, and on efforts to allocate some functions of the federal government to state and local levels. Reductions in government spending after the Korean War produced a slower rate of economic growth, to which the recessions of 1953–1954, 1957–1958, and 1960–1961 contributed significantly. Inflation, nevertheless, continued to spiral, as a result of the wage-profit cycles affecting basic industries such as steel. The administration also achieved mixed results in its determination to balance the budget and transfer federal functions to lower levels of government. Although budgetary surpluses were achieved during some years, the Eisenhower administration accumulated an overall deficit in excess of $18 billion. Meanwhile, only minor adjustments were made in the allocation of governmental responsibilities, leaving the federal government the mammoth organization that Eisenhower inherited from the Democrats. The persisting farm problem was particularly troublesome. Although the government spent billions of dollars on price support and soil bank programs, farm incomes dropped by nearly $4 billion from 1952 to 1959.

Election of 1956.   President Eisenhower's personal appeal as a national leader and a statesman above party outdistanced the narrower attraction of the Republican party. Voters reflected this dichotomy by providing President Eisenhower with an overwhelming popular vote in 1952 while awarding Republicans only narrow majorities in Congress. The elections of 1954 eliminated these slender margins, allowing Democrats to regain control of both houses with a 232–203 majority in the House of Representatives and a 48–47 majority in the Senate. As the 1956 elections approached, it was clear that Republican hopes rested mainly on the shoulders of an ailing President Eisenhower who suffered a heart attack in September 1955 and had an operation in June 1956. Richard Nixon was again chosen as the vice-presidential candidate after some controversy over the fairness of his campaign tactics and his identification with the party's conservative wing. After a first ballot victory again made Adlai Stevenson the standard-bearer for the Democrats, the convention, at Stevenson's behest, departed from the precedent of allowing the presidential candidate to choose his running mate and selected Tennessee Senator Estes Kefauver as the vice-presidential nominee. Deciding issues in the election were Eisenhower's continued popularity and the reluctance of voters to remove an experienced pilot from the helm when warfare was flaring up in the Middle East. Eisenhower's second victory over Stevenson was even more decisive than his first. The Republican ticket received nearly 10 million more popular votes and 457 electoral votes to 74 for the Democrats. Legislative returns, nevertheless, dramatized the personal nature of Eisenhower's triumph. Democrats maintained a 49–47 edge in the Senate and increased their margin in the House of Representatives from 29 to 33.

Desegregation.   After World War II, the Supreme Court's defense of the rights of blacks was an epochal development in American history. The court became increasingly liberal both on civil rights and civil liberties after Eisenhower appointed Governor Earl Warren of California chief justice in 1953. A series of cases had already weakened the Court's decision in *Plessy* v. *Ferguson* (1896), which interpreted the equal protection of the laws clause of the Constitution to mean that states could provide separate facilities for blacks so long as they were equal to those for whites. In the field of public education and later in other areas, the Supreme Court completely reversed the *Plessy* ruling. Separate educational facilities, the court declared in May 1954, were "inherently unequal." In a decision the following year, school authorities in the Southern and border states, where racial segregation existed by law, were ordered to submit plans for the integration of their school facilities with "all deliberate speed." Although border states reluctantly took steps to comply, resistance in the Deep South hardened as a consequence of President Eisenhower's ambivalence on the question, the organization of militant groups such as the White Citizen's Councils, and a manifesto by Southern congressmen condemning the school desegregation decision. Southern resistance to integrated schools reached a boiling point in 1957 when Governor Orval Faubus of Arkansas mobilized his state's national guard to prevent nine black students from enrolling at Little Rock's Central High School. Faced with this constitutional challenge, Eisenhower first persuaded Faubus to withdraw the National Guard and then sent federal troops to enforce the federal court order.

PRESIDENT KENNEDY'S THOUSAND DAYS

After Eisenhower's second term, the interlude of Republican rule came to an end. In both foreign and domestic affairs, the mood of the American electorate was again receptive to new leaders and programs. When Russia became the first nation to successfully test an intercontinental ballistic missile in August 1957, and later that year succeeded in launching *Sputnik I,* the first successful satellite, widespread apprehension developed over the future of American security and prestige. During Eisenhower's final year in office, Soviet-American relations worsened precipitously after showing marked signs of cordiality. A summit conference between Eisenhower and Khrushchev, scheduled for Paris in May 1960, was bitterly canceled by Russia after an American U-2 spy plane was brought down inside Soviet territory. There was further a broadening attitude that the persisting problems in race relations, poverty, and urban conditions could not be indefinitely obscured and postponed. Many believed that stronger presidential leadership would better enable the nation to fulfill the goals of social and economic progress. Massachusetts Senator John F. Kennedy skillfully exploited this mood as he vied for the presidency by declaring that "it's time America started moving again."

Election of 1960. After establishing himself as the most popular candidate in the primaries, John F. Kennedy won the Democratic nomination despite his youthful age (43) and his Roman Catholic faith, which had been thought to be insurmountable barriers. Kennedy's vigorous campaigning overcame the opposition first of Hubert Humphrey and later of Lyndon B. Johnson, the Senate majority leader, whom he chose as his running mate. Vice-President Richard M. Nixon won the Republican nomination as his control of the party machinery and position as heir apparent helped him overcome the opposition of his nearest rival, New York Governor Nelson Rockefeller. A series of television debates was influential during the campaign, allowing the self-confident and knowledgeable Kennedy to establish himself in the minds of many voters as a man of maturity and poise. Nixon's chances were further hurt by a business recession that began in 1960. Nevertheless, Kennedy won by the slimmest majority in a presidential election since 1884: a popular vote margin of 112,881 out of a total of over 68 million ballots cast. In the electoral college, his victory was more decisive, with a majority of 300 to 219. Democrats simultaneously strengthened their majorities in both houses, winnng in the Senate by 65 to 35 and in the House of Representatives by 261 to 176.

Foreign Affairs. With the aid of Secretary of Defense Robert F. McNamara, Kennedy moved away from the Eisenhower-Dulles policy of massive retaliation to more flexible deterrent plans that lessened dependence on nuclear weapons. As president, Kennedy soon learned that U.S. relations with other countries were more difficult to direct than he had supposed. Differences with de Gaulle thwarted his dream of a federated Europe closely allied with the United States. Despite Kennedy's desire to keep NATO strong, widening differences between the major Western powers, centering on control of nuclear weapons, created rifts that could not be bridged. America's involvement in the continuing postcolonial crises, including struggles in Laos, Vietnam, and the Congo, achieved only mixed results. In the Western Hemisphere, the administration's hopes were also unfulfilled. After approving the ill-fated Bay of Pigs invasion of Cuba (see pp. 307–308), the government launched the much-heralded Alliance for Progress, a program of massive aid designed to speed economic growth and raise living standards throughout Latin America. Although relations with Latin American nations improved, the goals of social and economic reform remained difficult to achieve.

In his arduous relations with Russia, Kennedy persistently sought a détente in the cold war. Nonetheless, a meeting in Vienna (June 1961) between Kennedy and Khrushchev did little to promote global tranquillity. Soon thereafter Khrushchev insisted that the German question be resolved in a way that would end Western access rights to West Berlin and convert the divided metropolis into a neutral city. When Kennedy responded with measures to strengthen American defenses, Soviet leaders reacted by erecting the Berlin Wall (see p. 302). In 1962, the Cuban missile crisis created perils to world peace that were more fully fraught with danger, bringing the world to the brink of nuclear destruction. Kennedy forced the dismantling of a Soviet missile buildup in Cuba by ordering a naval blockade to prevent further arms shipments to the island and warned that a missile fired from Cuba against the United States would be met by nuclear warfare against the

Soviet Union. A continuing quest of the Kennedy administration was for a nuclear test-ban treaty with Russia. Soviet negotiators were intransigent on this question when Kennedy assumed office, since they intended to resume the testing of nuclear devices in the atmosphere. Finally ratified in September 1963 after difficult negotiations, the test-ban treaty was the most momentous step toward easing East-West tensions since the end of World War II.

The New Frontier. Before his election, Kennedy had ambitions of opening his anticipated presidency with a comprehensive and dramatic legislative program comparable to President Roosevelt's Hundred Days. His New Frontier in the domestic arena envisioned medical care for the aged, federal aid to education, agricultural reforms, civil rights legislation, trade expansion, and tax renovations. Yet the narrow margin of Kennedy's victory could not be interpreted as a mandate for pervasive social change. Although Democratic majorities existed in both houses of Congress, the persisting coalition between Southern Democrats and conservative Republicans continued the congressional deadlock that had obstructed Truman's legislative proposals. For the liberal elements in his program, the president was assured of support only from Northern and Western Democrats, in addition to a small group of liberal Republicans from the Northeast. Kennedy therefore moved cautiously, attempting to conciliate Southerners by deferring action on civil rights bills while economic measures were enacted. The administration did succeed in obtaining passage during 1961–1962 of an increase in the minimum wage, provisions for trade expansion, a comprehensive housing bill, and broadened social security coverage. Other key measures were blocked by the conservative coalition in Congress.

Economy. Kennedy entered office in the midst of an economic recession that found sizable elements of the labor force unemployed. The administration's economic advisers concluded that the curbing of inflation was essential both to relieving the balance of payments problem and to protecting the dollar's value at home. Economists in the administration viewed the continuous cycle of wage and price increases, particularly in the steel industry, as the principal cause of inflation. To offset this trend, the government pressured business and labor leaders to accept wage and price guidelines based upon increases in productivity. Labor leaders yielded to these restraints during their contract negotiations in June 1962. When steel executives, on the other hand, announced price increases the following month, President Kennedy forced them to rescind their actions through public denunciations, antitrust proceedings, and the selective allocation of government con-

tracts. Despite a stock-market slump in May 1962, Kennedy's economic policies did encourage a return to business prosperity, which
produced average annual increases in the gross national product of
5.6 percent. Depreciation allowances and tax incentives encouraged
new investments, and the president in 1963 proposed a general reduction in taxes that was effected during 1964. Recognizing that large
segments of the American populace did not share in the nation's
affluence, President Kennedy had decided by 1963 upon the need for a
systematic "war on poverty."

Black Rebellion.   Almost a decade after the Supreme Court's historic integration decision of 1954, an imposing array of legal and
extralegal barriers still thwarted the civil rights movement for blacks.
The administration proceeded deliberately in this field, moving primarily in those areas where executive decisions did not require legislative
enactment. Federal authority was used to integrate the state universities of Mississippi and Alabama, two bastions of white supremacy in
higher education. Blacks were appointed to prestigious positions in
government, and efforts were made to remove segregationist barriers
in voting and interstate commerce. Nonetheless, the pace of change
fell far behind the rising expectations and demands of blacks. The
National Association for the Advancement of Colored People
(NAACP), which had led the gradual, legalistic struggle for change,
was joined by the more action-oriented Congress of Racial Equality
(CORE) and the Southern Christian Leadership Conference (SCLC).
A much smaller number of blacks were attracted to the militant Black
Panther and Black Muslim calls for black supremacy and racial separation. Efforts to desegregate facilities through sit-ins, which began in
1960, proved a decisive turning point. They were soon combined with
freedom rides, boycotts, and mass demonstrations. In April 1963, Dr.
Martin Luther King, Jr., director of the SCLC, inaugurated a crusade
of boycotts and marches to end public discrimination in Birmingham,
Alabama. The demonstrations were met by repeated acts of police
brutality and the bombing of a black church that resulted in the deaths
of four young girls. These acts created widespread sympathy for the
demonstrators. In August 1963, Dr. King also provided symbolic
leadership for the March on Washington of more than 200,000 participants. Under these circumstances, President Kennedy's commitment to the civil rights struggle became more unequivocal. He proclaimed that "race had no place in American life or law" and during
1963 announced plans for the most sweeping civil rights legislation in
the nation's history.

THE PRESIDENCY OF LYNDON B. JOHNSON

By the fall of 1963, President Kennedy was planning ahead to the election of 1964. He expected to win by a sizable majority, help elect a more liberal Congress, and thereby remove the logjam that obstructed many of his programs. These dreams ended on November 22, 1963, when during a motorcade in Dallas, Texas, the president was fatally shot by Lee Harvey Oswald, a loner whose political ideas had been influenced by Marxist thought. Vice-President Johnson was speedily sworn in as the nation's thirty-sixth president. Johnson's first priority was to maintain national unity while emphasizing his allegiance to the fallen leader by retaining his chief advisers and promoting New Frontier programs. Using the enormous political talents he had cultivated as Senate majority leader, President Johnson broke the legislative stalemate and steered more legislation through Congress than had been enacted since the New Deal. However, foreign affairs, and particularly the escalating Vietnam War, dominated most of his presidency.

New Frontier to Great Society. The central theme of President Johnson's address to a joint session of Congress on November 27, 1963, was "let us continue" the Kennedy policies. Congress responded speedily to this plea by enacting pending tax reduction and civil rights bills that President Kennedy had proposed. The landmark Civil Rights Act of 1964 prohibited discrimination in public facilities and the use of federal funds and created the Equal Employment Opportunity Commission (EEOC) to deal with complaints of discrimination in private employment. Also in 1964, President Johnson extended the New Frontier to include the Equal Opportunity Act. Designed as an antipoverty measure, this legislation established ten programs embracing provisions for volunteer social workers (VISTA), vocational and remedial education, and antipoverty grants to states and localities. The war on poverty became the foundation of the Great Society, President Johnson's distinctive label for his domestic programs.

Election of 1964. The 1964 presidential election was a contest between the moderate liberalism of President Johnson and the militant conservatism of Senator Barry Goldwater, the Republican nominee. From the outset, President Johnson had attempted to weld a national consensus that would embrace all except the most alienated of political extremes. With Goldwater commanding the Republican machinery as a hero of the radical right, heterogeneous alliances emerged across party lines in support of Johnson. Unlike most Republicans, Goldwater wanted to eradicate many of the welfare programs that represented fruits of the New Deal. He attacked the social security system and proposed abolition of the graduated income tax, TVA, and farm subsidies. In foreign affairs, his views were similarly unorthodox. His criticisms of Democratic policies included condemnations of peaceful coexistence with communism and appeals to escalate the Vietnam War by bombing North Vietnam. Goldwater's factional and ideological views induced massive defections from the Republican party. He virtually invited moderates to leave the party, causing prominent businessmen, such as Henry Ford II, to help form Republicans for Johnson clubs. Republicans lost marked support among blacks while simultaneously winning strong backing in the traditionally Democratic Deep South. The election outcome was predictable. With over 60 percent of the popular vote and 486 electoral votes to only 52 for the Republicans, the Johnson-Humphrey ticket was awarded the most overwhelming presidential victory since the election of 1936. Militant conservatism on the national ticket also proved disastrous for other Republicans, contributing to a loss of 34 seats in the House.

Great Society Legislation. With huge Democratic majorities in Congress and a convincing popular mandate, President Johnson succeeded in guiding more legislation through Congress than any president since Franklin D. Roosevelt. In 1965, for the first time in American history, a comprehensive program of direct federal aid to education was enacted. Also in 1965, after twenty years of debate, the federal government insured medical care for citizens over 65 through the Medicare-Social Security Act. Other groundbreaking legislation of 1965 included the Voting Rights Act empowering the federal government to end discriminatory registration practices, liberalization in the immigration laws, creation of the Department of Housing and Urban Affairs, rent subsidies for low income families, and the Appalachian Development Act. In 1966, Congress enacted laws empowering the national government to set safety standards on the highways and to control air and water pollution. After 1966, the tide of reform legislation ebbed as the president's popularity began to wane, but much of his program had already been enacted. An additional measure passed in 1968 was the Medicaid program, designed to supplement Medicare by providing financial assistance to the indigent sick below the age of 65.

Civil Rights to Black Power. During the middle and late 1960s, the black revolution moved decidedly to the left. While civil rights laws had achieved halting progress in the South, the gap between white and black incomes had widened nationwide. Frustration became particularly acute among blacks in urban areas of the North, where inadequate education and widespread unemployment seemed to make a mockery of the nominal civil rights they possessed. A growing mood of conservatism among whites, combined with the cost of the Vietnam War, aggravated bitterness among blacks by lessening the hope for programs to deal with their problems. Ghetto rioting and violence began on a major scale in Watts, a suburb of Los Angeles, in August 1965. Other uprisings occurred during the summers of 1966 and 1967 and after the assassination of Martin Luther King in April 1968. Within the civil rights movement, shifts occurred from interracial participation to black dominance of some organizations and also to the support of new groups, including CORE and the Black Panthers, at the expense of the more moderate organizations of the NAACP and the SCLC. Under the leadership of Stokely Carmichael and Floyd McKissick, CORE popularized the slogan *black power*, the interpretation of which ranged from the quest for local political and economic control in black communities to demands for the complete separation of the races.

The Problem of Vietnam.   In the election of 1964, the Vietnam War was rivaled by other issues. By 1968, America's unprecedented and continuing involvement in the Asian land war had made it the overriding national problem. President Johnson and his supporters reasoned that the Communist threat in South Vietnam was comparable with the Nazi threat in Europe during 1938 and 1939. They saw the North Vietnamese as the vanguard of a coordinated Communist plan to subvert all the free nations of Asia. Therefore, they argued, by demonstrating to the Communists that the West would meet their aggression with force, all of Asia would be made more secure. Many of those who opposed the war concluded that communism was not monolithic and that the struggle was essentially a civil war between the Vietnamese that the United States had no right to enter. In any case, victory remained elusive despite repeated administration promises that each new escalation would turn the tide. By 1968, over 500,000 American troops were involved in the war, which was costing over $20 billion annually. Meanwhile, American battle casualties had risen precipitously. Pressing domestic matters were relegated to lower levels of priority as some observers were commenting that the Great Society had become the sick society. The growth of an increasingly militant peace movement, combined with demonstrations of the administration's declining popularity through public opinion polls and the impressive victory of Senator Eugene McCarthy in New Hampshire's Democratic primary, finally persuaded Johnson to abandon hopes of again seeking the presidency.

PRESIDENT NIXON, 1967–1974

Major issues during the elections of 1968 were the Vietnam War, domestic disorders, inflation, and the rising crime rate. Primarily because of the war, the Democratic party entered the presidential race more bitterly divided than in any national election during this century. Profiting from these circumstances, the Republican ticket, consisting of Richard M. Nixon, former vice-president (1953–1961), and Spiro Agnew, the governor of Maryland, won a close election over Vice-President Humphrey and Maine Senator Edmund Muskie. Priorities in President Nixon's program gradually became evident. The United States would withdraw by degrees from the Vietnam War. Efforts would be made to prevent a recurrence of war in the Mideast. A quest for closer relations with China would be concurrent with continuing attempts to reach understandings with the Soviet Union, particularly in the area of arms limitation. In internal affairs, President Nixon devoted immediate attention to cooling domestic unrest generated by discontent among youth and blacks. Administration tactics toward this end included deescalation in Vietnam, repressive language and measures, and the maintenance by the president of a lower profile, which made his office difficult to attack directly. In attempts to satisfy demands of the white majority, the Nixon administration made ambivalent and frequently confusing retreats on major civil rights questions, notably school desegregation, voting rights, and housing. Highest priorities in the economic area were placed on efforts to reduce inflation, resolve the balance of payments problem, and stem the rising trend in unemployment. Although the president's legislative program during his first term was modest compared with that of his predecessor, strong opposition developed in the predominantly Democratic Congress. Polarized relations between legislative and executive branches affected many other issues as well. Nixon's second term began with an overwhelming victory in the 1972 election but was soon marred by revelations of administration scandals and allegations of criminal activities.

Election of 1968.   The election campaign of 1968 was filled with drama and pathos. Competition for the Democratic nomination became an open contest when President Johnson withdrew from the race following his poor showing in the New Hampshire primary. Senator Robert Kennedy's quest for the Democratic nomination was silenced with his assassination by Sirhan Sirhan, an Arab embittered over Kennedy's support of arms to Israel. Vice-President Humphrey was finally chosen as the Democratic nominee at a convention in Chicago, where the proceedings competed for attention with disruptions in the streets. It seemed as if Richard Nixon, the Republican nominee who had relentlessly sought the presidency for over two decades, would handily defeat the demoralized and divided Democrats. Yet the third-party candidacy of Alabama Governor George Wallace constituted one of the many election uncertainties, while Humphrey showed renewed strength in polls taken on the eve of the election. The final results were unusually close. Although both Nixon and Humphrey received approximately 43 percent of the popular vote, Nixon's majority in the electoral college was 302 to 191. Wallace carried five Southern states with 45 electoral votes. The Democratic margin in the House of Representatives was narrowed from 247–188 to 243–192 and in the Senate from 63–37 to 58–42.

Economy. From 1965 to 1969, dual expenditures for social programs and the Vietnam War sparked both domestic prosperity and accelerated inflation. In 1969, the Federal Reserve Board initiated policies to limit extensions of bank credit, precipitating the highest rise in interest rates in over a century. This deliberate economic slowdown, combined with sizable cuts in defense spending, were the motivating forces of a recession that developed during 1970–1971. By the end of 1970, industrial production had fallen more than 4 percent, and unemployment had risen from 4 percent to nearly 6 percent. In international exchange, sizable trade deficits were combined with assaults on the dollar's stability. To combat the nation's economic problems, the Nixon administration, during August 1971, dramatically announced a program involving a domestic wage and price freeze, a 10 percent surcharge on imports, and efforts to formulate a new system of currency exchange rates that would make American goods more competitive in foreign markets. As wage and price controls ingloriously ended (May 1974), the American economy was characterized by a condition of *stagflation*, combining high rates of unemployment with an annual increase in consumer prices exceeding 11 percent. Since retail prices were rising more swiftly than wages, retrenchments forced upon most American families were causing significant alterations in their life-styles.

Foreign Affairs. The development of President Nixon's policies in the international arena reflected a national mood of disenchantment with continuing postwar overseas involvement. In response, the Nixon administration promised a departure from the activist programs developed to fulfill the principle of collective security that prevailed from the Truman administration through the Johnson years. In Vietnam, the

disengagement was gradual yet persistent, with forces also being withdrawn from some other overseas bases. Total troop strength was cut
from 3.5 million in 1969 to 2.5 million in 1972. Critics condemned
the mixed nature of this protracted withdrawal, especially when President Nixon initiated the invasion of Cambodia, broadening involvement
in Laos, and the renewal of massive bombing over North Vietnam.
Results in the Mideast were also mixed, with the quest continuing for a
stable relationship between Israel and the Arab states.

East-West Détente. The president's most dramatic moves in his
search for an era of negotiations were the establishment of formal
contacts with China and continuing discussions covering a wide range
of cold war and economic issues with the Soviet Union. A Moscow
summit (June 1972) underscored the drive toward détente with agreements covering limitations on strategic nuclear weapons, cooperation in
space, and cultural exchanges. East-West rapprochement was furthered
by Leonid Brezhnev's visit to the United States (June 1973), which
culminated in a series of bilateral agreements to limit offensive nuclear
arms, exchange agricultural information and transportation technology, cooperate in oceanographic research, and establish broader contacts between businessmen from the United States and trading officials
from the Soviet Union. While the third Nixon-Brezhnev summit (July
1974) maintained the spirit of détente, it failed to reconcile major
differences over the curbing of nuclear arms.

Peace in Vietnam. During January 1973, the war that during a
dozen years cost Americans over 46,000 combat deaths and $146
billion was formally ended. The complex peace arrangements were
negotiated by American presidential adviser Henry Kissinger and North
Vietnamese Politburo member Le Duc Tho. Principal features included
the rapid completion of U. S. military withdrawal concurrent with the
return of all American prisoners from North Vietnam. The political
future of South Vietnam would be determined through free elections
planned by the National Council of National Reconciliation and Concord, comprising representatives from South Vietnam and the Viet
Cong's Provisional Revolutionary Government (PRG). Several bodies
were established to supervise the peace: the International Commission
of Control and Supervision (ICCS), composed of delegations and
forces from Canada, Indonesia, Hungary, and Poland; the Four-Party
Joint Military Commission, consisting of representatives from the
United States, North Vietnam, South Vietnam, and the PRG; and the
Two-Party Joint Military Commission, comprising delegates from
South Vietnam and the PRG.

Both in South Vietnam and elsewhere, objectives of the peace agreements proved elusive. Although the United States completed the withdrawal of its forces from South Vietnam while the North Vietnamese returned approximately 700 American prisoners of war, fighting persisted both in South Vietnam and elsewhere in Indochina. The North Vietnamese violated the demilitarized zone and continued to infiltrate men and supplies into the South. North Vietnam also refused to cooperate with the ICCS or withdraw its troops from Laos and Cambodia. Inadequate account for the more than 1,300 Americans missing in action was a further source of contention. Attempting to salvage the shaky truce, a communiqué signed by Henry Kissinger and Le Duc Tho (June 1973) called for stricter enforcement of the peace terms. After a congressional resolution ended U. S. air support to the Cambodian government, a sustained Communist incursion continued. In Laos, the formation of a coalition government between the Communist Pathet Lao and neutralist Premier Souvanna Phouma (August 1973) held greater promise for a stable peace. In Cambodia and Vietnam, however, successful military campaigns brought Communists to victory in both countries in 1975.

Space Travel.   Man's dream of extraterrestrial travel became a reality when the Soviet Union in October 1957 launched *Sputnik I,* the first man-made satellite of the earth. Apprehensive about the Soviet lead in rocketry for both prestige and military reasons, the United States soon committed itself fully to the space race. Plans announced by the Eisenhower administration for one-man flights under Project Mercury required the development of a powerful rocket, *Saturn I.* After a Soviet orbital flight in 1961 by Yuri Gagarin, President Kennedy announced the U. S. goal of reaching the moon by 1970. Project Mercury flights, beginning with the suborbital launching of astronaut Alan Shepard in 1961, included one other suborbital and four orbital flights by 1963. Under Project Gemini, there were ten two-man orbital flights during 1965 and 1966. These programs, which assured American equality with the Soviet Union in space, were followed by eleven Apollo flights from 1968 to 1972. In 1967, after a disastrous launching-pad fire killed three astronauts, there were two flights in earth orbit, three near the moon, and six highly dramatic and successful moon landings. In preparation for extended flights to Mars and beyond, the Skylab missions in 1973 tested man's ability to survive and work for extended times in a cramped and weightless environment.

While debates over national priorities led to reductions in the multibillion-dollar space program by the late 1960s, other notable

American ventures in space were still anticipated. Unmanned satellites were being designed to continue the exploration of earth's neighbors in the solar system. A joint Soviet-American orbital mission was scheduled during 1975. Envisioned by 1978 was a space shuttle to carry satellites. Already knowledge derived from the space program was being put to use: Orbiting satellites transmitted interhemispheric communication and meteorological information; some hospitals were using space-suit adaptations for neurosurgery; paralyzed patients were controlling their wheelchairs and turning book pages by manipulating switches with their eyes; and fire hazards on commercial airlines were being reduced through the use of heat-insulating paint developed for space vehicles.

New American Revolution? As the nation planned bicentennial celebrations of the American Revolution, President Nixon chose the New American Revolution as the label for his domestic reform program. He placed highest priorities on proposals to share revenue with states and cities and to renovate the welfare system. Ironically, the welfare scheme would centralize federal control while revenue-sharing would decentralize it. As a substitute for the problem-plagued state welfare operations, the president in August 1969 presented the Family Assistance Plan, which would guarantee a minimum annual income for families of both the unemployed and the working poor. Revenue-sharing was designed to relieve the financial agonies of cities and states. A percentage of the revenue derived from the personal income tax would be transferred to states and localities for their unrestricted use. Except for revenue-sharing, other measures, including a heralded water pollution bill, were stalemated in Congress during the last years of the Nixon administration. Government priorities shifted dramatically due to the Watergate investigations (see pp. 347–349) and the nation's intensifying economic malaise.

Supreme Court Appointees. During his first term, vacancies on the Supreme Court allowed President Nixon to appoint four of the nine justices, more than any president since Washington appointed in so short a time. Nixon had repeatedly criticized the Warren Court for weakening police forces against criminal elements. To reduce the power of the Court's liberals and activists, he appointed cautious men to the bench, thus providing the previously liberal Court with a decidedly conservative complexion. In 1965, Judge Warren E. Burger of Minnesota replaced Earl Warren as chief justice. Efforts to fill three subsequent vacancies were enveloped by controversy. The president in 1969 nominated Judge Clement F. Haynsworth of South Carolina to replace Abe Fortas, who resigned. Following debate in which Haynsworth was accused of being antiblack, antilabor, and indiscreet in possible financial conflicts of interest, the Senate refused to confirm him. Charging racism and judicial ineptness, the Senate also rejected the nomination of Judge G. Harrold Carswell of Florida. Fortas's seat was finally filled by Judge Harry A. Blackmun from Minnesota. The next two vacancies were created by the resignations of Justices John Harlan and Hugo Black. After considerable speculation, the president finally chose two men with conservative reputations and exceptional qualifications: Lewis F. Powell, former president of the American Bar Association, and William H. Rehnquist, an assistant U. S. attorney general. Both won easy confirmation.

Election of 1970. At stake in the midterm elections of 1970 were all seats in the House of Representatives, 35 seats in the Senate, 13 governorships, and numerous seats in state legislatures. The election campaign was particularly vitriolic. Leading the Republican crusade, Vice-President Agnew and President Nixon charged Democrats with being permissive on questions of extremism and crime, labeled them as exorbitant spenders who encouraged inflationary trends, and called upon the silent majority to support their quest for law and order. Democrats focused their major attacks on the administration's protracted withdrawal from Vietnam, its handling of economic troubles (particularly the high rate of unemployment), and on the Republicans' campaign tactics. The election results were contradictory enough for each party to claim victory. In congressional elections, the party in control of the presidency performed more ably than usual, with Republicans losing 9 seats in the House and gaining 2 in the Senate. Both houses, nevertheless, remained under the firm control of Democrats, whose differences with the president increased as the result of election bitterness. The Democrats scored their most dramatic victories in the statehouses where they were awarded a net total of 11 seats. Before the election, there were 32 Republican and 18 Democratic governors; after the ballots were counted, there were 21 Republican and 29 Democratic governors.

Social Trends. After World War II, the institutions and values of American society were profoundly influenced by continuously accelerating scientific and technological changes. Mass organizations, media, education, and advertising, combined with improved transportation and communications techniques, all encouraged trends toward social conformity. Both personal loneliness and a greater sense of national intimacy resulted. Increases in the number of white-collar in proportion to blue-collar workers further lessened differences in income, thereby creating higher levels of uniformity in the labor force. Books that analyzed these developments were appropriately titled *The Status Seekers, The Organization Man,* and *The Lonely Crowd.* Presidential administrations both mirrored and encouraged national moods. Cautious policies of the Eisenhower years legitimized the complacency of an affluent society unwilling to attack pressing problems of poverty, the cities, the environment, and social injustice. Still, there were rumblings of discontent that society could not long ignore. During the 1950s, civil rights activists and the so-called beat generation were increasing their attacks on contemporary values.

By the 1960s, these seeds of discontent erupted into a youth and black revolt characterized by recurring confrontations with the establishment through sit-ins, marches, and demonstrations. Disruptive acts forced the temporary closing of scores of college campuses, and major riots, releasing the anger and frustration of black ghettos, reverberated in widely separated cities. Although most of the disillusioned were committed to reforming the social system from within, a minority of dissidents decided that society could not be regenerated and formed militant extremist groups. The disenchanted created their own counterculture distinguished by social iconoclasm, long hair, plebeian dress, and liberalized ideas regarding sex and drugs. To a considerable degree, the sense of expectation and then disillusionment accompanying the presidencies of John F. Kennedy and Lyndon Johnson reflected and stimulated these trends. The long-range impact of this tumultuous decade remains unclear. Despite significant advances in some areas, notably civil rights, major goals of the reformers remained unfulfilled. Yet as the 1970s opened, many of the manifestations of discontent had dissipated. Repeated frustration had produced a state of disarray. Again, the administration in power was an important key. Under President Nixon, reformers expected less of their government; their demands were accordingly reduced.

Elections of 1972. The Democratic effort to unseat President Nixon and Vice-President Agnew was from the beginning an uphill battle. South Dakota Senator George McGovern, conducting a quest for the Democratic nomination that at first most analysts considered quixotic, overcame all his rivals to emerge victorious at the Democratic National Convention. Democratic strategy was to question the president's credibility, his conduct of the Vietnam War and the economy, and his campaign tactics; nevertheless, the temperament and character of George McGovern emerged as the principal campaign issue. A controversial $1,000 per person revenue-sharing plan, first proposed, then withdrawn, strengthened charges that the Democratic nominee was radical, unsound on economic issues, and uncertain about his own programs. A crisis was created in the Democratic campaign following public disclosures that McGovern's first choice as a running mate, Senator Thomas Eagleton from Missouri, had undergone psychiatric, including shock, treatment on several occasions. McGovern's own credibility was questioned after he first pledged unequivocal support of Eagleton and then undertook to replace him. (Sargent Shriver, former Peace Corps director, was his eventual choice.) Hopeful above all of projecting himself as the peace candidate, McGovern was deprived of this issue by recurring reports that a negotiated peace was imminent in Vietnam.

Election results confirmed the pollsters' predictions. Nixon won all but 17 of the 538 electoral ballots, capturing 49 states and over 60 percent of the popular vote. His commanding victory temporarily shattered as a national force the once dominant Democratic coalition that survived the popularity of President Eisenhower to win two presidential elections. In the South, where Democratic solidarity was splintered in 1968, nearly 72 percent voted for the Republican ticket; 61 percent of voters in the industrial mideast and even 59 percent in the liberal northeast cast their ballots for the conservative president. Widespread ticket-splitting, however, denied Republicans the broader victory they sought. In addition to the presidency, all 435 House seats, 35 Senate seats, and 18 governorships were being contested. In these races, Democrats maintained a commanding majority in the House (245–190) despite the loss of 12 seats, expanded their margin in the Senate by two (57–43), and added one governorship to their majority (31–19).

Domestic Scandals. After his landslide victory, President Nixon began 1973 at the peak of his power and prestige. But a few months later, the administration was in disarray with its confidence shattered. None of the government's economic experiments proved effective in controlling inflation. The peace achieved in Vietnam remained precarious. Above all, a series of rapidly unfolding scandals impugned the integrity and character of many high officials in the government. Troubling questions were raised regarding the extent to which both the president and vice-president might have participated in unsavory and even illegal activities. A crisis in leadership resulted, seriously affecting the administration's ability to govern effectively both at home and abroad.

Watergate. On June 17, 1972, five men were apprehended with bugging equipment and burglary tools inside the Democratic National Committee's headquarters at Washington's Watergate complex. Although one of the men, James McCord, was a security officer for the Committee to Re-elect the President, and notwithstanding the discovery that some money found on the men could be traced to that committee, for ten months the president and his top advisers adamantly denied any knowledge of the matter. What seemed an isolated crime by minor officials was gradually revealed (by April 1973) as part of a broad campaign of political espionage directed by officials in the government and the Committee to Re-elect the President. The activities were financed by secret campaign funds, which, after the arrest of the seven conspirators in the Watergate break-in, were used to pay their legal fees and allegedly to persuade them to deny the involvement of higher officials. The pinpointing of individual responsibility remained difficult due to conflicts and inconsistencies in the testimony of key officials and since the administration claimed broad prerogatives of executive privilege, national security, and separation of powers to justify its withholding of relevant information from the courts, the Congress, and the public.

Related Scandals. To many observers, the Watergate incident seemed to have been encouraged by a quest for power combined with a callousness toward legal requirements and individual rights that permeated many activities of the government. Top figures in the Watergate break-in were also participants in a White House "plumbers" unit, which not only employed illegal methods of surveillance to discourage security "leaks" but also was charged with forging State Department documents and exploiting a personal tragedy in efforts to discredit Senator Edward Kennedy, potentially Nixon's strongest campaign opponent. Related "dirty tricks" operators possessed considerable ingenuity and few scruples in efforts to disrupt and distort the Democrats' primary campaigns. There were persisting allegations that presidential advisers requested the Internal Revenue Service to use its regulatory powers for the purpose of rewarding the administration's friends and punishing its enemies, while some of the president's own tax deductions were questionable; that elevations in milk support prices were related to sizable campaign contributions from milk producers' associations; and that extraordinary government expenditures had been used to enhance the president's estates in San Clemente, California, and Key Biscayne, Florida. By the end of 1973, Watergate had thus become a code word denoting an array of questionable activities by administration officials.

Resignation of Vice-President Agnew. During his first term (1969–1972), Spiro Agnew distinguished himself as a strong and sometimes abrasive defender of administration policies. Untainted by the proliferating charges of illegal and unethical behavior, the popular and dynamic vice-president was a leading contender for his party's presidential nomination. Suddenly, he became instead the center of a new crisis. There were reports that the Justice Department possessed substantial evidence of his involvement in bribes, extortions, and kickbacks dating from years in Maryland politics and continuing during his tenure as vice-president. After first vehemently denying any guilt, the vice-president reached a compromise with the Justice Department, whereby he resigned his office (October 1973) and pleaded no contest to the charge of intentionally failing to report some 1967 taxable income. A three-year suspended sentence and a $10,000 fine left Agnew a free man since the more serious charges against him were terminated. For the first time, the Twenty-fifth Amendment to the Constitution (1967) became operational. President Nixon nominated Representative Gerald Ford, Republican leader in the House of Representatives, as the new vice-president, and Ford was confirmed in December 1973.

Resignation of President Nixon. As revelations of personal and political scandals surrounding the president unfolded during 1974, questions regarding Nixon's personal involvement both intrigued and troubled the nation. An inconclusive investigation by the Senate Judiciary Committee focused attention on the seriousness and dimensions of the scandals. Legal maneuvering centered on administration efforts to conceal an elaborate collection of recorded conversations between the president and his top aides. Erosions in the president's credibility and public support spread after mysterious gaps were found in some tapes and after discrepancies were discovered between tapes and transcripts the administration prepared. Nixon's defenses crumbled during July-August 1974. The Supreme Court unanimously ruled that tapes pertaining to criminal charges could not be withheld under claims of executive privilege. Shortly thereafter, a bipartisan majority on the House Judiciary Committee voted three articles of impeachment detailing ways in which the president had violated "his constitutional duty to take care that the laws be faithfully executed." Finally, incontrovertible evidence on three tapes that the president illegally ordered concealment of the Watergate break-in alienated his most faithful congressional defenders. Impeachment and conviction, or resignation, seemed the only options. Under these circumstances, Richard Nixon became the first American president to resign from office (August 9,

1974). He was succeeded by Vice-President Ford, who soon granted Nixon a "full, free and absolute pardon."

PRESIDENT FORD, 1974–

In the midst of national agonies over scandals of the Nixon administration, President Ford entered office with widespread public support. There were soon indications that the mood of euphoria would be short-lived. Bitter and prolonged criticism followed the president's pardon of Richard Nixon. Congressional elections (November 1974) increased Democratic majorities in the House of Representatives from 248 to 291 and in the Senate from 58 to 61. Governor Nelson Rockefeller, Ford's nominee as vice-president, was confirmed but only after a protracted and controversial investigation.

With the president's popular support waning and the legislative and executive branches at odds, the nation searched for direction in its domestic and foreign affairs during 1975. Priority matters at home were the continuing high rates of inflation and unemployment. Efforts were made to stimulate the economy through a tax bill that provided individual refunds and incentives for business investment. Abroad, the debate over Southeast Asia achieved renewed, though transient, intensity after successive Communist victories in Cambodia and South Vietnam. President Ford was thus faced with severe tests in his efforts to effectively manage the burdens of the presidency. Problems of the Middle East and Southeast Asia remained perplexing. Secretary of State Kissinger continued a graduated approach to permanent peace that would compromise Israeli concerns for its security and Arab claims to territory that Israel had conquered in previous wars.

Bibliography

Suggested readings, including annotations, are provided separately for each chapter.

CHAPTER 1

Ashworth, William. *A Short History of the International Economy, 1850–1950*. 2d ed. New York: McKay, 1962.
A descriptive and interpretative account that focuses on developments common to two or more countries.

Barraclough, Geoffrey. *An Introduction to Contemporary History*. Baltimore: Penguin, 1967.
Views the period of modernism (1890–1961) as a predecessor to the contemporary era.

Court, W. H. B. *A Concise Economic History of Britain*. Vol. 2: *From 1750 to Recent Times*. Cambridge, England: Cambridge University Press, 1954.
A readable and informative synthesis for nonspecialists.

Dangerfield, George. *The Strange Death of Liberal England: 1910–1914*. New York: Putnam, 1961.
A survey of England's political history from the death of Edward VII to the beginning of World War I.

Hayes, Carlton. *A Generation of Materialism, 1871–1900*. New York: Harper & Row, 1941.
This standard synthesis treats political, economic, military, artistic, and scientific developments.

Hellmann, Donald C. *Japan and East Asia: The New International Order*. New York: Praeger, 1972.
An assessment of Japan's changing role in Asia during the contemporary period.

Henderson, W. O. *The Industrialization of Europe: 1780–1914.* New York: Harcourt Brace Jovanovich, 1969.
Surveys major developments in a compact fashion.

Holmes, Vera B. *A History of the Americas.* Vol. 2: *From Nationhood to World Status.* New York: Ronald, 1964.
A narrative of developments in the United States, Latin America, and Canada from 1830 to the early 1960s.

Hughes, Henry Stuart. *Consciousness and Society: The Reorientation of European Social Thought, 1890–1930.* New York: Random House, 1961.
This pioneering and scholarly study focuses on intellectual history.

Kranzberg, Melvin, and Pursell, Carroll W., Jr., eds. *Technology in Western Civilization.* Vol. 1: *Emergence of Modern Industrial Society: Earliest Times to 1900.* Vol 2: *Technology in the Twentieth Century.* New York: Oxford University Press, 1967.
Volume 1 is a survey of technological advances from earliest periods to 1900; volume 2 treats the development of American dominance.

Munholland, J. Kim. *Origins of Contemporary Europe.* New York: Harcourt Brace Jovanovich, 1970.
A useful introduction to varied aspects of European life.

Paden, John N., and Soja, Edward W., eds. *The African Experience.* Vol. 1: *Essays.* Evanston, Ill.: Northwestern University Press, 1970.
Contains original short essays covering a wide range of topics from scholars in diverse academic fields.

Pinson, Koppel S. *Modern Germany.* 2d ed. New York: Macmillan, 1966.
The best one-volume study of Germany in English.

Ribeiro, Darcy. *The Americas and Civilization.* New York: Dutton, 1971.
An eminent Brazilian anthropologist interprets the forces that have produced varied national ethnic groups and their uneven development in the Americas.

Seaman, L. C. B. *Post-Victorian Britain: 1902–1951.* New York: Barnes & Noble, 1966.
An informative narrative that devotes principal attention to political matters.

Shafer, Boyd C. *Faces of Nationalism.* New York: Harcourt Brace Jovanovich, 1972.
An informative study of nineteenth- and twentieth-century nationalism for the nonspecialist.

Taylor, A. J. P. *The Struggle for Mastery in Europe, 1848–1918.* New York: Oxford University Press, 1954.
This first volume in the Oxford History of Modern Europe series is a lively and masterful treatment of diplomatic history.

Tuchman, Barbara. *The Proud Tower.* New York: Macmillan, 1966.
An examination of the broad themes in Western history during the generation preceding World War I.

Wright, Gordon. *France in Modern Times: 1760 to the Present.* 3d ed. Skokie, Ill.: Rand McNally, 1960.
The best one-volume study of French history in English.

CHAPTER 2

Beasley, William G. *The Modern History of Japan.* New York: Praeger, 1963.
A balanced one-volume study that covers the period from 1868 to contemporary times.

Black, Cyril, ed. *The Transformation of Russian Society: Aspects of Social Change Since 1861.* Cambridge, Mass.: Harvard University Press, 1960.
Includes 38 studies embracing the period from 1861 to contemporary times.

Fay, Sidney. *Origins of the World War.* Vol. 1. 2d ed. New York: Macmillan, 1941.
An authoritative and balanced survey that covers developments leading to the outbreak of World War I.

Haimson, Leopold H. *The Russian Marxists and the Origins of Bolshevism.* Cambridge, Mass.: Harvard University Press, 1955.
Considers the evolution of conflicting Marxist interpretations in the light of Russian realities.

Harcave, Sidney. *The Russian Revolution of 1905.* (Original title: *First Blood.*) New York: Macmillan, 1964.
An able analysis of the precedent-setting revolution against the czarist system.

Lockwood, William W. *The Economic Development of Japan: Growth and Structural Change, 1868–1938.* Princeton: Princeton University Press, 1954.
A thorough treatment of Japan's remarkable economic transformations.

May, Arthur J. *The Habsburg Monarchy, 1867–1914.* Cambridge, Mass.: Harvard University Press, 1951.

A sound study of one of Europe's most heterogeneous political and social structures.

May, Ernest. *Imperial Democracy*. New York: Harper & Row, 1973.
An examination of America's arrival on the world stage during the 1893–1898 period.

Mowry, George E. *The Era of Theodore Roosevelt: 1900–1912*. New York: Harper & Row, 1958.
A well-written synthesis of American history during the administrations of Theodore Roosevelt and William Howard Taft.

CHAPTER 3

Bruun, Geoffrey. *Clemenceau*. Hamden, Conn.: Shoe String, 1962.
A brief biography of a central figure in modern French history.

Chambers, Frank P. *The War Behind the War, 1914–1918: A History of the Political and Civilian Fronts*. New York: Arno, 1972.
Analyzes the impact of war on various home fronts.

Craig, Gordon A. *The Politics of the Prussian Army, 1640–1945*. New York: Oxford University Press, 1964.
A convincing study that examines the pervasive force of militarism in German life.

Crankshaw, Edward. *The Fall of the House of Habsburg*. New York: Viking, 1963.
This study of the Habsburg monarchy from 1848 to 1918 emphasizes its viability until the disintegrating impact of war.

Falls, Cyril. *The Great War: 1914–1918*. New York: Putnam, 1961.
A comprehensive military account.

Freidel, Frank. *Over There: The Story of America's First Great Overseas Crusade*. Boston: Little, Brown, 1964.
Diaries, letters, and photographs are used to convey the character and impact of America's participation during 1917 and 1918.

Gatzke, Hans W. *Germany's Drive to the West: A Study of Germany's Western War Aims During the First World War*. Baltimore: Johns Hopkins Press, 1950.
The author effectively illuminates an influential dimension of the war.

Jarausch, Konrad H. *The Enigmatic Chancellor*. New Haven: Yale University Press, 1973.
Portrays Bethmann-Hollweg as a practitioner of limited power.

King, Jere C. *Generals and Politicians: Conflict Between France's High Command, Parliament, and Government, 1914–1918.* Westport, Conn.: Greenwood, 1971.
An informed account that focuses on the four-year struggle over strategy between politicians and the military.

Panichas, George A., ed. *Promise of Greatness: The War of 1914–1918.* New York: John Day, 1968.
Absorbing recollections written in commemoration of the fiftieth anniversary of the end of the war.

Tapié, Victor L. *The Rise and Fall of the Habsburg Monarchy.* New York: Praeger, 1971.
The most comprehensive study in English of the Habsburg monarchy.

Tuchman, Barbara. *The Guns of August.* New York: Macmillan, 1962.
Events of the first month of World War I are related in an engaging literary style.

CHAPTER 4

Carr, Edward H. *History of Soviet Russia: The Bolshevik Revolution, 1917–1923.* 3 vols. Baltimore: Penguin.
These standard volumes deal successively with political institutions, economic institutions, and foreign policy.

————. *The October Revolution: Before and After.* New York: Knopf, 1969.
These essays by a specialist usefully supplement narrative studies.

Deutscher, Isaac. *The Prophet Armed: Trotsky, 1079–1921.* New York: Oxford University Press, 1954.
This first of a three-volume biography traces Trotsky's career through the Bolshevik Revolution.

Kennan, George F. *Soviet-American Relations, 1917–1920.* Vol. 1: *Russia Leaves the War.* Princeton: Princeton University Press, 1956.
An American expert in Russian affairs presents an absorbing study.

Pipes, Richard. *The Formation of the Soviet Union: Communism and Nationalism 1917–1923.* New York: Atheneum, 1968.
Traces political developments among nationalities in borderland areas during the Bolshevik Revolution's critical years.

Radkey, Oliver H., Jr. *The Elections to the Russians Constituent Assembly of 1917.* Cambridge, Mass.: Harvard University Press, 1950.
Emphasizes the degree to which these potentially crucial elections were valid.

Trotsky, Leon. *The History of the Russian Revolution*. 3 vols. Ann Arbor: University of Michigan Press, 1957.
Originally published in 1932, this is a provocative and interesting study by one of the foremost participants in the event.

Ulam, Adam B. *The Bolsheviks*. New York: Macmillan, 1955.
Primarily a critical biography of Lenin before and after the Bolshevik Revolution.

Wolfe, Bertram D. *An Ideology in Power: Reflections on the Russian Revolution*. New York: Stein and Day, 1969.
A collection of twenty-five essays by an informed observer of the Soviet scene.

CHAPTER 5

Birdsall, Paul. *Versailles Twenty Years After*. Hamden, Conn.: Shoe String, 1973.
The author strongly defends Woodrow Wilson and his principles.

Carr, Edward H. *International Relations Between the Two World Wars 1919–1939*. New York: St. Martin's, 1947.
A broad general account.

Kulischer, Eugene M. *Europe on the Move: War and Population Changes, 1917–1947*. Clifton, N. J.: Kelley.
The author advances the thesis that regulated migrations could help eliminate a major cause of war.

Landes, David. *The Unbound Prometheus: Technological Change and Industrial Development in Western Europe from 1750 to the Present*. Cambridge, England: Cambridge University Press, 1969.
A comparative study of industrial development that focuses on England, Germany, France, and the United States.

Mantoux, Étienne. *The Carthaginian Peace: Or the Economic Consequences of Mr. Keynes*. Pittsburgh: University of Pittsburgh Press, 1965.
Effectively repudiates Keynes's widely accepted view that the Treaty of Versailles permanently crippled Germany.

Mayer, Arno J. *Politics and Diplomacy of Peacemaking: Containment and Counterrevolution at Versailles, 1918–1919*. New York: Knopf, 1968.
An examination of the political and diplomatic climate within which particular decisions were made.

Walters, Francis. *A History of the League of Nations.* 2 vols. New York: Oxford University Press, 1960.
This definitive narrative covers the period from 1919 to 1946.

Wolfers, Arnold. *Britain and France Between Two Wars: Conflicting Strategies of Peace from Versailles to World War Two.* New York: Norton, 1966.
A valuable study that sheds light on the reasons why peace failed.

CHAPTER 6

Bonjour, Edgar, and Potter, G. R. *A Short History of Switzerland.* New York: Oxford University Press, 1952.
Treats the period between 1798 and 1950 in the last four chapters of this general history.

Carr, Raymond. *Spain 1808–1939.* New York: Oxford University Press, 1966.
This economic, political, and social survey examines the failures of Spanish liberalism.

Mowat, Charles. *Britain Between the Wars: 1918–1940.* Chicago: University of Chicago Press, 1955.
A broad textbook approach that covers politics, economics, and social developments, as well as the arts and sciences.

Thompson, David. *Democracy in France Since 1870.* 5th ed. New York: Oxford University Press, 1969.
A study of the evolution and status of democratic processes and institutions during the Third, Fourth, and Fifth French republics.

Thornton, Archibald P. *The Imperial Idea and Its Enemies: A Study in British Power.* New York: St. Martin's, 1959.
Traces the rise and decline of the idea of imperialism among politicians and the public.

CHAPTER 7

Borkenau, Franz. *World Communism: A History of the Communist International.* Ann Arbor: University of Michigan Press, 1962.
A former member of the German Communist party ably examines the vicissitudes of Comintern policy.

Eyck, Erich. *A History of the Weimar Republic.* 2 vols. Cambridge, Mass.: Harvard University Press, 1962–1963.
The first volume ends with Hindenburg's election to the presidency in 1925; the second volume covers the fateful years before Hitler's rise to power.

Halperin, Samuel W. *Germany Tried Democracy*. New York: Norton, 1965.
An impartial account of the Weimar Republic.

Seton-Watson, Hugh. *Eastern Europe Between the Wars, 1918–1941*. New York: Harper & Row, 1967.
Internal political developments, poverty, the peasant problem—all in the midst of great-power rivalries—are the common themes.

Tannenbaum, Edward R. *The Fascist Experience: Italian Society and Culture, 1922–1945*. New York: Basic Books, 1972.
Examines popular culture, literature, and intellectual life during the Fascist period.

Ulam, Adam B. *Stalin: The Man and His Era*. New York: Viking, 1973.
This comprehensive biography is also a history of the Bolshevik party, the Russian Revolution, and the Soviet regime to 1953.

CHAPTER 8

Benevolo, Leonardo. *History of Modern Architecture*. Cambridge, Mass.: M. I. T. Press, 1972.
Examines architecture and city planning within a social and political context from 1760 to the contemporary period.

Clark, Ronald W. *Einstein: The Life and Times*. New York: Avon, 1972.
An impressive study of the man and the intellectual era he helped to shape.

Collaer, Paul. *A History of Modern Music*. New York: Grosset & Dunlap, 1963.
Focuses on composers from Germany, Austria, France, and Russia during the period from 1910 to 1957.

Ellenberger, Henri F. *The Discovery of the Unconscious: The History and Evolution of Dynamic Psychiatry*. New York: Basic Books, 1970.
Treats the psychologies of Freud, Jung, Adler, and Janet.

Hughes, Henry S. *Consciousness and Society: The Reorientation of European Social Thought, 1890–1930*. New York: Random House, 1961.
An original and wide-ranging essay that covers the intellectual history of the period.

Kulski, Julian. *Architecture in a Revolutionary Era*. Nashville, Tenn.: Aurora, 1971.
Relates modern construction to revolutionary tendencies in contemporary culture.

Myers, Rollo. *Modern French Music: From Fauré to Boulez*. New York: Praeger, 1971.
Examines the works and lives of twenty French composers.

Pevsner, Nikolaus. *Pioneers of Modern Design: From William Morris to Walter Gropius*. Santa Fe, N. M.: Gannon.
Traces the rise of modernism to the beginning of World War I, with particular emphasis on architecture.

White, Morton, ed. *The Age of Analysis: Twentieth Century Philosophers*. New York: New American Library, 1955.
Clear editorial comments provide direction in this useful anthology.

Willard, Charlotte. *Famous Modern Artists from Cézanne to Pop Art*. New York: Platt & Munk, 1971.
Changes during the last century are concisely depicted by focusing on a representative group of artists.

Wilson, Edmund. *Axel's Castle*. 2d ed. New York: Scribner, 1959.
Traces trends in contemporary literature through careful essays on eight writers.

CHAPTER 9

Hicks, John D. *Republican Ascendancy, 1921–1933*. New York: Harper & Row, 1960.
A broad study of the entire epoch that highlights the triumph of business leadership.

Kazin, Alfred. *On Native Grounds*. New York: Harcourt Brace Jovanovich.
Examines American prose writers during the period between 1890 and 1940.

Leuchtenburg, William E. *The Perils of Prosperity, 1914–1932*. Chicago: University of Chicago Press, 1958.
American history, from the beginning of World War I to the Great Depression, is interpretatively surveyed.

Maddox, Robert J. *William E. Borah and American Foreign Policy*. Baton Rouge, La.: Louisiana State University Press, 1969.
Emphasizes Borah's consistent efforts to keep America free from overseas entanglements.

Neatby, H. Blair. *The Politics of Chaos: Canada in the Thirties.* Toronto: MacMillan, 1972.
A biographical approach that focuses on influential personalities.

Preston, William, Jr. *Aliens and Dissenters: Federal Suppression of Radicals, 1903–1933.* New York: Harper & Row, 1966.
A study of how American fear of foreigners produced new and significant restraints on civil liberties.

Wilson, Edmund. *O Canada: An American's Notes on Canadian Culture.* New York: Farrar, Strauss & Giroux, 1965.
A discursive, impressionistic collection of articles that previously appeared in the *New Yorker* magazine.

CHAPTER 10

Brzezinski, Zbigniew. *The Fragile Blossom: Crisis and Change in Japan.* New York: Harper & Row, 1972.
A Columbia University political scientist argues that Japan's economic growth and military potential rest on a delicate and unstable edifice.

Cameron, Meribeth; Mahoney, Thomas; and McReynolds, George. *China, Japan, and the Powers: A History of the Modern Far East.* 2d ed. New York: Ronald, 1960.
A survey of history, culture, politics, and foreign relations up to 1951.

Griffiths, Percival. *Modern India.* 4th rev. ed. New York: Praeger, 1965.
This compact account reviews political developments since 1947 in the perspective of earlier history.

Hookham, Hilda. *A Short History of China.* New York: St. Martin's, 1971.
A survey from prehistory to the People's Republic.

Lamb, Beatrice. *India, a World in Transition.* 3d ed. New York: Praeger, 1968.
A lucid survey that embraces historical analysis and a discussion of contemporary culture and problems.

Li, Dun J. *The Ageless Chinese: A History.* 2d ed. New York: Scribner, 1972.
A general survey that attempts to understand modern China by probing its historical forces.

Moseley, George. *China Since 1911.* New York: Harper & Row, 1969.
An introductory study that treats modern China from the revolution of 1911 to the consolidation of Communist control.

Peffer, Nathaniel. *The Far East: A Modern History.* Rev. and enl. ed. by Claude A. Buss. Ann Arbor: University of Michigan Press, 1968.
This condensed examination of interactions between Western and Far Eastern cultures is especially able when dealing with China.

Tien, Hung-Mao. *Government and Politics in Kuomintang China, 1927–1937.* Stanford, Calif.: Stanford University Press, 1972.
Analyzes government operations during this troubled period.

Yoshida, Shigeru. *Japan's Decisive Century: 1867–1967.* New York: Praeger, 1967.
A former prime minister of Japan interprets his nation's rise from feudal isolation to its triumphs and defeats as a world power.

CHAPTER 11

Abraham, Willie E. *The Mind of Africa.* Chicago: University of Chicago Press, 1963.
The author contrasts what he considers a metaphysical and spiritual African world view with the scientific and materialist philosophies of the West and Marxist East.

Abun-Nasr, Jamil M. *A History of the Maghrib.* Cambridge, England: Cambridge University Press, 1971.
This general history embraces Libya, Tunisia, Algeria, and Morocco.

Cohen, William B. *Rulers of Empire: The French Colonial Service in Africa.* Stanford, Calif.: Hoover Institution Press, 1971.
Examines the men who comprised the corps from the Third Republic to the end of empire.

Cole, Ernest, and Flaherty, Thomas. *House of Bondage.* New York: Random House, 1967.
A black South African depicts in photographs the conditions of apartheid.

Crowder, Michael. *West Africa Under Colonial Rule.* Evanston, Ill.: Northwestern University Press, 1968.
Analyzes the conquests and administrations of Britain, France, and Germany.

Davidson, Basil. *Africa: History of a Continent.* Rev. ed. New York: Macmillan, 1972.
Modern Africa is studied in the perspective of ancient civilizations and relations with Asia, Europe, and America.

Gifford, Prosser, and Louis, William R., eds. *France and Britain in Africa: Imperial Rivalry and Colonial Rule.* New Haven: Yale University Press, 1972.
Twenty-two essays focus on the motives, methods, and actions of the two major colonial powers.

Marlowe, John. *History of Modern Egypt and Anglo-Egyptian Relations 1800–1956.* 2d ed. Hamden, Conn.: Shoe String, 1965.
A British specialist in Near Eastern affairs provides a detailed account.

Meyer, Frank S., ed. *The African Nettle.* Freeport, N. Y.: BFL Communications, 1965.
Twelve essays treating modern problems.

Rotberg, Robert I., and Mazrui, A. A., eds. *Protest and Power in Black Africa.* New York: Oxford University Press, 1970.
Contains case studies of various African movements in resistance to colonial rule.

Suret-Canale, Jean. *French Colonialism in Tropical Africa, 1900–1945.* New York: Universe, 1971.
Views colonial rule as a source of contemporary unrest.

CHAPTER 12

Baum, Warren C. *The French Economy and the State.* Princeton: Princeton University Press, 1958.
This Rand Corporation study focuses on the state's directing role in the French economy.

Boardman, Fon W., Jr. *The Thirties: America and the Great Depression.* New York: H. Z. Walck, 1967.
Various aspects of society during the decade are lightly treated.

Galbraith, John K. *The Great Crash, 1929.* 3d ed. Boston: Houghton Mifflin, 1972.
A highly readable account that includes events leading up to and covering the stock market crash.

Leuchtenburg, William. *Franklin D. Roosevelt and the New Deal, 1932–1940.* New York: Harper & Row, 1963.
This concise history of the entire era focuses on the economic crisis and President Roosevelt's first two administrations.

Rauch, Basil. *The History of the New Deal, 1933–1938.* New York: Putnam, 1963.
One of the New Deal's advocates interprets this intensely controversial period in American history.

Rees, Goronwy. *The Great Slump: Capitalism in Crisis, 1929–1933*. New York: Harper & Row, 1971.
This study of the depression's early years concentrates primarily on Germany, Great Britain, and the United States.

Ryder, A. J. *Twentieth-Century Germany*. New York: Columbia University Press, 1972.
A survey that devotes unusual attention to social, economic, and cultural affairs.

Sobel, Robert. *The Great Bull Market: Wall Street in the 1920's*. New York: Norton, 1968.
In this insightful study, the actions of the stock market are related to other aspects of American life during the 1920s.

Swados, Harvey, ed. *The American Writer and the Great Depression*. Indianapolis, Ind.: Bobbs-Merrill, 1966.
This anthology includes selections from stories, poems, and other writings.

CHAPTER 13

Beloff, Max. *The Foreign Policy of Soviet Russia, 1929–1941*. 2 vols. New York: Oxford University Press, 1947, 1949.
Volume 1 painstakingly covers the period from 1929 to 1936; volume 2 continues this approach to 1941.

Brown, Edward J. *The Proletarian Episode in Russian Literature, 1928–1932*. New York: Farrar, Strauss & Giroux, 1971.
Traces the evolution and demise of the Russian Association of Proletarian Writers (RAPP).

Curtiss, John S. *The Russian Church and the Soviet State, 1917–1950*. Gloucester, Mass.: Peter Smith, 1953.
Chronicles Bolshevik policies toward the church from the early years of hostility to the more recent period of restrained toleration.

Deutscher, Isaac. *Stalin: A Political Biography*. 2d ed. New York: Oxford University Press, 1967.
A lucid and revealing study that focuses primarily on the period of the Russian Revolution to Stalin's death.

Jasny, Naum. *Soviet Industrialization, 1928–1952*. Chicago: University of Chicago Press, 1961.
Including an abundance of detailed information, the Soviet drive for industrialization is balanced against the costs that the Russians had to pay.

Payne, Robert. *The Rise and Fall of Stalin*. New York: Simon & Schuster, 1965.
A major strength of Payne's exhaustive biography is the intimate portrait he paints of Stalin the man.

Solzhenitsyn, Aleksandr. *The Gulag Archipelago, 1918–1956*. New York: Harper & Row, 1974.
A detailed account of the Soviet secret police and labor-camp system during these years.

CHAPTER 14

Bullock, Alan. *Hitler: A Study in Tyranny*. Rev. ed. New York: Harper & Row, 1964.
The standard full-length biography of Hitler.

Kubizek, August. *The Young Hitler I Knew*. New York: Belmont-Tower, 1971.
A childhood friend presents valuable intimate reminiscences of Hitler's formative years.

Mosse, George L., ed. *Nazi Culture*. New York: Grosset & Dunlap, 1968.
Uses excerpts from plays and novels, quotations from Hitler, newspaper articles, and other sources to depict German life between 1933 and 1939.

Nicholls, Anthony J. *Weimar and the Rise of Hitler*. New York: St. Martin's, 1969.
Narrates German political history from 1918 to 1933.

Nicholls, Anthony, and Matthias, Erich, eds. *East German Democracy and the Triumph of Hitler*. New York: St. Martin's, 1972.
Essays by British and German scholars, with emphasis on social and internal policies.

Reitlinger, Gerald. *The SS: Alibi of a Nation, 1922–1945*. New York: Viking, 1957.
In tracing the history of the SS, the author argues that its activities would not have been possible without widespread cooperation and tolerance by the German people.

Schweitzer, Arthur. *Big Business in the Third Reich*. Bloomington, Ind.: Indiana University Press, 1964.
Advances thesis that big business and large landowners were decisive influences during the Nazi regime's early years.

Shirer, William. *The Rise and Fall of the Third Reich: A History of Nazi Germany.* New York: Simon & Schuster, 1960.
A useful reference work for the entire period.

Speer, Albert. *Inside the Third Reich: Memoirs of Albert Speer.* New York: Macmillan, 1970.
The most revealing portrait to come from any of Hitler's close collaborators.

Stein, George H., ed. *Hitler.* Englewood Cliffs, N. J.: Prentice-Hall, 1968.
Revealing excerpts from Hitler's own words, firsthand impressions from contemporaries, and recollections of statesmen who knew him.

CHAPTER 15

Gargan, Edward T., ed. *The Intent of Toynbee's History.* Chicago: Loyola University Press, 1961.
Nine experts critically review Toynbee's ambitious works.

Harrod, Roy F. *The Life of John Maynard Keynes.* 2d ed. Clifton, N. J.: Kelley.
A perceptive study of one of the twentieth century's most influential economic theoreticians.

Milosz, Czeslaw. *The Captive Mind.* New York: Random House, 1953.
A Polish refugee from communism eloquently portrays the intellectual's dilemma under Communist rule.

Mosse, George L. *The Crisis of German Ideology: Intellectual Origins of the Third Reich.* New York: Grosset & Dunlap, 1964
From an examination of its roots and developments, the author concludes that the Nazi brand of fascism was a peculiarly German phenomenon.

Newman, Karl J. *European Democracy Between the Wars.* South Bend, Ind.: University of Notre Dame Press, 1971.
Examines the struggle between liberal and conservative forces.

Schoenbaum, David. *Hitler's Social Revolution: Class Status in Nazi Germany, 1933–1939.* Garden City, N. Y.: Doubleday, 1966.
A thought-provoking study that describes the effects of the Nazi revolution on various social groups.

Solzhenitsyn, Aleksandr. *One Day in the Life of Ivan Denisovich.* New York: Praeger, 1963.
An internationally acclaimed Soviet writer examines one day's existence of an inmate in a Siberian penal camp.

Talmon, Jacob L. *The Origins of Totalitarian Democracy.* New York: Norton, 1970.
The growth of twentieth-century totalitarianism is related to eighteenth-century liberal concepts.

Warnock, Mary. *Existentialism.* New York: Oxford University Press, 1970.
A modest book for the nonspecialist.

Wiskemann, Elizabeth. *Europe of the Dictators, 1919–1945.* New York: Harper & Row, 1966.
A condensed introduction to the general subject.

CHAPTER 16

Borg, Dorothy. *The United States and the Far Eastern Crisis of 1933–1938.* Cambridge, Mass.: Harvard University Press, 1964.
Superb assessment of both the context and the actual decisions made.

Carr, Raymond, ed. *The Republic and the Civil War in Spain.* New York: St. Martin's, 1971.
A group of modern Spanish scholars focus on Spain's crisis years, 1931–1939.

Cattell, David. *Communism and the Spanish Civil War.* New York: Harcourt Brace Jovanovich, 1955.
Examines the extent and limitations of Russian involvement.

Craig, Gordon A., and Gilbert, Felix, eds. *The Diplomats, 1919–1939.* 2 vols. New York: Atheneum, 1963.
A well-organized anthology emphasizing the men who served as diplomats and the special problems they faced.

Eubank, Keith. *Munich.* Norman, Okla.: University of Oklahoma Press, 1965.
Focuses on the pressures that persuaded Britain and France to betray Czechoslovakia.

Furnia, Arthur H. *The Diplomacy of Appeasement: Anglo-French Relations and the Prelude of World War II.* Washington, D.C.: University Press of Washington, 1960.
Contrasts frequently divergent Anglo-French policies with the evolving threat from Germany.

Maass, Walter B. *Assassination in Vienna.* New York: Scribner, 1972.
An account for the general reader of the abortive Nazi putsch in July 1934.

Namier, Lewis B. *Diplomatic Prelude, 1938–1939*. New York: Fertig.
A lively and masterful treatment that is useful for a study of the
origins of World War II.

Smith, Sara R. *The Manchurian Crisis, 1931–1932: A Tragedy in
International Relations*. Westport, Conn.: Greenwood.
This detailed study isolates for examination the first major act of
aggression during the 1930s.

Sontag, Raymond J. *A Broken World, 1919–1939*. New York: Harper
& Row, 1971.
A good introduction to interwar Europe.

Weinberg, Gerhard L. *The Foreign Policy of Hitler's Germany: 1933–
1936*. Chicago: University of Chicago Press, 1971.
The central theme is that Hitler achieved a diplomatic breakthrough
that made Germany the dominant European power.

CHAPTER 17

Boyle, John Hunter. *China and Japan at War, 1937–1945: The Politics
of Collaboration*. Stanford, Calif.: Stanford University Press, 1972.
Examines the complex relations between the Japanese-backed regional puppet governments and the Chinese people in a straight-
forward fashion.

Clark, Alan. *Barbarossa: The Russian-German Conflict, 1941–1945*.
New York: Morrow, 1965.
A readable account of the war on the Eastern front, from Hitler's
initial directive to the collapse of Germany.

Compton, James. *The Swastika and the Eagle: Hitler, the United
States, and the Origins of World War II*. Boston: Houghton
Mifflin, 1967.
Hitler's miscalculations, both of American intentions and of the
consequences of American intervention, are carefully examined.

Craig, William. *Enemy at the Gates: The Battle for Stalingrad*. New
York: Readers Digest Press, 1973.
Treats a decisive battle in a gripping manner.

Divine, Robert A. *The Reluctant Belligerent: American Entry into
the Second World War*. New York: Wiley, 1965.
Views British and French acts of appeasement as catalysts for the
withdrawal of the United States from the international scene during
the 1930s.

Fireside, Harvey. *Icon and Swastika: The Russian Orthodox Church Under Nazi and Soviet Control*. Cambridge, Mass.: Harvard University Press, 1971.
Focuses on efforts by Nazi and Soviet officials to manipulate the religious thinking of the Russian people during World War II.

Hoyt, Edwin P., ed. *The Battle of Leyte Gulf*. New York: Pinnacle, 1973.
An account of the decisive Japanese naval defeat.

Knapp, Wilfrid. *A History of War and Peace, 1939–1965*. New York: Oxford University Press, 1967.
A useful reference work that sensibly organizes the principal facts around a few central themes.

Maginnis, John. *Military Government Journal: Normandy to Berlin*. Amherst, Mass.: University of Massachusetts Press, 1971.
A day-by-day account of Allied operations in France, Belgium, and Germany.

McSherry, James E. *Stalin, Hitler, and Europe*. Vol. 1: *The Origins of World War II, 1933–1939*. Palo Alto, Calif.: Open-Door, 1973.
A study of Nazi-Soviet relations based principally upon German and British documents.

Michel, Henri. *The Shadow War: European Resistance 1939–1945*. New York: Harper & Row, 1973.
Examines resistance movements in various countries in their social and historical contexts.

Paxton, Robert O. *Vichy France: Old Guard and New Order, 1940–1944*. New York: Knopf, 1972.
A dispassionate and perceptive study of the foreign and domestic policies of the Vichy government.

Reitlinger, Gerald. *The Final Solution*. Rev. ed. Cranbury, N. J.: A. S. Barnes, 1961.
Emphasizes the development of events and the actual machinery used.

Snell, John L. *Illusion and Necessity; the Diplomacy of Global War, 1939–1945*. Boston: Houghton Mifflin, 1963.
This condensed study of wartime diplomacy sets the stage for the cold war.

Toland, John. *The Rising Sun: The Decline and Fall of the Japanese Empire: 1936–1945*. New York: Random House, 1970.
A dramatic account of the war from the Japanese viewpoint.

Tuchman, Barbara. *Stilwell and the American Experience in China, 1911–1945*. New York: Macmillan, 1971.
The implications of this study transcend the 1911–1945 period and the biographical attention devoted to Stilwell.

Wright, Gordon. *The Ordeal of Total War, 1939–1945*. New York: Harper & Row, 1968.
Using a broad canvas, the author evaluates military, psychological, and scientific dimensions of the war.

CHAPTER 18

Alperovitz, Gar. *Atomic Diplomacy*. New York: Simon & Schuster, 1965.
Examines the role of the atomic bomb in the development of American policy toward Russia during the period between April and August 1945.

Avineri, Shlomo, ed. *Israel and the Palestinians*. New York: St. Martin's, 1971.
A collection of essays by eight Israeli and two Arab writers.

Buttinger, Joseph. *Vietnam*. 2 vols. New York: Praeger, 1967.
Volume 1 covers the French colonial regime; volume 2 traces events from 1945 to the fall of Diem in 1963.

Collier, Basil. *The Lion and the Eagle*. New York: Putnam, 1972.
An interesting summary of how the United States replaced Britain as the leading world power.

Divine, Robert A., ed. *American Foreign Policy Since 1945*. New York: Grolier, 1969.
Twenty-four representative writings from the *New York Times* during the two decades following World War II.

Dobson, Christopher. *Black September*. New York: Macmillan, 1974.
A dramatic story of an Arab terrorist organization.

Fleming, Denna F. *The Cold War and Its Origins, 1917–1960*. 2 vols. Garden City, N. Y.: Doubleday, 1968.
In chronicling the conflict between East and West from the Bolshevik Revolution, these volumes place primary responsibility on the West for continuation of the cold war.

Halle, Louis J. *The Cold War As History*. New York: Harper & Row, 1967.
Though critical of both power blocs, Halle attributes the cold war initiatives to Russia.

Laqueur, Walter. *The Rebirth of Europe*. New York: Holt, Rinehart & Winston, 1970.
A comprehensive account of internal trends and common patterns for the general reader.

―――. *The Struggle for the Middle East: The Soviet Union and the Middle East, 1958–1968*. New York: Macmillan, 1969.
A useful introductory outline.

O'Ballance, Edgar. *Korea: 1950–1953*. Hamden, Conn.: Shoe String, 1969.
A brief understandable account that treats the Korean War as part of the worldwide conflict between East and West.

Schmitt, Hans A. *The Path to European Union: From the Marshall Plan to the Common Market*. Baton Rouge, La.: Louisiana State University Press, 1962.
Considers recent economic and political steps toward European union in a historical perspective.

Schurr, Sam H., and others. *Middle Eastern Oil and the Western World*. New York: Elsevier, 1971.
A clear and bold analysis of oil as the key economic variable in relations between the Middle East and Western nations.

CHAPTER 19

Buchan, Alastair. *Europe's Futures, Europe's Choices: Models of Western Europe in the 1970's*. New York: Columbia University Press, 1969.
Examines six possible choices, ranging from fragmentation to federation.

Charlot, Jean. *The Gaullist Phenomenon: The Gaullist Movement in the Fifth Republic*. New York: Praeger, 1972.
The many forms of Gaullism are concisely treated.

Clough, Shepard. *The Economic History of Modern Italy*. New York: Columbia University Press, 1964.
This broad and descriptive account covers the period since unification.

Coppa, Frank J. *Planning, Protectionism, and Politics in Liberal Italy: Economics and Politics in the Giolittian Age*. Washington, D. C.: Catholic University Press, 1971.
A sympathetic defense of Giolitti's policies.

Heath, Edward M. *Old World, New Horizons: Britain, Europe, and the Atlantic Alliance*. Cambridge, Mass.: Harvard University Press, 1970.
In his 1966–1967 Godkin lectures at Harvard, the later British prime minister argued for a more meaningful unity between Britain, Europe, and the United States.

Laqueur, Walter. *Europe Since Hitler*. Baltimore: Penguin, 1972.
A comprehensive account for the general reader.

Medlicott, William. *Contemporary England, 1914–1964*. New York: McKay, 1967.
A factual account that concentrates primarily on political developments.

Warnecke, Steven Joshua. *The European Community in the 1970s*. New York: Praeger, 1972.
Examines prospective economic and political developments in addition to relations between the community and the United States.

Williams, Philip M. *French Politicians and Elections, 1951–1968*. Cambridge, England: Cambridge University Press, 1970.
Twenty-five essays provide a valuable guide through the complexities of French politics.

Wilson, Frank L. *The French Democratic Left, 1963–1969: Toward a Modern Party System*. Stanford, Calif.: Stanford University Press, 1971.
Analyzes the unsuccessful efforts to merge the French non-Communist left into a modern political organization.

CHAPTER 20

Bromke, Adam, and Rakowska-Harmstone, Teresa, eds. *The Communist States in Disarray, 1965–1971*. Minneapolis, Minn.: University of Minnesota Press, 1972.
The fifteen selections examine general trends and patterns among and within Communist states.

Brzezinski, Zbigniew K. *The Soviet Bloc: Unity and Conflict*. Rev. and enl. ed. Cambridge, Mass.: Harvard University Press, 1967.
A full-length study that analyzes unifying and disintegrating forces within the Soviet orbit.

Crankshaw, Edward. *Khrushchev: A Career*. New York: Viking, 1966.
A Moscow correspondent for the *London Observer* chronicles Khrushchev's political life.

Debray, Regis. *The Chilean Revolution*. New York: Pantheon, 1971.
The dialogues included provide interesting insights into the aims
and methods of Chile's Marxist president.

Djilas, Milovan. *The New Class: An Analysis of the Communist System*. New York: Praeger, 1957.
A former associate and later victim of Marshal Tito analyzes discrepancies between the ideals and practices of the Communist
system.

Fenyo, Mario D. *Hitler, Horthy, and Hungary: German-Hungarian
Relations, 1941–1944*. New Haven: Yale University Press, 1972.
A scholarly treatment of Hungarian history during World War II.

Hazard, John. *The Soviet System of Government*. 4th ed. Chicago:
University of Chicago Press, 1968.
In a penetrating study, the Soviet system of government is com-
pared with those developed in the West.

Hoffman, George W. *Yugoslavia and the New Communism*. Millwood,
N. Y.: Kraus-Thompson, 1962.
A sympathetic study of Yugoslavia under Titoist rule.

Rothberg, Abraham. *The Heirs of Stalin: Dissidence and the Soviet
Regime, 1953–1970*. Ithaca, N. Y.: Cornell University Press, 1972.
Examines the troubled relationships between the Kremlin's rulers
and the intelligentsia.

Seton-Watson, Hugh. *The East European Revolution*. New York:
Praeger, 1956.
Surveys developments leading to Soviet and Communist domination.

Snow, Edgar. *Red China Today: The Other Side of the River*. Rev.
ed. New York: Random House, 1971.
A sympathetic journalist who traveled extensively in China assesses
China's strengths and weaknesses.

Trager, Frank N., and Henderson, William, eds. *Communist China,
1949–1969: A Twenty Year Assessment*. New York: New York
University Press, 1970.
Fourteen articles survey and analyze the first two decades of Communist rule in China.

Ulam, Adam B. *The New Face of Soviet Totalitarianism*. New York:
Praeger, 1965.
Seven interpretive essays.

Wilczynski, Jozef. *The Economics of Socialism*. Chicago: Aldine, 1971.
Stresses decentralization trends and the enhanced importance of profits.

CHAPTER 21

Berque, Jacques. *Egypt: Imperialism and Revolution*. New York: Praeger, 1972.
A comprehensive portrait of Egypt's social history during the period of British domination.

Duffy, James. *Portuguese Africa*. Cambridge, Mass.: Harvard University Press, 1959.
A penetrating and authoritative survey that examines the history of Portuguese colonialism in Angola and Mozambique.

Emerson, Rupert. *From Empire to Nation: The Rise to Self-Assertion of Asian and African Peoples*. Cambridge, Mass.: Harvard University Press, 1960.
A forceful synthesis that examines the rise of native nationalism and the related demise of Western colonialism.

Emerson, Rupert, and Kilson, Martin, eds. *The Political Awakening of Africa*. Englewood Cliffs, N. J.: Prentice-Hall, 1965.
An introductory collection of excerpts from addresses, articles, and books by African politicians.

Grierson, Edward. *The Death of the Imperial Dream*. Garden City, N. Y.: Doubleday, 1972.
The general subject is entertainingly and wittily introduced.

Mansergh, Nicholas. *The Commonwealth Experience: A Critical History of the British Commonwealth*. New York: Praeger, 1969.
Treats evolution of an empire based on force into a commonwealth based on freedom and mutual benefit.

Minter, William. *Portuguese Africa and the West*. New York: Monthly Review Press, 1973.
Criticizes America's role in the evolving colonial struggle against Portugal.

Strachey, John. *End of Empire*. New York: Praeger, 1964.
A Labour politician offers bold interpretations of British imperial history, with particular emphasis on India.

Von Albertini, Rudolf. *Decolonization: The Administration and Future of the Colonies, 1919–1960*. New York: Doubleday, 1971.
A comparative approach that examines the familiar difference between the French and British in their colonial philosophy.

Walshe, Peter. *The Rise of African Nationalism in South Africa: The African National Congress, 1912–1952*. Berkeley, Calif.: University of California Press, 1971.
A historical study of the first 40 years of the African National Congress.

CHAPTER 22

Abraham, Henry J. *Freedom and the Court: Civil Rights and Liberties in the United States*. 2d ed. New York: Oxford University Press, 1972.
Clearly interprets various Supreme Court cases affecting civil liberties and civil rights.

Ambrose, Stephen E. *Rise to Globalism: 1938–1970*. Baltimore: Penguin, 1971.
A survey of American foreign policy from the eve of World War II through the Johnson administration.

Boesel, David, and Rossi, Peter H., eds. *Cities Under Siege: An Anatomy of the Ghetto Riots*. New York: Basic Books, 1971.
This collection relates the ghetto riots of the 1960s to the history of violence in American cities.

Carson, Rachel. *Silent Spring*. Boston: Houghton Mifflin, 1962.
Angry exaggerations are employed in this campaign against chemical pollution of the environment.

Cohen, Carl. *Civil Disobedience: Conscience, Tactics, and the Law*. New York: Columbia University Press, 1971.
After defining and developing a general theory of civil disobedience, the author weighs the conflicting arguments.

Cox, Archibald. *The Warren Court: Constitutional Decision as an Instrument of Reform*. Cambridge, Mass.: Harvard University Press, 1968.
A former solicitor general provides a searching and compact summary of the Warren Court's landmark decisions.

Curtis, James C., and Gould, Lewis L., eds. *The Black Experience in America: Selected Essays*. Austin, Tex.: University of Texas Press, 1970.
Eight essays range from the colonial period to the present.

Divine, Robert A., ed. *The Cuban Missile Crisis*. New York: Grolier, 1971.
Uses the Cuban missile crisis as a case study of the political, ideological, and organizational pressures that influence American diplomacy in the atomic age.

Galbraith, John K. *The Affluent Society*. 2d ed. Boston: Houghton Mifflin, 1969.
In a wide-ranging reexamination of orthodox ideas, questions are raised regarding the effectiveness of monetary manipulations to control economic crises, and suggestions are offered for the restructuring of America's economy.

Goldman, Eric F. *The Tragedy of Lyndon Johnson: A Historian's Personal Interpretation*. New York: Knopf, 1969.
Memoirs of the Johnson era by a Princeton professor who served as a special White House consultant from 1963 to 1966.

———. *The Crucial Decade*. New York: Knopf, 1956.
A lively commentary, which recalls the fears, frustrations, and successes of the decade 1945–1955.

Harrington, Michael. *The Other America: Poverty in the United States*. Rev. ed. New York: Macmillan, 1970.
Filled with moral indignation, this book exhorts affluent Americans to recognize and remedy the disgrace of poverty.

Hole, Judith, and Levine, Ellen. *Rebirth of Feminism*. New York: Quadrangle, 1973.
An examination of the contemporary women's liberation movement.

King, Martin Luther, Jr. *Stride Toward Freedom*. New York: Harper & Row, 1958.
A prominent civil rights leader recalls the ethics and tactics of a crucial phase in the black struggle for equality.

Kissinger, Henry A. *The Necessity for Choice*. New York: Harper & Row, 1961.
A student of American foreign policy, later to become a principal formulator, defines the major issues confronting the United States during the 1960s.

Ordway, Frederick I.; Adams, Carsbie; and Sharpe, Mitchell. *Dividends from Space*. New York: T. Y. Crowell, 1972.
An authoritative demonstration that the technological achievements of the space age can help solve the problems of urban areas and the management of the earth's resources.

Rocks, Lawrence E., and Runyon, Richard. *The Energy Crisis*. New York: Crown, 1972.
Two scientists argue convincingly that the energy crisis could lead to widespread disaster.

Rosenberg, Bernard, and White, David Manning, eds. *Mass Culture Revisited*. New York: Van Nostrand Reinhold, 1971.
This anthology focuses on the nature of popular culture in the United States during the 1960s.

Seaborg, Glenn T., and Corliss, William R. *Man and Atom: Shaping a New World Through Nuclear Technology*. New York: Dutton, 1971.
Describes ways in which nuclear energy can help solve the problems of contemporary man.

Siegfried, André. *America Comes of Age: A French Analysis*. 2d ed. New York: Da Capo, 1969.
Makes interesting generalizations about diverse areas of American life.

Sorenson, Theodore. *Kennedy*. New York: Harper & Row, 1965.
A former adviser to President Kennedy writes a lucid and intimate biography.

Spanier, John W. *American Foreign Policy Since World War II*. 6th ed. New York: Praeger, 1973.
A reasoned account that condenses a considerable amount of useful information into a brief space.

Questions for Review and Discussion

Identifications and essay questions are provided for each chapter.

CHAPTER 1

Identify:

romanticism	socialism	cartels and trusts
realism	conservatism	Manchu dynasty
naturalism	nationalism	Otto von Bismarck
impressionism	militarism	Alfred Dreyfus
expressionism	the Left Coalition	Herbert Asquith
Social Darwinism	*les fauves*	Joseph Lister
fundamentalism	cubism	Paul Cézanne
imperialism	germ theory	Henrik Ibsen
liberalism	vertical integration	Franz Kafka

Essay Questions:

1. In what ways is it valid or invalid for one civilization to assume superiority over another? On the basis of what yardsticks was European civilization clearly preeminent as the twentieth century began?

2. Discuss the relationship between scientific and industrial advances, on the one hand, and population growth and urbanization on the other. What impact did these forces have on the political and social structure?

3. Compare and contrast the stages of industrial development and political party systems in Great Britain, Germany, and France.

4. Explain how the theories of Newton, Planck, and Einstein undermined the traditional view of man as a rational animal. Dis-

cuss the implications of this idea for liberal and democratic politics.

5. How and why did France and Great Britain end their isolation during the generation preceding World War I?

6. "During the late nineteenth and early twentieth centuries, trends in literature and the arts reflected developments in science and industry." Oppose or defend this statement.

7. "Protestants, Catholics, and Jews maintained their traditional dogmas in spite of the secularizing impact of science and industry." Oppose or defend this statement.

8. "Germany was an absolute government with constitutional forms." Explain this concept.

CHAPTER 2

Identify:

Roosevelt Corollary
dollar diplomacy
Open Door policy
Sino-Japanese War
Russo-Japanese War
Russian Revolution of 1905
Mark Twain
Augustus Saint-Gaudens
Mori Ōgai
Dupuy De Lôme
Vasilii Maklakov

Pëtr Stolypin
Charles William Eliot
First Duma
Third Duma
October Manifesto
muckrakers
the symbolists
Upton Sinclair
Sergei Witte
"Bloody Sunday"

Essay Questions:

1. Discuss the external and internal challenges to European supremacy.

2. What did the European powers have in common with the nations that were successfully challenging them?

3. Explain how the Triple Alliance and Triple Entente evolved. How did Bismarck's diplomacy lead to their formation? Why was the Triple Entente not also a triple alliance?

4. Discuss the origins, development, and consequences of the Progressive movement in the United States.

5. Why and in what ways did the United States expand beyond its continental boundaries during the two decades prior to World War I?

6. What were the principal domestic policies of Alexander II, Alexander III, and Nicholas II in Russia? How successful were they?

7. Compare the ways in which Japan and China responded to threats from the West. What lessons can be learned from the consequences?

CHAPTER 3

Identify:

Sarajevo	*Lusitania*	Erich Ludendorff
Central Powers	the Treaty of London (1915)	Georges Clemenceau
Allied Powers		David Lloyd George
the Schlieffen Plan	Friedrich Ebert	Admiral John Jellicoe
Battles of the Marne	Zimmermann note	Pavel Rennenkampf
Battle of Verdun	peace resolution (1917)	Joseph Caillaux
Battle of Jutland		
Greater Serbia	Marshal Foch	

Essay Questions:

1. Why did World War I erupt, after a century of comparative peace? Assess the significance of deeply rooted causes in relation to the immediate incidents that led to a general war. Is it true, as one historian states, that "none of the powers wanted a general war"?

2. Compare the expectations of August 1914 with the way the war actually developed. How did the changing popular mood strengthen the position of peace groups? Explain how the length and character of the struggle affected (a) the evolution of war aims and (b) the outcome of the conflict.

3. In what ways did the British blockade and the German submarine violate the rights of neutral nations? How did U.S. policy evolve in relation to these violations?

4. Examine the impact of the war upon the home fronts in belligerent countries. What mobilization measures were instituted? What impact did these have on relations between government power and individual rights? To what extent did the war produce domestic political changes?

5. Examine the influence that America's entrance and Russia's departure had on the closing stages and the outcome of the war.

6. Compare Woodrow Wilson's Fourteen Points with the war aims developed by the other Allied nations. Note the most prominent areas of agreement and disagreement.

7. How true was the postwar argument by German conservatives that the nation's army had been "stabbed in the back" by civilian weakness and opposition?

CHAPTER 4

Identify:

Constituent Assembly
Prince Georgi E. Lvov
Aleksandr Kerenski
Grigori Rasputin
Pavel Milyukov
Lavr Kornilov
July crisis
Provisional Government

Petrograd Soviet
Mensheviks
Socialist Revolutionaries
Treaty of Brest Litovsk
Nicholas II
Council of People's Commissars
Cheka

Essay Questions:

1. Describe the circumstances under which the Provisional Government was formed. What was its original composition? Why was the government "provisional"? Explain in detail the circumstances that produced three reshufflings of the Provisional Government before its eventual downfall.

2. Evaluate the attributes that made Lenin an effective revolutionary leader, considering especially his skills as theorizer and tactician.

3. List key individuals and events in the series of developments leading to the November Revolution. Discuss the role of each.

4. Compare the developments that produced two revolutions in Russia during a single year. Were there common circumstances? In what respects were there different causes? Evaluate the relative significance of social conditions, philosophic views, individuals, and chance as motive forces of each revolution.

5. Describe the evolving relationship between the Provisional Government and the Petrograd Soviet. What political groups supported each? Did the Petrograd Soviet contribute to, or detract from, the authority of the Provisional Government?

6. "The masses were a negligible influence in both revolutions of 1917." Oppose or defend this statement.

7. What was the attitude of the Provisional Government toward the Bolshevik program?

CHAPTER 5

Identify:

the Big Four
Aristide Briand
Gustav Stresemann
Mustafa Kemal
Geneva Protocol
Locarno agreements
Ruhr occupation
diktat
reparations

Henry Cabot Lodge
Charles Dawes
Treaty of Versailles
Treaty of Saint-Germain
Treaty of Trianon
Treaty of Neuilly
Treaties of Sèvres and Lausanne
Fiume

Essay Questions:

1. Why did Woodrow Wilson consider the League of Nations the most important part of the Paris peace settlements? How do you explain its subsequent rejection by the U.S. Senate?

2. In your opinion, did the Treaty of Versailles deal fairly and practically with Germany? Explain the reasoning that supports your decision.

3. Discuss the policies of the United States, Britain, and France toward Germany during the peace negotiations and throughout the 1920s. What factors motivated these policies?

4. Why is 1923 often considered a watershed in international relations during the 1920s? How valid is this assumption?

5. Compare the final peace settlements with the principles enunciated in Woodrow Wilson's Fourteen Points. Evaluate the particular reasons why he achieved some of his goals, yet failed in his quest for others.

6. Compare Germany's role as an imperial and European power before World War I with its position after the Treaty of Versailles.

7. Discuss the formulation and execution of reparations policies toward Germany from the Paris peace conference to 1929.

8. Relate the Draft Treaty of Mutual Assistance and the Geneva Protocol to the League Covenant's weak guarantees against aggression.

CHAPTER 6

Identify:

Ramsay MacDonald
Stanley Baldwin
Aristide Briand
Miguel Primo de Rivera y Orbneja
Antonio de Oliveira Salazar
Eamon De Valera
Raymond Poincaré

the dole
Ulster
Dail
Cartel des Gauches
Bloc National
Statute of Westminster
the strike of 1926 in England
the Low Countries

Essay Questions:

1. Relate the failure of France to secure strong guarantees against Germany in the peace settlement to France's postwar relations with Belgium, Poland, Czechoslovakia, Romania, and Yugoslavia.

2. Explain how international conditions following World War I permitted France to assume a directing role in European affairs.

3. Evaluate the impact of the following upon French domestic policy: (a) the reparations controversy and (b) the financial dilemma.

4. Explain the policies that successive British governments pursued relative to: (a) unemployment, (b) the Irish problem, and (c) Russia.

5. "During the postwar decade, the politics of coalition were impossible to maintain in Great Britain but were inevitably implemented in France." Explain this statement.

6. Relate Switzerland's federal structure to its geographic and cultural heritage.

7. List the common problems that the Low Countries faced during the 1920s. To what extent were their respective solutions similar or dissimilar?

8. "In Portugal and Spain, the military men continued to exercise a decisive political role." Explain this statement.

CHAPTER 7

Identify:

Max of Baden
Friedrich Ebert
Spartacists
rentenmark
Generals Lüttwitz and Kapp
Il Popola d'Italia
Black Shirts
March on Rome
Rapallo treaty
Giacomo Matteotti

War Communism
Kronshtadt rebellion
land reform
the Lateran treaty (1929)
Reds
Locarno treaties
New Economic Policy
Leon Trotsky
Joseph Stalin

Essay Questions:

1. Explain the transition from War Communism to the New Economic Policy (NEP) in Soviet Russia. To what extent did the NEP achieve its goals?

2. Discuss the succession struggle in Russia during the 1920s. What were the doctrinal and personal differences between Stalin and Trotsky? What circumstances led to Stalin's victory? In your opinion, would the evolution of Russia have differed significantly if Trotsky rather than Stalin had succeeded to the leadership?

3. Describe the rise of fascism in Italy. What were the postwar conditions that contributed to Mussolini's rise to power? Compare and contrast the theories and the practices of fascism.

4. How did World War I and the postwar settlements encourage the growth of small states in Central and Eastern Europe. Discuss the similar and dissimilar ways in which they evolved politically and economically.

CHAPTER 8

Identify:

Erich Maria Remarque
Gestalt school
Niels Bohr
Vienna circle
Martin Heidegger
Civilization and Its Discontents
Max Weber
fauves

Vilfredo Pareto
Franz Kafka
Marcel Proust
André Gide
T. S. Eliot
cubism
Arnold Schönberg
Walter Gropius

Essay Questions:

1. Define and discuss contemporary trends during the 1920s in the following areas: philosophy, science and technology, social thought, music, literature, art, and architecture.

2. In each of the areas listed in question 1, explain the extent to which modernist trends supplanted established patterns. To what extent did traditional patterns continue to hold sway?

3. "Pessimism and cynicism were the dominant impulses underlying cultural trends following World War I." Oppose or defend this statement, citing examples to support your opinion.

4. List the men whose theories, although formulated in one discipline, produced a widespread impact in others. Define and discuss these relationships.

CHAPTER 9

Identify:

"return to normalcy"
Red scare
Immigration Act of 1921
the "Coolidge prosperity"
F. Scott Fitzgerald
Daniel Chester French
Jazz Age
George Gershwin

Nicola Sacco
Albert Fall
Volstead Act
Huddie Ledbetter
mestizo
haciendas
Juan Vincente Gómez
estancia

Essay Questions:

1. Imagine that you are a Democrat campaigning against (a) Warren Harding and (b) Calvin Coolidge. How would you attack their economic programs?

2. Explain the trend toward isolationism in American foreign affairs during the 1920s. Were these policies justifiable? Can isolationism in foreign affairs be related to the attacks on minorities at home?

3. Discuss the postwar economic, political, and social tendencies in the United States.

4. Describe the trends in Canada toward: (a) independence, (b) continued loyalty to Great Britain, and (c) increasing dependence on the United States.

5. To what extent did the industrial and democratic revolutions succeed in transforming Mexico, Venezuela, Brazil, and Argentina during the years following World War I?

CHAPTER 10

Identify:

Sun Yat-sen	Twenty-One	Washington Confer-
Chiang Kai-shek	Demands	ence
Mohandas Gandhi	Amritsar massacre	Henry Stimson
Mohammed Ali	dyarchic	Nine-Power Treaty
Jinnah	National Congress	Government of India
Mikhail Borodin	Lansing-Ishii Treaty	acts

Essay Questions:

1. Describe the changes in Japanese domestic and foreign policies during the 1920s and 1930s.

2. Explain how warlordism, the Kuomintang-Communist separation, and the Yenan period were decisive events in Chinese history.

3. Summarize the objectives and achievements of Gandhi's passive resistance movement.

4. Describe American policies toward Japan from World War I to World War II.

5. How was the Kuomintang-Communist alliance formed?

6. Discuss the impact of Moslem-Hindu differences on the independence movement in India.

CHAPTER 11

Identify:

Anglo-Egyptian Condominium	Lord Frederick Lugard
Wafdists	Cecil Rhodes
Anglo-Egyptian Treaty of 1936	Savorgnan de Brazza
Haile Selassie	Henry Stanley
Walwal	assimilado
Young Tunisians	indigena
Habib Bourguiba	Sir Donald Cameron
Neo-Destour	White Highlands
Marshal Louis Lyautey	Buganda
Ferhat Abbas	African Native Congress
colons	

Essay Questions:

1. Discuss Africa's geographical, cultural, and religious variety.

2. Summarize the patterns of imperial control; in particular, contrast the theories and practices of British and French rule. In what areas did the following nations maintain mastery between the wars: France, Britain, Belgium, Italy, and Portugal?

3. Describe the evolving relationship between England and Egypt during the interwar period. How do you explain Britain's overriding interest in Egypt?

4. Explain why campaigns of national resistance were organized in North Africa before they formed in other areas of the continent.

5. What similar views regarding imperial rule in Africa were shared by Marshal Lyautey, Lord Lugard, Savorgnan de Brazza, and Sir Donald Cameron? Contrast their views with those of the French colons, the Dutch Boers, and the British whites in Kenya.

6. Describe the origins of the Union of South Africa and its development during the interwar years. What types of nationalism evolved? What consequences did they have on South African politics?

CHAPTER 12

Identify:

Credit-Anstalt	Hermann Müller
Reconstruction Finance Corporation	National Government
	Bonus March
Works Progress Administration	Pierre Laval
National Industrial Recovery Act	Lord Snowden
	André Tardieu
General Kurt von Schleicher	Arthur Henderson
Léon Blum	Stavisky affair
Securities Exchange Act	Heinrich Brüning
King Edward VIII	

Essay Questions:

1. Discuss the causes of the depression. Why did its effects become worldwide?

2. Relate the philosophy of President Hoover to the solutions that he supported for the widening economic crisis.

3. What were the similarities and contrasts between the first and second New Deals?

4. Explain the impact of depression politics on Britain's Labour ministry. How effective was the National Government in finding solutions to the economic crisis?

5. Explain the circumstances that produced the French Popular Front in 1936. To what extent were the promises of this experiment fulfilled?

6. How do parliamentary elections and the rise and fall of ministries demonstrate the conservative trend in German politics from 1930 to 1933?

CHAPTER 13

Identify:

Gosplan	socialist realism
sovkhozy	Maksim Litvinov
kolkhozy	popular fronts
"Dizzy with Success"	Anti-Comintern pact
kulaks	Russian-German pact
Stakhanovites	second Five-Year Plan
first Five-Year Plan	third Five-Year Plan
Nikolaiev	

Essay Questions:

1. Why did Stalin consider collectivization essential for the industrialization of Russia? From what sources did the principal resistance to collectivization come? How successful were government measures in overcoming this resistance?

2. Describe the principal changes that Stalinist rule achieved in Russia. Is it accurate to describe these transformations as a *Stalinist Revolution?*

3. Describe the origins and developments of the great purges. What were their consequences for Russia?

4. How do you explain the proclamation of a democratic constitution for Russia in 1936 at the time the purges were occurring? Contrast the theories underlying the constitution and its actual operation.

5. Given the mutual antagonisms between communism and fascism, how do you explain the German-Soviet nonaggression pact of 1939?

6. Weighing the influential economic achievements under Stalin against the cost in human lives and freedom, do you consider the methods employed by Stalin justifiable?

CHAPTER 14

Identify:

putsch of 1923	Reichstag fire
Storm Troopers	Enabling Act
Gleichschaltung	Gerhard Ritter
anti-Semitism	"Night of the Long Knives"
Nuremburg Laws	Confessional Church
Ernst Röhm	Pope Pius XI
German Christians' Faith	Pope Pius XII
Movement	Anschluss

Essay Questions:

1. What immediate political effects did the Great Depression have in Germany during the period from 1929 to 1933?

2. "With or without the Great Depression, a totalitarian regime was Germany's fate." Oppose or defend this statement.

3. Compare Hitler's purge of 1934 with Stalin's purges in the 1930s. Note the similarities and differences between the objectives and results of each.

4. Explain how and why the Enabling Act of 1933 was enacted. Why was it a key step in the formation of Hitler's dictatorship?

5. Evaluate Hitler's attributes as a leader. How did he attract a large popular following? What were his major weaknesses?

6. Compare the ideological program of National Socialism with Nazi rule in practice.

7. Describe responses of the following to the evolution of Nazi policies: (a) industry, (b) labor, (c) the army, and (d) churches.

8. Discuss Nazi attitudes toward Jews. What were the sources of their anti-Semitic views? How were these reflected in Nazi policies? What impact did these policies have on Jewish life prior to World War II?

CHAPTER 15

Identify:

John Maynard Keynes
fascism
communism
totalitarianism
Oswald Spengler
Arnold Joseph Toynbee
Benedetto Croce

Thomas Mann
Les Thibaults
The Grapes of Wrath
Quadragesimo Anno
Karl Barth
Margaret Mead

Essay Questions:

1. Discuss the appropriateness of a chapter dealing with the 1930s titled "Western Civilization at the Crossroads." What values, institutions, and social groups were at stake? For what reasons?

2. Compare the theories of historical progression in general and the development of Western civilization in particular offered by Spengler, Toynbee, and Croce. What are the strengths and weaknesses of each view?

3. Compare orthodox economic principles with John Maynard Keynes's New Economics. What role in the economy did each advocate for the government? Why?

4. Explain how intellectual and religious leaders reacted to the spread of totalitarian values.

CHAPTER 16

Identify:

Manchukuo
Lytton commission
Henry L. Stimson
World Disarmament Conference (1932–1933)
Jean Louis Barthou
Saar plebiscite
Walwal
Rhineland crisis
Alfonso XIII
Loyalists
General Francisco Franco
Kurt von Schuschnigg

Artur von Seyss-Inquart
Sudetenland
Berchtesgaden
Bad Godesberg
Nazi-Soviet pact
appeasement
Eduard Beneš
Édouard Daladier
Rome-Berlin Axis
anti-Comintern Pact
Munich Conference
Stresa Front

Essay Questions:

1. "Due to widespread feelings of disillusionment, varying conceptions of national interests, and internal divisions, neither the United States, Great Britain, nor France consistently pursued forceful policies during the 1930s." Discuss in detail.

2. In contrast with the major democracies, explain the willingness of totalitarian powers to use force in order to achieve their objectives.

3. Evaluate the role of the Great Depression and the Versailles treaty in the breakdown of world peace.

4. Describe the origins, development, and consequences (domestic and international) of each of the following:
   a. the Japanese-Chinese conflict
   b. the Italo-Ethiopian War
   c. the Spanish civil war

5. List the series of world crises that Hitler precipitated between 1933 and 1938. How did the leading Western powers respond to each of these challenges?

6. Oppose or defend each of the following statements:
   a. "After the Nazi regime was established in Germany, a world war at some point became inevitable."
   b. "Ideological differences were of subordinate importance in the crises of the 1930s."
   c. "The Nazi-Soviet pact of August 1939 was inconsistent with the national interests of both signatories."

CHAPTER 17

Identify:

blitzkrieg	Lend-Lease
Maginot Line	Operation Barbarossa
Siegfried Line	General Douglas MacArthur
Danzig	El Alamein
Polish Corridor	Battle of Stalingrad
Russo-Finnish War	*Il Duce*
Vidkun Quisling	Pietro Badoglio
Sedan	Normandy Invasion
Dunkirk	Leyte Gulf
the Vichy government	Iwo Jima
General Charles de Gaulle	Okinawa
Operation Sea Lion	Nagasaki
Hermann Göring	Battle of Moscow

Essay Questions:

1. Explain how and why the Nazi invasion of Poland erupted into war involving all the European states.

2. Expain the meaning of "phony war." How did it end?

3. Contrast the military strategy that Germany used against France in May and June of 1940 with that used in August and September of 1914. Explain Germany's speedy success in subjugating France. What impact did military defeat have on the political and constitutional system in France?

4. Considering the fall of France, how and why did Britain endure?

5. Describe the extent and nature of Nazi rule in Europe by the summer of 1940; by the winter of 1942.

6. Discuss the origins, development, and consequences of Hitler's invasion of Russia in 1941.

7. How did the United States respond to Nazi triumphs between 1939–1941?

8. Discuss the war in the Pacific. Why did Japan decide to wage war against the United States? To what extent did Japan achieve its objectives during the opening months of war? When and how did the Allies achieve supremacy in the Pacific?

9. Explain how the tide of battle in Europe turned in favor of the Allies during 1942–1943. What major victories were won by the Soviet Union? By the Western Allies?

10. Describe the attitudes of Roosevelt, Churchill, and Stalin toward the Normandy invasion. Why did the invasion succeed? Relate its effectiveness to the outcome of the war.

11. Discuss the final stages of the war in Europe and the Pacific.

CHAPTER 18

Identify:

containment	Viet Minh
peaceful coexistence	Ngo Dinh Diem
Yalta conference	David Ben-Gurion
Potsdam conference	Six-Day War
Allied Control Council	third world
COMECON	Jawaharlal Nehru
NATO	Warsaw Pact

OEEC   17th parallel
EDC   38th parallel
Seoul

Essay Questions:

1. Describe the origin, meaning, and application of the Truman Doctrine, the Eisenhower Doctrine, and European integration.

2. Explain how the following areas have been issues of the cold war: the Oder-Neisse Line, Poland, Berlin, Israel, Korea, and Vietnam.

3. Describe the impact of third world nations on relations between the two superpowers.

4. In what ways have Eastern and Western alliances evolved?

CHAPTER 19

Identify:

Clement Attlee   Jean Monnet
Winston Churchill   Georges Pompidou
Sir Stafford Cripps   Basic Law
Steel Nationalization Bill   Konrad Adenauer
Sir Anthony Eden   Free Democrats
Suez crisis   Franz Joseph Strauss
Harold Macmillan   *Ostpolitik*
Profumo affair   *Spiegel* affair
Edward Heath   grand coalition
Enoch Powell   Treaty of Warsaw
Georges Bidault   opening to the Left
Pierre Poujade   Amintore Fanfani
Alcide De Gasperi

Essay Questions:

1. Assess the government of West Germany under the leadership of Konrad Adenauer and the government of France under the leadership of Charles de Gaulle. In what ways did each man fashion his regime? Describe the impact of each in world affairs.

2. To what extent have the successors of Konrad Adenauer and Charles de Gaulle continued or deviated from their policies?

3. Christian Democracy has been a potent postwar force in Italy, Germany, and France. Summarize its achievements and failures in each country.

4. Compare the policies and programs of the British government under the alternating rule of the Conservative and Labour parties. What recurring and what unique problems have been faced by each party? Examine the policies that leaders of each party have devised to meet them. How successful were they?

5. Discuss the causes, development, and consequences of the Suez and Algerian crises. How did each help reveal the illusion of Western omnipotence?

6. In French politics, what is meant by the phrase *from tripartism to the third force?* What meaning did de Gaulle give to the expression *third force* in world politics?

7. What major powers in Western Europe have adopted new constitutions since World War II? Describe the circumstances that prompted these changes and the actual innovations made in each case.

8. What general observations may be made about economic developments in Great Britain, France, West Germany, and Italy since World War II? Analyze the principal events that have shaped these trends.

9. Discuss the role of the Free Democrats in the politics of West Germany since 1949.

CHAPTER 20

Identify:

Chiang Kai-shek
Mao Tse-tung
Marshal Tito
Georgi Malenkov
Lavrenti Beria
Twentieth Party Congress
U-2 incident
Libermanism
people's democracy
National Democratic Bloc
Nicolae Ceausescu
Wladyslaw Gomulka

Mátyás Rákosi
Klement Gottwald
Alexander Dubček
Walter Ulbricht
socialist market economy
New Democracy
great proletarian cultural revolution
Chou En-lai
Bay of Pigs
Cuban missile crisis
Salvador Allende

Essay Questions:

1. Discuss the evolution of the Soviet government from the last years of Stalin to the rise of Brezhnev and Kosygin. Pay particular attention to the period of Nikita Khrushchev. How did he acquire power? What goals did he pursue? Summarize the probable reasons for his downfall.

2. Describe the broadening of Communist rule in Eastern Europe after World War II. What circumstances favored this expansion? Summarize the procedures that brought Communist regimes to power.

3. Analyze the evolution of the satellite states since the death of Stalin. Summarize the major domestic developments in each country. How has each state unfolded in its relations with Russia?

4. What were the causes and consequences of the civil war in China, which ended in 1949?

5. Discuss the foreign relations and principal domestic developments of Communist China since 1949.

6. "Alone among the Communist states of Eastern Europe, Yugoslavia from the beginning was able to defy Kremlin controls and create its own brand of socialist rule." Explain this statement.

7. Discuss the origins, development, and significance of Communist rule in Cuba and Chile.

CHAPTER 21

Identify:

British Commonwealth	Patrice Lumumba
Indian National Congress	Antonio Salazar
the Federation of Malaysia	Jomo Kenyatta
Achmed Sukarno	Buganda
Netherlands New Guinea	Malawi
King Faruk I	Zambia
the National Liberation Front	the Federation of Rhodesia and
the Secret Army Organization	Nyasaland
loi-cadre	Ian Smith
Sékou Touré	apartheid
Katanga	Dr. H. F. Verwoerd

Essay Questions:

1. Explain the general causes of the colonial revolts in Africa and Asia after World War II.

2. Discuss the evolution of independence for India. What significance did Indian independence have for other colonial areas?

3. Write essays covering each of the following topics:
   (a) the end of Dutch rule in Indonesia
   (b) the colonial struggle in Indochina
   (c) Belgian liberation of the Congo

4. Explain the process by which the French liberated North Africa. What circumstances made Algeria a special problem? Describe the development and outcome of the Algerian war of independence. What impact did this conflict have on French politics?

5. Contrast the French withdrawal from North Africa with its departure from sub-Saharan Africa.

6. The British Commonwealth and the French Community were attempts to grant independence without separation. How successful has each experiment been?

7. Explain the circumstances that persuaded Kenyan nationalists to resort to violence. What effect did the bitter struggle in Kenya have on the liberation of other British colonies in East Africa?

8. Explain how the Union of South Africa and Rhodesia remained exceptions to the trend toward native rule in Africa.

CHAPTER 22

Identify:

Truman Doctrine
Marshall Plan
Alger Hiss
Joseph McCarthy
Dean Acheson
modern Republicanism
John Foster Dulles
White Citizen's Councils
Orval Faubus
Bay of Pigs
Alliance for Progress
Berlin Wall

NATO
Martin Luther King, Jr.
march on Washington
black power
Lee Harvey Oswald
Yuri Gagarin
Alan Shepard
William H. Rehnquist
Family Assistance Plan
Strom Thurmond
Watergate

Essay Questions:

1. Compare and contrast the objectives and programs of the Fair Deal, the New Frontier, and the Great Society. How successful was each?

2. Explain the evolution from the principle of containment to the goal of détente in U.S. relations with the Communist world.

3. Discuss the origins, development, and termination of the Korean War.

4. How did U.S. involvement in Vietnam evolve and decline? Explain how the conduct of the Vietnam War produced profound effects on American politics.

5. Assess the origins and nature of the varied attacks on contemporary values during the 1960s.

6. What were the reasons for the shattering Republican defeat in the presidential election of 1964 in contrast with the party's overwhelming victories in 1968 and 1972?

7. Describe the advancements in space travel and their implications for life on earth.

8. Discuss the legal and political implications of the scandals uncovered in the Nixon administration.

Index